Pandita Ramabai's America

Pandita Ramabai's America

Conditions of Life in the United States

Edited, with a Biographical Introduction, by

Robert Eric Frykenberg

Kshitija Gomes, *Translator*

Philip C. Engblom, *Translation Editor*

William B. Eerdmans Publishing Company

Grand Rapids, Michigan / Cambridge, U.K.

Wm. B. Eerdmans Publishing Co.
255 Jefferson Ave. S.E., Grand Rapids, Michigan 49503 /
P.O. Box 163, Cambridge CB3 9PU U.K.

Printed in the United States of America

08 07 06 05 04 03 7 6 5 4 3 2 1

Library of Congress Cataloging-in-Publication Data

Ramabai Sarasvati, Pandita, 1858-1922.
[Speeches. English] Pandita Ramabai's America /
edited, with a biographical introduction by Robert Eric Frykenberg;
translated by Kshitija Gomes; translation editor, Philip Engblom.
p. cm.
Includes bibliographical references.
ISBN 0-8028-1293-7 (alk. paper)
1. United States — Description and travel. 2. United States — Social
conditions — 1865-1918. 3. United States — Civilization — 1865-1918.
4. Ramabai Sarasvati, Pandita, 1858-1922 — Journeys — United States.
5. Women, East Indian — Travel — United States. 6. Women, East Indian — Biography.
7. Women social reformers — India — Biography. I. Frykenberg, Robert Eric.
II. Gomes, Kshitija. III. Engblom, Philip C., 1951- IV. Title.
E168.R156 2003
917.304′8 — dc21

2003044355

www.eerdmans.com

To Carol

Beloved

— REF

Contents

Editor's Preface to the English Translation

The significance of Pandita Ramabai, and her place among India's great national figures, is well known. Arguably among the most notable women India has ever produced,[1] she can be ranked alongside Gandhi. Like him, she too can be seen as a "Mahatma" — or "Great Soul" — one such as is seldom seen in any age. The fame of this tiny woman, especially during her early twenties when she first surfaced, was such that even the title of "Pandita" was deemed insufficient. After subjecting her to a long and searching examination, learned scholars in Calcutta threw up their hands and exclaimed in astonishment, "We do not feel that you belong to this world since the great Pandits have been dazzled and amazed by your superhuman ability. The very Goddess of Learning 'Saraswati' has come down amidst us in human form."[2]

Such an opinion of Ramabai has not, however, been universal. Today, as during her own day, that positive perspective is being contested, and her significance is certainly a matter for debate. Throughout most of her life, Ramabai vehemently protested against conditions of life in India. These were conditions which she herself had personally experienced and observed, systemic evils she had confronted since early childhood — injustices suffered by

1. In the exaggerated prose of A. B. Shah, ed., introduction to *The Letters and Correspondence of Pandita Ramabai* (Bombay: Maharashtra State Board for Literature and Culture, 1977), p. xi: "Pandita Ramabai Saraswati . . . was the greatest woman produced by Modern India and one of the greatest Indians of all history. Her achievements as a champion of women's rights . . . remain unrivalled even after the lapse of . . . a century. . . ."

2. Padmini Sengupta, *Pandita Ramabai Saraswati: Her Life and Work* (New York: Asia Publishing House, 1970), p. 1.

women, by children, and by those whose birth condemned them to lives of deprivation, oppression, and poverty. Those who dispute her place among historic figures of modern India do so because they feel that Ramabai turned against her own — against her own birth, her own family and lineage *(vamsha)*, her own caste and class *(jāti* and *varna)*, her own "religion" and the traditional order *(sanāthana dharma)*, and her own nation *(rāshtriya)*. Worst of all, in such eyes, she is seen as having abandoned or betrayed her own by forsaking ancient *Shastras* for the "*Veda*" of Christ. Those who turned their back on Ramabai during her lifetime did so even though she vehemently maintained, to the very end of her life, that she was still a "Hindu."[3]

There can be little doubt that many of the nationalist reformers who had become her staunch friends and supporters and who had joined her in her early efforts to eradicate social evils by building a special boarding school for Brahman child widows became disenchanted. The gradual process through which she embraced the gospel of Christ made her somewhat suspect, and suspicions existed even before she came to Pune from Bengal. That alone did not provoke reaction and resistance, however; among her friends and supporters were prominent reformers such as Ranade and Gokhale and their wives. But after her return from America, and after some of her young charges began to "turn to Christ," many of these friends began to turn away. From the perspective of high-caste Hindu reformers, a courageous and heroic champion had fallen. It was only later (after 1898), however, after she began to care for female famine victims and child widows of low ("impure" or "polluted") birth, that most upper-caste Hindus left her. Supporters in India abandoned her when actions at her Sharada Sadan and at her newly established Mukti Sadan in Kedgaon, just outside Pune, threatened to bring pollution upon themselves and upon families of their high-born friends. For most Maratha Brahman kindred and friends, pollution was more disturbing than devotion to Christ. If her espousal of belief in a single, common humanity and her actions based on belief in a common and universal birth *(jāt)* for all humankind cooled ardor and turned many people away, the danger of becoming outcastes was even more terrifying. What she had brought back with her from her travels in the United States, and what she put into practice in

3. Of course, her view of what it meant to be "Hindu" might not have accorded with that of her critics. She perhaps only meant that, culturally, she was still as "Indian" as ever. Certainly, her love for Sanskrit, the "Divine Language," which was "the most beautiful and the oldest language of my dear native land," never left her. Cf. R. E. Frykenberg, "The Emergence of Modern 'Hinduism' As a Concept and As an Institution: A Reappraisal With Special Reference to South India," in *Hinduism Reconsidered*, ed. Gunther Sontheimer and Hermann Kulke (Heidelberg: South Asia Institute, 1989), pp. 1-29.

Pune and Kedgaon, brought increasingly bitter disappointment and led, stage by stage, to deepening disillusionment and sadness, alienation and anger.

Yet, for many others in the world, the name Ramabai still rings like a bell.[4] If anything, her fame and name seem greater today than ever. Reasons for this may lie in her having, throughout her life, stood as a champion of the lowly, the weak, and the poor, particularly downtrodden women and children. Memory of her special concern for child widows, for those suffering thralldom under systemic degradation and oppression, is again being awakened.

No single word, in fact, so epitomized or symbolized Ramabai's life — her ideals, her calling, and what she stood for — as "liberty" *(mukti)*. It was no accident that the name she chose for her periodical was *The Mukti Prayer Bell* and that the emblem she emblazoned on the cover was that of a large, cracked bell, for she idealized the Liberty Bell,[5] which represented all that she had ever striven to obtain, both for herself and for others. The words on the bell come from sacred writ, one verse from the Torah and the other from the prophets. Like a bell clapper, the first sings out, "Proclaim Liberty throughout all the land unto all the inhabitants thereof" (Lev. 25:10), and the other answers back, "The Lord hath anointed Me to preach Good Tidings unto the meek and to bind up the brokenhearted, to Proclaim Liberty to the captives and the Opening of the prison to them that are bound" (Isa. 61:1).

Nothing meant more to Ramabai than liberty, and she spoke of it and wrote about it over and over. This was something that those who upheld authoritarian and hierarchically organized power structures — whether caste- and gender-based oppression or colonial oppression — could never tolerate nor quite understand. Those who struggled with her, whether reactionary "Hindutva" nationalists or reactionary European imperialists, never saw the inherent contradiction and utter incompatibility between Ramabai's love for liberty and their own insistence on unquestioning conformity. This incon-

4. Her periodical newsletter from Kedgaon to supporters was called *The Mukti Prayer Bell.*

5. The Liberty Bell still rests in the Tower Room of Independence Hall in Philadelphia. Weighing more than twenty-eight hundred pounds, it was purchased in 1752 for three hundred dollars from a firm in England for the Colony of Pennsylvania. Although it broke almost immediately, it was recast in Philadelphia, with the same inscription, in 1753. On July 8, 1776, it was rung along with other church bells in the thirteen colonies to announce the Declaration of Independence. It was rung again each year on the fourth of July to celebrate the anniversary of that momentous event until a large crack rendered it unringable. Nevertheless, the Liberty Bell is still "rung" (symbolically tapped) at important moments, and it remains a national treasure, both a relic and a symbol of all that America, in its loftiest ideals, represents and proclaims — both to itself and to the whole world.

gruity could be seen clearly in her standoffs against Western Christendom, as found in the established (or Anglican) church, and particularly in her experiences with the Anglo-Catholics of Wantage. Forces both in the East and in the West, both of the High Church and of Brahman Orthodoxy, could accuse her of arrogance and betrayal. Like her father and mother before her, however, she was herself always implacably opposed to all oppression, wherever it existed, and especially if those afflicted were child widows and women.

Nowhere on earth at any time in history have so many women (and children) been made to suffer so much as have low-caste and poor women and children in India. Had they voices, the millions of infants whose lives have been and are being casually extinguished, the millions of child brides whose aged spouses died and left them child widows (deaths for which they were blamed), and the millions more who, prior to 1827, were immolated as *satis* (or "true wives") upon the funeral pyres of their husbands, would cry out against what was done. In her own day, it was Ramabai, even before Gandhi, who heard and heeded this cry. Against inhuman deeds being done and deeds apparently destined to continue, she raised her voice and exercised her pen. She continued to do so down to the day she drew her last breath.

But the importance of the ideas contained within this volume lies in more than Ramabai's authorship or her cause. Significant as she herself and her contributions may have been, there are at least two other factors making this work noteworthy. First, as far as we know, notwithstanding excellent work done by Meera Kosambi,[6] who is undoubtedly the foremost authority on Ramabai in our day, this is the very first time the entire text of Ramabai's work on America *(Conditions of Life in the United States and Travels There)* has been translated and published in English. This is also the first time the full text has been made available to the world at large — the world outside of India, and, to be specific, the world outside of Maharashtra. Ramabai's words, originally in the Marathi language, were perhaps written as a diary or journal in which she recorded the fascinating things she had observed. Ramabai seems to have intended that her own impressions and insights, ponderings and reflections — everything her mind had gathered during her extensive travels back and forth across North America during the years of 1886 and 1887 — should be shared and made available for the Marathi-speaking peoples of her own country.

Second, Ramabai's work on America is important because of the astute-

6. See *Pandita Ramabai Through Her Own Words: Selected Works* (Oxford: Oxford University Press, 2000), pp. 181-244. Compiled and edited, with translations, by Meera Kosambi, this work contains two chapters of what is being published in its entirety here.

ness of her observations. What she conveyed to the reading public in her own country in her own tongue still provides a wonderful mirror by which Americans and Indians, over a century later, can catch a glimpse of themselves as they once were and compare this with what they are today. The work enables us to make assessments, comparisons, and measurements — to see what has happened to our own ideals and what we have become as a society. For this reason alone, her work can properly be compared with Alexis de Tocqueville's classic, *Democracy in America.* While obviously shorter and perhaps simpler and less sophisticated, Ramabai's work gives us a clear-eyed and deeply penetrating look into the circumstances of real life among peoples of America, as she herself saw them. Her cultural and sociopolitical findings are insightful, whether hilariously entertaining and funny, as they often are, or starkly sobering. The mirror put before us as Americans and as Indians in our own day, as for Marathi readers over a century ago, enables us to see for ourselves, for the very first time, what this truly remarkable woman saw and what she understood about the people of America. The beautiful and serene are described, along with the ugly blemishes that still exist in America. These Ramabai did not attempt to gloss over or hide.

Tocqueville's work is widely known and quoted. Ramabai's work is virtually unknown. Part of the reason for this is that Tocqueville was soon translated and acclaimed, something that has hitherto never happened to Ramabai's Marathi work. Perhaps if her work had been translated and published in 1890, soon after its first appearance in India, it might now be recognized as a classic insight into the inner workings of America.

Of course, the importance of her views on America cannot be properly appreciated without knowing something about the background and life of Pandita Ramabai herself. To that end, a biographical introduction is included to provide an overview of the multiple contexts out of which her reflections emerged. The introduction describes the stark conditions of Ramabai's early life; the Raj within which she suddenly emerged in 1878; her rise as a popular public figure in Bengal, Assam, and Bombay (from 1878 to 1882); the circumstances that led her to question customs and traditions long held sacred within her own society; her lifelong religious quest, which, beginning during her childhood wanderings, accompanied her to Britain in 1883 and then to America in 1886; the reception she received in America and her activities there; the events which then followed her return to India; and, finally, her later experiences as a social reformer and scholar, down to the time of her death at Kedgaon in 1922. Without a sketch of the salient events and features of her life and her career, neither her remarkable work on the United States nor the significance of publishing this translation can be comprehended.

Editor's Preface to the English Translation

The story of the book and its construction is very briefly and simply told. The idea of doing it came originally from Professor Uma Chakravarti, during her visit to the Wisconsin campus in the spring of 1995.[7] At that time, while she and I were discussing Pandita Ramabai over coffee with Professor Edith Blumhofer of Wheaton College (who had come to Madison to present a paper on Ramabai in America[8]), Professor Chakravarti indicated that there was a classic work by Ramabai which the world did not know and which her own country no longer remembered. This was a book in Marathi that Ramabai had published shortly after her return from the United States in 1889. As far as Professor Chakravarti knew, the book still slumbered quietly in the Mukti Mission at Kedgaon. She was herself writing a book on Ramabai and strongly recommended that someone be recruited to do something about this archival lapse. All three of us became excited and discussed what might be needed for such an undertaking to be launched.

It just so happened that, at that time, I was directly engaged in overseeing a multi-pronged Research Advancement Project generously funded by the Pew Charitable Trusts. While there were already a dozen or more projects at various stages of progress, I hoped there might still be sufficient funding for this project. Indeed, in a subsequent report, I recommended that, if possible, this translation be undertaken and that, if it turned out well, funds be provided for publication. Meanwhile, as months dragged on, I kept pondering this matter and wondered how it might be possible, within an already stretched budget, to both fund and implement such a project.

Finally, in 1997, I asked my project/research assistant, Chandra Mallampalli, who was then doing field research in the wonderfully rich archives and library at UTC (Union Theological College), Bangalore, to journey to Pune and Kedgaon to look into the matter. I also asked him to keep a sharp eye open while he was doing so for a scholar who might be able undertake this task. I wanted to find someone who not only possessed a high level of learning both in Marathi and English languages and literatures but also had substantial experience in Marathi-to-English translation. On both counts, Chandra was soon successful. He returned from Kedgaon with a photocopy

7. A letter from R. E. Frykenberg to Uma Chakravarti (dated August 25, 1995) is still lodged in my computer files.

8. Edith Blumhofer, "Pandita Ramabai and Indian Christianity: A North American Perspective" (Wheaton: n.d., unpublished).

of the book; and, at the same time, he had located just the right scholar — someone both competent and willing to undertake this project. Mrs. Kshitija Gomes, the wife of Professor Jules Gomes (an Old Testament Scholar at UTC), had herself been a lecturer in English Literature at Ahmednagar College for a number of years; moreover, being a native Marathi speaker who was proficient in both languages, she had already been engaged in translation work for nearly five years. She was appointed in January 1998 and immediately set to work. During the entire time that she worked on the translation, she kept in close touch and sent me copies of each chapter as it was completed. By the late spring of 1999, the initial translation work was done. But previous experience with a translation project had taught that this initial work was only phase one.

The second phase was begun before the end of the year. This involved engaging a second expert to carefully go over and vet the work of the first expert. I had long known of just the person to do this; moreover, he lived only an hour's drive away. Philip Engblom, born and reared in Maharashtra, not only had written his doctoral dissertation on Marathi Literature but also had critically examined and reviewed the work of other Marathi scholars and had formally taught students Marathi. Well acquainted with academic research, he was just the right person to compare the original Marathi text with the English translation, double-checking the accuracy and appropriateness of the terminology and giving special attention to difficult concepts found in the more sophisticated portions of Ramabai's discourse. The purpose of this procedure, in short, was to check for both accuracy and style. By employing both Kshitija Gomes and Philip Engblom, both of them experts in Marathi and both proficient in English, I was aiming for quality control. Both translators, in addition, added a number of helpful explanatory notes in the text, which appear along with Ramabai's own notes.

It should be pointed out that, as editor, I myself do not handle Marathi, and that I am not a specialist on Maharashtra. My own scholarly work in the history of South India has dealt with Telugu-speaking peoples of Andhra Pradesh, with special reference to Company rule. The greatest authority on Pandita Ramabai today, in my opinion, is Professor Meera Kosambi. In addition, Professor Uma Chakravarti has produced a revision of the history of modern Maharashtra, with special reference to Pandita Ramabai that is no less cogent, powerful, and sophisticated. Certainly her insights on the cultural legacy of the Peshwai have saliency for understanding Ramabai that stands well beside the work of Professor Kosambi. Both scholars have also long been preoccupied with feminist concerns, but always with solid empirical grounding beneath what they do. A third and earlier authority on Ramabai, Padmini

Sengupta, produced a detailed work revealing a comprehensive grasp of the intricacies of Ramabai's life, from a scholarly Christian perspective. Unlike the host of other Christian writers who have written on Ramabai, her work is almost entirely free of pietistic cant or unduly biased polemic. The little book by Nicol Macnicol, written just four years after Ramabai's death, has perhaps also become a durable classic. In comparison to such authorities, Gauri Viswanathan's chapter on Ramabai in *Outside the Fold* (1998), which follows the footsteps of her mentor Edward Said, is a venture in literary criticism that contributes little historical understanding.

Finally, I unhesitatingly acknowledge my debt to many who have made the production of this book possible. Among them I would count a number of colleagues and friends, not only at Wisconsin but around the world. Without the support of officers of the Pew Charitable Trusts and of those who have participated in many of the conferences connected to the studies in the historical currents in Christianity, not only in India but around the world, a translation work such as this would never have come about. Of course, this book could never have been produced without the heavy labors of Kshitija Gomes and Philip Engblom. It has been a joy to work with both of them. Among many not named, I would only thank my close colleague and friend Brian Stanley, Director of the Henry Martyn Center at Cambridge, who, as co-editor of the Curzon/Eerdmans series of scholarly works entitled Studies in the History of Christian Missions, broadened my understandings. At the same time, I must express my gratitude to William B. Eerdmans for help in the production of this volume. And last of all, I must acknowledge, with profound thankfulness, the faithful encouragement of my beloved wife, Carol. As my closest and dearest companion and friend, she has patiently endured far too many lonely hours while I "burned the midnight oil" trying to unravel the tangles and complexities of Ramabai's life. To her, for whom no words are adequate, I dedicate this book.

Robert Eric Frykenberg
University of Wisconsin–Madison
August 25, 2001

Translation Editor's Preface

Pandita Ramabai was a twenty-five-year-old widow when she came, with her infant daughter, from India to England in May 1883, and she was not quite twenty-eight when she traveled from England to the United States in March 1886. Already, for one so young, she had lived the equivalent of several average lifetimes. The sheer variety of her life experience — the unprecedented achievements and acclaim as well as the most grievous personal losses and hardships — had given her life even then an aspect almost of myth. Some part of her fame within her homeland and in England, as the most learned Indian woman of her day and as an outspoken advocate of the advancement of her countrywomen, preceded her; but by the time her two-and-a-half years' residence in the United States ended it can justly be said that she had become the most widely known and widely acclaimed Indian woman (if not indeed Indian person) of the nineteenth century.

Ramabai came to the United States with the intention of staying only a brief time, but her reception in America was so enthusiastic and her own always insatiable curiosity was so piqued by the extraordinary novelties she found in this strange new land that she extended her stay many times over. Although she had not known the English language before she went to England, by the time she came to the United States three years later she was able to speak it not just confidently but eloquently in public meetings in cities and towns all across the land. She traveled by her own estimate over thirty thousand miles by railway in every region of the country, meeting people belonging to every level of American society, from the intellectual elite to former slaves. Everywhere she went, always as an invited guest, she spoke passionately about the conditions and the needs of the women of her homeland. During the second year of her stay, this became formalized as a hugely successful project to raise support in America for the creation of a residential school for Hindu widows in India.

As part and parcel of this effort Ramabai wrote the short English book for which she is most widely remembered, *The High-Caste Hindu Woman.* Published privately in Philadelphia in 1887, partly through the efforts of Ramabai's chief American sponsor, Dr. Rachel Bodley, Dean of the Woman's Medical College of Pennsylvania, *The High-Caste Hindu Woman* seeks to explain to her American audience more completely than she could in any single lecture the motives for her mission on behalf of Hindu widows. Quoting liberally from the Hindu law code, the *Manusmṛti,* both by way of illustration and as support for her argument, she presents a devastating picture of the deprivations and outright oppression suffered in those days most particularly by high-caste Hindu widows but also more generally by all Indian women in the name of sanctified tradition. It is a passionate, polemical book, but what gave it the ring of particular authority was her own status as a widow speaking (albeit as a highly exceptional case) for other widows. By the time Ramabai left the United States in November 1888, the book had sold ten thousand copies.[1]

Remarkably, during the same time that she was writing *The High-Caste Hindu Woman* and endlessly travelling about the United States promoting her project, Ramabai also found the time to write an even larger and much more ambitious book in the opposite direction — a book, that is, written in her mother tongue, Marathi, in which she seeks to explain the society and culture of the United States to her compatriots at home in India. *The Conditions of Life in the United States and a Travelogue (yunaited stetsaci lokasthiti va pravasavarnana)* was published in Bombay in 1889 upon her return from the United States. If sales ever reached even a few hundred copies, it was doing well by the standards of the time; yet there is evidence that people did read it then with considerable interest. No less an authority than M. G. Ranade lists it, as part of a survey he compiled in 1898, as one of the sixty selected "standard books" published in Marathi up to that point in the nineteenth century (out of a total of 9,287) that were "fairly equivalent, in standard, to the text books in English . . . prescribed by the University."[2] Over the

1. A. B. Shah, introduction to *The Letters and Correspondence of Pandita Ramabai* (Bombay: Maharashtra Board for Literature and Culture, 1977), p. xx.

2. "A Note on the Growth of Marathi Literature, 1898," *Writings of the Late Hon'ble Mr. Justice M. G. Ranade* (Bombay: Manoranjan Press, 1915), p. 47.

course of most of the twentieth century, however, the book came to share the same fate its author suffered in her own land, of being "almost totally obscured from the official histories of Western India, condemned both during her lifetime and after her death for her challenge to the Hindu, patriarchal social order of the day."[3] Only a few copies of the book have survived down to the present day, when a re-emergent interest in Pandita Ramabai and a general reappraisal of her great contribution to the cause of Indian women have brought this unique and revealing Marathi text the renewed attention it has long deserved.

The question presents itself: Why did Ramabai choose to undertake such a major task as this at a time when so much else was being demanded of her? Perhaps partly she wrote it for her own benefit, as a way to make more coherent to herself a culture and a society that must have seemed profoundly alien to her — even if for the most part she found herself admiring it. But like so many others of the Marathi-speaking intellectual elite of that era, she also clearly felt a responsibility to use her unique situation, in her case as one of the very first visitors from India to the United States, to educate her compatriots at home about what was then still largely a blank space in their cognitive map of the world.

This does not mean that she wrote in the manner of a schoolteacher to ignorant students. Quite the contrary, as her own erudite and complex Marathi prose style amply demonstrates, she wrote as one who is both conscious of and thoroughly conversant in the prevailing medium of intellectual exchange, which even at that very time during the 1880s was emerging as the style of modern Marathi discursive prose. The principal architects of this style — among them notably Vishnushastri Chiplunkar in his journal *Nibandhamala,* Bal Gangadhar ("Lokmanya") Tilak in his newspaper *Kesari,* and Gopal Ganesh Agarkar in his journal *Sudharaka* — were all graduates of Deccan College. They had enjoyed the full benefits of a formal education under the system introduced in stages after the British conquest of the Marathas in 1818, culminating in the establishment of the university system in 1857. Most of them by virtue of their education were also major actors in the intellectual and cultural life of the city of Pune, the focal point of Marathi culture since the early eighteenth century. All of them were also, it goes without saying, men.

Ramabai, on the other hand, never had access to a day of formal educa-

3. Meera Kosambi, "Multiple Contestations: Pandita Ramabai's Educational and Missionary Activities in the Late Nineteenth-Century India and Abroad," *Women's History Review* 7, no. 2 (1998): 194.

tion in the established system before her two years at Cheltenham Ladies' College in England, where she studied sciences, math, and English literature. Until then she had learned everything she knew of literate knowledge through private instruction within an enlightened family of traditional Sanskrit scholars and through her own indefatigable need to read everything. Yet she was able, in *Conditions of Life in the United States,* as elsewhere, to address the reigning intellectual elite of Pune with serene confidence as an intellectual equal.

The challenge for the translators has been to find a translation medium, a variety of English, that would not only preserve something of the distinctively Indian (in her own usage, "Hindusthani") flavor of Ramabai's manner but that could at the same time do justice to the full complexity of thought and of style of such a remarkably erudite and broad-ranging mind as Ramabai had. The nineteenth-century Brahminical, Sanskritic, learned, "Puneri" culture that so inevitably informs Ramabai's Marathi — this was, after all, what constituted both her own cultural-linguistic roots and those of her acknowledged audience — is something that she both addresses respectfully and vigorously challenges. Situated within the strenuous cultural polemics of that era in Maharashtra between the "traditionalists" (e.g., Vishnushastri Chiplunkar and Lokmanya Tilak) and the "reformers" (e.g., M. G. Ranade, Gopal Ganesh Agarkar, and G. K. Gokhale), Ramabai's writing is both a party to that ongoing controversy and a startling anomaly within it — if only because of her unprecedented position in that era as an unarguably serious woman writer of Marathi who could not be ignored and because of her unabashed feminist advocacy.

Ramabai brings to her description, analysis, and cultural critique of the United States distinctly Indian ("Hindusthani") categories of both seeing and thinking; but at the same time a very important part of what she is consciously doing is turning her critique back upon the very Indian culture out of which she is writing. There is an element of Ramabai's style of thought that is a kind of two-edged sword with respect to many things that are (or at one time were) Indian. This was certainly not lost upon her audience at home, and she suffered for it. Yet it is constantly rewarding to see how Ramabai's very bright and brave mind works. She has a particular talent for irony (often amounting indeed to outright sarcasm) that would have made her Chitpavan Brahman ancestors proud. There is a voice, at once erudite and yet colloquial, that belongs uniquely to her in the original text. Some part of that perhaps can be seen to come through the translation.

The problems encountered in the process of a translation of this kind can be complex and daunting. Decades of effort by numerous scholars in the

West, as documented notably in the book *India through Hindu Categories* edited by McKim Marriott some years ago, have gone into developing a sociology that allows an approach to interpreting the culture of India "by reasoning in terms derived from the civilization's own recognized systems of categories."[4] Imagine, then, the quite salutary problem of reversing the direction and seeking to apply these systems of categories — these "Hindusthani" categories as Ramabai might have preferred to think of them — to the problem of describing, analyzing, and interpreting the culture and society of the United States, a United States moreover as it existed over a hundred years ago, at the very apex of triumphal Western colonialism. This was the very real, very concrete problem Ramabai confronted when she undertook the task of thinking and writing about the United States through the medium of late nineteenth-century Marathi prose, which itself was still undergoing the process of metamorphosing into its characteristically modern form. From "simple" descriptions of the apparently most mundane of physical artifacts — bathtubs, for instance, or window screens — to the self-evidently absurd and harmful American practice of putting ice in drinking water during the heat of the summer, to the ever-widening ambiguities associated with applying the convenient "Hindusthani" social categorization of *jata* (commonly rendered in the context of India as "caste") to the vast diversity of ethnic and social communities constituting the American union, the problems of rendering a Marathi United States proliferate on every page of Ramabai's text. The challenge has been not to hide or to gloss over these rough spots in the grain of the text (and indeed to foreground them where that adds important texture) while at the same time producing a readable translation.

A native speaker of Marathi hailing from the same area as the author, Kshitija Gomes played a creative role in interpreting the original text and in translating it into English, striving to remain faithful to the intent, thought processes, and characteristic style of the author. The division of labor was such that, after Kshitija Gomes's crucial primary work of translation, of getting onto the page the English words that reflect the original in a coherent way, my role, as translation editor, was to go back over the translation, sentence by sentence, in tandem with the original, making sure that important details (both of substance and of Ramabai's characteristic style) were not lost or glossed over, while at the same time ensuring that the style of the translation avoids the common pitfalls of the Marathi-to-English translation process and reflects lucidly the characteristic flow of Ramabai's thought process.

4. McKim Marriott, introduction to *India through Hindu Categories* (New Delhi: Sage, 1990), p. xiii.

No translation can ever be totally transparent, of course, but any translator's hope must be to minimize as much as possible her or his intrusion on the author's place of privilege. In the case of her *Conditions of Life in the United States,* the hope is that this English version will bring to a new reading public, a century after the work nearly fell into oblivion, a renewed appreciation for the remarkable person Pandita Ramabai truly was.

PHILIP C. ENGBLOM
University of Chicago
January 23, 2003

Pandita Ramabai Saraswati: A Biographical Introduction

Early Years

Life for Ramabai Dongre began on the twenty-third of April, 1858, high atop Gangamal peak in the Western Ghats, not far from Mangalore. At six months, she and her surviving siblings (Krishnabai and Srinivas) were carried down from the family's idyllic forest retreat *(ashram)* when her parents embarked upon a perilous, never-ending "pilgrimage." For twenty years they wandered ceaselessly on foot back and forth across the subcontinent. Her immensely learned and pious father, having exhausted all his material resources providing hospitality for students *(sishiyas)* and pilgrims, had decided to begin a new life for himself and his family. Traveling to famous shrines far and near, he recited and taught Sanskritic lore, subsisting on the generosity of those who listened and made contributions. Ramabai's earliest memories were of trudging and camping along roadsides. What made such a life possible was the enormous storehouse of learning her father had accumulated over his many years. From this, he was able to take and share and dazzle.

Anant Shastri Dongre, born in 1795, was a Chitpavan (or "Konkanestha") Brahman of ancient lineage whose family had migrated from Maharashtra to Mangalore country in the sixteenth century. His high learning had begun at age sixteen, when he went to Pune to study under the greatly renowned Ramachandra Shastri Sathé. Since Ramachandra also served as a royal pandit of the Peshwa, Baji Rao II, and his gifted wife, Shrimati Varanasibai Sahiba, young Anant listened with awe and wonder as this woman recited huge collections of Sanskrit verses. Her accomplishments convinced him that he should dedicate himself to the provision of learning for women, something hitherto unheard of.

In 1818, after Maratha armies suffered defeat by forces of the East India Company and the British Raj spread across India, Ramachandra Shastri decided to follow the Peshwa into exile in North India. But before departing he took care to bestow the title of *Shastri* upon his disciple *(sishiya)*. Returning south to his family, Anant Shastri was obliged to marry a child bride. Both she and his family, however, fiercely resisted all his attempts to impart Sanskrit learning to her. Sharing such knowledge with any female was still viewed as a violation of the sacred laws of the *Manusmṛti*. Later, after his father squandered the family's wealth, Anant Shastri was obliged to seek employment in the kingdom of Mysore. There his brilliance immediately caught the eye of the Maharaja. After years of royal service brought him honor and wealth, he retired and embarked on a great pilgrimage.[1] Along the way, after his wife Yamunabai died, he decided to send his parents back to Mysore in the care of servants so that he could remain in Varanasi and devote himself to studying the *Darshan Shastra*. As a result of these studies, Anant Shastri turned away from the Shaiva *(Ādvaita)* tradition and embraced the Vaishnava *sampradayia*.[2]

In 1839 Anant Shastri acquired his second wife, Ramabai's mother. He was on his homeward journey when, having stopped to bathe along the banks of the sacred Godavari, near Paithan, he met a Brahman also on pilgrimage with his family. This Brahman, a fellow Chitpavan named Madhavarao Abhyankar, became so impressed by Anant Shastri's learning and outlook that, on the spot, he offered him the hand of his nine-year-old daughter. As Ramabai put it nearly fifty years later, "All [was] settled in an hour or so; next day the marriage concluded; and the little girl was placed in the possession of a stranger, who took her nearly nine hundred miles away from her home. . . . Fortunately, the little girl had fallen in good hands, and was well and tenderly cared for."[3] No

1. There is an interesting coincidence between Anant Shastri's departure from Mysore and the divesting of political power from the Mysore Maharaja, which occurred on October 3, 1831. Diwan Purnayya, a Maratha Brahman, became famous (or infamous) for "his partiality for members of the brahman community" and the "monopoly of government posts" he had given them. If only for his strict aversion to pollution, Anant Shastri would certainly have fled from the British-run Raj. Cf.: K. N. V. Sastri, *The Administration of Mysore under Sir Mark Cubbon (1834-1861)* (London: George Allen and Unwin, 1932), pp. 15-31.

2. Sir Monier Monier-Williams, *A Sanskrit-English Dictionary* (Oxford: Oxford University Press, 1982 [1899]), p. 1175, col. 1, defines this as "tradition; established doctrine transmitted from one teacher to another; traditional belief or usage; . . . any peculiar or sectarian system of religious teaching, sect."

3. Pandita Ramabai Sarasvati, *The High-Caste Hindu Woman*, with an introduction by Rachel L. Bodley (Philadelphia: J. B. Rogers Printing Co., 1887), p. 20.

sooner had he changed his bride's name (from Ambabai) to Lakshmibai (as was the custom) than he began to put into practice his radical scheme for female education.

> My father, although a very orthodox Hindu and strictly adhering to caste and other religious rules, was yet a reformer. . . . He could not see why women and people of the Shudra caste should not read and write the Sanskrit language and learn sacred literature. . . . He thought it better to try the experiment at home instead of preaching to others. He found an apt pupil in my mother, who fell in line with his plan, and became an excellent Sanskrit scholar.[4]

Thus, along with cooking, washing, serving guests, and caring for young children as a dutiful wife, Lakshmibai spent hours each night studying Sanskrit texts and memorizing Puranic lore.

Anant Shastri's radical scheme did not go unchallenged. Brahman pandits near the family's ancestral village did all in their power to dissuade him: the "language of the gods" was not for women. When he quoted sacred texts to show that teaching Sanskrit to women (and Shudras) was legal, his foes appealed to higher authority. Before the chief guru of Madhava Vaishnavas in Udipi, Anant Shastri confounded his opponents, quoting texts to show that what he was doing was not wrong. Yet, while not excommunicated or made an outcaste, he became a marked man; wherever he went, he was shunned and harassed by members of his community.

To free himself and his family from ceaseless censure, Anant Shastri retreated deep into the forests of Gangamal. There he built a house, and within a square mile of cleared fields and orchards, watered by brooks of the sacred Tungabhadra, he established a retreat. This provided a location for a self-sufficient residential school and the teaching of students and pilgrims he attracted. Such a venture was not, however, inexpensive. As Ramabai later recalled,

> The place he had selected for his home happened to be a sacred place of pilgrimage, where pilgrims came all the year around. He thought it was his duty to entertain them at his expense, as hospital-

4. Pandita Ramabai Sarasvati, *A Testimony of Our Inexhaustible Treasure* (Kedgaon: Mukti Mission, 1907 [11th ed. 1992]), p. 1. Reprinted in *Pandita Ramabai Through Her Own Words,* compiled and edited by Meera Kosambi (New Delhi: Oxford University Press, 2000), pp. 295ff.

Anant Shastri and his family; Ramabai is second from the left

> ity was a part of his religion. For thirteen years he stayed there and did his work quietly, but lost all his property because of the great expense he incurred.[5]

It was in 1858, after he had exhausted his resources, that Anant Shastri put his six-month-old daughter in a basket and headed down the mountain with his family. Forced to abandon his idyllic retreat, he decided to seek his living as a *puranika* (reader/reciter/preacher of Puranas). Accompanied by Lakshmibai his wife and their three surviving children, he set out on his unending pilgrimage. For Ramabai, these wanderings would continue until 1878, four years after his death. By then, only she and her brother Srinivas Shastri survived.

Ramabai's own education began at the age of eight. Her father, by then too blind to read, left all instruction to her mother. Awakened well before dawn, before the others were stirring, Ramabai would be drilled relentlessly. In the *gurukul* system, single words, then phrases, and finally sentences would be recited twice; these would then be repeated back five or ten times until exact words and phrases had been indelibly recorded into memory. With increasing proficiency, lessons increased in size — to a thousand and then two thousand

5. Ramabai Sarasvati, *A Testimony,* pp. 11-12.

spoken lines — each uttered twice and then repeated back five times, or ten times. Her parents had carefully wrapped in cloth and preserved hundreds of palm-leaf books and manuscripts, which would be taken out and transcribed one by one. Paper and ink and printed books, deemed too defiling to touch, were strictly avoided. Repeating each lesson aloud, committing all words to memory, and inscribing them on palm leaves was exhausting. Among the works Ramabai memorized were whole vocabularies, dictionaries, grammars, commentaries, and classics such as the Bhagavata Purana and Bhagavata Gita.

By age fifteen, Ramabai took her place as each member of the family was able to take turns at giving public recitations or readings from classical works. Traveling from one sacred place to another, ever crossing and re-crossing India, they only stayed in any one place for a few months. Sitting cross-legged, manuscript in hand — by the roadside, in the shade of a great tree, at the confluence of two rivers, on the banks of a tank, or inside a temple hall — one family member after another would intone the sacred sounds. Passers-by would pause to listen and would make offerings of flowers, fruits, food, clothing, or money, hoping thereby to gain expiation and merit *(puniya).*

This pattern of life continued for sixteen years, until Ramabai's eighty-year-old father became too feeble to travel. At that time, the entire country, especially the region known as the Madras Presidency, was suffering from a terrible famine. The family wandered desperately in search of food and water. In a forest near Tirupati, they prayed that some tiger or snake might end their miseries. Then, first her father, next her mother, and finally her sister starved to death. Only Ramabai and Srinivas remained. They managed not only to survive but to remain free from pollution; even as they continued their studies and wanderings, they also gradually became more and more disillusioned, both with their old religion *(sanāthana dharma)* and with their means of livelihood:

> We wandered from place to place, visiting many temples, washing in many rivers, fasting and performing penances . . . [this was] all that we knew for more than three years after the death of our parents and elder sister. We had walked more than four thousand miles on foot without any sort of comfort; sometimes eating what kind people gave us, and sometimes going without food, with poor, coarse clothing, and finding but little shelter except in Dharma Shalas . . . free lodging places for the poor.[6]

6. Ramabai Sarasvati, *A Testimony,* p. 16. In other accounts, she wrote of living on a handful of grain soaked in water, walking barefoot, sleeping under trees or roadside bridges, digging pits to keep warm, and swallowing wild, hard berries. See, for example, *Pandita Ramabai: The*

After wandering from the south as far north as Kashmir, Ramabai and her brother decided they would no longer disdain to earn a livelihood by some other means than their itinerant life. In 1878, they journeyed to Calcutta.

Entry into Public Life

Calcutta, like all of India, was just then emerging into the modern world. In fact, the very name "India" was new, signifying things the people of India, including Ramabai, had never before known. While the many cultures, hundreds of kingdoms, and the myriad of village communities on the subcontinent were very old, some having existed from earliest antiquity, at no time had the entire region been unified under a single system of government. Prior to this, over the centuries, countless peoples and tribes had entered the continent from the northwest — as military invaders, migrants, merchants, and mendicants. Domains of different size and strength had formed and fallen, expanded and crumbled, merged and split. What had been left behind was a rich mosaic of diverse cultures.

In recent centuries, however, more intruders had also come from the sea. Eventually, by gradual processes of collaboration, conquest, and consolidation, some groups of these Europeans, known locally as *Farangi,* had grown wealthy and powerful. Indeed, in the century before Ramabai's birth, the entire subcontinent had been brought together and consolidated under a single over-arching political system.

Yet this system, known as "India, " the "Indian Empire," or the "Raj," had never been solely the handiwork of aliens from Europe. Rather, from its earliest, most fragile beginnings in the seventeenth century, this had been a joint venture, a collaborative experiment in which indigenous elite communities had played pivotal roles. Without Indian manpower, Indian money, and Indian methods there could never have been an India. Merchant partners, Indian and European, made huge fortunes through mercantile activities, especially in the merchandizing of handmade cotton textiles. These partnerships then, when compelled by turbulent events, turned to the manufacturing and merchandizing of modern military machines — again, by using indigenous manpower and materials. High-quality armies, regiments of professional mercenaries recruited from warrior castes, were rented out to princes. Reve-

Widows' Friend, second ed. (Melbourne: George Robertson and Co., 1903), p. 14, the Australian edition of *The High-Caste Hindu Woman,* which was edited and includes a sequel by her daughter, Manoramabai.

nue from such rentals, on terms that became institutionalized, paid for the making and maintaining of more and more military establishments. Such establishments within princely states, like so many Trojan horses, brought about the undoing of such princes. Thus, just as merchant bankers and entrepreneurs of India had helped to construct the East India Company's commercial empire, so military manpower of India enabled conquests by which the Company gained a huge territorial empire. Between 1773 and 1793, first under Warren Hastings and then under Lord Cornwallis, structures for stabilizing internal security and codes for applying a regular and systematic rule of law had been developed and then strengthened.

By the time Ramabai's father left Pune in 1818, standing armies of the Indian Empire's three presidencies sometimes numbered from as many as 150,000 to 300,000 Indian soldiers (sepoys). Comparable numbers of native civil servants provided the administrative skills without which this vast imperial system could not be governed. By then, the Government of India, created in 1773, had become "paramount" over the whole subcontinent. This system of rule — this Raj — continued to expand until, by the time of Ramabai's birth in 1858, just after the Great Mutiny (or Revolt), the Company itself was swept away and a more alien and distant British Crown put in its place. But by then, the sway of the Raj encircled the Indian Ocean, reaching across the Arabian Sea into the Persian Gulf, Red Sea, and Africa, and across the Bay of Bengal into Burma, the Malay Peninsula, and beyond.

Twenty years after Ramabai's birth, by the time she and her brother reached Calcutta in 1878, new forces were starting to challenge this Raj. These new challenges were coming from within the very same elite communities that had helped to construct the Raj in the first place — from those whose indispensable sinews of manpower and money and method had made it possible. Challenges came from those who, through their own intellectual curiosity and dexterity, had not only demanded modern educational institutions for themselves but also gained a remarkable mastery over the English language, English channels of communication, and English technology. The newly aspiring and affluent classes within British India were the professional people of a "New India" — enlightened journalists, lawyers, physicians, teachers, bureaucrats, and even some of the landed gentry. Challenges to the Raj were coming mostly from among those who belonged to the most advanced, forward-looking, and self-reforming elements in India's social system. Most important of all, challenges were being mounted by those who, while engaged in efforts to influence imperial policy through increasing numbers of voluntary associations, were also beginning to think of themselves as nationalists. They were now seeing themselves as the "true Indians," as distinct from the tiny group of Europeans (Britons) who occupied the highest seats in government and whose colonial society was increasingly perceived as "alien" and "foreign." Two reformist societies in particular were to strongly influence Ramabai's life — the older Brahmo Samaj of Bengal (Calcutta) and the newer Prarthana Samaj of Maharashtra (Pune). Ramabai soon counted herself among the most ardent nationalists of India.

It was in Calcutta, not long after her arrival, that Ramabai suddenly entered this new world. Just twenty years old, her brilliance startled and astounded all. Learned Brahmans and Europeans, Sanskrit experts of Calcutta who examined her, could hardly believe their ears. This tiny young woman could recite from memory all eighteen thousand verses of the Bhagavata Purana, together with the whole of Panini's famous Grammar. Laboriously they composed a Sanskrit verse in her honor. She responded by quickly composing verses for them on the spot. Having already called her "Pandita," they now added the title "Saraswati" ("Goddess of Learning"). Overnight she became a national sensation. Newspapers throughout the land reported her scholarly debut, and local institutions vied with each other to have her as a speaker. Wherever she went, her fame went before her. She became a sought-after celebrity, a symbol of rising national pride. Her words and deeds were closely followed, and not just in India but in remote parts of the world.

It was in Calcutta also that Ramabai's disillusionment with the Hindu religion deepened. The terrible deaths of her parents had deeply disturbed her beliefs and raised doubts. As the Brahmo Samaj, especially Kesheb Chandra Sen and his family, dared her to read texts forbidden to women (and those of low caste), she examined the Manusmritri Dharmashastras, the Upanishads, and even the Vedas and found contradictions: sacred texts informing her that "women of high- and low-castes, as a class, were bad, very bad, worse than demons, unholy . . . and that they could not get Moksha [release, salvation] . . .";[7] that a woman's sole hope of admission to *svarga* (heaven) lay in worshiping her husband and utterly abandoning herself to him as his slave; that low-caste people had "no hope of any sort . . . being very like the lower species of animal, such as pigs."[8]

Institutional injustices that had held all women in helpless thralldom for so long, she concluded, had been invoked in the name of the "old religion" *(sanāthana dharma).* Thus, she later confessed, her ceaseless quest for greater liberty *(mukti)* began. She became a Brahmo, or monotheist, forsaking graven

7. Ramabai Sarasvati, *A Testimony,* pp. 18-19.

8. Rambai Sarasvati, *A Testimony,* pp. 19-20. She also read that molten lead was to be poured into the ears of any Shudra who just happened to overhear the Vedas being recited.

images and pilgrimages to sacred places. She ceased her work as a *puranika* and, instead, began her career as a public speaker, speaking on behalf of women in particular. The story-telling skills that had served her so well since childhood, enlivened by her captivating and charismatic personal magnetism, held audiences spellbound. Championing women's education and emancipation, she took every opportunity to repudiate the idea that women were not fit to read the Vedas. Eventually, even the contradictions and eclecticism of the Brahmo Samaj began to dismay her,[9] especially when the Kesheb, the very person who had spoken so vehemently against child marriage, forced his own daughter to marry before the age of consent. Even so, Ramabai's popularity increased, and invitations poured in upon her from all sides.

Then, in the midst of personal triumphs, Ramabai was again struck by sudden personal tragedies. Srinivas Shastri Dongre, her remaining brother, died. They had been on an extended speaking tour in Assam and had returned to Dacca as guests in the home of Sri Shebhoy Charan Das when Srinivas was struck down by cholera. The shock was profound: without her brother, she lost the companion who had been with her since earliest childhood and provided her with a sense of security. Deeply devoted to him and safe under his protection, she had felt no compelling need to marry, despite proposals. (Unlike most women of her time, Ramabai had of course never been given in marriage in her youth; her father had been dissuaded from arranging the customary early marriage for her by the early and unhappy marriage of her elder sister.)

News of Ramabai's plight quickly reached Maharashtra. There hopes arose, especially among the social reformers, that this "priceless gem" might be brought back to "her native homeland." One newspaper, the *Subodh Patrika,* suggested that she might run a school for "adult women . . . desirous of a further knowledge of Marathi and Sanskrit," and that, in any case, "it [would be] highly blameworthy to allow Ramabai to stay in a foreign country [sic] and face calamities in such a destitute condition."[10]

But suddenly, other news arrived. Ramabai announced that, in accord with her brother's last wishes, she was marrying Babu Bepin Behari Das

9. A. B. Shah, ed., and Sister Geraldine, compiler, *The Letters and Correspondence of Pandita Ramabai* (Bombay: Maharashtra State Board for Literature and Culture, 1977), p. xv, n. 5.

10. In Meera Kosambi, *Pandita Ramabai's Feminist and Christian Conversions* (Bombay: Research Centre for Women's Studies, S.N.D.T. Women's University, 1995), p. 45, as quoted directly from Pandita Ramabai's *Pandita Ramabai yancha Englandcha Pravas,* second ed. (Bombay: Maharashtra State Board of Literature and Culture, 1883), p. 36. Bengal was viewed as a foreign country by the people of Maharashtra.

Medhavi.[11] Bepin Babu, handsome and talented, was a pleader in the District Court at Sylhet (Assam). Having previously served as headmaster of Gauhati Normal School, he had already published a textbook in Bengali entitled *Introduction to Chemistry.* Ramabai had met him in Calcutta, and, in due time, they had become well acquainted. In her words,

> About a year before my brother's death, we were invited to come and stay in a town [Sylhet, Assam] where we stayed for ten months. There lived my dearly beloved late husband, Babu Bepin Behari, M.A., M.L., a very learned, humble, and kindly gentleman. He became an intimate friend of my brother. I too became very much attached to him. After some time, Mr. Bepin, as it usually happens, wrote a letter to me and asked my consent for marriage with him. I did not answer. After that, he asked me again four or five times. "It would be possible if my brother is agreeable to the proposition," I said. After a few days we were invited to visit Dacca. Before proceeding there Mr. Bepin made me promise that I would not give my consent to marry anyone else, and that I would marry him if my brother gave his consent.[12]

Bepin Behari Babu was a Kayastha. That Kayasthas ranked highly in North India seems never to have quite registered with Ramabai: she often later referred to him as "low caste" and "Shudra."[13] For a Maratha Brahman of Chitpavan or Konkanestha birth, someone who normally would not even have mar-

11. Padmini Sengupta, *Pandita Ramabai Saraswati: Her Life and Work* (Bombay: Asia Publishing House, 1970), p. 68. Sengupta quotes from *The Statesmen and Friend of India* (January 18, 1879): "The *Sulabha Samachar* hears that the well known Roma Bye is about to be married to an educated Bengali — an M.A. of Calcutta University in the service of the Dholipore Raj. The accomplished lady has left Calcutta for the purpose. The proposed announcement, if true, is an interesting sign of the times, it being, we believe, the first time when a Bengali has succeeded in winning the love of a Marathi lady."

12. Quoted in Sengupta, *Pandita Ramabai Saraswati,* p. 77. Quote from the *Subodh Patrika* (November 17, 1882).

In *Letters and Correspondence,* pp. 17-18, we read that Ramabai married "a great friend of her brother" six months after her brother's death, that she had already known him for two years, that he had been born in the Sylhet District of Assam, that having lost his parents he was brought up by an uncle, and that he had gained his education and become headmaster of a government normal school in Assam.

13. In *A Testimony,* p. 22, she wrote, "Having lost all faith in the religion of my ancestors, I married a Bengali gentleman of the Shudra caste." Almost the same words are found in a short autobiography quoted in a letter of Sister Geraldine (dated Wantage: November 1, 1883) in *Letters and Correspondence,* pp. 17-18.

ried a Brahman from some other caste, she may never have really known very much about people of lower castes — especially since it was customary for Brahmans to speak and think of all who were immediately below them, even if respectable, as Shudra. In any case, since no orthodox priest would officiate in an inter-caste marriage, their wedding was a civil ceremony. It was duly registered on October 13, 1880 (under Act III of 1872, by which such marriages could be recognized). Husband and wife lived happily together in Cachar (Silchar), Assam, for nineteen months.[14] Then, suddenly, like her brother, Bepin too came down with cholera and died (on February 4, 1882).[15] Once again, Ramabai found herself alone, now a widow of twenty-four with an infant daughter (who had been born in July of 1881). Moreover, she not only had to fend for herself, but she had to pay off the debts her late husband had accumulated.

Once again, when news of Ramabai's plight spread across the land, new offers arrived. One Chitpavan couple living in Serampore (Bengal) invited her to come and live with them. This gesture, by Anandibai and Gopalrao Joshi, she never forgot. It was, indeed, the gesture that would later prompt Ramabai's visit to America.[16] Meanwhile, Maratha Brahmans of the Prarthana Samaj, those from her own Konkanestha community in Maharashtra who had previously hailed her proudly as a "native daughter" and "one of our own," also renewed their efforts to bring her back to Pune. Ramabai was cautious. She did not want to suffer any loss of her newfound liberty. Having suffered years of shunning and slights, from "friends" and relatives fearful of losing caste, she was determined to accept no charity: she would make her own way, as best she could, caring for herself and her child. She would be beholden to no one. Moreover, as a woman with a mission, she solemnly vowed before the genteel women of Dacca that she would henceforth dedicate herself entirely to the betterment of women in India. As she pondered how to render such service to the women of India, she decided that modern medicine would best serve this purpose. Thus, even as invitations came to her from Pune, she

14. It was during this happy time in Assam that Ramabai composed and sent to the Orientalist Congress in Berlin her poem entitled "Ode to Sanskrit: Addressed to the Congress at Berlin, September 1881, by the Lady, Pandit Ramabai of Silchar, Cachar, Assam, with a translation by Sir Monier-Williams, K.C.I.E., D.C., M.A., Boden Professor of Sanskrit at the University of Oxford" (Oxford: December 21, 1881). See Sengupta, *Pandita Ramabai Saraswati,* pp. 340-47, for the entire text, in both Sanskrit and English.

15. Sengupta, *Pandita Ramabai Saraswati,* pp. 68-73. At the birthplace of Bepin Behari, in Marjatkandi (Cachar, Assam), institutions in their memory, erected to serve the oppressed, have been named the Bepin Bhavan and the Ramabai Seva Sadan.

16. Caroline Wells Healey Dall, *The Life of Dr. Anandabai Joshee, a Kinswoman of the Pundita Ramabai* (Boston: Roberts Brothers, 1888), pp. vi-viii, 131-34.

was traveling down to Madras to enquire into the possibilities of pursuing a medical education.

Controversy in Pune

Ramabai's eventual arrival in Pune attracted immediate and widespread attention — and controversy. No sooner had she settled as a guest in the Abhyanker's residence *(wada)* than invitations plunged her into a strenuous schedule of public speaking engagements. Her clear and stated purpose, with encouragement from such prominent social reformers as Raosaheb Mahdeo Govind Ranade and Sir Ramakrishna Gopal Bhandarkar, was to campaign for the emancipation and advancement of women. To that end, she soon founded the Arya Mahila Samaj, a women's association dedicated to promoting social awareness. At its first meeting, on June 1, 1882, before one hundred and fifty prominent ladies, she called upon on all women to free themselves — from oppressive customs, from child marriage, from illiteracy and denial of basic education, and, especially, from oppression suffered by high-caste child widows. The impression she made was vividly described by Mrs. Ramabai Ranade:

> The sweet and musical flow of her speech and the manner in which she presented her subject were alike admirable. In addition, she had amazing skill in winning the hearts of her hearers for whatever she had to say. The result was that every educated person, young and old, in the city who desired to learn, was filled with pride and admiration.[17]

Within a few weeks Ramabai also wrote and published her first book. Entitled *Stree Dharma-Neeti,* it appeared in June of 1882.[18] In stilted and heavily Sanskritized Marathi that some found difficult to read or understand, and

17. Nicol Macnicol, *Pandita Ramabai: A Builder of Modern India* (New Delhi: Good Books, 1996), p. 100, quotes from Ramabai Ranade's Marathi *Athvani* (Recollections), p. 106. The same passage can be found in Kusumavati Deshpande's translation of Ramabai Ranade's *Amchya Ayushatil Kahi Ashavai* (Pune: Dnyanaprakash Press, 1910) entitled *Ranade: His Wife's Reminiscences* (Delhi: Government of India, 1963). It reads: "Her exposition was excellent. She had the power of drawing and holding the attention of her listeners. With all these qualities, she became an object of pride and admiration for all lovers of education, new and old, in the city" (p. 83).

18. Under the mandatory registration required for all vernacular books, it was given the English title *Morals for Women.*

opponents soon disparaged, she castigated Brahman men for the way they had long treated their women. She also chided Brahman women for slothful and slovenly habits that earned disrespect from their husbands.

Opposition to Ramabai came from women within her own Brahman community. Nowhere was this more pronounced than within the Ranade house. As the Pandita's foremost sponsor in Pune, Raosaheb Ranade had decided to have her deliver her first major discourse within his own home. His second wife,[19] the young woman also named Ramabai already mentioned (who was sometimes also known as Vahinibai), was utterly committed to her husband's causes. Educated by him, she recorded her recollections of how this event aroused animosity (not unmingled with fear) among the women of her own family:

> Since my husband and I were inclined towards her, the women of our family had a priceless opportunity to pour ridicule upon us, along with the Pandita. . . . They seemed to detest Panditabai more and more every day. If she called on us, they would say to me, "She is a wretched convert. Don't touch anything in our house, after touching her. . . . We cannot tolerate such sacrilege. What an accursed thing! Her father turned her into a devotee and wedded her to the heavenly bridegroom, Shri Dwarkanath. And yet, this wretch married a Bengali baboo and polluted herself. She brought utter ruin on everyone connected with her and is now out to pollute the whole world!"[20]

Predictably, Ramabai's campaign also evoked heavy criticism from Chitpavan men. Kashinath Trimbak Telang, Bal Gangadhar (later "Lokmanya") Tilak, and others gave priority to political reforms rather than to social reforms. Through newspapers, such as *Kesari* (in Marathi) and *The Mahratta* (in English), they mobilized public opposition against her. Mingling grudging respect with scorn, they reacted against anything that could interfere with "larger" or national issues and anything that might threaten their own dominance. Having hesitantly approved the moderate tone of Ramabai's *Stree Dharma-Neeti,* even while condemning its overly Sanskritized vocabulary, dense and convoluted

19. Despite his strong opposition to child marriage, Ranade had been forced against his will into this second marriage when she was eleven and he thirty-two. Although totally illiterate at the time of their marriage, she had become a dedicated scholar by the time she met Pandita Ramabai.

20. Ranade, *Ranade: His Wife's Reminiscences,* p. 232. See also Ramabai Ranade, *Himself: The Autobiography of a Hindu Lady* (New York: Longmans, Green and Co., 1938), translated and adapted by Katherine Van Akin Gates from Ranade's original Marathi book.

syntax, and awkward Marathi terminology, they took special exception to her radical calls for female literacy, medical training, and liberation.

What hardened this opposition was Ramabai's decision to give testimony before the Hunter Commission on Education.[21] Appearing before the commission on September 5, 1882, she declared,

> I am the child of a man who had to suffer a great deal on account of advocating Female Education, and who was compelled to discuss the subject, as well as to carry out his own views amidst great opposition. . . . I consider it my duty, to the very end of my life, to maintain this cause, and to advocate the proper position of women in this land.[22]

She went on to explain that women needed better educational facilities and opportunities for female teachers in both general and medical education. Without such changes, the oppression which India's women had suffered for so long would never come to an end. Dr. W. W. Hunter, president of the commission, had previously heard Ramabai speak in Bengal, and had been impressed.[23] Now he immediately ordered her testimony translated and published in a separate pamphlet and also ordered a government purchase of six hundred copies of her book.

Nevertheless, seeing her efforts being blocked and frustrated, Ramabai began to look at other options. Unable to see how the plight of India's women could be improved until Indian women started studying medicine and becoming physicians, she decided to take lessons in English and to use the proceeds from her book to purchase passage aboard a ship. She sailed from Bombay on April 20, 1883, bound for England.

21. *Report of the Indian Education Commission, appointed by the resolution of the Government of India, dated February 3, 1882* (Calcutta: 1883), vol. 2.

22. From a portion of the English translation of Ramabai's deposition, which she took to America and inserted in her most renowned English book, *The High-Caste Hindu Woman* (see pp. xvi-xvii).

23. Sengupta, *Pandita Ramabai Saraswati*, pp. 11-14. Sir William Wilson Hunter, "A Lady Lecturer in India," in *England's Work in India* (London: Smith, Elder and Co., 1881), pp. 50-51, recounts that at a lecture he heard on the banks of the Ganga, "The clear blue sky and the broad river . . . sweeping down . . . dominated everything else. It was a place such as Buddha might have chosen to address his followers. This young lady is twenty-two years of age, slight and girlish looking, with a fair complexion and light grey eyes. She is now engaged to be married to a Bengali pleader, an M.A. from Calcutta University."

Turning Points, and Ramabai's English Experience

Conversions marked the course of Ramabai's life. From infancy onward, from her journey down from the mountain abode of Gangamal, she was constantly exposed to new insights and perspectives. As new vistas opened, her outlook changed, producing a pattern of pivotal turning points. Acutely conscious of the sufferings her parents had endured and the price they had paid for turning against established, age-old taboos which would have denied her access to "the divine language" of Sanskrit, Ramabai continued the pattern of turning against the expected which her parents had established. The events of her life — her own turning away from *sanāthana dharma* long before she and Srinivas had reached Calcutta; her turning to and then away from the Brahmo Samaj; her dedication of herself, in turn, to campaigning on behalf of oppressed women; and, finally, her marriage outside of caste and "outside the fold" of conventional Hindu *dharma* — all had accustomed her to a life of turning and turning and turning again.

Many of these turnings can be seen as distinct conversions marking important events in the evolution of her Christian faith. Each brought her more deeply into a personal faith, moving her progressively from an intellectual to a more devotional relationship with God. The first of these (to go back briefly in time) occurred long before her journey from Bombay to England, while she and her husband were living in Silchar (Cachar District, Assam). It began as a chance encounter.[24] One day, while looking among books in her home, she came upon a little Bengali pamphlet. Not knowing what it was, she picked it up and started to read. It was a copy of Luke's Gospel. Fascinated and curious, she began to ask questions. Answers came to her from her husband's long-time friend, a Baptist missionary by the name of Isaac Allen, who explained many things to her including the Genesis story of creation. He left her a small card on which the words "Incline your heart to the Lord" were printed. Of this time, she later wrote, "Having lost all faith in my former religion, and with my heart hungering after something better, I eagerly learnt everything I could about the Christian re-

24. This was not, however, Ramabai's first experience with anything Christian. Previously, while in Calcutta, she had gone to a meeting of Christians and had been astonished at how they knelt with their faces to the back of their chairs and prayed with their eyes closed. Someone in Calcutta had then presented her with a Sanskrit copy of the Bible.

Ramabai would also relate the story of her first contact with missionaries when, while still a child, she was bathing on the banks of the Ganges and two words — "Yeshu Khrista" (Jesus Christ) — had stuck with her and come to her lips, a name she'd never forgotten. See "Ramabai Sings Magnificat," in *Letters and Correspondence*, p. 428.

ligion, and declared my intention to become a Christian. . . ." But her husband became upset: he had gone to a Christian school and appreciated what the Bible taught, but he did not wish to become identified as a Christian, nor "did he like the idea of his wife being publicly baptized and joining the despised Christian community."[25]

After her husband's death and her own arrival in Pune, Ramabai's continuing interest in Christian ideas soon brought her into contact with a Chitpavan Brahman convert by the name of Nehemiah Goreh.[26] Goreh, a learned and ordained Anglican missionary well-versed in Sanskrit literature, took pains to answer difficult questions, both doctrinal and philosophical, and did so with patience. At the same time, in her efforts to find someone who could teach her English, Ramabai learned that Ranade was employing someone to teach his wife English. Panditabai immediately asked if she too could attend these lessons. The teacher was an Anglo-Catholic missionary sister by the name of Miss Hurford. She came regularly to the Ranade house, and there she used an English New Testament as her textbook, and also a Marathi New Testament.

Miss Hurford would become an important figure in the story of Ramabai's journey to England, as it was she who brought Ramabai into contact with other sisters of her Anglo-Catholic mission. From the sisters of this mission, the Community of St. Mary the Virgin (CSMV), Ramabai soon received an invitation to stay and to train at their headquarters in Wantage, England. Since she was adamantly opposed to accepting charity, an arrangement was eventually worked out whereby she would give Sanskrit lessons to fledgling missionary sisters in return for what was given her. Even so, Ramabai wanted it clearly understood that these arrangements would in no way oblige her to become a Christian.

Ramabai embarked from Bombay, as noted, on April 20. She landed in England on May 17, 1883. With her was her young daughter Manorama and a Brahman companion named Anandibai Bhagat. Soon after her arrival, she met the former governor of the Bombay Presidency, Sir Bartle Frere. Encouraged by their conversation, she carefully crafted a public letter entitled "The Cry of the Indian Women." In it, she appealed to the British public on behalf of the Arya Mahila Samaj and proposed setting up a "destitute home" for female victims of oppression.

This letter may well have been inspired by her visit to a "Rescue Home" run by the CSMV Sisters at Fulham. What she saw there made her realize that

25. Ramabai Sarasvati, *A Testimony*, p. 23.

26. See C. E. Gardner, *Life of Father Goreh* (London: Longmans, Green and Co., 1900).

it was possible for fallen women, in conditions of abject and utter destitution, to be totally transformed by "the love of Christ and compassion for suffering humanity." Lives of dedicated service to homeless, sick, and infirm women, she realized, could really make a radical difference in the world. "Here for the first time in my life," she would later recall, "I came to know that something could be done to reclaim the so-called fallen women and that Christians, whom Hindus considered outcastes and cruel, were kind to these unfortunate women. . . . I had never heard or seen anything of the kind done for this class of women by the Hindus of my own country."[27] Reading the story of Jesus and the Samaritan woman, she learned about "the Infinite Love of Christ for sinners" and saw that Christ came not to condemn but to save all who turned to him. "I had never read or heard anything like this," she wrote; "I realized, after reading the fourth chapter of St. John's Gospel, that Christ was truly the Divine Saviour he claimed to be, and no one but He could transform and uplift the downtrodden women of India. . . . Thus my heart was drawn to the religion of Christ. I was intellectually convinced. . . ."[28] On September 29, 1883, Ramabai and her daughter Manorama were baptized.[29] She later confessed, "I never regretted having taken that step. I was hungry for something better. I found it in the Christian Bible and was satisfied."[30]

The simplicity of this later confession, however, seems to belie the traumatic experiences she suffered in the weeks just after her arrival in England. Her companion from India, Anandibai Bhagat, had become deeply depressed and frightened. Some sense of what happened can be found in a letter Professor Max Müller wrote to his daughter on October 27, 1883:

> We had a nice visit from Ramabai, a Bramin lady who knows Sanskrit splendidly. She knows books as long as Homer by heart from beginning to end, speaks correctly and writes Sanskrit poetry. Although she came to England to study and take a degree, she is very unhappy. . . . What happened was quite terrible. Her friend was frighted by the idea that she and Ramabai would be made Christians by force; and to save Ramabai and herself, she tried one night

27. Ramabai Sarasvati, *A Testimony,* pp. 25-26. Full text also found in Kosambi, *Pandita Ramabai Through Her Own Words,* pp. 307-8.

28.Ramabai Sarasvati, *A Testimony,* pp. 25-26.

29. Quoted in the introduction to *Letters and Correspondence,* p. xv. Canon (Dean) Butler officiated, while Sister Geraldine and others listened to her speak her confession and the Apostles' Creed. Ramabai was christened "Mary Rama" and her daughter "Manorama Mary" (pp. 14-15).

30. Ramabai Sarasvati, *A Testimony,* pp. 25-26.

to strangle her. Failing that, she committed suicide herself. It was at this terrible catastrophe at Wantage that Ramabai came to stay with us at Oxford, and such was her nervous prostration that we had to give her a maidservant to sleep every night in the same room with her.[31]

Exactly how this tragedy came about remains unclear. Both Anandibai and Ramabai seem to have been suffering what in our day is called culture shock, and the pressures they encountered were very heavy.

As if these experiences were not enough, Ramabai also faced a head-on encounter with political forces of Western Christendom. This came in the form of cultural and racial, if not clerical and colonial, domination by authorities within the Church of England. Initial pressure came from Sister Geraldine, the sister at Wantage charged by the Mother Superior with mentoring Ramabai.[32] As arguments between Ramabai and Sister Geraldine intensified, the Pandita soon realized that her stay with the Wantage Sisters would not provide the help she needed and wanted.[33] The cloying confinement of Wantage, with its strict discipline, regimentation, and dogma, was too much for her. On top of everything, Ramabai discovered at this critical juncture that a hearing defect would preclude her obtaining a medical education. Nevertheless, she became no less determined to equip herself to provide basic education for high-caste child widows in India.

Ramabai was a free spirit. She yearned for liberty, for answers to her questions, and for freedom to pursue her own vision. These she found in Dorothea Beale. Beale was an intellectual with Broad Church leanings and a philosophical bent of mind, and she herself had recently struggled with doubts about her faith.[34] As founder and principal of the Cheltenham Ladies'

31. Friedrich Max Müller, *Auld Lang Syne, Second Series: My Indian Friends* (New York: C. Scribner's Sons, 1899), pp. 127-28. See also "Pandita Ramabai," by Sister Geraldine, and Mother Harriet's letter (September 1, 1883), enclosing Anandibai's suicide note, both in *Letters and Correspondence*, pp. 9-14.

32. See "Apologia Pro Opere," "1917," and "Pandita Ramabai," by Sister Geraldine, in *Letters and Correspondence*, pp. 3-9.

33. Sister Geraldine later confessed (Wantage: March 19, 1917), "I was not equipped for such a work as instructing Ramabai. . . . [N]either my natural gifts nor my educational advantages would have fitted me for the work. This is why it was decided to send her to Cheltenham Ladies' College, that she might have the advantage of instruction by women of the highest education and culture" (*Letters and Correspondence*, p. 5).

34. See Elizabeth Raikes, *Dorothea Beale of Cheltenham* (London: Archibald Constable and Company, 1908), pp. 197-98. Raikes writes that "at a time when long accepted opinions were unsettled for many, by new scientific theories, Beale struggled. Her resignation letter, written

College, she was a forceful champion of women's education, someone who shared Ramabai's vision.[35] Beale, with encouragement from Professor Max Müller at Oxford and with support from the Royal Bounty Fund (via William Gladstone, on behalf of the Queen),[36] invited Ramabai to study at Cheltenham. By early 1884, arrangements had been completed: Ramabai would learn mathematics, science, and literature under Beale's direction,[37] and, as professor of Sanskrit, she would share some her own learning with others. During the next two years, midst ongoing discussions with Dorothea Beale, she regained her balance and confidence.[38] Beale provided sympathetic support, intellectual and rational reinforcement, and the constant emotional and moral encouragement that Ramabai needed in her ongoing struggles with Sister Geraldine and the Anglo-Catholic bishops.

At issue was Ramabai's adamant refusal to allow her thought to be controlled or dominated by anyone. Relentless efforts to steer her and make her conform ran up against an iron will. The Anglo-Catholic establishment failed to perceive what Max Müller had so quickly grasped — that "this truly heroic Hindu lady, in appearance small, delicate, and timid, [was] in reality strong and bold as a lioness. . . ."[39] Adamantly refusing to bend to church discipline, to accept any doctrine imposed by the Wantage Community, or to bow to ecclesiastical dictates from bishops with the Church of England, Ramabai remained dauntless. Attempts to control her beliefs or to force her faith into any mold of cultural and national identity other than her own utterly failed. In July 1884, she made her position clear:

---

10 August 1882, was not submitted, after doubts left her." Ramabai's long letters to Dorothea Beale regarding her own religious difficulties were answered at equal length.

35. Raikes, *Dorothea Beale of Cheltenham;* also, Amy Key Clarke, *A History of the Cheltenham Ladies' College, 1853-1953* (London: Faber and Faber, 1953). Ramabai's enthusiasm and unsparing devotion to the cause of her unhappy sisters in India touched Dorothea Beale deeply, and when the home for widows was established Beale because a generous subscriber.

36. Dorothea Beale to Sister Geraldine (Cheltenham: January 2, 1884), pp. 21-22, and Beale to Geraldine (January 3 and 12, 1885), pp. 30-31, both in *Letters and Correspondence.* These notes reveal that the Queen, through William Gladstone, supported Ramabai. So also did Professor Max Müller, Gladstone himself, and others. After Ramabai acquired funds in America, she remitted £300 to pay off debts.

37. Dorothea Beale to Bishop of Bombay (Cheltenham Ladies' College: May 22, 1884), in *Letters and Correspondence,* pp. 40-41. A month later (Wantage: June 17), Bishop William Butler wrote Beale: "All that she needs is an English development of her Indian brains" (p. 45).

38. *Letters and Correspondence,* pp. xxxvi. Ramabai's letters during this time show that, once she was in Cheltenham, she read widely — from Ferishta to Raja Ram Mohan Roy to Bishop Brook Foss Westcott.

39. Friedrich Max Müller, *The Life and Letters of the Right Honourable Friedrich Max Müller* (London: Longmans, Green and Co., 1902), vol. 2, p. 149.

> It is quite true that we cannot know what will come in the next moment, yet we have a great gift from God, i.e. *our own free will.* By it we are to decide for our self what we are to do. . . . I am arguing with those people who give their opinion or decide anything for me without knowing my will, and above all God's will. . . . I am always surprised when I see or hear people troubling themselves to decide my future.[40]

A year later, when accused of insubordination, she retorted:

> [The bishops] have gone too far. . . . It was very kind of you to give me a home in this country . . . [but] I must tell you that when I find out that you or your friends have no trust in me, and they want, whether directly or indirectly, to interfere with my personal liberty, I must say "good-bye" to you and go my way, by which my Lord God will guide me. I have long since taken all matters which concern me into my own hand and shall by no means let others lay a hand on my liberty.[41]

A few days later she wrote again to Sister Geraldine:

> I have a conscience, and mind and a judgment of my own. I must myself think and do everything which GOD has given me the power of doing. . . . I am, it is true, a member of the Church of Christ, but I am not bound to accept every word that falls down from the lips of priests or bishops. . . . I have just with great efforts freed myself from the yoke of the Indian priestly tribe, so I am not at present willing to place myself under a similar yoke by accepting everything which comes from the priests as authorised command of the Most High.[42]

Clearly exasperated, Sister Geraldine chided Ramabai for a lack of "humility, childlike simplicity, obedience, truthfulness, and trustfulness" and declared

40. Pandita Ramabai to Sister Geraldine (Cheltenham: July 1884), in *Letters and Correspondence,* p. 25.

41. Pandita Ramabai to Sister Geraldine (Cheltenham: May 8, 1885), in *Letters and Correspondence,* p. 50.

42. Pandita Ramabai to Sister Geraldine (Ladies' College, Cheltenham: May 12, 1885), in *Letters and Correspondence,* pp. 58-61.

that the "germ of new life given [her] in baptism . . . [had] become overgrown by rank and poisonous weeds of heresy."[43]

Throughout all these ordeals, Ramabai continued to see herself as both Hindu and Christian. She was a convert searching for a way to resolve inner conflicts and bring about a transformation both within her own self and within the culture of her people. Steadfastly refusing to become a clone or proselyte — whether of Anglicanism or of any other kind of Western cultural institution[44] — she withstood constant onslaughts and kept her balance. Behind her own inner resources lay a toughness of mind forged on the anvil of hard experience: survival amid the perils and privations of her early life on the Indian road and inspiration from her initial conversion in Assam, where she first encountered the gospel. It was in Assam that Isaac Allen, the Baptist missionary, first imparted biblical basics to her, and in Assam that she ceaselessly strove for rational answers to her questions. This background enabled her to make clear and firm distinctions between scriptural content and church dogma. In addition, her studies in the West had uncovered contradictions and dissensions between denominational groups, each of which claimed the Bible for its ultimate authority.

> Besides meeting people of the most prominent sects, the High Church, Low Church, Baptist, Methodist, Presbyterian, Friends, Unitarian, Universalist, Roman Catholic, Jew, and others, I met with Spiritualists, Theosophists, Mormons, Christian Scientists, and followers of what they call the occult religions. No one can have any idea of what my feelings were at finding such a Babel of religions in Christian countries.[45]

Interestingly, just when relations with her Anglican "handlers" were reaching a crisis, Ramabai found help in Bristol. There, at Clifton, during the

43. Sister Geraldine to Pandita Ramabai (Wantage: October 5, 1885), in *Letters and Correspondence,* pp. 91-92. The heresies at issue were Unitarianism (questioning the divinity of Christ) and "protestant" rebellion against the Catholic church. Ramabai's searching eventually led her, through later conversions, to Trinitarian monotheism and holiness. The only catholic church she ever recognized was the universal (catholic) church, the Body of Christ: namely, all followers of Christ, visible and invisible, in all ages and in all places.

44. Historian Dana Robert (Boston University), paraphrasing Andrew Walls (Aberdeen University): "Conversion involves introducing the Gospel into a culture so that it transforms itself from within, according to its own internal logic, while proselytism involves making clones of the messenger"; review of Kevin Ward and Brian Stanley, *The Church Mission Society and World Christianity, 1799-1999* (Grand Rapids: Eerdmans, 2000), in *Books & Culture* (forthcoming).

45. Ramabai Sarasvati, *A Testimony,* pp. 26-28. These contentions she compared with dissensions between various Hindu groups she knew.

Easter weekend of May 8-11, 1885, she arranged to meet her old friend from Assam, Isaac Allen. Allen, at that time convalescing at the home of the Reverend Richard Glover, pastor of Tyndale Baptist Church and a leader of the Baptist Missionary Society, gave her the support she wanted.[46] After her return to Cheltenham, she wrote Sister Geraldine:

> I was so pleased to see my old friend again, you may have heard about him from me. . . . Mr. and Mrs. Glover who knew me long since through him had invited me (last term). . . . This time, Mr. Allen who was staying with them asked me to go there and see him. He is not very well; his health broke down in Cachar, so he had to leave that station and come home in order to save his life from the malarial fever. I enjoyed my visit to Bristol very much. On my arrival there on Saturday afternoon, Mrs. Glover took me to the Arnos Vail Cemetery to see the tomb of Raja Ram Mohan Roy. . . . Yesterday I went with Mrs. Glover to see the portrait of Raja Ram Mohan Roy in the Bristol Mission.[47]

This Easter holiday visit was significant: it marked a turning point in the battle over whether the church or the Bible would have the highest claim to Ramabai's allegiance. To Canon William Butler, founder of the CSMV (and the one who had baptized her), she wrote: "I believe in Christ. . . . But at the same time I shall not bind myself to believe in and accept everything that is taught by the church; before I accept it I must be convinced that it is according to Christ's teaching. . . ."[48] A few days later, after Beale had cautioned Butler against impatience, Ramabai wrote him in even stronger terms:

> I believe the Bible says in detail all that is necessary for the salvation of mankind. There are in the Bible all the essential articles of faith

46. Richard Glover was the father of T. R. Glover. The younger Glover, who was sixteen years old in 1885, recalled Ramabai's coming to Bristol when later, on behalf of the BMS, he visited India (1915-1916) and tried without success to get to Mukti to see her in 1916. See Brian Stanley, "A Cambridge Passage through India: The Making of T. R. Glover's 'The Jesus of History'," *Cambridge Review* 119, no. 2331 (November 1998): 60-69.

47. Pandita Ramabai to Sister Geraldine (May 12, 1885), in *Letters and Correspondence,* p. 58.

48. Pandita Ramabai to Canon William Butler (Cheltenham: July 3, 1885), in *Letters and Correspondence,* p. 76 (pp. 72-76). William Butler to Dorothea Beale at Cheltenham (Wantage: July 5, 1885), in *Letters and Correspondence,* pp. 76-77: "What I crave for her is a *humble* heart. . . . [T]o a neophyte in the Faith. . . self-reliance is intensely dangerous."

to be found. . . . All the days of the week are as much holy in God's sight as the first or the last day of the week. . . . An honest and contrite heart and true words are acceptable to God, and not outward ceremonies. Inspired books are proofs of themselves, their own honest words prove their truthfulness. And so a great many things which are not essential are left to man's choice.[49]

Again admonished by Geraldine against having anything to do with dissenters, nonconformists, and other dangerous or heretical sects, and reminded that she had been "baptised into the Church of England," Ramabai replied: "Baptism and the solemn oath which we take before GOD do not belong exclusively to one person or to one church with particular beliefs and customs. They are Catholic, i.e. Universal. . . ." She added, "in the Roman, Greek, English or Dissent [sic] Church, if a person believes with all his heart Christ to be the Son of God, might he not say with the [Ethiopian] Eunuch, 'Behold here is water, what doth hinder me to be baptised?' . . . Baptism does not bind a person to obey certain rules laid down by uninspired men . . ."; it only "binds [one] to obey Christ."[50] To this, Geraldine retorted, "you are not in a position, dear Ramabai, to argue or lay down the law as to the prerogatives of the Catholic Church. You are . . . but a babe in the Faith, and your duty is to sit as a humble learner. . . . 'Let a woman learn in quietness with all subjection.'"[51] By November 1885, the relationship between the two women was clearly becoming more strained. In gentle but firm words, Ramabai reproached her "dear old Ajeebai" (Sister Geraldine): "You seem to be very hard upon the Baptists, Congregationalists, Wesleyans, and among other bodies, mostly upon Unitarians."[52]

49. Pandita Ramabai to Canon William Butler (21 Lansdown Crescent, Cheltenham: July 2, 1885), in *Letters and Correspondence*, p. 80. Earlier, on Ash Wednesday, she had written to Sister Geraldine from Cheltenham: "My object in telling you this [on the Lord's prayer] is to show you or rather to tell you from my own experience how Indian people are touched by the simplicity of Christ's teaching. Take away all outward shows of your words and grand ceremonies and teach simply the words of Christ as they fell from His lips, without making any comments and you will see what power they have of enchanting the people's hearts."

50. Pandita Ramabai to Sister Geraldine (Wantage: September 22 night, 1885), in *Letters and Correspondence*, p. 88 (pp. 87-90).

51. Sister Geraldine to Pandita Ramabai (St. Mary's Home, Wantage: October 5, 1885), in *Letters and Correspondence*, p. 95. Geraldine also replied (Bath: October 1885) that "such bodies as the Wesleyans could not be said to belong to the Church because they were not knit together by the rites which Christ appointed" (p. 102).

52. Pandita Ramabai to Sister Geraldine (Ladies' College, Cheltenham: November 7, 1885), in *Letters and Correspondence*, p. 112.

By the time she left for America in February 1886, Ramabai's views on what constituted the one, holy, catholic (universal) church had become fixed. Henceforth, and increasingly over later years, her ecclesiology moved away from conformity and away from any single earthly community. Yet, while arguments over clerical and earthly authority were going on, Ramabai also struggled with other doubts and uncertainties. Even as news of her conversion reached India, with predictions that her days of public influence were over, she herself remained far from settled in her own mind about what she actually believed. A convinced monotheist since her days as a Brahmo in Calcutta, she continued to grapple with Trinitarian monotheism. Not yet sure about the divinity of Christ, she found herself accused of the heresy of Unitarianism. These inner struggles were still going on when her days in England came to an end, and would continue even after her sojourn in America and her return to India; deeper peace, resolution, and tranquility still lay years ahead of her. Yet, while adamantly refusing to surrender her freedom to speak and to think for herself, her words remained restrained and sensitive to those with whom she disagreed. She never broke off relations with Wantage, but continued to be grateful for the help she had received.

Sojourn in America

Ramabai had just completed two years of study at Cheltenham Ladies' College, and her relations with Wantage had come close to a breaking point, when she received an invitation to attend and celebrate the graduation of her kinswoman from Women's Medical College in Philadelphia.

The story of Anandibai Joshi is itself one of the more stirring episodes in the history of India's women and, especially, in the history of efforts to gain emancipation from shackles imposed by family and caste. The significance of Anandibai's remarkable life, along with that of Ramabai, cannot be fully appreciated without considering the cultural and social contexts within which other late-nineteenth-century women (as well as several men, whether fathers or husbands) were beginning to raise their voices.[53] Anandibai, the first Indian

53. All too briefly, a few of the most significant of these women can be mentioned: (1) Tarabai Shinde, from an elite Maratha family of Vidarbha, published *Stree Purushal-Tulana* (which came out in early 1882, just before Ramabai's book), in which she lamented double standards of morality for men and women. (2) Dr. Rakhmabai, while fighting a lawsuit by her husband, published letters in *The Times of India* under the name of "A Hindu Lady"; in these letters (entitled "Infant Marriage," June 26, 1885, and "Enforced Widowhood," September 18, 1885) she charged, "We are treated worse than beasts. We are regarded as play-things . . . ." (3) Muktabai, a

woman to earn an M.D., had been a child bride. She had also, however, been extremely fortunate in both her father and her husband. Had they not valued the traditions of learning common to all Konkanestha Chitpavan Brahmans, and done much to encourage her learning, her story would not have been remarkable. Gopal Vinayak Joshi had been her teacher for three years when, at the age of eight, she begged her father to arrange for her marry to him. Thereafter, she accompanied Gopal when he went on various assignments in the Indian Postal Service. This enabled her not only to pursue her scholarly interests but also to become well learned. The death of her only child, because of the lack of competent medical treatment for women, led her to decide that she would devote her life to trying to provide modern medicine to women. To that end, while her husband was serving as postmaster of Serampore, far from their native homeland of Maharashtra, she studied English and prepared herself for medical training overseas. It was while they were living in Serampore that she and her husband invited the just-widowed but already renowned Ramabai to come live with them. (One can assume that Anandibai had taken the trouble to read Ramabai's deposition before the Hunter Commission in the Marathi newspapers to which she and her husband subscribed.) Such was her determination to go abroad to study medicine that she sold her wedding jewelry to pay for ship passage to Philadelphia. When her plans became known, there was public outcry against any woman doing such a shocking thing, and against crossing the forbidden "Black Water" *(Kala Pani)*, which was seen as polluting. Anandibai then decided, for the first time in her life, to speak out publicly in defense of her decision to go to America. Staunch Hindu that she was, this action took great courage and determination. On February 24, 1883, to a packed audience in College Hall, Serampore, she declared: "There is probably no country so barbarous as India. . . . The want of female physicians in India is keenly felt. . . . In my humble opinion, there is a growing need for Hindu lady doctors in India, and I volunteer to qualify myself for one."[54]

Thus it transpired that the very same month that Ramabai had embarked from Bombay for England, Anandibai herself boarded a ship in Calcutta bound for America. Three years later, in the midst of taking and passing her final examinations, utterly exhausted and already fatally ill (with tubercu-

---

fourteen-year-old Mang girl in Jyotiba Phule's school, wrote an essay about griefs suffered by Mangs and Mahars *(Mana Mahrachya Dukha Visaiyi)*, which vividly catalogued the inhuman sufferings caused by untouchability among low-caste women. (4) Savitribai Phule wrote a famous letter to her husband against Brahman domination. Cf. Kosambi, *Ramabai's Feminist and Christian Conversions*, pp. 199-202; and Uma Chakravarti, *Rewriting History: The Life and Times of Pandita Ramabai* (New Delhi: Kali for Women, 1998), pp. 74-78.

54. Quoted in Dall, *Life of Dr. Anandabai Joshee*, p. 84 (pp. 81-91).

losis), Anandibai stood two days on a cold, windy, and icebound wharf waiting for Ramabai to land (March 6, 1886). Later that night, hardly able to keep her eyes open or her hand steady, she wrote her first impression of the relative she had hitherto never met: "She is a woman, tender with feeling, as tender as a flower, timid as can be, and impatient of pain, but her courage has outweighed that of the sternest and bravest warrior."[55] Shortly after this meeting, one of Anandibai's closest American friends and supporters, who came from Washington for the graduation, also penned a vivid description in her journal: "Ramabai is strikingly beautiful. Her face is clean-cut oval; her eyes, dark and large, glow with feeling. She is brunette, but her cheeks are full of color. Her white widow's saree is drawn closely over her head and fastened under her chin."[56]

One day after the graduation, on March 12, 1886, Ramabai delivered her first address in America. An hour before she rose to speak, "about eighty ladies of the highest social position" attended a special tea in honor of the occasion. Her fame had already preceded her by several years; and many came to hear what she would say. The crowd of five to six hundred who jammed the Hall "was reverent, struck by the speaker's beauty and awed by her enthusiasm and eloquence. . . . The hush which followed her appeal when, after clasping her hands in silence for a few moments, she lifted her voice to God in earnest entreaty for her countrywomen" made such an impression that, according to Caroline Dall, "The whole city echoed the next day with wondering inquiry and explanation."[57] When news of this event reached India, *The Mahratta* (May 2, 1886) reported that "a Hindoo woman of high caste, her slight figure wrapped in the white robe of Indian widowhood, out of which looked a face of most picturesque beauty," spoke without a text, and, "standing in an easy attitude, with her hands clasped upon the desk before her and speaking with a voice of musical sweetness and distinction, and with the unembarrassed manner of genuine simplicity . . . told the story of Hindoo womanhood."[58]

Overnight, Pandita Ramabai became a national sensation. Her name was heard and seen across the length and breadth of America. What she did and said was followed closely. Articles poured forth by the hundreds, especially in women's magazines. Invitations and speaking engagements multiplied. In lecture tours across the land, Ramabai told her story and challenged Americans to help their less fortunate sisters in India. Her message included a

55. Anandibai Joshi to Mrs. Carpenter (Philadelphia: March 7, 1886), in *Life of Dr. Anandabai Joshee,* pp. 128-29.

56. A letter of March 10, 1886, in Dall, *Life of Dr. Anandabai Joshee,* pp. 130-31.

57. Dall, *Life of Dr. Anandabai Joshee,* pp. 135-36.

58. Quoted in Kosambi, *Pandita Ramabai's Feminist and Christian Conversions,* pp. 152-53.

Ramabai on her first visit to America, 1886

practical proposal, something she had been developing in her mind for some time. What she wanted was a special residential boarding school for high-caste widows. This institution would provide shelter, basic training, and literacy and practical (vocational) skills. A secular or nonsectarian institution would enable all its high-caste boarding inmates to avoid pollution and to preserve caste purity. Well aware that, to be successful, anything faintly hinting of proselytism or religious indoctrination would have to be avoided, Ramabai also knew that, in order to succeed, such an institution would need not only whole-hearted participation from reform-minded leaders in India (especially her old friends and supporters of the Arya Mahila Samaj and the Prarthana Samaj) but also financial support from her new friends in America. What she envisioned was a voluntary association governed by a two-headed administrative apparatus — a local governing board made up of prominent Indians and an overseas board or committee made up of prominent Americans (and, eventually, others).

All in all, Ramabai's reception in America, much like her reception in Maharashta, drew enormous publicity. Within both societies, the imaginations of prominent, upper-class notables were awakened. Those who were idealistic and reform-minded were especially excited by her arrival. At the same time, it is apparent that Ramabai's time of reflection and study in England had prepared her for the whirlwind of activity in America. As after her time in Assam, so again after her time in England: Ramabai's many months of meditation and study seem to have been followed by an unleashing of pent-up energy and a furious outburst of productivity.

Behind Ramabai, in all these strenuous and tireless activities — all the ceaseless thinking, writing, and lecturing — lay the encouraging and directing hand of Rachel Bodley. Dr. Rachel L. Bodley, president of the Women's Medical College, was distinguished, devout, and well connected. Having already watched over Anandibai, she now determined to provide Ramabai with her fullest support. Within a few days of her arrival, Ramabai was taken to visit several kindergartens and was shown the principles upon which they were run. She acquired copies of the most advanced and approved textbooks, and, once they were in hand, she set about translating these into Marathi, and adapting them to Hindu needs. By July of 1886, she had begun to prepare schoolbooks in Marathi, based on the American model (with American designed wood-cuts but with printing delayed until her return to Bombay). By September, Bodley had helped Ramabai to enroll in a "kindergarten training-school," where, despite Ramabai's heavy lecturing schedule, she was able to faithfully complete a full year of academic coursework.

Most important of all, again at the behest of Bodley, Ramabai soon turned her lectures into a book manuscript. What she published, much enriched by her many months of research and study at Cheltenham, was entitled *The High-Caste Hindu Woman.* This, Ramabai's first book in English, became her most famous publication. With its introduction written by Bodley and dedications to the memory of Ramabai's mother, Lakshmibai Dongre, and to Anandibai Joshi (who had died in Pune on February 26, 1887), the book's success was both immediate and widespread. Before the year was out, a second edition (in a much larger print run) appeared, and later printings followed. Bodley herself hoped that profits generated from sales would help to provide support for a network of schools for high-caste Brahman widows:

> If, therefore, every American woman who during the last twelvemonth, has taken Ramabai by the hand, every college student who has heard the Pundita speak in college halls, every reader of this book whose heart has been stirred to compassion by the perusal of its sorrowful pages, will at once purchase a copy of the book and induce a friend to do the same, each reader being responsible for the sale of one copy, the work is done, and the large fund needed to prepay three passages to India, to purchase the illustrative material for the school-rooms, to illustrate and print the school-books, and secure the needed school property in India, is at once assured.[59]

Bodley's wish was fulfilled, and instant and wide acclaim throughout the English-speaking world helped to launch the venture.[60]

The Ramabai Association was formally brought into existence in a crowded meeting in Channing Hall, Boston, on Tuesday, December 13, 1887. It was headed by many of the most prominent figures of the day. Among those taking part and serving on the Board of Trustees were Edward Everett Hale (president), and Phillips Brooks, George A. Gordon, Rachel L. Bodley, Frances Willard, and Mary Hemenway (vice presidents). Before "sailing through the Golden Gate" after four months in San Francisco, Ramabai summed up successes beyond her imagination in a letter to Dorothea Beale (October 7,

59. From Rachel L. Bodley's introduction to Ramabai Sarasvati's *The High-Caste Hindu Woman*, pp. xxiii-iv.

60. In Shah's introduction to *Letters and Correspondence* we read: "The book made a tremendous impact in America. 10,000 copies . . . were sold out before Ramabai left the US . . . and brought her a profit of Rs. 25,000 [over $8,000]" (p. xx). See also Mrs. C. M. Cayley to Dorothea Beale (May 25, 1888), in *Letters and Correspondence*, p. 181; and Kosambi, *Pandita Ramabai's Feminist and Christian Conversions*, p. 154, citing Max Müller to *The Times* (August 22, 1887), p. 3.

1888): sixty-three Ramabai Circles had pledged some $5,000 (Rs. 15,000) annually; $11,000 was in hand for building a residential hall and another $14,000 was expected for building a schoolhouse.[61]

Details of Ramabai's triumphant two-year sojourn in the United States, reflecting the depth of her penetration into the consciousness of public life and, especially, into circles of high society ladies, as well as churches, colleges, and universities, have been well and carefully explored by Dr. Edith L. Blumhofer.[62] Just how comprehensively and profoundly she had come to understand America and its institutions could be seen in the book, written and published in Marathi, that was released not long after her return to India. Entitled *Conditions of Life in the United States and Travels There*, this remarkable work, reminiscent of Alexis de Tocqueville, stands as a monument to her insights. Suffice it to say that, by the time of her departure to India in late 1888, after several months on the West Coast, Ramabai could leave for her home country confident in the knowledge that some of America's most renowned, forward-looking religious leaders, reflecting a broad spectrum of denominational and doctrinal positions, from Universalists to evangelicals, had pledged themselves to her cause. After a voyage of over three months, with stops in Japan and China, she reached Bombay on February 1, 1889.

Travails of the Sharada Sadan

Ramabai no sooner stepped ashore at the "Gateway of India" than she went into high gear. During a quick trip to Pune to see her daughter (Manorama had been brought to India by the Wantage Sisters, to whom she had been sent from America), she met with her Advisory Board. This board, led by Raosahib Ranade, advised her to open her school in Bombay, away from the center of reactionary Chitpavan-Hindu elite who were already girding them-

61. Shah, *Letters and Correspondence*, pp. 182-84. The same letter tells us that word of Bodley's death had reached Ramabai in May while she was in Iowa, and that she returned seventeen hundred miles to Philadelphia before resuming her "travel in the Great West" in July 1888. By then she was also confessing that the nearer she came to her homeward journey, the more she shrank from the thought of "what unknown things" lay in wait for her in India.

62. Edith L. Blumhofer, "Consuming Fire: Pandita Ramabai and the Global Pentecostal Impulse," in *Interpreting Contemporary Christianity: Global Processes and Identities* (Pretoria: University of Pretoria, Currents in World Christianity Conference Paper, 3-7 July 2001); Edith L. Blumhofer, "'From India's Coral Strand': Pandita Ramabai and U.S. Support for Foreign Missions," in *The Foreign Missionary Enterprise at Home: Explorations in North American Cultural History*, ed. Daniel H. Bays and Grant Wacker (Tuscaloosa and London: University of Alabama Press, 2003), pp. 152-70..

selves to do battle against her. In Bombay, she worked "like a steam engine"—renting and furnishing a house, buying school equipment and materials, advertising, and doing "a hundred nameless things."

On March 11, a gathering of 150 "ladies and gentlemen" selected from among the city's reformist elite attended the grand opening of Sharada Sadan ("Home of Learning," or, more literally, "House of the Goddess of Learning"). After a benedictory prayer, "encouraging speeches" from prominent notables, and the election of Mrs. Kashibai Kanikar as president, Ramabai gave an inaugural address. In this she reviewed efforts on behalf of high-caste widows, obstacles encountered, and the results of her mission to England and America. She appealed for support and rendered a financial statement, showing funds that Ramabai Circles had already pledged. Finally, she outlined how rules of the Home would protect high-caste women from pollution, how the curriculum would provide high literacy and practical self-sufficiency for each young woman in the Home, and how much care was being taken to avoid any hint of religious propaganda.[63]

Public reaction to this "strictly neutral" and secular venture was initially positive. Still, many Christian missionaries did not think such neutrality would work, and many Hindu nationalists remained deeply suspicious. While Ramabai's "change of religion" was viewed as a "misfortune" by Hindus, many could also see that she had "not given up her national pride."[64] Yet, even as the Sharada Sadan began to slowly gain in respect and as enrollment of high-caste child widows increased, shadows were gathering. By December of 1890, twenty-one months later, these shadows over the Sharada Sadan had deepened.

First, due to the "expensiveness" of Bombay, Ramabai moved the Sharada Sadan to Pune.[65] This move into the very teeth of Chitpavan power and Hindu nationalism would seem, on its face, to have been foolhardy and fraught with danger. Second, just after the move to Pune, Ramabai herself began to experience the most momentous and radical conversion experience of her life. This "personal encounter" with Christ and "not merely His religion"

63. *Dnyānodaya* (March 14, 1889), pp. 81-82; quoted in Kosambi, *Pandita Ramabai's Feminist and Christian Conversions,* pp. 157-58. Nevertheless, the editor of this Marathi Christian periodical, probably the respected Vaman Narayan Tilak, felt that neutrality was a mistake: "One cannot be true to God and man, and be neutral in questions referring to the relation between them. . . ."

64. *Kesari* (May 28, 1889), p. 2; quoted in *Pandita Ramabai's Feminist and Christian Conversions,* by Kosambi, p. 159.

65. Pandita Ramabai to Sister Geraldine (November 9, 1890), in *Letters and Correspondence,* p. 259.

brought her such joy that she could not contain herself.[66] As a result, her time of daily devotion and worship (prayer and praise), in which she kept her door open, became a focal point of interest among some of her adoring young charges. As she herself later explained:

> When starting from San Francisco, and on landing in Bombay, I had resolved in my mind, that although no direct religious instruction was to be given to the inmates of my home, yet I would daily read aloud and pray to the only True God in the name of Christ; that my countrywomen, seeing and hearing . . . might be led to enquire about the true religion. . . . No one was urged to become a Christian, nor was anyone compelled to study the Bible. But the Book was in the library along with other religious books. The daily testimony to the goodness of the True God awakened new thoughts in many a heart.[67]

Serious trouble erupted when rumors were published, as early as January 28, 1890, that girls were being converted.[68] In December 1890, one month after the move to Pune, *Kesari* was grumbling that any institution funded by Christians was not likely to gain approval from Hindus.[69] Later, when one conversion actually did occur, there was an immediate reaction. Amidst outcries of "scandal," a dramatic war of words between rival Marathi and English newspapers broke out, lasting for more than two years. This turned ugly when, in June 1891, *Kesari,* by then under the control of Bal Gangadhar ("Lokmanya") Tilak, attacked Ramabai and accused her Hindu supporters of being gullible: "We consider the Christian women, who try to make inroads into our society under the garb of female education . . . to be the enemies of our society, of Hinduism, and even of female education."[70]

66. Ramabai Sarasvati, *A Testimony,* pp. 28-29. See also Kosambi, *Pandita Ramabai's Feminist and Christian Conversions,* p. 189.

67. Ramabai Sarasvati, *A Testimony,* pp. 40-41. See also Kosambi, *Pandita Ramabai's Feminist and Christian Conversions,* pp. 160-61, and Kosambi, *Pandita Ramabai Through Her Own Words,* pp. 319-20.

68. An item published by over-zealous well-meaning "friends" in the *Christian Weekly* of New York had been picked up and published in *Kesari. Kesari* (November 25, 1890), p. 3, also published remarks by a Miss Hamlin, an American Ramabai Association "helper," on how Ramabai's private devotions were really a form of religious instruction. Hamlin soon left India, leaving Ramabai to deal with the consequences: See Ramabai to the ARA (September 15, 1891), in *Letters and Correspondence,* pp. 263-70.

69. Kosambi, *Pandita Ramabai's Feminist and Christian Conversions,* p. 160.

70. Quoted in Kosambi, *Pandita Ramabai's Feminist and Christian Conversions,* pp. 161-62.

Allegations and counter-allegations mounted as attackers and defenders marshaled witnesses and gathered testimonials to prove their claims. Attackers accused Ramabai of disregarding warnings (after Miss Hamlin departed); of getting the Ramabai Association in Boston to officially dissolve the Board so that she would be accountable to no one; and of forming an institution with American (Christian) funds solely for the purpose of propagating their religion. Defenders, in turn, accused attackers of "contemptible" hypocrisy and of trying to "deceive the ignorant" so as to malign Ramabai: "Surely, if she had truly wanted to pursue a Christian agenda, Ramabai would never have enlisted Hindu advisors."[71] One writer for the *Indu-Prakash,* weighing evidence presented by both sides, concluded that Ramabai had not founded the Sharada Sadan in order "to draw Bramin widows into the Christian flock."[72] Nevertheless, attacks by *Kesari* and *Mahratta,*[73] and rebuttals by the Marathi *Sudharak* and *Subodh Patrika,* backed by the English *Indu-Prakash* (of Bombay), dragged on for more than two years.

Ultimately, the controversy turned not on the concepts of religious neutrality and secularism but on the issue of religious liberty itself. While Ramabai never actively attempted to bring about the conversion of any of the high-caste widows under her care, neither was she prepared to give up her own personal freedom to act, pray, and worship in accordance with her own conscience. Nor was she prepared to infringe upon the freedom of anyone else within the Sharada Sadan — either to prevent anyone from being exposed to Christian influences or to make sure that they left the Sharada Sadan as completely untainted (and "Hindu") as when they arrived. To have done so, in her view, would have vitiated the whole purpose of her campaign on behalf of high-caste child widows. Her stand, she repeated, accorded with that of the Ramabai Association in America, which insisted that the Sharada Sadan remain entirely secular in its influence and that secular instruction did not mean that Ramabai must cease to act, in her private life, as a believing Christian. Thus, when a member of the initial Advisory Board in India wrote the Ramabai Association in America, claiming to speak for all members and insisting that the Sharada Sadan should not only scrupulously observe

71. From the *Sudharak* (July 6, 1891), p. 2; quoted in Kosambi, *Pandita Ramabai's Feminist and Christian Conversions,* p. 162.

72. From the *Indu-Prakash* (August 17, 1891), p. 4; quoted in Kosambi, *Pandita Ramabai's Feminist and Christian Conversions,* p. 162.

73. Bal Gangadhar Tilak, the famous Hindu nationalist leader who owned and ran both papers, Marathi and English, took control in mid 1993, and ran editorials attacking Ramabai and her Sharada Sadan.

Brahmanical caste restrictions but also actively discriminate in favor of Hindu customs and rites, the situation became extremely difficult, if not impossible.[74]

As if she did not have troubles enough, one newspaper reported that Gopalrao Joshi, the widower husband of the late Dr. Anandibai Joshi, had been "baptised . . . into the Christian fold";[75] and another *(Pune-Vaibhav)* further scandalized readers with word that Gopalrao had done so in order to marry Ramabai. Ramabai sued for defamation and the matter was settled out of court, with a published retraction and apology; in addition, another paper *(Indu-Prakash)* soon indicated that Gopalrao had performed rituals required for returning to the Hindu fold.[76] Nevertheless, the waters of public esteem were muddied and her reputation suffered.

Eventually, in August 1893, after warnings from Tilak that the situation in Pune could erupt in bloodshed comparable to Hindu-Muslim riots then raging in Bombay, Ramabai's Indian Advisory Board collapsed. Tilak's continual and persistent sniping seems to have intimidated the softer members of her Advisory Board and worn them down. As it was, most of them, as members of the Prarthana Samaj, had not been as concerned with social reform as with religious reform. On August 13, they dispatched and circulated a formal but open letter to the Ramabai Association in Boston, formally severing their connection with the Sadan. In this letter, published in *Kesari* on August 22, they accused the Ramabai Association in America, and Ramabai herself, of having "departed from the lines of strict neutrality on which the institution was started and managed for some time"; of having induced girls "to attend her private prayers regularly and read the Bible"; of asking guardians and parents to allow their girls to attend such prayers; of doing nothing when one girl had become a Christian; and of alienating public Hindu support necessary for the stability of the institution.[77]

The result of this letter was immediate. Guardians and parents withdrew their widowed relatives, daughters, or daughters-in-law, and the Sadan was boycotted by Chitpavan Brahmans. Anti-Christian and Hindutva senti-

74. Introduction to *Letters and Correspondence*, pp. xxiii-xxv; for Ramabai's responses, cf. pp. 285, 320-21. To make matters more confusing, a new Advisory Board was appointed after the Sharada Sadan moved to Pune, with some names from the old managing board being included.

75. *Mahratta* (July 5, 1891), p. 3; quoted in Kosambi, *Pandita Ramabai's Feminist and Christian Conversions*, p. 164.

76. Kosambi, *Pandita Ramabai's Feminist and Christian Conversions*, p. 164.

77. *Kesari* (August 22, 1893), p. 3; quoted in Kosambi, *Pandita Ramabai's Feminist and Christian Conversions*, p. 163. See also *Letters and Correspondence*, pp. 302ff.

ments prevailed at the expense of religious freedom, secularism, and toleration. Never again did Ramabai enjoy support from the Hindu public at large, and the event marked the end of her career on the All-India stage. Even as her public visibility shrank within the society she had so strenuously sought to help, however, and as her influence among Hindu elites became marginalized, her purpose remained fixed and unaltered. Years before, when preparing to depart for India from San Francisco, she had already written Dorothea Beale that "people who are mine . . . look [upon] me as a foe and a stranger,"[78] and, later, that she would have been glad if such people could either take over the Sharada Sadan itself or, failing that, if they would establish a similar institution for themselves. In a letter to *Kesari* three years earlier (February 2, 1890) she had written,

> If my countrymen had given me adequate support and encouragement, there would have been no need for the Sharada Sadan to become a Christian institution. . . . [But since] the Hindus would not give the funds for establishing such a school, I had to beg from the Christians. If you are prepared to run the school now, our Christian patrons will make no difficulty at all. In this [relieving the plight of Hindu widows], we Christians will only help you.[79]

Yet, in the end, Ramabai's original cause survived. A Hindu Sharada Sadan was established in 1896 (though not actually opened until 1899). Located within Pune and then moved to Hinge beyond the city limits, this Hindu Widows' Home (or *Anath Balikashram*) owed its inspiration directly to Ramabai.[80] D. K. ("Maharshi") Karve, its founder, was a professor at Fergusson College. Having lost his wife, and determined to marry a widow even at the risk of excommunication, he married again (March 11, 1893). His new wife, Godubai Natu (who he renamed Anandibai) was a former child widow who had been one of Ramabai's first students in the Sharada Sadan, both in Bombay and then in Pune.[81] Since pollution rules were strictly ob-

78. Pandita Ramabai to Dorothea Beale (October 7, 1888), in *Letters and Correspondence*, p. 184.

79. Quoted in introduction to *Letters and Correspondence*, p. xxv.

80. Kosambi, *Pandita Ramabai's Feminist and Christian Conversions*, pp. 164ff. Eventually, in 1916, this Home became what is now known as the S.N.D.T. Women's University (now in Santa Cruz, Bombay).

81. Anandibai, "Autobiography," pp. 58-79 in *The New Brahmans: Five Maharashtrian Families* (Berkeley: University of California Press, 1963), selected and translated by D. D. Karve with the editorial assistance of Ellen E. McDonald.

served in this new Home, it was closed to non-Brahman widows. This enabled Ramabai to turn her attention to less privileged segments of Hindu society, which for centuries had been treated as less than human. By 1902, when the Sharada Sadan itself was moved to Kedgaon, both Ramabai and her Sadan had ceased to exist as far as most Chitpavan Brahmans of Pune were concerned.[82]

Thus, while both Ramabai and the Ramabai Association had striven during its first ten years (1889-1899) to fulfill the mandate of maintaining the Sharada Sadan as a totally secular institution, thereafter, with no small regret, she and the Board changed the Association's constitution. No longer would its mission be other than avowedly and explicitly Christian. Both Ramabai's critics and her foes, whether Hindu or Christian, seem never to have realized that her conscience, grounded in deeply held convictions concerning each person's inherent right to freedom and liberty, would never have allowed her to take advantage of her position in such a way as to exert coercion or to make attempts to proselytize. She did not believe that genuine conversion was something that human agency alone could accomplish: only God could truly change and inwardly transform the human condition. Also, therefore, her critics never quite realized that Ramabai saw herself as both Hindu *and* Christian. She did not see the two as being, either essentially or necessarily, in conflict, nor did she believe she was betraying either her family or her nation. Her love for India and for India's peoples remained steadfast. It was the pole upon which her entire life's work turned. This being so, she never saw the British as superior or as worthy, in themselves, of emulation. She did not hesitate, therefore, to strike out boldly and publicly at degrading and inhuman treatment by plague officials and at "the shameful way in which women were made to submit to treatment by male doctors." Such attitudes revealed to her that Europeans "did not believe that Indian women [were] modest and in need of special consideration."[83]

Years later, looking back on these events and viewing the whole situation from afar, Max Müller rendered his own assessment of what had happened. He had no doubt that Ramabai's becoming a Christian had proved to be a serious obstacle to the ultimate success and usefulness of her initial venture:

> Though we may trust her that she never made an attempt at proselytizing among the little widows committed to her care, yet how

82. Karve, *the New Brahmans,* p. xxvi.

83. *Letters and Correspondence,* pp. 362, xxviii. For saying this she was castigated by many, including Sister Geraldine of Wantage.

could it be otherwise than that those to whom the world had been so unkind and Ramabai so kind should wish to be what their friend was, Christian?!! Her very goodness was the real proselytizing power that could not be hidden; but she lost, of course, the support of her native friends and has even now to fight her battles alone, in order to secure the pecuniary assistance necessary for the support of her little army of child-widows. She is, indeed, a noble and unselfish woman, and deserves every help which those who sympathize with her objects can give.[84]

The Mukti Mission

In 1893, just when Ramabai was encountering her worst opposition over the Sharada Sadan, Swami Vivekananda was making his grand tour of the United States, capped by his address to the First World Parliament of Religions in Chicago.[85] During that tour, he succeeded in convincing liberally minded, generous, and eclectic Western clerics, some of whom were on the board of the Ramabai Association, that Hinduism should be "finally recognized" and "elevated" to the rank of a world religion.[86] At the same time, he also became a self-appointed one-man "truth squad," seeking to blunt or nullify Ramabai's impact on North America. Wherever he went, he denigrated what she had said and done. Word of what he was saying, together with attacks she was already suffering in Pune, may partially account for the more strident tone of the rhetoric she employed in what she saw as her part in an all-out war against darkness and evil. Ramabai urged Western thinkers not to allow themselves to be so charmed by the "grand philosophies" of India but to "open the trap-doors into the dark cellars where they [would] see the real workings of the philosophies they admire so much . . . and go round Jagannathpuri, Benares, Gaya, Allahabad, Mathura, Brindaban, Dwarka, Pandharpur, Udippi, Tirupaty and such sacred cities, the strongholds of Hinduism," where she had seen how thousands of priests and men learned in sa-

84. Müller, *Auld Lang Syne,* p. 128.

85. Eric J. Ziolkowski, "Heavenly Visions and Worldly Intentions: Chicago's Columbian Exposition and World's Parliament of Religions (1893)," *Journal of American Culture* 13, no. 4 (1990): 11-12, documents this American "discovery" and "validation." For details, cf. John Henry Barrows, *The World's Parliament of Religions . . . of 1893,* 2 vols. (Chicago: Parliament Publishing, 1893).

86. Robert Eric Frykenberg, "Constructions of Hinduism at the Nexus of History and Religion," *Journal of Interdisciplinary History* 23, no. 3 (Winter 1993): 523-50.

cred lore "oppress the widows and devour widows' houses" and "trample the poor, ignorant, low-caste people under their heels."[87]

Perhaps as a consequence of these attacks, in 1895 Ramabai decided to don the apparel of a *sannyasini* (female mendicant) and take to the road, traveling to sacred sites she had not seen since her youth. She wanted to learn what, if anything, could be done to rescue abandoned or destitute widows who, in one way or another, were still being enticed or forced into temples where they fell prey to sexual depredation.[88] After spending a fortnight in Brindaban, she wrote: "I had known something of the condition of widows in this and other places . . . , but I had no real idea of the terrible facts which I came to know. . . ."[89] She described how hundreds of agents were being sent out into the countryside

> to look for young widows and bring them by hundreds and thousands to sacred cities to rob them of their money and their virtue. They entice the poor, ignorant women to leave their own homes, to live in the *Kshetras* — i.e., the holy places — and then after robbing them tempt them to yield to their unholy desires. They shut the young, helpless widows into their large *maths* (monasteries), sell and hire them out to wicked men . . . and, when the poor miserable slaves are no longer pleasing to their cruel masters, turn them out in the streets to beg . . . [and to] die a death worse than [that] of starved street [pariah] dogs.[90]

Yet, Ramabai's venture was not successful and very nearly cost her her life: seven widows whom she tried to rescue were forcibly taken away from her and locked up.

From 1896 onward, as severe drought and famine once more ravaged the land, Ramabai launched herself into a massive rescue and relief campaign. At Sohapur, while walking by the doors of the local poor house — which was "no poor house at all" — she managed to save "three little famished skeleton-like orphans." There, seeing girls and women waylaid and carried off to carnal markets, she recalled how, twenty-two years earlier, when she was but a girl of eighteen, she herself had also suffered privation and could just as easily have "fallen into the cruel hands of wicked people." She found that "parents were

87. Quoted in *Letters and Correspondence,* pp. 312-13.

88. Macnicol, *Pandita Ramabai,* pp. 90-91; Sengupta, *Pandita Ramabai Saraswati,* p. 228.

89. Pandita Ramabai, "A Short History of Kripa Sadan or Home of Mercy," reproduced from Mukti Mission archives in Kosambi, *Pandita Ramabai Through Her Own Words,* p. 279.

90. *Letters and Correspondence,* pp. 312-13.

Ramabai disguised as a *sannyasini* or pilgrim

selling their girl-children . . . for a rupee or a few annas, or even for a few sears of grain."[91] She returned from her first relief expedition in January 1897 with some sixty female famine victims she had rescued. In May of the same year, she went back into the worst-stricken areas to pick up more victims. This time she and her volunteer helpers traveled into the famine zone in a convoy of bullock carts, slowly jolting along the tiresome road day and night; sometimes stopping briefly by the roadside to rest or by a riverside to bathe and wash clothes; and sometimes stopping in the jungle at night to pick up small, destitute girls lest they fall prey to "beasts prowling in search of food."[92]

While she was on this second journey of mercy Ramabai was suddenly called back to Pune. A serious crisis had arisen over her domicile for female famine victims. Due to the severe epidemic of bubonic plague then afflicting the people of Pune, municipality health officials had delivered an edict ordering the removal from Pune, within forty-eight hours, of all the famine victims Ramabai had recently settled in a hastily erected new building within the Sharada Sadan compound. Fortunately, the means for dealing with such a contingency existed. Back in 1892 and 1893, just as troubles besetting the Sharada Sadan had reached a boiling point, Ramabai had begun to think about how her institution might have to survive and become self-supporting without outside assistance. She had foreseen that the best means for achieving this end would be for her to acquire a piece of undeveloped land and to turn it into an income-producing fruit farm for the Sharada Sadan. She and her assistant, Soondarabai Powar, had not only made this a matter of continual prayer, but had also begun to search for a suitable place. In 1894, at the small town of Kedgaon, a railway station just thirty-four miles from Pune, they had located what they thought would be an ideal piece of property. Ramabai had then gone to Bombay to see if her life insurance could serve as collateral for a loan. But before this transaction could be completed, a "miracle" had occurred: a cablegram arrived with a special contribution of funds sufficient to pay for the property. She had immediately purchased one hundred acres and had begun to organize a workforce to clear away scrub, dig a well, plant orchards of orange, lime, and mango trees, and prepare fields for crop cultivation. Now, two years later, land that had once been "bare, stone, treeless, and

91. Letter of January 1997 in *The Widows' Friend,* p. 135; cited by Sengupta, *Pandita Ramabai Saraswati,* p. 238, and Kosambi, *Pandita Ramabai's Feminist and Christian Conversions,* pp. 166-68. Of her experience, Ramabai wrote, "The agony and dismay I felt at seeing that sight cannot be told in words."

92. Ramabai Saraswati, *The Widows' Friend,* pp. 136-42; cited in Sengupta, *Pandita Ramabai Saraswati,* pp. 139-43, and Kosambi, *Pandita Rambai's Feminist and Christian Conversions,* pp. 167-68.

waterless" was ready to provide sufficient space for the erecting of shelters for the famine victims under her care.[93]

An encampment of rented tents and hastily erected sheds soon sprang into being. As increasing numbers of famine victims arrived from villages in the north, they were moved to Kedgaon, along with staff to assist and teach them. Each group of girls and women refugees, as soon as they arrived, had to be speedily rehabilitated. Incredibly filthy, clad in rags, suffering from sores, assorted ailments, and vermin, and faint from malnourishment, their appearance was pitiful. Volunteer students and staff from Sharada Sadan, directed by Soondarabai Powar, were recruited to scrub each and every body and to shave every head, as well as to provide such basics as clothes and combs, food, and sleeping mats. Since newly planted trees had not yet grown enough to provide shade, there was little escape from the burning sun, and conditions in general were harsh:

> Sunstrokes, fever, sore eyes, and other such things were inevitable. . . . The girls lived in sheds not good enough for horses. Snakes crawled on their bodies while sleeping in the night. Numberless scorpions, centipedes and other poisonous insects found their way into the bedding . . . and not a few were stung. But the good Father of the fatherless protected the children, so that no harm came.[94]

But dealing with physical need was only the beginning. Rescuing the girls from degradation and starvation was not, by itself, enough, nor was feeding, cleaning, and nursing them back to health. Complete rehabilitation called for dealing with the effects of emotional and psychological trauma as well. Moreover, many of the girls had backgrounds, customs, and habits that were less than compatible with the community's peace. Endless hours of coaching, comforting, and counseling were required; and the girls were taught to develop the gifts they possessed and to lead productive and useful lives — for example, to be employed in various forms of teaching or in various technical vocations such as agriculture, brick-laying, wood-working, printing, tailoring, or some other craft. This massive rescue operation profoundly altered Ramabai's work.

93. Sengupta, *Pandita Ramabai Saraswati*, pp. 235-39. See also Ramabai Sarasvati, *A Testimony*, p. 24.

94. Ramabai Saraswati, *The Widows' Friend*, pp. 140-41; cited in Sengupta, *Pandita Ramabai Saraswati*, p. 242; Kosambi, *Pandita Ramabai's Feminist and Christian Conversions*, p. 169; Helen S. Dyer, *Pandita Ramabai: The Story of Her Life* (New York: Fleming H. Revell, 1900), p. 58.

The chapel and schoolhouse at Mukti

Thus was Mukti[95] — both the Mukti Sadan and the Mukti Mission — born. At the same time, construction was finished on a separate home and school for famine victims within the Sharada Sadan compound at Pune. This building, although probably begun in 1896 or 1897, if not earlier, was not formally inaugurated until September 1898. As fresh funds, in response to appeals, poured in from all over the world, dormitories, schools, a meeting hall, and other buildings sprang up on Mukti lands at Kedgaon. More land was acquired, more wells were dug, and more land was put under cultivation. What her father had once done, long ago on Gangamal mountain before she was born, Ramabai now more than replicated. The campus at Kedgaon soon also provided buildings for more newly formed institutions — for the Kripa Sadan (Home of Mercy for the "fallen"), the Prita Sadan (Home for the Aged and Infirm), Sadanand Sadan (Home for Boys), and Bartan Sadan (Home for the Blind, whose residents learned to read Braille and to do useful crafts). By the turn of the century, there were almost two thousand residents occupying beds within various halls at Kedgaon.

By then, Ramabai's staff for the first three institutions, not counting

95. The term *mukti* (or *moksha*) can have more than one meaning: "salvation" is one, but "release," "freedom," and "liberty" are also important dimensions of the term. Ramabai's outlook, and her use of the Liberty Bell as her symbol, cannot be ignored.

those who managed the buildings and grounds, had risen to eighty-five. These were her own women and girls: ten were matrons, thirty-five teachers in letters and science, and forty-two in industrial crafts. In its first eleven years (1889-1900), the still steadfastly nonsectarian, religiously neutral, and secular Sharada Sadan had trained some eighty high-caste (though decreasingly Brahman) girls to earn their own living. Sixty-five of these had either married or were earning their living as teachers and workers in different positions. Nor was this all. Out of continuing royalties from her *High-Caste Hindu Woman,* Ramabai was able to acquire scientific and laboratory equipment; instruments and models; a printing press to publish illustrated science textbooks in Marathi; a Braille system for Marathi readers; and a publishing house to provide both for in-house needs and for commercial distribution.[96] All in all, what she had accomplished, albeit with the worldwide support she had harnessed, was truly remarkable, especially when seen within the context of her background, the age in which she lived and worked, and the opposition she encountered. This tiny Indian woman possessed a strength that belied her size.

The Struggle over Mano: Christianity vs Christendom

It was, in fact, Ramabai's distinctly Indian perspective as a Christian that, again and again, brought her into head-on collision with Sister Geraldine of Wantage. Since the underlying conflict was theological and ecclesiastical, the same old arguments recurred. The central issue, at its heart, revolved around relationships with the church, as defined by Sister Geraldine; and the struggle itself was over the training of Ramabai's daughter, "Mano" (Manorama or Manoramabai). Having failed with Ramabai, Geraldine was determined that the church should not lose Mano. The grounds for her frustration were clear:

> Individuals and nations who reject Catholic teaching, or who are only half-hearted or half-educated Christians are terribly afraid of the influence of the Truth. . . . They fail to reason this out, but they are aware that given a free hand the teaching and influence of the Catholic Church are irresistible. The Church is the Truth, she teaches the Truth, she sets forth not a pittance of the Truth, but the whole Body of the Truth.[97]

96. Introduction to *Letters and Correspondence,* pp. xxvi-xxvii.
97. In *Letters and Correspondence,* pp. 317-18.

Like her mother, Mano had never known anything but change. Born in Assam and soon brought to Pune, she had been placed in the infant school at Wantage. In 1885, after a furious clash over what Ramabai saw as unfair indoctrination and usurpation of her parental authority, Mano had gone with her mother to America, only to be sent back when her mother's itinerary made adequate care impossible. She had been brought to Bombay to join her mother in 1889. In 1891, after home schooling, she had been enrolled in the Epiphany School in Pune (run by CSMV sisters); there she had benefited from instruction by Mary Samuel, a very gifted English teacher. But when Miss Samuel left the Epiphany School in 1895 and took a position as head English teacher at the Sharada Sadan, Mano followed her. In May 1896, just when she was about to take her matriculation examination at Bombay University, plans abruptly changed again and she was sent to England.[98]

In quick succession, letters reached Sister Geraldine informing her of these changes. Sister Benigna Mary informed her that Mano, very much in awe of her mother, was attending the "dissenting Chapel" of the "Methodist Society," adding: "We must keep constantly before her the duty of returning to the Church as soon as she is old enough to act for herself. . . ."[99] Mary Samuel also sent a "private" note indicating that, on finding that the behavior of some girls made them "not fit companions for her daughter," Ramabai had decided to send her at once to London to complete her studies.[100] These changed plans were soon confirmed by Ramabai herself. Declaring that what Geraldine had written Mano about her mother preventing her from studying was not true and requesting that, in Mano's own spiritual interests, Geraldine should not press Mano to be confirmed, Ramabai added, "Let the Holy Spirit do the work of converting and sanctifying her." Mano was sent to England with the Reverend Alfred Dyer (of Bombay), a Methodist missionary, with instructions to place her somewhere in London "to get the kind of education I want her to get."[101] On the third of June Sister Geraldine responded:

98. *Letters and Correspondence,* pp. 324, 328-29.

99. Benigna Mary to Sister Geraldine (May 4, 1896) and Mary Samuel to Sister Geraldine (May 6, 1896), in *Letters and Corresondence,* pp. 326-28.

100. Mary Samuel to Sister Geraldine (May 6, 1896), in *Letters and Correspondence,* pp. 328-29.

101. Pandita Ramabai to Sister Geraldine (May 11, 1896), in *Letters and Correspondence,* pp. 329-30. Soon enrolled at North London Collegiate School, Mano prepared to pass the matriculation examination of London University and to enter a missionary training school in Brighton.

> I cannot understand why, having once brought your child to the Font to be baptized, and having heard the solemn exhortation, "Ye are to take care that this child be brought to the Bishop to be Confirmed so soon as she can say the Creed, the Lord's Prayer and the Ten Commandments . . ." you should now sweep aside your act and refuse your child that further Gift of Grace . . . : namely, the sevenfold Gift of the Holy Spirit, whereby her intellectual faculties will receive illumination in the mysteries of the Faith.
>
> But since you refuse this inestimable privilege for your child, I would be the last person to put her into the difficulty of urging her to it contrary to your wishes. . . . I do not, however, understand how in the matter of her following the Methodist persuasion you should consider that she is old enough to judge for herself, and yet in the matter of her Confirmation you do not consider her old enough to make a decision.[102]

Seven weeks after her arrival in London, Sister Geraldine wrote to Dyer, indicating that the Pandita's letter of May the third said that Mano was to visit Wantage "as soon as possible." Dyer wrote back that, while Mano did wish to see Geraldine, she was also dreading the prospect of a visit to Wantage. He added,

> Manorama is a true child of God and disciple of Jesus Christ . . . her mother is not dissatisfied with her religious state. As the terms in which Pandita Ramabai committed Manorama to my charge cause her to stand in a position of a ward to me, . . . I cannot allow her to go anywhere where she would be subjected to pressure to change the religious views which she holds. . . .[103]

Many months later, in late November, after months of silence, Ramabai wrote Sister Geraldine that she had been very ill and that, beset as she had been, she could not bear to read letters; guessing what Geraldine's letter might contain, she had left it sealed until she could find heart to open it. Trying to express her personal love and asking Geraldine to forgive and "forget all our shortcomings," she pleaded:

102. Sister Geraldine to Pandita Ramabai (June 3, 1896), in *Letters and Correspondence,* pp. 332-34.

103. Sister Geraldine to Dyer (July 11, 1896) and Dyer to Geraldine (July 13, 1896), in *Letters and Correspondence,* pp. 330-32.

> Let the differences of opinion alone. We serve the same Master and believe in the same God wherever we are. She [Mano] has joined the Methodist Church of her own free will and I do not want to disturb her in her belief or unsettle her mind. It is very harmful to unsettle the minds of the young — I have suffered a great deal from it. . . .
>
> I believe in the Universal Church of Christ which includes all the members of His body, and am not particular about others being the members of different sects. . . . And now I enjoy the peace of God which passeth all understanding and do not trouble myself with small matters of opinion and its differences. So please, let Mano alone in this matter.[104]

This Sister Geraldine refused to do. She had suffered "nine months without so much as the courtesy of a visit from Mano." Worse, having "learnt from Mano the wicked, venomous and foul lies [without] a grain of truth with which he [Dyer] had filled her mind, for the purpose of weaning her . . . , such righteous indignation is kindled as cannot be extinguished. . . ."[105] In Geraldine's long reply to Ramabai, dated December 14, she minced no words:

> Your letter has caused me great pain. . . . It is not I who wish to unsettle Mano's mind: it is you who *have already done so*. . . . The same arrogance and wilfulness which characterized your life when you set up your own opinions against the Ministers of God's Church . . . — that same arrogance and wilfulness characterizes your life at the present time. . . . Your *want of faith* in the teaching of the Catholic Church may arise from your loving the praise of men.[106]

The year that followed brought no response from Ramabai. For her, Christian faith did not entail submission to Western Christendom, and Mano's faith and mission did not entail more words from others about what was best. With accusations of sedition and blame for inciting the murder of plague officials being hurled against her (accusations with which Geraldine concurred), Ramabai's hands were by then too full with the overwhelming task of bringing many hundreds of famine victims to Mukti and caring for

104. Pandita Ramabai to Sister Geraldine (November 25, 1896), in *Letters and Correspondence*, pp. 334-37.

105. In *Letters and Correspondence*, p. 324; on p. 350, she indicates that "nearly eight months" elapsed before Mano could "revisit her friends at Wantage."

106. *Letters and Correspondence*, pp. 338-42.

them. By the end of 1897, new tidings came to Sister Geraldine that 108 girls and women had been baptized in the river at Kedgaon (116 "girl-widows and women" at Sharada Sadan), and that Ramabai too had been baptized by immersion or re-baptized.[107]

On "Advent 1897" Geraldine sent another grave letter warning Ramabai that her "best friends [were now] greatly grieved" over how she was bringing up her child. But the letter did not arrive in time; Ramabai, exhausted and realizing her need for recuperation, had already left India. The ten-year anniversary of the Ramabai Circles in America was coming up (in March 1898), and invitations urging her to return to America, if only to help with the reconstruction of the Association, had increased her sense of obligation. By then, moreover, Minnie Abrams (an American Methodist) and Soondarabai Powar were fully able to carry on with the combined operations at the Sharada Sadan and Mukti Mission. Ramabai sailed in early January, taking two of her most gifted girls (having already sent three the year before). She stopped in England only long enough to pick up Manorama and bring her along.

Soon after reaching America, Manorama was admitted to a women's college ("seminary") in New York. There, after successfully completing her first year, she asked to be allowed to compress two academic years of work into one. While such an undertaking was considered impossible, Mano was so insistent that she was allowed to make the attempt. This she was able to accomplish. With discipline and determination, by rising early and retiring late, she not only managed to do it but also, at the same time, to win the friendship of fellow students and the high approval of her teachers. All the while, she also managed to help the five other Indian girls from the Sharada Sadan. At her graduation (June 19, 1900) she won first place, having gained honors in all but two of ten subjects, including extra science courses and extra distinction as a pianist. Greatly impressed, the Ramabai Association commissioned Mano, upon her arrival in India, to take charge of the Sharada Sadan (which by then had nearly two hundred students and a high school).

Manoramabai was only nineteen when she became principal of Sharada Sadan. Such a position for one so young was extremely delicate and potentially disturbing. Above her in rank stood her beloved and proud mother who, despite her tiny frame, was a towering giant of authority. Below her was Mary Samuel, the head teacher, who, like all the other teachers, was considerably

107. *Letters and Correspondence*, pp. 349-50. By then, Ramabai had come a long way in her religious journey. She had migrated from High Church affiliations in England and distinguished and theologically liberal supporters in America to dissenter and populist links with strong Anabaptist and Pentecostal overtones. Yet, while all these groups tried to "own" her and use her, she stoutly remained free of all.

Manoramabai

older than Mano. Despite all the commendations and favorable reports she received, small difficulties and frictions were bound to arise, and hidden jealousies were almost inescapable. Ramabai herself constantly counted on Mano's help with correspondence and accounts and expected her at Mukti at least once a week to be at her right hand. The overall burden eventually became so heavy that Mano's health began to suffer. Even after a respite in the hills, she returned to find the school growing rapidly, along with problems, difficulties, and annoyances. In mid 1902, there was friction with the Ramabai Association over the sale of the by then much-enlarged property of the Sharada Sadan. In addition, Ramabai began to realize more fully the extent of her standing in the world at large, together with the possibilities of raising funds from countries other than America. Thus, in order to remove Manorama from the predicament in which both of them found themselves, Ramabai dispatched her daughter and Minnie Abrams to represent their cause in Australia.[108]

The Search for Ultimate Mukti

All of Ramabai's life — from her earliest struggles to her experiences in England, America, and India — can be seen as stages along her road of conversion. Her first Christian conversion began, as we already saw, in Assam, where she encountered the gospel and sought its explication. Her second conversion was more intellectual; mainly as a result of her experiences in England and America, her theological position became increasingly broad and clear, if not also liberal. Her third conversion, however, was even more profound and satisfying. It was also more *bhakti* — more emotional and devotional, more personal and spiritual.

This new "turning" which came less than two years after her return from America, did not begin until 1891. Looking back sixteen years later, in 1907, on what had happened, she recounted how many months and years of inner spiritual turmoil had finally come to an end and how, at last, she had found a deep inner peace:

> Although I was quite contented with my newly-found religion, so far as I understood it, still I was labouring under great intellectual difficulties, and my heart longed for something better. . . . I came to know after eight years from the time of my baptism that I had found the Christian *religion,* which was good enough for me; *but I had not found Christ, Who is the Life of the religion and the Light of every man that cometh into the world.*[109]

108. Mary Samuel to Sister Geraldine (Poona: September 12, 1902), in *Letters and Correspondence,* pp. 353-74: "Mano . . . could not leave Kedgaon till she was told to sail with Miss Abrams . . . at a day's notice. There have been so many changes since the sudden removal of the school from Poona in June, and such conflicting rumours . . . you cannot imagine how I miss her." By then Samuel, who had opposed the move to Kedgaon, was no longer on the staff.

109. Ramabai Sarasvati, *A Testimony,* pp. 26-28 (emphasis in original text); Kosambi, *Pandita Ramabai's Feminist and Christian Conversions,* pp. 188-89; Kosambi, *Pandita Ramabai through Her Own Words,* p. 309.

Unhappy and dissatisfied, having given more time to studying books about the Bible than to the Bible itself, she decided to read the Bible for herself, regularly. This she had been doing for two years when one day, while in Bombay, she happened upon a book entitled *From Death unto Life.* Its author, an evangelist named Halsam, related how a lady had informed him he was trying too hard to "build from the top" and that he had not yet "experienced regeneration and salvation in Christ." The words made Ramabai stop and think. She realized, suddenly, that she had failed to understand the most elemental and essential truth of all: that she needed Christ personally, not his religion, and that she was groping in darkness like someone born blind. In her words:

> I can give only an idea of what I felt when my mental eyes were opened, and when I, who was "sitting in darkness[,] saw Great Light," and when I felt sure that to me, who but a few moments ago "sat in the region and shadow of death, Light *had* sprung up." . . . O the love, the unspeakable love of the Father for me, a lost sinner, which gave His only son to die for me! I had not merited this love, but that was the very reason why He showed it to me.[110]

This, she realized, was not some merit that one could earn, some heaven *(svarga)* one could attain by serving one's husband or some Brahman:

> No caste, no sex, no work, and no man was to be depended upon to get . . . this everlasting life, but God gave it freely to any one and every one who believed in His Son Whom He sent to be the "propitiation for our sins." And there was not a particle of doubt left. . . . I did not have to wait till after undergoing births and deaths for countless millions of times, when I should become a Brahman man, in order to get to know the Brahma. . . . The Holy Spirit made it clear to me from the Word of God, that the salvation which God gives through Christ, is present and not something in the future.[111]

The fourth and final major turning point in Ramabai's life came in 1905. If Ramabai's initial conversion and baptism had led her first to an intellectual development of her faith and public acknowledgement of her relationship to God the Father of Jesus Christ, and then to a more personal *bhakti* experience

110. Ramabai Sarasvati, *A Testimony,* p. 31. Also found in Kosambi, *Pandita Ramabai's Feminist and Christian Conversions,* p. 189; and Kosambi, *Pandita Ramabai through Her Own Words,* pp. 311-13.

111. Ramabai Sarasvati, *A Testimony,* p. 31.

of Jesus Christ as divine Son of God and personal Lord and Savior, her final conversion was her "baptism of the Holy Spirit."[112] It occurred fourteen years after she, in her own words, had "come to know the Lord Jesus Christ as [her] personal Saviour" and when, as she put it, her life had become so full of joy and song that she was possessed by a constant urge to tell others of what God had done and could do in anyone's life.[113] It happened after she had established the Mukti Sadan as a Christian ashram and school for child widows and after she had launched a famine relief campaign bringing hundreds of starving girls, regardless of caste, into the Mukti community.

What happened began within the Mukti Mission itself, in the wake of news about revivals or spiritual awakenings, first in Wales and then in the Khasi Hills of Assam. Ramabai herself described how this came about:

> I was led by the Lord to start a special prayer circle at the beginning of 1905. There were about seventy of us who met together each morning and prayed for the true conversion of all Indian Christians, including ourselves, and for a special outpouring of the Holy Spirit on all Christians in every land. Six months from the time we began to pray in this manner, the Lord graciously sent a glorious Holy Ghost revival among us, and also in many schools and churches in this country. The results of this have been most satisfactory.[114]

This event, later referred to as the "Great Revival," began among girls at her own school. Many were young women who, due to horrible experiences earlier in their lives, had struggled to overcome depression, deceit, and varied illnesses. *Mukti,* liberty, had come suddenly. Released from these manifold miseries, they rejoiced with loud and joyful outbursts — prayers, songs, healings, "consuming fire," and speaking in tongues *(glossolalia).*

Ramabai herself confessed to having had ecstatic experiences that she could not explain: a consciousness of the Holy Spirit as a burning flame within her and times when, alone in prayer, she involuntarily uttered some sentences in Hebrew. Nevertheless, she remained quietly restrained about much of what happened, fearing that the events and her words about them might be misunderstood. As a result, while not forbidding or hindering charismatic tongue-speaking, her personal approach to such phenomena re-

112. For an analysis of this episode, see Gary B. McGee, "'Latter Rain' Falling in the East: Early-Twentieth-Century Pentecostalism in India and the Debate over Speaking in Tongues," *Church History* 68, no. 3 (September 1999): 648-65.

113. Ramabai Sarasvati, *A Testimony,* p. 34.

114. Ramabai Sarasvati, *A Testimony,* p. 42.

mained self-controlled. She maintained that "Love, perfect divine love, [was] the only and most necessary sign of the baptism of the Holy Spirit" and took to quietly quoting prophecies and psalms, prayer and praise from the Old Testament, extolling the manifold goodness and mercies of God. But she also spoke of apocalyptic visions and of waiting eagerly for "the return" or "second coming of the Lord Jesus Christ."[115]

Most of those who commented publicly on these events were critical, but some were more cautious. One observer, L. B. Butcher of the C.M.S., indicated that, while loud sounds of tongue-speaking had become "a common phenomenon," the Pandita herself had "maintained a very sane attitude" and avoided extremes and sensationalizing to which some proponents of the movement were prone. He saw that what mattered most to Ramabai was what she saw as evidence that the Holy Spirit was at work in the midst of the Mukti Mission. This was most manifest in "the true conversion of hundreds of women" and "the full consecration of large numbers" to the "the witness and work for Christ."[116]

From 1905 onward, and for the remainder of her life, the influence of this "Great Revival" continued to be evident both in Ramabai's inner life and in the work she did at Mukti. She herself came to be seen as a "great soul" *(mahatma)* or "living saint" and was especially seen as such by many of the women who, from this time onward, went out from the mission into lives of service.[117] For the Pandita herself, having prayed with passion for God to bring about a revival and having seen for herself the awakening that had occurred, the event was life-changing. Her constant refrain thereafter was to recite prayers of thanksgiving and to repeat the words in the Gospel uttered by the beggar born blind: "One thing I know, that once I was blind but now I can see."[118]

Despite the complications of administering her by then huge institutional complex, Ramabai had by 1903 (and especially after the Great Revival of 1905) attained a remarkable depth of peace and tranquility, both within herself and with regard to forces arrayed against her. Drawing upon these inner resources she managed not only to survive but to thrive. Neither the reac-

115. From *Mukti Prayer Bell* (Kedgaon: September 1907), p. 11: found in Nicol Macnicol, *Pandita Ramabai* (Calcutta: Association Press, 1926), pp. 116-19. Letters from Manoramabai show that she too was profoundly influenced by these events.

116. Quoted in Macnicol, *Pandita Ramabai*, p. 121.

117. Macnicol, *Pandita Ramabai*, pp. 132, 116ff. Ramabai made daily intercessions for these women. Pasted inside her Bible were blank pages with "lists of hundreds and hundreds of her girls, whom she knew and whose needs she knew and whose cause she pleaded continually."

118. John 9:25.

tionary forces of Hindutva in India nor the reactionary forces of Christendom in the West nor even forces that were coercively liberal, populist, or secular had been able to crush her spirit, defeat her mission, or exploit her for their own ends. Indeed, as she often declared, it was liberty *(mukti)* she had attained, and the Lord to whom she turned who had made this possible.

A Final Project

The last decades of Ramabai's life were grounded in ceaseless prayer and joyfully satisfying work. Three main projects consumed her energies during the latter part of her life. The first of these, as we saw, was a constantly expanding outreach to ever widening circles of the downtrodden and oppressed; this was accompanied by a continuing enlargement of the institutional infrastructures to sustain this outreach and by the expansion of her influence to ever wider circles of Christian communities, both within India and around the world. Using her enormous corpus of classical learning as her weapon in her war to end the oppression of high-caste widows, she had been able to marshal the resources of Hindu reformers in India; she had been able to recruit supporters in England and America; and she had raised funds enough to launch a truly radical institution. Although it was finally rejected by high-caste Hindus, it had blazed a path by which other Hindu reformers had been able to found their own institutions for high-caste child widows. By this point, having done all she could for high-caste women and children, she had broadened her mission.

Her second major concern was the upbringing, education, and vocation of her only child Manorama. In this, despite the renewed conflict with Wantage that it provoked, she was remarkably successful. Moreover, by taking over many of Ramabai's duties at the Mukti Mission, Manorama aided Ramabai greatly in her third and final project: a new translation of the Marathi Bible.

For the last twenty years of her life, Ramabai devoted herself to her first love — Scripture — and it was this Bible translation project that absorbed virtually all of her remaining energy. Though a love of Scripture was not unique to her final years, her perspective had evolved and her horizons had been broadened due to her experiences over the years. Her own understandings of ritual purity and pollution had gradually changed until, by the time of her work among famine victims, her conception of what constituted humanity was radically different from what she had known as a child. Since each was made in the image of God, no longer was any human being to be excluded from the blessings of liberty and liberation from oppression. Rather, since all persons were both made by God and redeemed by God, through the sacrificial atonement of Christ, any and all could be born again, or born from above, and so attain "second-birth" or "twice-born" *(dvija)* status. That being so, and since no one should be denied access to the Divine Language, something had to be done to enhance and increase access to truth. Sanskrit alone was no longer enough; it was no longer the only divine language. All language, Ramabai believed, and hence all languages, had the capacity, as gifts from God, to be divine. It followed from such reasoning that each human being should have immediate access to the Word of God in her or his own mother tongue. That was the ultimate message of Pentecost and of "speaking in tongues." This then meant that Marathi was potentially as divine and sacred as Sanskrit.

It was this realization, along with her return to the centrality of language, that took hold of Ramabai's last years. Her father and mother (whom she now expected to see "in Glory") had passed along their love of the divine language, and she never lost that; but in her view, the Marathi Bible was too heavily Sanskritized, too full of terms and concepts which the lowly, oppressed, and poor could not grasp — not because they were not intelligent but because their own mother tongue was not being used. The great task, therefore, was to bring the Word of God to the level of the common people of Maharashtra. Ramabai had only one life and only so much time, and thus work in India's other languages she left to others; and, indeed, for some languages, such as Tamil, this work had already been done. With her great ability to master new languages and her command of other languages in India, Ramabai had only to acquire the necessary volumes on Greek, Hebrew, and Latin in order to accomplish what needed to be done. This was a huge task. But, with the help of her gifted daughter and others who took over the various tasks of the Mukti Mission, she was free at last to undertake her project.

Thereafter, day by day, month by month, and year by year, she toiled away. She had just managed to complete this task when, on the twenty-fourth of July, 1921, Mano unexpectedly died. This sudden death of her only child and potential successor took away Ramabai's desire to linger any longer on the earth. She was only too glad to follow Mano, and this she did before another year had passed, only a few days before her sixty-fourth birthday, on April 5, 1922.

Robert Eric Frykenberg

A Word to the Reader

There are no doubt many who have heard the name "United States" or the "United States of America," and there may be many who have seen the map of this country when they were studying geography in school. But there must be very few people in our country who know the true praiseworthiness of the United States, what the people there do, and what their social conditions and system of government are like. At the beginning of 1886 I went to the United States from England. At the time I did not know anything about this country except its name. But when I began, a few days after my arrival there, to understand bit by bit the worthiness of this nation, I formed the wish to stay there longer and get to know it better. Accordingly, I stayed there from March 1886 to the end of November 1888, traveled about thirty thousand miles around the country, and gathered information about a number of things. The joy that I felt in the United States in seeing the amazing things that are to be seen there would be incomplete if I did not share some portion of it with the dear brothers and sisters of my own land;[1] and that is why I am publishing this small book. A large portion of it I wrote while I was still in the United States; the rest of it I have written since my return here.

A few days ago I delivered eight or nine lectures in Mumbai and Pune on "The Conditions of Life in the United States." Some who came to hear them may have felt that there was an element of exaggeration in what I said. But I can assure you that I have not exaggerated. If anyone has doubts about the truthfulness of the extravagant numbers related to commerce, business,

1. *Deśabandhubhaginī:* literally, "country brothers and sisters." — *PCE*

the system of education, and so on, that I quoted, they should go take a look at the U.S. Census figures for 1880. If there is anything false in what I have written, I request the many learned American gentlemen and women living in this city of Mumbai who know Marathi to correct my mistakes.

A group of those belonging to another party has accused me of speaking only good of the United States and of excluding anything bad. I have only this to say to them, that they *will* encounter at various places in the course of their reading of this book reference to those evil things that everybody would notice there. But I will at least admit that I have not found fault with the people of the United States to the extent so many think I should have. One of our pious countrymen,[2] who visited that country before I did, has found ample fault with American society already. (Apparently he found nothing in America but its faults — and this is not to mention, to be sure, the fact that all his expenses for traveling as much as he wanted all around that country and even back to Hindusthan were paid for him!) When I was traveling in the state of New York, a certain gentleman asked me, "What is the most despicable thing you have seen in our country?" I replied, "My friend, I have not come to see the faults of your country. I want only your merits. I seek only them, and I find only them." I had occasion to see the faults of the American people as rarely as when a stone or a thorn unexpectedly hurts somebody's foot on a fine, large, spacious road; and this is why I had no choice but to mention them here. There are good and bad people everywhere. All people have their merits and their faults. If we search for their merits, we will find only their merits; and if we do the opposite, we will reap a contrary harvest. No one should need to be told this afresh.

Although the greatest of care has been taken in correcting the proofs of this book, there is nothing I can do about the occasional errors that remain.

If the reading of this book instills even a little more love of hard work and goodwill toward the service of our Mother Bharat[3] in the hearts of the dear brothers and sisters of my homeland than what they have at present, I shall know that this small effort of mine has been worthwhile.

Ramabai
Sharada Sadan[4]
December, AD 1889

2. *Deśabandhū:* literally, "country brother." It has not been established who this person was. — *KG*

3. *Bhāratamātā:* "Mother India." This is the one occasion in the text when Ramabai does not use the name "Hindusthan" for India. — *PCE*

4. *Śāradāsadana:* literally, "house of the goddess of learning." This was the school for high-caste widows that Ramabai opened in Mumbai upon her return from the United States. — *KG*

Pandita Ramabai's America

or

"Conditions of Life in the United States"

CHAPTER 1

The Journey from Liverpool to Philadelphia

Dr. Rachel Bodley,[1] Dean of the Women's Medical College in Philadelphia, wrote to me in January 1885 earnestly inviting me to come to Philadelphia and witness the graduation of *Sau.* Anandi*bāī* Joshi,[2] which was to be held in March 1886. I was then teaching and studying at Cheltenham Ladies' College in England. I had a particular reason initially not to accept her invitation, but she herself once again urged me to come, and she also got Sau. Anandibai Joshi and Raosahib Gopalrao Joshi[3] to write letters urging me to

1. Trans.: Rachel Littler Bodley (1831-1888), American chemist and botanist, graduate of Wesleyan Female College (1849), was the first chair of chemistry at the Women's Medical College (1865-1874), and then dean of the college for fourteen years until her death. — *PCE*

2. Trans.: Anandibai Joshi (1865-1887) was one of the first Indian women to study medicine and the first to obtain a medical degree from a medical school in the West. Tragically, she died of tuberculosis within weeks of her return to her homeland. *Sau.*, the standard Marathi equivalent for "Mrs.," is the abbreviated form of *saubhāgyavatī:* "A woman possessing *saubhāgya* or the excellence and blessedness consisting in the possession of a husband; a married and unwidowed woman" (James Thomas Molesworth, *A Dictionary, Maráthí and English* [Bombay: Bombay Education Society's Press, 1857]. Future references to Molesworth's dictionary throughout the text will be cited simply as "Molesworth"). *Bāī*, a Marathi term of respect for women generally, is added as a suffix to either their given names or their surnames. — *KG*

Ed.: Diacritical marks are used on the first use of a foreign word or on infrequently used words to aid in pronunciation but are dropped in frequently appearing words and names. — REF

3. Trans.: Gopalrao Joshi was Anandibai's husband, under whose tutelage she had prepared for her education in the United States. Raosaheb is a title of honor for men of distinction. *Rao* is also used as an honorific suffix to a man's name. — *KG*

visit America. So no matter what the obstacles might be, I felt I could not decline her invitation any longer: first of all, because even though Bodley*bāī* may belong to a different social group *(jāta)*[4] and even to a different religion, she has shown such compassion for Hindu women it puts us all under the greatest obligation; and second, because Anandibai Joshi is the very first instance of a Hindu woman studying a science as difficult as medicine and obtaining a degree in it.

That is why I earnestly desired to see the joyous occasion of her graduation; and that is why, although I had many obstacles in the way of my coming to America, I put all my burden on Almighty God and, together with my daughter, left Liverpool port on February 17, 1886, aboard the *British Princess*, bound for America. My English friends did not want me to go to America at all; so, needless to say, they did not appreciate the fact that I actually came here. Many of these women friends in England had predicted that our ship would be wrecked and that we would drown at sea because February is not a favorable month for a sea voyage. What is more, during this month that year, there were many storms, and many ships were wrecked near the American coast. Because of the severe cold near New York City and in the area twenty-five to thirty miles around it, the water had frozen and the continent of America was hemmed-in by ice.

But be that as it may! For three days after leaving Liverpool port we saw no sign of any storm. There is a spot in the Atlantic Ocean, however, somewhere between England and America that is called the Devil's Pot. On the fourth day, as our ship approached this spot, a terrific storm broke, and we truly were given to see the dreadful power of the sea.

Because this was not a good time for a sea voyage, there weren't that many passengers on board the ship. There were four men and three women in first class and about 190 men, women, and children in third class. These 190 people had come from various parts of Europe to settle in America. (See the brief information I give later on in one place about the conditions of those who come to settle here.)

Some devout people from this group of 190 passengers gathered in the open space of the middle deck on Sunday, where they sang songs and worshipped God. That very night there was a terrible storm. I must mention the strange story I heard from one of the women on this occasion. Since this woman was staying in the first-class cabin adjacent to ours, I had come into

4. Trans.: In the American context (not to mention here the Indian), the word "caste," which is typically used to translate *jāta,* seems highly problematical. The better equivalent here would seem to be "social community" or "social group." — *PCE*

close contact with her. She was a Roman Catholic. A certain man on board, she told me, was unable to bear the singing of the passengers. He complained about their behavior and predicted that there would be a storm that same night. He said that these people were infuriating Satan by worshipping God and that Satan would definitely make war on us by bringing on a storm that very day. By some coincidence a storm broke that same night, and his prediction came true. Once again later on, when the same people began to sing hymns one evening, he grew very angry and predicted that there would be a storm just as before. And once again it came true. The following Sunday, as it was pleasant and not very stormy, some boys came up on deck and began singing, "Hallelujah, Hallelujah!" (This Hebrew word means "sing praises to God.") Our helmsman could not contain his anger. He immediately went out and shut those thoughtless boys' mouths. But Satan must have really had it in for him. Our ship almost sank that day. If the story about this helmsman is true, then it must be said that many educated and progressive people in England still firmly believe in the power of spirits and demons. But let that be as it may.

We truly were severely afflicted by this storm. Moment by moment huge waves would dash against our portholes, and we feared that the ship would sink at any time. For three or four days we could not even raise our heads, much less think of walking about. Finally the air in our cabin grew so stale and unclean it became difficult to breathe. So, come what may, we decided we had to get up to the upper deck at least once; and with our hearts in our mouths we left the cabin. But how was I even going to walk upstairs when I couldn't hold my feet steady on the ship's deck because of the movement the ship made? Somehow, finally, I did manage to get upstairs and sit down on a deck chair. Within about a quarter of an hour, refreshed by the clean sea breeze, I felt as if a new life force had entered my body. Just moments before, every time a wave dashed against the porthole, I couldn't even look in that direction I was gripped by such a strange fear. I felt my stomach sinking within me. But then see what a wonderful miracle took place in just those few moments! Now as I stood on the upper deck of the ship, a ship that seemed almost on the point of sinking, and looked at the wild and dreadful sea, I felt not the slightest fear in me. On the contrary, enthusiasm, joy, and peace began to rise up in my heart like the sun. I shall never forget the lesson I learned from this naturally occurring event. Just as long as a person does not face his adversities and his enemies with courage, they will remain a terrifying bogeyman to him. The more a coward is inclined to hide himself away, the more his fears increase and his entire life becomes darkened by despair. But my friend, once and for all take this decision: *kāryaṃ vā sādhayeyaṃ, dehaṃ vā pātayeyaṃ* (i.e., "Either I shall accomplish my task or I shall renounce my body");[5] and face up to your enemies and adversities such as despair. Then the word "fear" will vanish from your memory; and like one who has found liberation,[6] you will be utterly fearless; and even though the entire world should go against you, you will accomplish what you have to do, relying on truth and courage. How many are the storms our frail ships must face in this unfathomable ocean of life! If only we fight the fearsome, tumultuous ocean with courage, we will surely triumph, and our minds find peace. But if while climbing the ship's mast, either to let the sail out or to gather it in, the spirit of false fear possesses our hearts and we start to tremble, then our plight will be even worse than a dog's.

Our ship continued to rock violently in the Devil's Pot for five or six days. Its steam engine was not working properly even when it entered this spot. It would have sunk without further delay if they had driven it on at the usual speed without fixing it; and fixing it was easier said than done in the face of the sea's tumult, in which they could not hold it steady anywhere. The poor captain was in a real fix. But in the end the engine was gradually put right, and the ship sailed on as before. Even after leaving the Devil's Pot the intensity of the storm did not seem to abate. The force of the mountainous waves was such that our ship would be raised to the skies and in the next instant hurled down to the depths; so it was quite natural to wonder if it was going to sink now or in the very next moment. In that vast and unbounded sea, with the globose awning of the sky above us (sometimes clear, sometimes over-clouded) and here below the tumultuous billows like little Himalayan mountains and our ship dashing up against them, what could be the harm in saying that in contrast to the surrounding scene our ship must have looked like a little flying fish floating on the water. I cannot begin to describe what varied ripples of thought this pleasing, dreadful, and strange scene created in the minds of the onlookers. When there is a storm, the sort of sea birds that they call "gulls" can be seen floating everywhere on the sea. These birds are

5. Trans.: Prof. K. S. Arjunwadkar of Pune identifies this quotation as being "current among the Sanskritists and Sanskrit-lovers in Maharashtra [and] handed down from generation to generation without reference to a specific text. My version of it is slightly different: *arthaṃ vā sādhayet, dehaṃ vā pātayet,* where *artha* means object, goal. I got it from my father. This is equivalent to the English 'Do or die,' which (in the English version) Gandhiji made popular during the 1942 Freedom Fight. You can compare it with the following from Valmiki's *Rāmāyaṇa: adya me maranaṃ vā ayat taranaṃ sāgarasya vā* ('Today will see either my death or crossing over the sea.') This is Rama's utterance just before he built a bridge on the sea [to Sri Lanka]." Grateful acknowledgements to Gudrun Buhnemann. — *PCE*

6. Trans.: *Jīvanmukta:* One who is "[p]urified by divine knowledge, and exonerated whilst living from future births and from all ceremonies and rites at present; emancipated although in the body" (Molesworth). — *KG*

really and truly the harbingers of the storm. Before a storm breaks they come flying over the sea at great speed, and during the storm they alight on the ocean waves and with great delight begin sporting on the water. Huge waves rise up from all directions and dash against each other, the wind blows furiously, the surface of the sea is covered with impenetrable fog, and people's ears are stunned by the thunder both from the sea and from the clouds. Yet these joyful birds think nothing of it. Totally at their ease, they delight themselves. They ride the huge waves as if racing each other — just as an Arab might take his young, bright steed for a gallop at the speed of the wind itself. Sometimes when the sun would break through the curtain of clouds and shine in the sky like some mighty conqueror, we would to our great delight catch sight of a rainbow against the sky. Sometimes one-and-a-half or two full rainbows would appear together in the sky. Sometimes a rainbow would be created by the sunlight falling on the spray of water that was flung a great distance by the force of the wind as the ocean waves dashed against the ship or against each other. Oh, how indescribable was the splendor of the sky and the sea at such a moment! The sight of it was so pleasing and so fascinating it was hard to take your eyes away from it. When the storm had abated somewhat and while our ship was still three days away from the American continent, we got to see a great many flying fish soaring over the water.

On March 3, at around 4:30 in the evening, we caught our first sight of land: the North American continent of the Western Hemisphere, which in 1492 Christopher Columbus, thinking he had circumnavigated the earth, had concluded to be Hindusthan. I cannot describe the joy I experienced then. I said to myself, "Well, my Hindusthani friends, here we are, the soles of our feet exactly opposed to the soles of your feet. Here it is broad daylight, but your side of the earth is covered now in night. Here we are strolling around on the deck and talking, and over there you are snoring in your beds! Just see what a miracle this is!"

As I have mentioned above, because of the intense cold the ocean water along the shores had frozen, and the continent of America was hemmed-in by a layer of ice. The sun reflecting off it, when you looked at it, almost blinded your eyes. By evening, when our ship reached the mouth of the Delaware River, a pilot who knew the interior of the Delaware well came on board our ship, and our captain handed over the ship to him.

No matter how well-versed people are in whatever kind of work they do, it is inevitable that at times they make mistakes. It wasn't so surprising then that this pilot made a mistake. Either he was sleepy or intoxicated, but he got our ship, which he was piloting at great speed, stuck in the mud of the Delaware when we were still sixty or sixty-five miles away from Philadelphia, and it could not be budged for two or three days. We had not had sight of land for sixteen or seventeen days. It had taken us seventeen days to accomplish a journey that normally took just twelve days. At last we had, if nothing else, a *sight* of the land. But now even though the desired destination was so close, this new obstacle prevented us from reaching it. We had planned on finishing our voyage that very night and disembarking in Philadelphia at dawn. I can't express how disappointed we were when our plan was suddenly thwarted in this way. Yet we thanked God profusely for protecting our ship in the storm, for saving it from being carried away when the engine failed, and for bringing us safely to this hemisphere.

The next morning when we got up we saw that our ship was hemmed-in by ice. That day and the following a number of small steamers gathered around our ship and cleared the way for us by breaking the sheets of ice with their pointed prows. But still our ship wouldn't budge. Then, at high tide, several of the boats together tried to tow it out of the mud with a massive rope but all in vain. It didn't move an inch. So on the morning of March 6, the passengers from our class were shifted to another ship and sent on to Philadelphia. There wasn't enough room for the second-class passengers on this other ship, so as we were leaving, these poor people were looking at us with very disappointed faces. We felt so sorry for them, but what could we do? There was no option but to leave them behind on the bigger ship and be on our way. (The very next day arrangements were made to transport the remaining passengers to Philadelphia.) We reached Philadelphia on March 6, at 8 P.M. Both Raosaheb Gopalrao and Sau. Anandibai Joshi came to meet us at the dock on the river. They welcomed us most warmly and took us to their lodgings, where we immediately went to bed, as we were completely exhausted.

On March 11, 1886, at 11 A.M., we went to the auditorium in Philadelphia that is called the Academy of Science. About three thousand or thirty-five hundred men and women had gathered in the hall to witness the graduation of the women students who had studied in the medical college there. That same day our countrywoman Sau. Anandibai Joshi was awarded a degree in medicine. The ceremony was extremely interesting. This was a day of great joy for us because Anandibai was the first Hindu woman to acquire a degree in medicine. Besides, we are naturally very proud of her because she is our kinswoman.

Four years ago there was no provision for women to study medicine in Hindusthan except in Madras, and even in Madras there was no provision for obtaining a medical education of a high standard. Public opinion did not favor even general education for women. Needless to say, it was strictly against offering an education in medicine to women. I was invited to Pune by the Education Commission in 1882 to give my opinions on what changes and improvements were needed in the present system of women's education. My recommendation was that women most definitely should be allowed to receive an education in medicine. Later, the chairman of the commission, Dr. Hunter, told me that since medical education does not come under the purview of general education, the commission would not be able to make any official recommendation about it to the government but that he would bring it up before the government in private. Later on, owing to the efforts of many good people, a sizable subscription fund was collected to bring a woman doctor from England; and the government also made certain appointments and opened classes in men's medical schools for women to study this subject.

But following established custom, they first asked the most learned people of the land what their opinions were. It goes without saying that the government received widely varying opinions from a host of different people. What was most surprising, as it turned out, was that some reformers and those who claim to favor the advancement of women were against offering medical education to women. It was the opinion of Kesheb Chandra Sen, the Bengali leader of the Brahmo Samaj of India,[7] that women should not be granted the freedom to appear for university exams, that they would lose their femininity if they studied medicine, that they are not fit to study such a difficult subject, and so on. Nevertheless, many learned gentlemen *were* convinced that women had the capacity to study this branch of knowledge, that the structure of their bodies and their "inferior" brains would not prevent them from studying it, and that, moreover, they would not lose their femininity by doing so! The government accepted the favorable opinions of these gentlemen and opened the doors of medical schools to women. But as yet not very many Hindu women have dared to come forward for a medical education. Two girls in Madras and one woman in Bengal were studying medicine, but I have not yet heard the news that these women have passed their exams. Women doctors are badly needed in Hindusthan. Our shy Hindu women feel great shame about letting men know their condition when they are suffering from many kinds of women's diseases and especially during childbirth. On too many occasions they would rather die than tell their plight to a male doctor. In a situation such as this, you would think everybody must realize the need for women doctors. But men continue to be obstinate no matter what country they come from. Some oppose medical education for women out of ignorance, some out of jealousy, and some out of simple selfish interest.

7. Trans.: The Brahmo Samaj was a movement to reform Hinduism founded by Raja Ram Mohan Roy (1774-1833) and greatly expanded under the leadership of Kesheb Chandra Sen (1838-1894). — *KG*

Just as Sau. Anandibai is the first Hindu woman to study medicine and to obtain a degree in it, the medical college in which she studied it is the very first medical college in the entire world that has been established just for women. It underwent its rites of inauguration in 1850.[8] Initially, public opinion was set against it. The founder and first teacher of this college had to endure immense hardships, including poverty and public ridicule. But today, by God's grace, the school is flourishing. It is supported financially and otherwise by many people. Mrs. Rachel Bodley, the dean of this college, labors devotedly day and night, striving in every way to make it prosper. It has been during her tenure that the school has acquired such eminence. It is our prayer that God grant her ever greater and greater success in this task. The "Friends" — that is, the Quakers — are of tremendous help in this task. I have said elsewhere that the Quakers are generally large-hearted and not at all set in their ways.

When female medical graduates, especially from this college in Philadelphia, began to practice medicine in the same way that male doctors in this country do, the association of male doctors known as the Philadelphia County Medical Society passed a regulation stating that since they did not approve of teaching by women, their members should not consult female doctors and should not encourage women in any way to go for medical education.[9] But this regulation did not hinder either the passage of time or the advancement of women. With the changes brought by time, the advancement of women inevitably took place.

8. Trans.: The word Ramabai uses here is *prāṇapratiṣṭhā*, i.e., the Hindu ritual of instilling breath in an icon or image. — *KG*

9. But in June 1888, the County Medical Society, after humbly beseeching her, made the learned Dean Bodley, the director of the Women's Medical College, a member of their association. Some days later I heard the news that she had died very unexpectedly. Dean Bodley was my very dear friend. She loved both Dr. Anandibai and me selflessly. I am ever grateful to her for her compassion towards our countrywomen and for the help she extended to both of us in our efforts. Dean Bodley left her mortal body and departed from this world. Her absence is so hard to bear. Nevertheless, we take great comfort in knowing that incarnate in the high and sacred repute of her name she will remain on this earth forever. It is our prayer that God may be merciful and send virtuous women like her to this earth to uplift our greatly distressed and needy womankind. — *PRS*

C H A P T E R 2

The Nether World or the American Continent

Before I tell you what I saw in the United States of America after I arrived here and what its living conditions are like, it is essential that I relate a brief history of this land. My fellow countrymen and countrywomen[1] who are well-educated will probably be familiar with its unique history; but if those who haven't had the chance to read the history of the discovery of America and of the colonies that were established by Western people there, were to try to read this book, they would not understand how the foundations of the system of government and of the living conditions of the United States came to be laid there. So I have given here a brief account of the discovery of America, of its original inhabitants, and of the origin of the United States.

Centuries ago when people did not have an adequate knowledge of the shape of our earth, they each imagined it to be however they saw fit. Our Hindu ancestors as well as the ancestors of the people of other communities *(jātī)* believed that the earth was flat; and that is why they thought that, just as large houses in big cities have many stories, this world also must have many levels built on top of the other and that the human world[2] must be the middle level. According to the Hindu Puranas, this world is like a fourteen-storied mansion. There are six stories or levels of existence above the earth and seven stories or levels of existence below the earth. The lowest level of them all is given the name *Pātāḷa* — the Nether World.[3] These things have now been

1. Trans.: *Deśabandhubhaginī:* literally, "country brothers and sisters." — *PCE*

2. Trans.: *Bhūloka:* "The earth as the habitation of man" (Molesworth). — *KG*

3. Trans.: *Pātāḷa,* the last of the seven regions under the earth, is the abode of the *Nāgas* or serpents. — *PCE*

proven false through careful investigation. Everyone has begun to understand that the world does not resemble a fourteen-story building and that the earth is not flat.

In 1435 a certain boy named Christopher Columbus was born in the town of Genoa, Italy, on the continent of Europe. While he was still a child no one understood his true worth. His father was poor and worked as a wool-carder. But when Christopher reached adolescence, he expressed a desire to become a sailor and to travel the seas. In order to become a good sailor, he studied geography, mathematics, and the science of navigation thoroughly. At the age of fourteen he made his first sea voyage.

About seven or eight hundred years ago, the Christian people of Europe went to war against the Turks and other Muslim peoples over the issue of religion. These wars, which were called the Crusades, were the means by which the Europeans came into contact with the Muslims, and the Europeans learned a great many things from them. It was from the mouths of Muslims that they heard a description of our own land of Hindusthan. In ancient times it was customary for people, particularly Muslims, to exaggerate a hundredfold both the good and the bad of anything they were describing. So it isn't very surprising that when the Turks told stories about Hindusthan to the Europeans they made an entire crow out of what was no more than a feather and a mountain of gold out of a single coin. In short, when it came to describing Hindusthan, they would say, "Hindusthan is a veritable golden bird" — by which they meant that Hindusthan was brimming over everywhere with gold it was such a wealthy land.

Beginning in the latter part of the tenth century of the Christian era, the Muslims invaded Hindusthan time after time and plundered her people of gold, silver, and precious stones. When they heard coming from the mouths of Muslims stories of such massive plunder, the mouths of the Europeans began to water out of greed for the riches of Hindusthan, and they began to search for an easy route for them to get to Hindusthan. Since there were many difficulties if you came overland from the north by way of Afghanistan, they began to search for an independent sea route. Many of them had gotten the idea that by circumnavigating the continent of Africa you could reach Hindusthan by sea. But when Christopher grew up to be a great authority in mathematics, geography, and the science of navigation, he said, "Since the earth is round, I shall sail westward and thereby, in the process of circumnavigating the earth, reach Hindusthan directly."

Christopher vowed that he would prove his idea to be the right one. He approached the kings of Italy, Portugal, England, and France for help. But the people in each of these lands decided he was quite mad and refused to give him any help. In spite of this discouragement, he did not give up. He met the king of Spain and told him, "I will find for you an easy route to Hindusthan, a land of enormous wealth. Give me the help I need to do this." The king paid no heed, but Queen Isabella of Spain took pity on him. She summoned him to her and promised to get for him the money he needed for his venture by selling her jewels. So Christopher Columbus took three ships, a few promising men, and a supply of food and water that would last for many days, and sailing off westward, set out in pursuit of the "golden bird" called Hindusthan.

After a journey of many days Columbus's ships arrived at the Canary Islands, which are northwest of Africa. When they left these islands behind them and when the last trace of land disappeared and they saw nothing but the vastness of the sea surrounding them on all sides, Columbus's companions were frightened to death. But Columbus encouraged them by saying, "Don't worry. Don't be afraid. We must keep moving onward." On October 12, 1492, in the third month after leaving his homeland, Columbus caught sight of an island. It was covered everywhere in wild forests *(rāna),* and many wild *(rānaṭī)* people were wandering about it. The next morning when it was possible to see more clearly, Columbus was the first to set foot on the island, bearing the flag of Spain in his hands. Then, with an unsheathed sword in one hand and the flag of Spain in the other, he claimed possession of the island on behalf of the king of Spain. It was he who established the practice of calling the people there "Indians" (i.e., Hindusthanis), because he thought this island must be close to Hindusthan. Thereafter he traveled onward some ways, and there he saw the island called Haiti. Columbus visited this new country four times in all. He went on still further and also discovered South America.

Because Columbus firmly believed that the land he had discovered was Hindusthan, it was he who started the fashion of calling it the "Indies" — that is, Hindusthan. Later on, after further exploration, when the Europeans realized that this land was not Hindusthan, they gave it the name "America." The reason for this was that after the death of Columbus, his friend Amerigo Vespucci traveled to this newly discovered land. On his return voyage, he described the new land he had seen in a large number of letters. These letters were published by a German geographer, who expressed it as his wish that this new land be known by the name of Amerigo. From that time on, the continent of America was known by the name of Amerigo (or "Ameriko," as it can also be pronounced). In fact, the land that Columbus discovered should be named Columbia; but it must have been in conformity with the ancient custom of this world, as expressed in the maxim "One shall sow and another shall reap," that the land brought to people's knowledge through the efforts of

Columbus was given the name of "Ameriko." The islands to the east of Mexico and Central America are still customarily called the West Indies, i.e., the "Western Hindi Islands." The custom of calling the native people of America "Indians," i.e., Hindusthanis, has still not changed. In order to distinguish between the people of our land and them, the nickname "Red" has been added to their name. It was in this manner that the discovery of our Red Indian brothers and sisters and of their Nether World *(pātāḷaloka)* took place in the fifteenth century of the Christian era.

Robbing Peter to Pay Paul

Readers may find the title of this section a bit strange. Gossipmongers, cheats, and misers, while taking care not to spend a single copper coin of their own, will engage in acts of benevolence and charity — either through words alone or by using the plundered wealth of others. To describe the acts of such people we have a saying: "Being generous at the cost of others," i.e., "Robbing Peter to pay Paul."[4] An unparalleled example of such "charitable" robbery is found in a very significant story from European history. I must tell it to you because it is closely related to us as well as to our Nether-World-dwelling Red Indian brothers and sisters.

This is how it goes. There is a country called Italy on the continent of Europe. Rome, the capital city of Italy, became very famous during the ascendancy of the Romans. Later on, during the time of the Roman people's decline, this city rose to great eminence again through its connection with the pope. Now the papacy is also in a state of decline. Even though there isn't much left of the former glory of the popes, many learned people and lovers of antiquity visit Rome because it is such an ancient city. The pope, about whom I have spoken, is the chief guru of the Catholic church, which is one of the orders of Christianity. Just as in our own land the disciples of the Shri Shankaracharya have conferred on him, as their chief guru, the title of *Jagadguru*,[5] the Christian people belonging to the Catholic church have conferred the title of "pope" on their chief guru. The word "pope" means "papa" or father. The glory and greatness of the popes flourished all across Europe for about a thousand years from the fifth to the fifteenth century of the Chris-

4. Trans.: *Halavāyācyā dukānāvar brahmārpaṇa,* literally, "an act of charity at the expense of [somebody else's] sweetshop." See *Mahārāṣṭra vāksampradāya kośa,* ed. Y. R. Date and C. G. Karve (Pune: Varda Books, 1988 [1941]), p. 625. — *KG and PCE*

5. Trans.: *Jagadguru,* a title conferred on the Shankaracharya, the chief proponent of the Advaita Vedanta philosophy, means "teacher of the world." — *KG*

tian era. In the beginning, the pope was nothing more than the superior of a monastery of poor and pious Catholic ascetic monks. He had no connection at all with moneymaking and affairs of state. From the time that the Roman Emperor Constantine embraced the Christian religion in the fourth century of the Christian era, however, this father superior began gradually to make his entry into matters of statecraft. As time went by, the pope's influence grew so overpowering that he could take away a monarch's kingdom, without so much as a by your leave, and give it to somebody else who was more in his favor. Eventually the pope began to think of himself in these terms: "There is no guru in all the world beside me. And not only am I guru among gurus *(jagadguru);* next only to God, I am master of this earth. God himself has given me the power to turn whomever I wish into a king or into a pauper. I am without sin and I am without error. Should I decide to call the West the East, then so it must be." Millions of credulous people began to accept as the literal truth every opinion expressed by the *Jagadguru* pope*jī*[6] and to worship him and to obey his orders without question. If anyone stubbornly refused to obey him, the pope could excommunicate the person. Not only could such people be excommunicated during this present life, however; the credulous people were kept in awe of the pope by their belief that he had the power to make sure that the excommunicated would never find a place in heaven during the next life either. Leave aside ordinary indigent folk; even great and powerful rulers and scholars trembled out of fear of the pope. Even so, it certainly was not the case that all monarchs paid homage to the pope out of genuine religious sentiment; some two-faced kings flattered the pope only to accomplish their own ends.

Around the time when determined and erudite people like Columbus had gotten ready to travel hither and yon all around the globe in search of ever new and wealthy lands, one of the popes of Rome really managed to do the job — of robbing Peter to pay Paul. During the fifteenth century, the king of Spain and the king of Portugal were two of the favored disciples of the pope. In 1493, Pope Alexander VI, being very pleased with them both, bestowed on these two beloved disciples of his two very large gifts. He published a decree called a papal bull in which he proclaimed that whatever new lands or islands might be discovered through the agency of the two kingdoms of Spain and Portugal would become the possessions of these kingdoms. In order to avoid any dispute between them, he drew an imaginary line of demarcation in the middle of the Atlantic, from north to south, and told them that whatever continents or islands such as America had been discovered or would

6. Trans.: The suffix *jī* is an additional honorific, used here with evident sarcasm. — *KG*

yet be discovered within the western half of the sphere would belong to the king of Spain; while Africa, Hindusthan, and the islands in their vicinity, which lie within the eastern half of the sphere, on the right side of the line of demarcation mentioned above, would belong to the king of Portugal.

What possible connection could the pope have had with Africa, America, Hindusthan, and the islands in their vicinity? From where did he get the right to bestow these territories on the kings of Spain and Portugal? But there is no limit or rule to what hypocrites and impostors will do. That is why I think that "Robbing Peter to Pay Paul" is an apt title for this pope's action.

Bring Gold, More Gold!

Following Columbus's return from his voyage westward in 1492 to America (which he presumed to be Hindusthan), undertaken with the support of the Queen of Spain, Vasco da Gama, in the year[s] 1497[-1498] and with the help of the Portuguese government, successfully circumnavigated Africa and journeyed all the way to Hindusthan.[7] The Spanish and the Portuguese went in search of new lands for no other reason than to find gold. If a newly discovered land was ruled by a people of strength, they adopted a policy of trimming their sails to whatever the prevailing wind happened to be and would request these powerful people for the freedom to carry on trade within their country. But if the people there were ignorant, uncivilized,[8] and incapable of fighting them, they would simply attach the land to their own kingdom. And that the intention of the Europeans was to enslave these people, either by force or by oppression, and to bring them like cattle to market for sale is perfectly clear from their actual behavior. When Columbus arrived in these new lands and when the people who were the original inhabitants of the island of San Salvador[9] first encountered the pale skin, the imposing figures, and the

7. See Mr. Vinayak Kondadev Oak's very fine description of Vasco da Gama's voyage under the title "*Hindusthānāta portugīja lokāṇca praveśa*" [The Entry of the Portuguese into India] in his book *Hindusthānakathārasa* [Stories of Hindusthan]. — *PRS*

8. Trans.: The word Ramabai uses here (and in many other places throughout the text) is the colloquial Marathi word *rānaṭī,* literally, of the *rāna* (forest or wilds). In his dictionary, Molesworth defines the term thus: "Wild, growing spontaneously. 2 Boorish, rustic." "Uncultivated," in both an agricultural and a cultural sense, is the prevailing connotation of the word — and "savage" or "uncivilized" seems to be the sense at which Ramabai is aiming. — *PCE*

9. This was the first island on which Columbus set foot. It is one of the Western Hindi or West Indies islands, belonging to the Bahamas. Its original name was Guanahani. Columbus named it San Salvador, which means "holy savior." — *PRS*

strange names of Columbus and his companions, they thought they were gods. So they began to worship these fair-skinned gods with the most sincere devotion. And what did these fair-skinned gods do but straightway (without so much as inquiring whether their red devotees had a right to that island or not) attach this island to their own kingdom, all in the name of King Ferdinand and Queen Isabella of Spain! Nor did they stop at this; later on, after Columbus's second voyage when many more Spaniards began to arrive, they made slaves of these poor harmless inhabitants of the Nether World and brought them for sale back to Spain. And many others they enslaved right there where they were and forced them to dig gold mines. As a consequence, hundreds of these red people quickly died from hard labor and from oppression. If anyone stubbornly refused to work as a slave, the Spaniard gods would give him a beating. If this did not subdue his stubbornness, they would torture him to death in front of the people of his own community *(jāta)*. And so, out of fear that they would suffer the same plight if they were obstinate, the red devotees of these white fiends would do whatever work their lords commanded them to do, without so much as a murmur. But since they were unaccustomed to incessant labor of this kind they died very quickly. These red people, the inhabitants of the Nether World, had been born free, and they were totally unaccustomed to being anybody's slave. When the Spaniards and numerous other Europeans first started to use force to enslave them, they often would take their own lives by starving or hanging themselves. They preferred death to enduring a lifetime of oppression as slaves to greedy and cruel people like the Spaniards.

On one occasion it so happened that in order to escape from the hands of these cruel foreign lords, a large number of these red people settled upon a certain day when they would all gather together as a group and hang themselves. One of the white men who held them in slavery learned of this plot. He was by nature especially cruel, and he oppressed the red people he had forced into slavery by regularly beating them. When they gathered together on the appointed day at a secret place bringing along ropes with which to hang themselves, this cruel man unexpectedly showed up in their midst carrying a piece of rope in his own hands. Words cannot express how frightened and shocked these poor people were to see him there. And then he said to them, "My slaves, did you really think that I would not know about your plot? I can understand even the thoughts inside your heads. Go ahead, hang yourselves. But do you see this rope I'm holding in my hands? Go on, hang yourselves if you want. But then I'll take this rope, you see, and hang myself as well. That way I will die along with you — so that in the afterlife I can oppress you a hundred times worse than here in this life!" These poor, gullible people took what he said to be the truth. Fearing that if he really did die with them, he would make them suffer in the afterlife more than he did here in the present life, they gave up their plan of hanging themselves. And they submitted themselves as before to their white masters and carried on working to the point of death for them. From this story we see quite clearly how the whites had become thoroughly expert in the art of imposing an impression of their own superiority on the minds of credulous people through duplicitous tricks — when force could not accomplish their ends.

Even great men like Columbus did not fail to resort to such duplicity. Columbus had incurred enormous debts because of the vast expense of his voyages. In order to repay his debts he devised a scheme whereby on various occasions he captured some five hundred red people from the West Indies, by trick or by force, and transported them on his ships to be sold as slaves in Spain. He paid off some of his debts with the money he got by selling them! What is especially worth bearing in mind in all of this is that Columbus and those who came here after him all thought that everything they did was in conformity with God's will. Columbus actually thought that he had done a great favor to these poor, innocent people — people who were deprived of everything — their kith and kin, their households and homes, the joy of liberty, their homeland, and numerous other priceless things (the very things that give people a reason to live); who were deprived of every hope of happiness and sold in Spain as slaves; and who were forced to endure there the unspeakable agonies of slavery. And all for what reason? Because they were idolaters. He presumed that he had served God to the fullness of his abilities by sending these people to a Christian country like Spain, thus making it possible for them to be given initiation into the Christian Catholic church. How evil it is that the conduct of great people should be tarnished by such monstrous deeds!

The conscious faculty *(buddhi)* in the human heart that distinguishes good from evil is called the conscience. An evil deed while it is being committed or one that has already been committed preys on a person's heart. So in order to assuage the pain in his heart, he has to come up with some sort of remedy — any sort at all — that will give at least the appearance of goodness to his evil deed. One remedy of this kind is to issue religious mandates. When the king of Spain gave Columbus (and those who later followed him) his generous support and sent them back to the Nether World, he (along with the other kings who sent such people) got them to pledge three things. The first and the most important was that they search for gold and bring it back. The second was that they convert the Red Indians to Christianity; and the third was that they search out new lands and if possible conquer them and attach them to their own kingdoms. Their primary purpose was to go to foreign lands and plunder their wealth; but since their consciences were not likely to be satisfied by this, they made a great to-do out of their second pledge — that of spreading their own religion. Along with those who went only in search of gold, many good and benevolent people went to the Nether World with the heartfelt purpose of spreading their faith. They sincerely sought the welfare of the red people. On many occasions they came to stand between the Europeans who were greedy only for gold and these poor people; and they acted to prevent their oppression. It is not just we but the people of every community *(jāta)* in every land who would commend and praise the goodness of these virtuous souls.

Our Red Indian Brothers and Sisters and Their Customs

I have already mentioned that the people of the Nether World have been given the nickname "Red." Now my purpose is to inform you briefly about how they got this nickname, what customs they had, and what their living conditions were in various places. It is always very helpful in understanding and remembering the stories you hear about the people or the things of any country if, before you hear the stories, you come to some understanding of what those people or things are like and what their various qualities, good and bad, are.

In our own land we see people with a variety of skin colors every day. All of us are aware that some of our native people are fair-skinned, some are quite black, some brown, some pale, some reddish brown, and some (in keeping with the Marathi proverb, "Neither wholly a donkey nor wholly a *brahmacārī*"[10]) do not fit in any color category.

As I mentioned earlier, when the Spaniards discovered the Nether World, the people there had skin the color of what appeared to them as brick dust. At first, not knowing any better, they called these red people by the name "Hindusthani," but later when they realized their mistake, they established the custom of calling these original inhabitants of the Nether World "red people" or "Red Indians," on the basis of their skin color. Nobody knows when these people came to North America or from where. Many surmise that some other group *(jāta)* of people must have lived there before these people settled in North America. This is because it seems clear when you look at the evidence — the ruins of ancient buildings in various parts of this land, the

10. Trans.: *Na dhaḍa gāḍhava na dhaḍa brahmacārī.* A. Manwaring, in *Marathi Proverbs* (New Delhi: Asian Educational Service, 1991 [1899]), p. 196, renders this proverb as "Not wholly a donkey nor an ascetic." It is equivalent to the English "Neither fish nor fowl." — *PCE*

caves carved into mountains, the large dams, and the clay pots and cooking utensils, ornaments, and arrowheads, etc., that have been found in deep excavations — that they do not belong to the period of the Red Indians.

Red Indian men are physically very strongly built, tall, full of strength, agile, and good-looking. The women are somewhat shorter than the men, and many of them are quite beautiful. Their natural disposition is not different in kind from that of people of other nationalities. Unless they are provoked, they do not harm anyone unnecessarily; but if they are used badly, they know very well how to take their revenge. And who wouldn't understand that? Some white people say that the red people are cheats, that they are dishonest, treacherous, malicious, and cruel; but this is not true. Many white people of good disposition have lived among the "Reds" and have made the test of experience. They tell us that the Red Indians are highly reputable people, grateful for kindness, extremely hospitable toward strangers, and affectionate by nature. Not that every last one of them is good, but then who would be willing to say that all whites are good? In short, whether people are good or bad does not depend upon their community *(jāta)* or their country. Good people and bad people are found in all communities *(jātī)* and in all lands, and by the same rule they are present among the Red Indians as well.

In the fifteenth century of the Christian era the red people were for the most part in an uncivilized *(rānaṭī)* state. They painted their bodies with different colors. They tanned the hides of animals killed in the hunt, made shirts and other clothes out of them, and adorned the clothes by sticking colorful feathers to them. This custom continues even to this day. Recently, through contact with the Europeans, they have become accustomed to wearing cotton and woolen clothes and have acquired many of the other habits of advanced communities *(jātī)* of people. Previously they did not know the use of iron. They used to manage everything by cutting flint stones to make arrowheads, spears, javelins, and so on. They were skillful archers and expert at wielding clubs and cudgels. They were absolutely ignorant about the use of bullets, swords, guns, cannons, and such weapons. Building houses with bricks, stones, and mortar was unknown to them. They did not cultivate the land very much but made their livelihood from products such as maize, which in certain places produced abundant grain without much effort; wild fruit; the fish and game they killed in the hunt; and so on. They did not have a script with which to write letters or books. Although there were many different tribes *(jātī)*[11] and each tribe had its own language, to a certain degree, these

11. Trans.: Although *jamātī* (sing. *jamāta*) is the more common Marathi word for "tribes," it appears from the context that Ramabai uses *jātī* here in that sense. — *PCE*

languages were similar to each other. The people of Mexico, at the southernmost end of North America, were not in an altogether uncivilized *(rānaṭī)* state, but were advanced to a considerable extent.

The houses of these uncivilized *(rānaṭī)* people were nothing more than small huts: about a dozen very long, straight, slender tree trunks planted in the ground and spaced evenly in a large circle with their top ends tied together, and, covering that, the skins of animals, the bark of trees, or mats to form small tents. They had a small hole at the center of the roof to let out smoke and a small door at the front. This door was not made of wood but was a small curtain. As you came in or went out, all you had to do was lift this curtain. Hunting, fishing, the making of small boats from the bark of trees, the making of weapons from flint stones, fish bones, etc., and the dressing of animal hides were the everyday occupations of the men. The women for the most part had to do all the rest of the work, of which their principal tasks were cultivating the land, keeping watch over the fields, planting, and cooking. They grew mainly maize, tobacco, pumpkins, gourds, beans, and so on. These people have a great fondness for smoking. Four hundred years ago people in the Eastern Hemisphere didn't know anything about tobacco. This gem came to Europe from the Nether World, and ever since, people in most of the countries of the world have been falling prey to the vice of smoking tobacco.

Although the uncivilized *(rānaṭī)* red people did not give very great importance to trade, those in the East made bead strings or necklaces called "wampum," while those in the West mined copper, and they used to sell these things. Wampum is a kind of bead string or necklace made by stringing together the black, white, or purple cowry shells of certain species *(jātī)*. Not only were these bead strings used in place of rupees, paisas, gold coins, and so on, but when two kings or tribes were arranging a truce, belts made from them were exchanged and took the place of a written peace treaty. Many tribes also had the custom of exchanging eagle feathers and of smoking tobacco through a particular kind of pipe in order to make peace.

Their system of government was also very simple. All the people in the tribe *(jāta)* would choose by consensus a strong man to be their king and then act in obedience to him. It was the rule among them that kingship was hereditary. When there was occasion to fight a neighboring tribe *(jāta)* and the king was weak, he would appoint, by general consensus, some brave and shrewd man from his own tribe to be the general. If the king himself was brave, he himself would become the general. There were a great many different tribes *(jātī)*, and there were a great many quarrels and disputes among them.

Their religion (to tell about it very briefly) was as follows. There is a Supreme Being who is the Creator and Protector of all. He rules over all. Under his authority there are many smaller deities and spirits, some of whom are good by nature and some bad. The good ones bring happiness and the bad bring sorrow. To keep bad spirits from doing harm, they have to be worshipped with blood sacrifices. Future events can be known through dreams and omens. After death virtuous people become immortal, and they can then go hunting happily forever. According to them, good hunting is the greatest happiness.

It was their custom, when they brought back somebody captured in battle, either to offer them as a sacrifice in the temple or to torture them to death. A person would be judged as more or less brave according to how much torture he could endure. The fact that torturing people to death was a custom they had as a tribe does not mean that they are by nature cruel. There are many perverse customs that prevail in human societies while they are as yet in an uncivilized *(rānaṭī)* and ignorant state. The people of England, while they were still in an uncivilized *(rānaṭī)* state, used to offer human sacrifices. Later on, even though these people were steadily advancing through the spread of Christianity across the whole of Europe, the practice remained among them of burning people — those who were convicted of crimes against the church or the state — alive at the stake or of torturing them to death in various other ways. Just very recently there has been (and continues to be) a great hue and cry everywhere over the terrible torture inflicted upon the Burmese rebels after Burma was brought under British dominion.[12]

The Red Indians belonging to numerous tribes ate the sanctified flesh of humans whom they had sacrificed to their gods. Experience has shown that, with the exception of aquatic animals, none of Nature's other creatures eats the flesh of its own kind. It is very sad that even though man is such a superior creature, he yet eats the flesh of his own kind. It is true, of course, that advanced peoples do not in literal fact eat the flesh of other humans; but they certainly have acquired the art, to a quite superior degree, of devouring fellow members of their own species in numerous other ways! The pages of history telling of every nation and tribe are replete with descriptions of this kind of cannibalism. In our own times, ever new devices for committing cannibalism are flowing continually out of Europe. Someone may prefer to eat his neighbor raw, while someone else may eat him roasted, fried, or chopped up like a chutney — and that is all the difference there is. Indeed, it cannot be said that cannibalism has as yet disappeared from any country. Watch yourself, be

12. Trans.: Following the Anglo-Burmese War of 1885, Burma was made a province of India in 1886. — *PCE*

alert, but whatever else you do, don't devour one another. If you manage not to, you will surely have attained something great.

The Reasons for the Red People's Loss of Freedom and Their Ruin

Thus far I have narrated the customs of our red brothers and sisters in brief. Now I will close this portion by summarizing the reasons for the loss of their freedom and their current predominant state of ruin.

I have already described above in what an ignorant and uncivilized *(rānaṭī)* state the red people were when the Europeans began coming to the Nether World, excavating the gold, and bringing the people back as slaves. They knew absolutely nothing about the use of deadly weapons such as gunpowder and bullets, cannons and guns — or even what these were. What is more, there were no horses in America at that time. These uncivilized people naturally assumed that those whose merest command these remarkably majestic, agile, and powerful animals obeyed, must not be ordinary human beings at all but some kind of demigods. We hear stories from the Puranas about the *agnyastra* (fire weapon), the *vajrāstra* (lightning weapon), the *vāyavyāstra* (aerial weapon) and other marvelous and invincible weapons used by the immortals, but we do not know what these weapons actually are, what they even look like, or how they are used. Given this situation, if some person who knew the use of these weapons were to come to our land and take it in his mind to conquer us by mere intimidation, he could easily do so. In the face of such a foe the resistance even of millions of people who are ignorant of these weapons would not last long; and not only that but the very fact of his having this marvelous knowledge would be reason sufficient to make ignorant people presume that he is superior to them — if not indeed part god. And that is why they would be more intimidated by him than they might need.

This was precisely the plight that befell these poor Red Indians. Not that they were inherently weaker than the Europeans or that they did not love freedom or that when the Europeans began to interfere with their freedom the red people did not resist them. But they were ignorant, credulous, and superstitious. Sometimes they did not resist their enemies out of fear of portents or bad omens. Sometimes they were cowed by the very sight of the enemy's fire weapons *(agnyastreṃ)* such as guns and cannons and of their horses as well. Poor people, what were they to do? Even if you were to come in your thousands ready to do battle with the enemy and if just one of them were to rain fire and burning bullets on you, you would not be able to stand before him because you yourself do not have weapons that are of any use to fight him. In that event it is not very surprising that a few thousand Europeans could slaughter hundreds of thousands of Indians. This deed of theirs was about equivalent to a powerful, armed man coming along and chopping off the heads of hundreds of thousands of orphaned, ignorant, and weaponless nursling infants. Nobody would ever call such a deed an act of true valor. Had these Europeans put aside their fire weapons and conquered the Red Indians by wrestling them or by fighting them with weapons they used, such as bows and arrows, flint knives, bone spears, and so on, then the Europeans would have proven themselves to be truly brave. But it pains me grievously to tell you that those who called themselves religious and who said they came to give knowledge to the ignorant and to show the way to heaven to the hell-bound, adopted an evil ethic of deceit, persecution, cruelty, and dishonesty from start to finish so as to destroy these poor and blameless Indians.

Now I don't mean to say that the Red Indians were absolutely without reproach from beginning to end of the story, but they never of themselves provoked the Europeans. They never of themselves started deceiving them. On the contrary, when the Europeans first came to their land, they welcomed them with the greatest respect, even imagining them to be sons of the Sun. They tried to please them as best they could with gifts such as gold and fruit. Even then these white gods remained unsatisfied with them; and when they discovered just how sweet the Indian's sugar cane crop was, they devoured it root and all.[13] What person on the face of this earth would not resist such omnivorous gods? It is certainly not for me to blame them for trying in every possible way to preserve their rights. It was their ignorance that was their misfortune. At that time they did not have access to any of the means to overcome this ignorance. It goes without saying that the person who possesses the means to overcome his own ignorance but who still makes no effort to do so, deserves to be blamed. But if he fails to do so because he does not have the means to do so, how can the poor man be blamed? If you read the history of the Indians, it is quite evident that this ignorance (and their credulousness, superstitiousness, fear of portents and bad omens, fear of ghosts and spirits, and so on, were all aspects of it) was one of the main reasons for their destruction.

The Marathi proverb says, "Two people quarrel, a third profits."[14] Being

13. Trans.: This alludes to the Marathi proverb *Ūsa goḍa mulyā soḍa,* which A. Manwaring renders, "The sugar cane is sweet but leave the roots," and of which he gives the common sense, "Do not utterly beggar a benevolent man." See *Marathi Proverbs,* p. 2. — *PCE*

14. Trans.: *Doghāṃceṃ bhāṇḍaṇa tisaryāsa lābha.* See Manwaring, *Marathi Proverbs,* p. 83. — *PCE*

jealous of one another is an altogether ruinous thing — for families, great or small, as well as for societies and for countries. Truth to tell it is ignorance that is the root cause of jealousy. The misunderstandings people have about each other, arising out of the most trivial of causes, are what create jealousy in a person's mind. And the creation of jealousy brings with it palmy days for fighting and quarreling. Then, because of their fighting and quarreling, men come to think of each other as enemies; and making every possible effort they seek to defeat their enemies. If the enemy is too powerful, it might very well seem necessary to seek the help of some third party in order to defeat him. And once a third party has entered the fray, it is he who makes the people of both the quarreling parties dance to *his* tune and thus accomplishes his own aims. And so it inevitably comes to the point that is described in the proverb: "Not to you, not to me — give it to the dog!"[15] Fighting and quarreling among its members is always extremely harmful for any family or for any country. Everyone who has read the history of Hindusthan knows that it was because of the bickering and quarreling among themselves of the people of our land that foreigners were able to enter among us and we began to lose our sovereignty. It was this very same plight that befell our red brothers and sisters. While they were fighting among themselves, the white people made their entry into the Nether World. The weaker people among them, who could not get along with a more powerful tribe, would take it in mind to get the aid of the whites, who came from outside, to destroy their more powerful enemies, who were of their own kind. They brought the whites into their own country and gave them whatever help they needed. As a consequence, with the help of the whites they certainly did destroy their enemies who were of their own kind; but not only did they not gain the slightest benefit for themselves from this, they themselves suffered the greatest loss. Once the whites had destroyed their enemies, they turned and seized them too by the scruff of their necks and drove them out of their own country; and the white lords themselves became the sovereign rulers of their land. It is very clear, then, that the weaker Indians who aided the whites in order to defeat enemies of their own kind — as also the very same kind of contemptible people in our own land — are perfect examples of the proverb, "The handle of the axe is death to its own kin."[16]

Europeans of various kinds *(jātī)*, such as the Spaniards, the Portuguese, the French, the English, and the Dutch, seeing opportunities like the one mentioned above, devised various stratagems and seized the Indians'

15. Trans.: *Na tulā na malān ghāla kutryālā.* This particular proverb is not listed in any of the standard references. — *PCE*

16. Trans.: *Kurhāḍīcā dāṇḍā gotālā kāḷā.* See Manwaring, *Marathi Proverbs*, p. 156. — *PCE*

motherland from them; and there they set up new colonies and established their own sovereign states. By now, the Indian people all across America have been smashed to pieces like a broken glass vase and utterly scattered. All that the Indian people can look to now as the final attainment of their life is this: to eat whatever their white enemies, who now rule over their land, give them to eat; to quench their thirst with but a handful of water; to be born and so to live for some brief time upon this earth; to be hunted and killed by the white people; and to die like the birds and beasts of the wilds. But that is enough on this subject.

A Brief History of the United States

Following Columbus, during the reign of England's Henry VII, a man by the name of Cabot visited America in 1494.[17] And right behind him numerous others such as the French, the Spanish, the Portuguese, and the Dutch went to America and established colonies there. Since the intended subject of this book relates to none of them except the English colonies, I won't refer to the others here. A man by the name of Sir Walter Raleigh went to America in 1585 and attempted to set up a colony there.[18] The people who accompanied him at that time, instead of bringing the land of their new colony under cultivation and living like proper, well-bred folk, showed nothing but a dreadful hurry to explore for gold and to oppress the Indians. Needless to say, their settlement on this new land did not turn out at all happily for them. Later still, a man by the name of John Smith went to Virginia, a region discovered by Raleigh, and began the task of establishing a colony there. As there were many women among the people who accompanied him, these newest settlers in America began to live there in family groups. It was this one man, John Smith, who succeeded in establishing the first English colony in America. Later on some people belonging to the Puritan sect came to America and established the colonies called New England. In this way, one after the other, English colonies began to come into existence in North America. The settlers who lived in these colonies endured calamities and adversities of many different kinds; but never giving up their firm determination, they brought the land of America under cultivation and, where there had been nothing but forests, established great cities and towns. Everywhere in the land their talents and skills

17. Trans.: John Cabot's first voyage to America actually took place in 1497. — *PCE*

18. Trans.: Raleigh in fact never himself visited the Roanoke Island settlement, even though it was he who obtained the patent authorizing it. — *PCE*

were made to flourish. All the characteristics they showed — daring, courage, determination, and unflagging industriousness — call for nothing but praise.

There were altogether thirteen English colonies in North America by the end of the eighteenth century. When they saw the prosperity of their fellow countrymen living in these colonies, the English people who lived in England started to become increasingly envious. They began to feel that they themselves ought to profit much more from these colonies in America. What was the point of discovering a country if the produce of the country they had discovered did not make England rich? Once their minds were seized by this, they devised various schemes to extract a great deal of money from these colonies. Principal among them were the obstacles they raised through an act of Parliament as a hindrance to the commerce and the development of the American colonies. This act of Parliament stated that the people living in the English colonies should extract metals such as gold, silver, copper, and iron from the mines in America but that they should not manufacture anything from them. No matter how much ore was produced, it must all be sent to England — and not to any other country. These colonies were not to conduct any trade directly with countries other than England. Because of this and other oppressive laws like it, the colonists who lived in America began to find England to be nothing but trouble.

But even after making laws like these, the greed of the English was not satisfied. They decided to implement a new law called the Stamp Act in the American colonies for the purpose of paying off the debts they had incurred in the French and Indian War. In order to make their legal documents such as receipts and contracts valid and legal, every American was compelled by this act to buy and use stamps that were printed in England. They lost their right to create any legal document without first buying and using stamp paper printed in England. The American colonists all agreed then that this act was tyrannical. They took to task the English authorities who were implementing it. Ultimately the English government realized that the matter had reached a perilous point — that owing to the Stamp Act peace in the colonies was being threatened — and this law was implemented in America for only about a year. During this period the English government received sixteen thousand pounds from the sale of these stamps; and this was of course what it cost the American people to buy these stamps under duress. But at the very same time, in order to cover the cost of the army that had to be maintained there to uphold English rule, the English government had to spend five times that amount — that is, eighty thousand pounds a year!

There were at that time two political parties among the American people. The Tories were favorably inclined toward England; but the Whigs were against all parliamentary laws. When they saw that the Stamp Act brought them no profit, the English government canceled it — only to impose a tax on tea and on many other essential commodities. The Americans did not like this either. The English people who lived in England had representatives in the English Parliament, but the people who lived in the colonies did not have the right to send their own representatives. The American people began to think of this as a terrible humiliation: the people of England made the laws according to their own whims while they themselves were expected quietly to obey them. They said that, no matter what, they would not buy the commodities that were being taxed. After the Stamp Act took effect virtually all the American people made the decision not to use any product which, because it was produced in England, would harm the commerce of their own country. This resolution of theirs had a profound effect on the business of English traders — upon whose request, consequently, the English government canceled the taxes on every essential commodity except tea. This was not a very profitable tax, but it did still symbolize England's dominion. The American people, however, would no longer tolerate even that. As a test of its dominion over the American people, the English government had sailing ships laden with tea sent from the *East India Company*[19] to America. They arrived at important American ports such as Philadelphia in 1773. When they saw that nobody was buying their cargo in New York and Philadelphia, the captains of these ships set sail back to England. It is true that the tea was unloaded in the city of Charleston, but the people there did not buy it. It was stored in warehouses and there it rotted away. When three ships filled with English tea arrived in Boston, a large number of young Boston men boarded the ships, broke open three hundred boxes of tea, and dumped the tea into the sea. The people of the United States still humorously call this gang the "Boston tea party" — that is, the band of Bostonians that went out for a convivial cup of tea.

When news of the Boston revolt reached England, the English government was incensed. They immediately implemented a law called the Boston Port Bill, which decreed that no English trader could maintain any business relations with the city of Boston. The residents of that city had to endure a great deal of hardship because of this. People from other places, however, gave them much help by supplying them with essential commodities. Following

19. Trans.: As at other places throughout the text, this is Ramabai's own emphasis (rendered with bold print in the original text). We have placed all of these points of emphasis — here the name of the company that had brought India under British dominion — in italics. — *PCE*

this, all across the American colonies, a great clamor arose in denunciation of the tyranny of the English government. In order to punish the Bostonians, in 1774 an English army was landed in the state of Massachusetts. In time this affair reached the point of no return. The American colonists began to say, "We do not have a single representative in the English Parliament. It is absolutely essential, however, that our opinions be consulted when framing the laws that affect our welfare for good or ill. The actions of the English government in imposing taxes exactly as it pleases without consulting our opinions can never be just." Not only did the English government reject this logical and legal demand of theirs but they also arranged that the expense of maintaining in America the army they had sent to hold the American people in subjection should be paid by *them* — much to the displeasure of the American people.

Given these circumstances, the American people, now all of one mind, made every effort to hold fast to their just and due rights. They elected their own representatives from the different colonies and sent them to Philadelphia, where the American people's *Continental Congress* was instituted.[20] Through their very highest-ranking public servants in this Congress, the American people undertook the task of governing and ordering their own nation. There followed many battles between the English and the Americans. At the end of 1775 the American Congress appointed George Washington as the general of their army — whereupon the American people began to have some hope that they would win their battle against the English. On the fourth of July, 1776, the American people declared to the world at large that they had completely severed all connection with the English government and were now independent. At that time the population of the American States was approximately thirty lakh (3,000,000) men, women, and children. They did not have much money, nor did they have the excellent instruments of war that the English government had. But their desire for independence was so powerful that the mountainous adversities that time and again faced them came to seem no bigger than sesame seeds. They fought the English for eight long years. By 1781 they had prevailed enough that they could truly make of their *United States* an independent nation. The English government continued fighting them sporadically until 1783; but in the independent states of America, they couldn't get their pot to boil.

This war reduced the nation to dire poverty, and it had to face all the difficulties that any newly established nation quite naturally has to face. But on the strength of the intellect and the statesmanship of learned, foresighted,

20. Trans.: *Rāṣṭrīyasabhā* (literally "national council") is the word Ramabai uses here. — *KG*

and public-spirited people such as Washington, Franklin, and Jefferson, all these difficulties were overcome. In 1887 the *Continental Congress* of the United States drafted a *national system of government* and implemented it. This was how the political system of the United States was made to work so well and peace and order were established everywhere. This is why the people of these independent states enjoy every happiness and why their nation has become the most wealthy and developed nation in all the world. And it is this national system of government of these United States that we shall briefly consider now.

CHAPTER 3

The System of Government

In the ancient precepts governing royal polity in our country there are seven constituents of the state enumerated: the *swāmī* (lord or king), the *amātya* (minister or counselor), the *mitra* (friend or ally), the *kośa* (treasury), the *rāṣṭra* (nation), the *kille* (forts), and the *senā* (army). It is simply accepted that by "state" *(rājya)* is meant all the land ruled over by a king and that the principal constituent part of the state is in turn the king. From this it is commonly understood by everyone that the nation, the treasury (that is, all the wealth of the state), the subjects, and all other such things are created for the pleasure and convenience of the king. In keeping with the uncouth *(rānaṭī)* custom expounded in the Marathi proverb that has come down from ancient times, "The strong man will twist your ear,"[1] the king is god, and he holds in his hands alone the reins of his subjects' destinies. From proverbs such as "As the king is, so are his subjects"[2] and "The king brings both the good times and the bad,"[3] we see very clearly how deeply the king's sovereignty over his subjects and his right freely to do exactly as he pleased were impressed on people's minds. It did not even occur to the people of ancient times that any country could prosper without a king — that is, without some strong person

1. Trans.: *Baḷī to kāna piḷī.* See A. Manwaring, *Marathi Proverbs* (New Delhi: Asian Educational Service, 1991 [1899]), p. 60. — *PCE*

2. Trans.: *Yathā rājā tathā prajā,* also commonly rendered in Marathi as *Jasā rājā taśī prajā.* See V. V. Bhide, ed., *Marāṭhī bhāṣece vākpracāra va mhaṇī* (Pune: Chitrashala Prakashan, 1959 [1918]), p. 400. — *PCE*

3. Trans.: *Rājā kālasya kāraṇam.* See Bhide, *Marāṭhī bhāṣece vākpracāra va mhaṇī,* p. 401. — *PCE*

to govern it. And that is why they must have used the word *arājaka* (which means "kingless" or "the country where there is no king in power") for "misrule" or "anarchy."

Such an understanding of things simply does not exist in the republic of the United States. Although there is no king and there are no subjects here, this nation's system of government is superior to all, and there is neither anarchy nor misrule. The aim of this chapter is to explain the main reasons for this. In the sentence quoted below, we find the essence of the superior ethic upon whose solid foundation the building of this remarkable democratic country is built: *"All human beings have been created free and equal, and the creator has given them numerous unexpropriatable* (anapaharaṇīya)[4] *gifts, such as life, liberty, and the endeavor to obtain happiness; these truths are self-evidential* (svataḥpramāṇa)[5] *so we believe."*[6]

Upon the foundational principles of these things, the equality among themselves of all the human inhabitants of this country has been established. All their laws, all their traditions, customs, and ideas are dependent upon this timeless truth. It leaves absolutely no room for any interpretation that entitles one person to a particular right and deprives another of it; so the possibility does not even arise of discrimination along the lines of high and low caste *(jāta)* or in accordance with family line. This American caste *(jāta)* is one. Just as in our country *there was only one pure caste*[7] *during the* kṛtayuga,[8] *which is why all people acted then with one mind and why in the* krtayuga *all the people were happy and equal;* here in *this* country, owing to the fact that they have only one caste *(jāta)*, they have achieved the supreme happiness which arises out of such concord. Here in America they consider it an insult to the great caste *(mahājāta)* called "American" if anyone brags about their own particu-

4. That is, not liable to be expropriated *(apaharaṇa)*. — *PRS*

5. That which does not need any other proof *(pramāṇa)* to establish its truth; that which is its own proof *(pramāṇa)*. — *PRS*

6. Trans.: The original wording in the Declaration of Independence is as follows: "We hold these Truths to be self-evident, that all Men are created equal, that they are endowed by their Creator with certain unalienable Rights, that among these are Life, Liberty, and the pursuit of Happiness." The emphasis here (as in italicized passages that follow) is Ramabai's own. — *PCE*

7. Trans.: *Śuklavarṇa* is the word Ramabai uses here. It means literally "white color" (or "white category" of castes) but can be used in the sense of "pure caste." — *KG*

8. Trans.: According to the *Manusmṛti* the four *yugas* or ages of the world (the *mahajuga*) are *kṛta* or *satya, tretā, dvāpāra,* and *kali.* The duration of each is said to be respectively 1,728,000; 1,296,000; 846,000; and 432,000 years of men. The diminishing length of each of the *yugas* represents a corresponding physical and moral deterioration of the people living in each, *krta* being called the golden age and *kali* or the present age being called the dark age. — *KG*

lar social group *(jāta)* or their own particular family line. The Goddess of Liberty, who is the household deity of the Americans, writes "American Citizen"[9] on the forehead of every human being (with the exception of the Chinese) who comes to America. The fortunate person who has this name shining on his forehead feels himself as being more select and more highly decorated than all the thousands of people who wear bejeweled crowns. Indeed, it should not come as a surprise were these crowned princes and kings to envy *him.*

The basic *mantra* of the American citizen is this: "This country belongs to the people, has been brought into existence by the people, and is ruled by the people."[10] Here in America the vote[11] of presidents such as Washington, Lincoln, and Grant or of learned people such as Franklin, Jefferson, and Emerson counts not one whit more than the vote of the most ordinary Negro citizen; and what is more, there is not a single citizen in this country who does not possess all the same rights as a citizen that those famous men did.

There are many differences in the systems of government of the various states of the United States. And their laws are also of varying kinds. When the people of this nation assumed power, they made some changes to the English laws that were then in effect here, but on the whole they left them the way they were. As the people developed and their opinions continued to change, however, the old laws also continued to be changed. More recently, the states that have been joined to this nation during the last forty years or so, being of an altogether American sort, have had simpler laws. And day by day the older states are imitating their newer brethren.

9. The word Ramabai uses here for citizen is *jānapada,* which she introduces from Sanskrit for the reasons she herself has given in the following note: "I have translated 'American citizen' as *Amerikecā jānapada.* The common meaning of the word 'citizen' is city-dweller. But in the United States of America, the meaning given to this word is much more complex and much more important than the sense of it given above. Here in America 'citizen' is understood to mean 'That person who is a resident of the nation and who is under its governing authority.' In our language we do not have a single word that conveys the sense of this word. The Sanskrit word *jānapada,* however, does somewhat approach the meaning of 'citizen' in America. If *jānapada* means 'country' or 'nation,' a person who resides in it is a *jānapada.* If we were to take this basic sense of the word and change it slightly to make it refer more broadly to him 'whose country *(jānapada)* it is, who is subject to its power,' and were we then to make *jānapada* the equivalent for the American 'citizen,' no one should take offense." — *PRS*

10. Trans.: This appears to be a rendering of the famous phrase in the last sentence of Lincoln's Gettysburg Address: "government of the people, by the people, for the people." — *PCE*

11. Trans.: The Marathi word for "vote" *(mata)* is the same word used for "opinion." Here, as elsewhere in the text, it is not always clear which sense Ramabai intends. — *PCE*

The Local Structure of Government

The national government is only a larger form of the structure of local and regional government. It is a self-evident truth that the local structure of government is like a seed, that the tree of the national government that is produced from it belongs to the very same species *(jāta)* as the seed, and that its fitness and fruitfulness must depend entirely on the fitness of that seed. So before turning our thoughts to the democratic system of national government, we shall look first at the nature of its originating causes.

Since the state of Iowa belongs to the newer American type, it would be useful to call it a prototypical state of this nation. At one point this state was nothing but wilderness. Some time ago when I was in Iowa, I happened to make the acquaintance of quite a number of the people who had first come and settled there. In what follows I shall recount for you the pattern in which they settled there and established the local structure of government.

To start with, one adventuresome, industrious man leaves his home, taking his wife with him or else going alone, to test his fortune in a new and untamed region. He has nothing more with him than an axe, some tools, plows, a team of horses, and some seed. When he arrives at the place of his choosing, he himself fells the trees and builds a cabin. Then he clears and plows the land, plants a small field with the seeds he has brought along, and plants some fruit trees. After some days several more people arrive, following his example, and start to build cabins or houses on their own plots of land a short distance apart and next to his and begin to live there. By the time ten or fifteen families have begun to live comfortably in one place, their attention is drawn to two essential things: first, to the building of roads to allow them to get about conveniently between home and market or anywhere else; and second, to the establishing of schools for their children. Since there is no government there as yet to provide these amenities, the people of this tiny settlement make the effort themselves to fill this need. After some days, an assembly of twenty or twenty-five of the people gathers, and its members pledge to one another to pay a certain amount in taxes for this work. Now, at the point when it becomes necessary to have individuals assume responsibility for the various tasks — someone to decide how much the tax should be, someone to collect it, someone to appropriate it in the proper way, and someone to maintain the accounts — the offices of tax assessor, tax collector, village supervisor, keeper of accounts,[12] and so on, are

12. Trans.: Ramabai uses here the name of the traditional Maharashtrian office of

created; following which, the sheriffs[13] and lower-level magistrates are appointed.

The establishment in this way of these duties and of these offices all for the convenience of the residents is accomplished by means of voting. One person among the assembled residents might propose the name of some man for a certain job and a certain amount of money for some particular task; and everybody's opinion is then sought about the matter — this opinion being called a "vote." Whereupon that person is appointed to do the stipulated work. All other similar matters are worked out according to which person or which matter is favored by the majority of votes. And as they are soliciting public opinion in this way in all matters, nobody questions anyone about the superiority or the inferiority of their family or about their social group *(jāta)* — and hence their worthiness. The person may belong to any social group *(jāta);* it is sufficient only that he have these things in his favor: that he be a resident of the village of respectable (i.e., lawful) conduct, that he not be a criminal or insane or mentally incompetent, that he not be under the age of twenty-one, and that he be a man. (Women have still not received their full rights under the law — only in Wyoming and Kansas do they have them.) Whether he be rich or poor, learned or unlearned, black or white, his vote counts not one whit more or less than that of the president of the country.

Within the overall national system of government, the structure of village (i.e., local) government is extremely important. Within the governing structure of every town can be seen almost all the very same basic principles underlying the system of the national government. It would not be far wrong to say that every village is an independent nation in its own right. It is a very good thing that the structure of local government in the United States does not have, on the one hand, the deficiencies and the lack of independence that undermine the structure of local government in our own country nor, on the other hand, the excess of independence that led to the destruction of the independence of ancient Greece. The structure of local government in our own country actually does possess many of the fundamental principles of self-rule *(svarājya).* It would not be far wrong to say that what our people call by the name of *pañcāyata*[14] constitutes one kind of assembly of people's representa-

---

kuḷakaraṇī: "an officer of a village under the *pāṭīl* [headman]. His business is to keep the accounts of the cultivators with Government and all the public records" (Molesworth). — *PCE*

13. Trans.: The word Ramabai uses is *caukīdār:* "a watchman or guard" (Molesworth). — *PCE*

14. Trans.: Originally an assembly of five witnesses or arbitrators usually appointed by disputing parties or influential people of the village, in present-day India the *pañcāyata* is the form of local self-government at the village level. Its officers are now democratically elected. The term

tives. But it does not have the effectiveness of a body elected by the people in a democratic state for the simple reason that the *pañcāyata* is chosen by a select few of the prominent people in a village. There is a vast difference between this and a body that is elected thoughtfully and publicly by a vote of all the people. The *pañcāyata* does not have the support of common public opinion. There is no possibility of it having the same degree of importance and effectiveness as something that is constituted legally and with all proper and due order. Moreover, sometimes the selection of the *pañcas*[15] is in the hands of two parties that have a quarrel going on between them. There is absolutely nothing of public-spiritedness[16] about it. It is impossible that something that lacks *public-spiritedness* can have a *concern for the common good*[17] (i.e., beneficialness for all the people); which is the reason why, although we have had the *pañcāyata* system in our country, our people have yet to see such things as a true knowledge of local self-rule *(svarājya)*, the benefits that stem from it, and the unity that infuses human society by means of it.

During the time when ancient Greece was under democratic rule, the Hellenic people held local independence to be of paramount importance. A united democratic state, such as the United States, was never established in that country. The Greek people neither created nor implemented a common system of state government that was strong and that looked to the future — and that would thus make their self-rule *(svarājya)* permanent. The democratic state of ancient Greece was of such a kind that each city was independent and totally sovereign. With many totally sovereign cities existing side by side in this way, occasional disputes were unavoidable — whether over some quite common or some very particular issue. Now when one small city began a war against another small city, one or the other of the two sides was inevitably the victor. And thus the fire of animosity between them was constantly kept smoldering. How could small towns that were fighting each other like this hold out in a war with some really powerful country? Even supposing they wanted to have friendly relations with each other and unite themselves, they fundamentally lacked a universally accepted, common

---

has also entered the English dictionary as "panchayat"; see the *Chambers 20th Century Dictionary* (1983). — *KG*

15. Trans.: Members of the *pañcāyata*. — *KG*

16. Trans.: The word Ramabai uses here is *sārvajanikatā*, an abstract noun formed from the adjective *sārvajanika* ("public"), hence literally "public-ness." — *PCE*

17. Trans.: The word Ramabai uses here is *sārvajanīnatva*, which is not fundamentally different in sense from the preceding *sārvajanikatā*. In Ramabai's usage, however (as indicated in her own parenthetical definition that follows it in the text), it has the sense of concern for, attention to, the public good. — *PCE*

constitution[18] that would weave them all together within a net of unity. Each one of them was independent in its own right. Each felt free to act as it wished. Because of this lack of regulation within each independent city, when these disunited democratic states of Greece suffered the full force of foreign invasion, they fell one after the other and were utterly destroyed. At one point there was an attempt made in the region of Greece called Attica to unite several cities into one nation, but this did not succeed. And the reason for this was that, for one thing, the various independent cities did not voluntarily surrender as many of their important rights to the unified nation as was necessary in order to make it a strong nation; and, for another, they did not get the time they needed, after they realized their need for unity, to do what was necessary to make it work. Before the deathless vine of unity could germinate and take firm root in the soil of Attica, two of its enemies, Macedonia and Rome, attacked it. The idea never occurred to the Greeks or to the Romans that the inhabitants of every city and every town should elect their own representatives, appoint them as their leaders, give them full authority to speak and work on their behalf, send them to a general legislative assembly at the state or national level, and then implement the laws that were approved there by majority vote in their own cities. It is not surprising that these people should have felt it as an insult to their independent, sovereign cities to implement there the laws made in some other city. The ideas both the Greeks and the Romans had about the independence of towns or even of larger districts were for the most part the same.

Once you arrive at an understanding of how the system of government in the United States works, it is easy to see that the local governments of this country have neither too little nor too much independence — just as I have described it above. In this system of government, there is just that degree of independence granted to local, regional, and state governments as is required to maintain their stability and effectiveness. But this system does not allow that degree of independence that would create hostility between towns, districts, and states and, owing to this discord, pose a threat to the nation.

A township is an area of land six miles in length and six miles in breadth. Along these same lines, the entire nation has been divided into counties, states, and so forth, by actual measurements of the land with the aid of government surveyors. When new towns begin to be settled here and there in the manner described earlier, twelve or fifteen townships are consolidated to form a county.

18. Trans.: *Rāṣṭrīya nīti* is Ramabai's phrase here — meaning the national *(rāṣṭrīya)* "laws and rules of dealing and conduct" (Molesworth). The contexts in which she uses this same phrase later on in the chapter clearly show that she means "constitution" by it. — *PCE*

The Counties

All the officials in a county, like the officials of a town, are elected by popular vote to their various offices. For the most part they occupy their positions for a period of two years. In several states the elections for these officials take place annually. The officials are paid monthly salaries according to what is decided by their respective communities. But the salaries are as a rule extremely modest. Which town will serve as the county seat is decided upon with the consent of all the people in the county. At quite short intervals elections are held for the appointment of such officeholders as the sheriff, the criminal magistrate, road inspectors, and superintendents of education, as well as other officials. But that is not all. Even the lowest-ranking justices of the peace are appointed by popular consent. That the system of appointing judges is dependent on popular consent is a very good thing because public matters like justice have a very close connection with all the people. The fortunes of the poorest and neediest people, of family men who must drudge for a living, lie primarily in the hands of officials like the judge. No one needs to be told that if these officials are careless, callous, arrogant, or tyrannical, then the life, the property, and the very dignity of the poor and the powerless are placed in jeopardy. Examples of these things can be found wherever you turn in monarchies, especially in those states where the kings indulge themselves with nothing but luxury and ease while leaving everything that needs to be done in the hands of ignorant officials who have managed to curry their favor. When the rights and offices that are most closely linked with the joys and sufferings of all the people are placed in the hands of one man or of some select class of great imaginary rank and when the people do not have the power to seize these rights from them, it is a most lamentable thing. This is why the poor never receive proper justice, even as the rich, the powerful, and those who hold office invariably get the upper hand — and an unceasing sacrifice is made of the Goddess of Justice to injustice.

The States

Several counties of the kind described above together constitute a state. Just as the county government is a larger form of local government, the government of a state is a grander form of the county government. Every state has a chief official who is called the governor. He is chosen by the consent of all the people of the state. The governor is related to the state in the same manner that the president of the United States is related to the entire nation. The state government has two or three more constituent parts than the local and county governments do, and these are very important. Each state has the authority to make its own laws. In the capital city of each state there is a state assembly hall. The state's legislative assembly, the office of the governor, the supreme court of the state, and the office of the head official of the state's department of education are all located there. The legislative assembly of each state is divided into two parts. One of them is called the House of Representatives[19] and the other is called the Senate.[20] The representatives and senators are both elected by all the rank and file people of the state. These two assemblies together make all the necessary laws for the state. The state government has the authority to make only those laws that do not conflict with the larger national system of government of the United States. It is the task of the governor to implement the laws of the state. The justices of the state supreme court are appointed by the president of the country with the consent of the Congress of the United States.[21] They decide the cases that are brought before them in accordance with the laws of their respective state governments.

The chief official of a state's department of education superintends all the schools within a state. Each state has its own separate treasury. The state government itself manages the levying and collecting of state revenues and other such matters. And in a similar vein, each state has its own separate army reserve department. But the various states within the nation do not make use of this department in disputes among themselves. And none of the states within the United States has the authority to declare war on or to make a treaty with any foreign country. That authority is the preserve of the national government alone. The rule is that all the expenses for the state's department of education, for its army reserve, and so on are to be borne by the state alone. In brief, all the rights and all the constituent functions that any independent state or nation would have, are to be found as part of a state's government. The state government has, however, voluntarily entrusted numerous rights,

19. Trans.: *Lokapratinidhīṃcī sabhā* (assembly of people's representatives) is the phrase Ramabai consistently uses; but in what follows we will continue to use the established American term "House of Representatives." — *PCE*

20. Trans.: *Kārabhāryāṃcī sabhā* (assembly of *kārabhārīs*) is the phrase Ramabai coins and consistently uses. Molesworth defines *kārabhārī* thus: "One that carries on or conducts (some extensive business); a conductor, manager, deputy, Major domo, minister of state etc." The clearly executive functions of a *kārabhārī* are inconsistent with the sense of "senator" in its established American usage. But since "senator" and "senate" are Ramabai's referents here, in what follows we will continue to use the established American terms. — *PCE*

21. Trans.: Here Ramabai is perhaps confusing the appointment procedures of the federal Courts of Appeal with those of the various state supreme courts. — *PCE*

such as the authority to make treaties with foreign nations, to the national government for the sake of everyone's convenience and in order to maintain unity among the states. Other than this, in virtually all respects each state is an independent nation in its own right.

The Territories

Next to the state in importance is the territory. The people of a territory do not have the right to choose their own governor because a territory is considered to be part of the common fixed assets of the entire nation. When the population of a territory reaches the number that is required to become a state, it assumes statehood. It receives all the rights that pertain to a state at the point when the national Congress passes a resolution, in accordance with the system of government of the United States, that it should be included as one state among all the rest. The local and county governments of a territory work independently just as they do in any state. Even in a territory there has to be a governor and a supreme court. The kinds of authority possessed by its officials are exactly like those of officials in any state. It is the president who, with the consent of Congress, appoints these officials to their various offices in a territory. Although a territory does not have the right to send a representative or a senator to Congress, each territory does send a delegate to live in Washington, where, although he cannot enter Congress as a member, he can advise the members of Congress in important ways whenever they are making resolutions and laws regarding his territory. Because the territories do not have the right to send representatives, they have no part to play in electing the president or vice president of the country.

The Nation

Thirty-eight states of this kind and twelve territories together constitute this great democratic nation called the *United States.* Since there is no rule about the number of states the country can have, any number of new states may be added to it. I have already mentioned that these states are not just insignificant little districts but virtually independent countries. Because each state separately possesses all the constituent elements of a state — a legislative assembly with both representatives and senators, an executive head of the state (the governor), state supreme court justices, an army reserve, a treasury, and an administrative system — all of the states, each in its own right, are their own sovereign authorities. Clearly, these states would not be able to hold out against foreign aggression if they remained as separate entities entirely, and this would constitute a serious blow both to commerce and to the progress of the country as a whole; so they have agreed to certain constraints among themselves, and by following these established rules they are able to act with one accord. In order to solidify this unity, and to strengthen their own governance, they have voluntarily ceded numerous sovereign rights in order to create one united government. The reins of this united government are in the hands of the president. But he is not a law unto himself. He must oversee the government, taking into consideration the opinions of the representatives and senators who represent all the citizens of the country. The seat of this united government, the city of Washington, is the capital of the United States of America. It is located in the small zone called the District of Columbia. This zone is not a special state. In accordance with the provisions of their united government, it is the common property of all the states of the United States. All those things over which the states share equal rights — such as the national treasury, courts of justice, the department of education, and scientific academies[22] — are located in Washington.

The National Court of Justice

A very great and excellent instrument for bringing stability and strength to this united nation is the *Supreme Court* of the United States. The Supreme Court decides those cases arising from disputes between the state governments and the federal government over who has which rights and how far they extend as well as those arising from other issues of national importance. Both the state and federal governments have to abide by any verdict handed down by the Supreme Court unless and until the federal government enacts a new law after seeking the opinion of all the states. If the Congress of the United States enacts and seeks to implement a new law that violates the Constitution,[23] which was

22. Trans.: *Śāṣṭrīya vicārālayeṃ* is Ramabai's obsolete and very obscure usage here. *Śāṣṭrīya* is defined by Molesworth in the 1857 edition of his Marathi-English dictionary thus: "Relating to the Shastras, scriptural." Shortly thereafter, however, the word began to develop into one of the two common Marathi terms for "scientific." *Vicārālaya* is literally "house of thought," hence "academy" in our translation. Ramabai may very well be referring here to federal institutions such as the Smithsonian Institution (created by an act of Congress in 1846) or even the Library of Congress (created by an act of Congress in 1800). — *PCE*

23. Trans.: *Rāṣṭrīya nīti* is Ramabai's phrase here — meaning the national *(rāṣṭrīya)* "laws and rules for dealing and conduct" (Molesworth). — *PCE*

adopted by consent of all the states when this democratic country was founded, the Supreme Court considers the suitability or unsuitability of the law and issues a decree overturning it. But no one should assume from this that the Supreme Court has unlimited power. Certainly Congress, the president, and the other members of the governing body of the United States obey the court's orders with profound respect; but the court does not have the authority to do just anything it pleases, only to decide the cases that come before it in conformity with the Constitution. Nor does it have the power to frame new laws or to implement the laws that already exist. When a particular matter is brought before it in the established manner, the Supreme Court considers whether it is in agreement with the Constitution or not and hands down either a favorable or an unfavorable decision accordingly. In this way the Court is denied the right to interfere in the administration of the states, of local governments, or of the president unless and until a particular matter is brought before it in the established manner. And it is also obligated to inform all the people of what its decisions are and the reasons for them. Nobody in this nation has the power to set aside (at least in a legal manner) any decision that this court hands down — within the bounds of these rules and with the constitutional power vested in it by the nation — on the suitability or unsuitability of any matter.

Although the legislative assemblies of the various states are free within their own states to make the laws they want, these assemblies take extreme care while framing these laws that they do not violate the Constitution, because everybody knows that the Supreme Court has the power to overturn these laws if they violate the Constitution in any way. No reason exists fundamentally anyway for making laws that violate the Constitution because, in the first place, the residents of the states themselves would not vote to allow the creation of laws that are against the Constitution of their united nation — for which all the states, out of concern for their own security, have yielded up certain rights in order to establish it as their common governing authority. But should such an occasion arise and one of the states did act outside the provisions of the Constitution, someone has to have the power to say that this is wrong; and it is only right that the Supreme Court has that power. From the founding of the United States up to the present day, only once has such a case come before the Supreme Court. About twenty-five years ago some southern states that held Africans[24] in slavery, with the aim solely of filling their own pockets, declared that they would secede from the United States — and that

24. Trans.: *Habaśī* is the word Ramabai uses here, from the Arabic word for "Abyssinian" (Molesworth). — *PCE*

they had the right to do so. And they did try to separate themselves from the national union. At that time the Supreme Court decided that this was a violation of the Constitution and that these states did not have the right to secede from the nation. The southern states defied the court's decision and rose up in rebellion; but the northern states, together with those states that wanted to maintain national integrity, put the rebellion down.

Although there are extremely few court cases concerning restrictions on the rights of the states and although the Supreme Court does not have many occasions to hand down decisions on them, residents of the various states who have disputes with each other over large sums of money or other significant matters can bring them before the Supreme Court for settlement. So this court does not have any time to sit back and be idle.

There are nine justices on this court. Unlike other government officials (the president, his secretaries, etc.), new members are not appointed to the Supreme Court every few years to replace the sitting justices. Once they are appointed to the court, they can be removed by the federal government only when and if it becomes apparent that they are incapable of carrying out their duties or they are impeached by Congress and proven guilty of the charges against them. Otherwise, the provision is for them to remain in office as long as they have the strength to carry out their duties. If one of them should die or his seat fall vacant for whatever reason, the president chooses a worthy person and appoints that person to the position; but before doing so he must request the Senate to give its consent. The president does not have the right to appoint a new member to the Supreme Court without consulting the Senate or in defiance of its wishes. Each member of the Supreme Court receives a salary of $10,000 a year, while the Chief Justice receives $500 more, or a total of $10,500. Those who have reached the age of seventy are expected to retire, following which they continue as long as they live to receive the same salary they did while in office.

There are plenty of other officials and lawyers in the United States who probably earn ten times more than this. From the point of view of acquiring wealth, the position occupied by the members of the Supreme Court is not that desirable. A lawyer or even a doctor earns three or four times more than they. But the honor and respect attached to their position isn't something that can be obtained through mere money. Their exalted position is itself the reason for the honor and respect they enjoy. All the citizens of this country show them the highest esteem. The governors of the states, the president of the nation, and important bodies such as Congress obey their orders without question. As the representatives of the Goddess of Justice, they occupy an exalted position as if on a veritable throne of national justice. Nowhere in the world is there likely to be any position equal to this. If greed for money were to become the basis for rising to such a rank, what would be left of any honor or respect for the Goddess of Justice? So it can only be for the good that there is no powerful attraction of something like wealth to inspire people to seek this position. The members of the Supreme Court are generally persons of good character, influential, erudite, judicious, and experienced. Their manner of living and their style of clothing is very modest, which makes their honorableness even more imposing.

The Supreme Court has its headquarters in the city of Washington, where its work is normally conducted; but its members each take their own turn every year at appointed times to visit all the regions of the country and assist the judges in these various places with such things as the examination of lawsuits. In order to make the administration of justice more convenient, the federal government has divided the country into nine sections and then further divided these into separate districts. There are courts and judges in all of these districts. Because these are federal courts, the judges are appointed to them by nomination of the president and approval by the Senate. The judges who are appointed to these positions serve for life — that is, unless they are found, through substantiated proof, to be unfit for the work or guilty of serious misbehavior.

The National Assembly: "Congress"

We shall consider now the legislative body that makes the laws on the basis of which the judges resolve the people's disputes and maintain social, commercial, and constitutional order in the country. There are two branches of the national legislative body called Congress: the House of Representatives and the Senate.[25] Both of these assemblies are located in the city of Washington and conduct their business there. Every year they assemble in March and in December on appointed dates to begin their work. At present there are 325 members of the House of Representatives. The number of representatives sent from each state depends upon the population of that state. Every ten years the federal government conducts a census and determines, on the basis of its population, the number of representatives each state is entitled to send

25. Trans.: Once again Ramabai uses the terms *lokapratinidhīṃcī sabhā* (assembly of people's representatives) and *kārabhāryāṃcī sabhā* (assembly of the *kārabhārīs*); and again in what follows we shall consistently use the terms of established American usage, "House of Representatives" and "Senate." — *PCE*

to the Congress. As the population of this country continues to rise, the number of voters per representative also increases. In 1870 it was determined that there would be one lakh thirty-eight thousand (138,000) state residents for each representative. In 1880 this was changed to one lakh fifty-four thousand (154,000) people per representative. This provision gives all the states an equal right in choosing their representatives, based on each state's population, so no one has any reason to quarrel with anyone else.

The representatives have a two-year term of office. When Congress ends its work on March 4,[26] the representatives' terms of office also come to an end. But if they are competent in what they do and popular, they can be re-elected and are then entitled to work in the Congress for another two years. That is why those who come new to this important position find themselves under the supervision of well-seasoned older political leaders. Every representative receives an annual salary of $5,000 in addition to some money for travel expenses. The officials of the federal government receive their salaries from the national treasury in accordance with the regulations of the Constitution.

The Senate

Two members are elected and sent to the Senate from each of the states. It is the legislative assembly, which has been established in each of the states by the will of the people, that chooses each state's senators and sends them to work on behalf of the state.[27] The senators' term of office is six years, and they also receive a salary of $5,000 a year plus travel expenses. It has prudently been arranged that all the senators' terms of office should not begin at the same time. Every two years one third of the members of the Senate tender their resignations. But if they are bright and popular, they can be elected again and resume their duties for another six years. It is true that senators have an obligation to support whatever the ruling party happens to be in each of their states; but unlike the House of Representatives, the political bearing of this assembly

26. Ed.: The first session of the first Congress under the Constitution met on March 4, 1789, but in subsequent years March 4 came to be the adjourning date rather than a convening date. In 1933 the twentieth amendment to the Constitution was ratified, establishing noon on the third of January as the convening date for Congress, unless Congress by law appoints a different day. — *REF*

27. Trans.: This system of selecting senators did not change until the seventeenth amendment to the Constitution, passed in 1913, provided for their election by direct popular vote. — *PCE*

does not change abruptly with the whims of public opinion. The Senate has some very large and important rights and responsibilities, owing to which this constituent part of Congress is very powerful. After the House of Representatives approves the first draft of new laws they are brought before the Senate. Without the Senate's approval no law can be implemented. Unless two-thirds of the Senate votes in favor of treaties with foreign countries, they cannot be ratified.

The ambassadors and representatives of the United States government to foreign countries must be approved by the Senate. It is true that the president can appoint many officials of his own choice to various offices; but if they are not approved by the Senate, then not just any single president but even ten presidents would not be able to bestow these positions upon the people they favor. It is held to be a sign of great honor in American society for members who have worked in the House of Representatives to be promoted to the Senate. The great pride that this nation takes in its Senate is not empty. Just as in the case of the Supreme Court, you will not find assemblies anywhere else that can equal this assembly in worthiness and power. Even the English Parliament can boast no assembly that can compare with it. The English Parliament is composed of two parts: the House of Commons, which is of the common people; and the House of Lords, which is of the nobility. Only in the House of Commons is some respect paid to common public opinion. In the House of Lords public opinion isn't worth a straw; and only the rich have access to it. So what does it matter whether ordinary people even like or admire these overbearing paragons or not? The queen of England's present prime minister, Lord Salisbury, says, "I envy the Americans for the Supreme Court they have. And as you know, they also have a Senate. My ardent wish is that we might also have such an assembly in our country. The effectiveness and the power of this assembly are altogether extraordinary." It must be remembered that behind this extraordinary effectiveness and power lies the tremendous support of public opinion. The principal strength of the nation indeed is this, that ordinary people have the right to consider their own future interests and to vote on how the nation's business is to be conducted. Why shouldn't the vine that is the Senate possess such extraordinary power and effectiveness — when it finds its origin in such a strong root and when it takes its growth only from the strength of the sap-filled leaf of public approval?

No one in the country has the right to make a treaty with or to wage a war against foreign countries without the approval of the Senate. This and many other things like it are responsible for the greatness of this country. Because of the thoughtful behavior of the Senate, this country has not had to suffer the terrible consequences of many thoughtless actions. In a nation where the reins of its destiny are held for a long time by a single person or by a coterie of maybe ten at most, it is only too likely that the intense temptation these officials face to gratify their own ambition and to win the acclaim of the people will bear its inevitable fruit — when they do terrible things that may seem good at the moment and that may look dazzling on the surface but that lead the entire country into desperate straits. These men think first not of what is ultimately for the good of the country but of what for the present moment will startle and amaze the people and bring themselves popular acclaim. The blows of the ax of divine retribution[28] that fall upon a monarchy — where the reins of its destiny are in the hands solely of its ministers or generals — are most unlikely to strike a democratic nation. Here in this country it is out of the question that, by doing some particular ill-considered action, some particular individual's glory should be enhanced — and failing to do which, be obliged to idle his time away sitting on the sidelines. Nobody's honor or dishonor depends upon his doing or his not doing something with which that individual has no real connection — so nobody has any reason to insist that it has to be done. When the Senate (which is the assembly of the representatives of the entire nation) votes for or against some matter after giving it the deepest deliberation, it is universally accepted. Only those actions that ultimately benefit the nation are held to be worth doing and worth being universally accepted; nobody assigns any importance at all here to actions that, even as they ignore all costs or benefits to the nation, help keep some particular person in power or bring acclaim to some particular person. If the occasion should ever arise for making war on a foreign country, the government of the United States does not commit itself to such a monstrous action unless and until the representatives, the senators, and the president debate and consider the reasons for the war, whether these are compelling enough to bring matters to the point of shedding human blood, and what will be gained or lost by the war — and then all of them agree by majority vote to declare war. It takes a long time to discuss these matters and to arrive at a decision. This period of time affords all the citizens of the country the chance to express their opinions about the government's actions; and sometimes it happens that with the passage of time the very reasons for the quarrel with a foreign country disappear and the necessity for war no longer remains.

28. Trans.: The Marathi idiom here is *ākāśācī kurhāḍa* (literally, "ax of the sky"), the sense of which Bhide renders as "a calamity brought about because of divine anger" (see *Marāṭhī bhāṣece vākpracāra va mhaṇī*, p. 292). This comes from the Marathi proverb *ākāśācī kurhāḍa kolhyācyā dātāvara,* which Manwaring renders, "Heaven's axe on the teeth of the jackal," and of which he gives the common sense, "God's punishment falls on the leader" (*Marathi Proverbs*, p. 217). — *PCE*

If war is in fact declared, however, the responsibility for this is borne by all the nation's representatives, senators, and the president. It is simply out of the question that any particular high-ranking official, reacting to an insult from any particular person, should act arbitrarily and unilaterally and go to war out of simple revenge — and then have the consequences borne by innocent people.

The superiority of the rules of this democratic country becomes especially evident when they are compared with so many of the rules underlying the British system of government. In Britain, if any action intended for the public good is undertaken, it is necessary to get a favorable vote of the entire Parliament and to pass a law to that effect. But to wage war on Egypt, Burma, Afghanistan, and other such nations — in the process sacrificing the lives of thousands, even hundreds of thousands of people in the fires of war — and to suffocate a poor country like Hindusthan under a stifling burden of debt, nothing more is needed than a mere nod of the head of one or two or at most six or seven ministers of state. No one seeks the consent of Parliament for this. Five or six selfish people, in the name of the queen (and it must be remembered that the king or the queen is not an individual who holds real power but a weak person who is made to dance like a puppet in the hands of the serving ministers of state), are all it takes to wreak havoc with the entire nation or to make an ill-considered treaty with a foreign country that allows their own country and their dependent nations to be given to slaughter. And they call this the highly developed governing polity of a highly developed nation.

How much better it would have been if the British government had followed the example of this democratic country, acted upon the advice of thoughtful people, and not allowed a mere handful of people to meddle in the internal affairs of foreign countries. The established policy of the government of the United States is that they will not interfere in the affairs of foreign nations and will not allow anyone else to meddle in their own internal affairs. There are two strong political parties in this country. However they may wish to treat one another, if there are compelling reasons for confronting a foreign nation, they are both pledged, before taking any hasty action, to think through these reasons with the mediation of a neutral party and to try calmly to reach a settlement of the matter. Not very long ago the governments of the United States and England signed a treaty with each other that if and when disputes arise between them they will settle them through the mediation of a neutral nation and without recourse to arms. This action is a great adornment to their common decency. The government of the United States is ready to make such agreements with other countries as well. But if, after the government of the United States has communicated its desire to settle a dispute through mediation, the other party to the dispute disregards that proposal and insists on war, this government will not hesitate to go to war with them as a last resort.

The President

Up to this point we have considered the governing bodies of this country. Now we shall consider their chief executive,[29] the leader of these bodies who executes the laws that they have determined to be good and proper for the country. This chief executive is called the president of the United States. He accepts the responsibilities entrusted to him by the nation with the consent of Congress and executes all the nation's work on its behalf. His term of service is four years. If he is very popular, when his term expires the people of the United States reelect him in the customary way to the position of president for another four years. George Washington, Thomas Jefferson, James Madison, James Monroe, Andrew Jackson, and Ulysses Grant were all elected president of the United States twice, and each enjoyed the position for eight years. No one is elected president for more than eight years. Just as George Washington refused to be made a king and thereby won for himself immortal fame, he also refused a third term in office out of consideration for the welfare of the nation, even though the people wanted it. He recognized that if one person were to hold the president's position for three or four terms, it would be a major threat to the independence of the United States; so he refused the presidency the third time around, leaving a fine memorial to his patriotism and setting an excellent example for future presidents of the United States.

The president of the United States is not a mere puppet who has been placed on the throne in name only and is made to dance to the tune of the ministers of state. He is the president of the entire nation, as also the nation's chief law-enforcement officer and the commander in chief of the Army and the Navy. While in office, his political power is vast. Without orders from him there can be no changes made or much work of any kind carried out in the departments of justice, interior, defense, and so on. The moment he issues an order everyone is prepared to carry it out. Including the army reserves of all the states, the standing army of the United States does not even amount to twenty-five or twenty-six thousand men, which is next to nothing; but the moment the president issues the order, as many as sixty or seventy lakhs

29. Trans.: *Mukhtyāra* is the obsolete Perso-Arabic term Ramabai uses here: "a plenipotentiary or any one to whom full powers have been delegated" (Molesworth). — *PCE*

(seven million) strong men could prepare themselves to go to war for the defense of their country against whomever the president tells them. All these soldiers are not paid for the rest of their lives out of the national treasury; only as long as they are in service is it the duty of the nation to maintain them. They fight not to place the nation under obligation to themselves; they fight *for the protection of the country. They do not fight for the glory of any one particular person, but they are prepared to give up their lives freely for the defense of the country.* The president can, according to his wishes, dismiss any officer in the army if there is a valid reason. Because the people have made him their representative, no one wishes to put limits on his vast power. If the people do not like what the president does, they reserve their opinions about it until the next presidential elections. There is no reason for the people to regard him spitefully for making use of his vast power because it is not beyond the power of the people to remove him from office — should this, their highest-ranking official, who is appointed by the people, abuse his power. As long as the president is in office he receives a salary of $50,000 a year. He is also given the use of a large mansion in which to live in the city of Washington not far from Congress as well as a garden house a few miles outside the city whenever he goes away for a rest. Every week at an appointed time, he receives visitors for some hours. Everyone, from the richest tycoon to the most penniless laborer, who lives in this nation has an equal right to the president's time. Anybody who wants to may meet the president at the appointed time; and the president must show proper respect toward all. Owing to this and to many other such customs, the president is continually reminded that the power of the nation does not lie in the hands of one individual but with all its citizens in equal measure.

When this person, who is elected by the people, first begins his term of office as the nation's president, he himself appoints his own cabinet.[30] Because the president acts as his own prime minister, there is no gradation in the importance of the ranks of his "ministers" — all of whom enjoy the same respect. These "ministers" are called secretaries, such as, for instance, the Secretary of War, the Secretary of the Treasury, and so on. These cabinet mem-

30. There are altogether seven members of the cabinet in the order given here: the Secretary of State, the Secretary of the Treasury, the Secretary of War, the Attorney General, the Postmaster General, the Secretary of the Navy, and the Secretary of the Interior. At the time the president is elected, a vice president is also elected. His term of office is the same as that of the president. He receives a salary of $9,000 a year. If the president dies during his term or if he is removed from office, the vice president is appointed as president until his term expires. And if the vice president also dies or is removed from office, one of the members of the cabinet, in the order mentioned above, is given the authority of the president until the term expires. — *PRS*

bers are not permanent. If they prove unfit, it is not difficult to replace them. The cabinet does not normally appear before Congress. If they have any recommendations to make, they do so in writing. Previously the president used to attend each session of Congress and give an inaugural address. But ever since it came to be understood how important it is for the person responsible for executing the law not to be present while the laws are being made, this custom has been discontinued. Now whatever recommendations need to be made to Congress are sent by the president in writing. He also is at liberty to inform Congress about any matter that he feels paying more or less attention to would benefit the nation.

I have already said that the president has enormous power, one of the most important tokens of which is his veto authority. A veto is the power by which, if the president doesn't approve of a piece of draft legislation that has been passed by the representatives[31] and senators and sent to him for approval, he can, after showing valid reasons, reject it — that is, not give it his consent. Any draft legislation that is vetoed by the president does not become a law. If it is felt that the president's reasons for his veto are not valid and if two-thirds of the members of both houses of Congress vote in favor of the law, it is reconsidered and passed. In this way, even though the president has vast powers, it is well within the sphere of the power of Congress to keep them under check.

The American people have not been responsible for making many mistakes in electing their presidents. All the presidents who have served so far have turned out for the most part quite well. And any number of presidents such as Washington, Adams, Jefferson, Lincoln, and Garfield, by virtue of their peerless good conduct, statesmanship, and other such virtues, have been worthy in all respects of becoming the popular presidents they were. Neither Lincoln nor Garfield were millionaires; nor did they come from great families of sages or princes. Overcoming their disadvantaged birth, the impediments to their education, their lack of wealth, and all such obstacles by the strength of their hard work and good conduct, these children of the poorest, most common and ordinary farmers became learned men, teachers, lawyers, and presidents of the United States — and made their names immortal by virtue of their own intrinsic decency. When we consider these things, we can't help but react with joyful surprise; and when we learn that the most common and ordinary people of the United States, without depending at all on those three

31. Trans.: Here Ramabai is inconsistent in the term she uses for "representatives," although the context makes her sense clear: *mukhtyāra* (here used in the plural), as we have seen, is used earlier to describe the function of the president. — *PCE*

mighty powers of caste *(jāta),* family, and money, can ascend to high positions on the strength of their own worthiness, our hearts can only be filled with worshipful admiration for this nation.

Should the American people discover, however, that they have made a mistake in electing a particular president, they have remedies available to rectify it. All the people keep their eyes on the president's behavior and on his way of doing things. Just one or two actions of his that the people do not like and bingo! — all across the nation the newspapers raise a hue and cry. People discuss them in all the most noteworthy places. Everyone begins to talk about the need to elect a more virtuous and competent president than the current one in the next elections. When he hears this, a president who is inclined toward immorality usually takes it as a warning. If he doesn't, efforts usually are already well in hand to get somebody else elected in his place when his term expires. If his conduct violates the laws of the United States, he can be tried like any ordinary person before the Supreme Court and he can be removed from office. After the president's term of office is over, he engages himself in whatever work he wants to do just like any other ordinary citizen. Some engage in business as lawyers and some in farming. Some become elected representatives of the states to which they belong and serve the nation by remaining in Congress. An ex-president does not receive a pension. He retains all the rights of a citizen of the United States even while he is president; and if during that time there is an election for the governor of the state to which he belongs, he goes to the place he calls home just as any ordinary citizen and casts his vote in the election. His vote, just because he is the president, does not carry a straw's more weight than that of James, the farmer, or Samuel, the coal merchant. Just because he is visiting his hometown, the municipality does not squander the money of its poor people arranging some sort of big function for him, unless there is a very special reason for it. Nevertheless, the people are always very eager to honor him properly. It should be understood that this honor is not for the individual but for the power of the people that shines through him. Just because a person was previously the president, no one pays him more than the normal respect. On the contrary, he himself is grateful to the American citizens for giving him the finest honor of making him the president.

It is the people as a whole who elect the president, but they do not do so directly. Each state sends to Congress a greater or lesser number of representatives depending on its population. By the same rule, it can elect a greater or lesser number of "electors." These electors are to take the results of the popular vote in their own states and go to Washington where they are to declare which candidates get how many of their votes; then whoever receives the most votes is appointed president. Once every four years, on November 6, there is a presidential election. And four months later, on March 4, the old president hands his job over to the new president. At that time the new president takes a pledge that he will implement the laws of the United States honestly and dependably[32] and will serve the country faithfully. The cost involved in electing a president each time comes to six lakh dollars ($600,000) — which is approximately eighteen lakh rupees (Rs. 1,800,000). But it cannot be said that this entire expense relates solely to the election of the president. The presidential electors from each state have to be elected at the same time that each state's representatives are elected, so the cost of the one election is absorbed by the other.

Just as in England, there are two major political parties in the United States. There have been many such parties up to the present time. The purpose of these parties is to take some important matter as their goal and then to work hard to achieve it. The Republican Party came into existence some twenty-five or thirty years ago with the aim of setting free the African slaves. The original purpose of the Democratic Party, which was to protect individual liberty, was very fine. But now that this party has passed its sixtieth year, it is not that surprising that its original character is getting increasingly corrupted. Even the Republican Party is approaching middle age. Of late, three new parties have emerged. Among them the Prohibition Party is extremely important. Even though it has not been that many years since this party came into existence, it is growing stronger every day with the help of men and women of strong moral character throughout the United States. Just as previously it was the Democratic Party that had its day in the sun and now the Republican Party that is in power, many people hope that in the future the Prohibition Party will succeed in its efforts and the United States will be freed from the clutches of its mortal enemy, liquor.

Because everyone is in favor of freedom of thought and opinion, no one harbors real animosity toward the people of an opposing party. The followers of each party support their own party with arguments pro and con in the most forthright manner possible; and if, in the heat of the moment, somebody exaggerates one way or the other, nobody takes offense. Even if two persons from one family (brother and brother or father and son) are independent followers of two different parties, their mutual love and admiration does not diminish. The officials who are to be elected at the national level (such as the president), the state level, or the local level are all usually candidates se-

32. Trans.: Interestingly, here Ramabai uses (in the obsolete Marathi instrumental case) the Arabic *imānem̨ itabārem̨:* with "trust, confidence, reliance" (Molesworth). — *PCE*

lected by some particular party or other. Those who win a majority of the popular vote, no matter what party they belong to, are appointed to the various positions I have already described above.

The Income of the United States Government

In keeping with the present system of government of the United States, each town, each county, and each state takes responsibility for its own expenses. Compared to the vast size of this country, what debt it has is very small. Many states have no debt at all, and what each of them produces is sufficient to run its own government. The total combined debt of cities and municipalities in the United States is approximately fifty-seven crore fifty lakh dollars ($575,000,000). The per capita debt of the whole population is thirty dollars — which comes to a total national debt amounting to one billion *(abja)* fifty crore dollars ($1,500,000,000). In 1835 not only did the United States have no debts whatsoever, but the directors of the Treasury Department did not know what to do with all the money accumulated in the treasury. The terrible civil war that took place in America between 1861 and 1865, however, imposed a great load of debt on the United States. In 1866 this country had more than three billion dollars in debt, on which they were paying fourteen crore sixty lakh dollars ($146,000,000) annually in interest. By 1885 more than half of this debt had been paid off. It now appears that within ten or twelve years most of the debt will be paid off. Recently — during the past two years — when it was realized that twenty-seven crore dollars ($270,000,000) of debt had been paid off, many of the taxes were canceled outright. At the same time, the soldiers who fought for the government in the Civil War and their widows have been given a 25 percent increase in their pensions. When it came to his notice that the United States government pays off its debts eight times faster than the government of England, Mr. Gladstone said somewhere that the virtues of wisdom, self-sacrifice, self-control, and foresightedness possessed by the government of the United States are eight times greater than those possessed by the British government. That a statesman of the stature of this gentleman should give such an opinion about this democratic government is no small or trivial praise.

In 1830 the annual income of the United States government was one and a quarter dollars per capita. In 1860 it rose to one and three-quarters dollars, which amounted to a total income of five crore sixty lakh dollars ($56,000,000). This income used to come mainly from tariffs on imports and from the sale of public lands. Numerous taxes were imposed for a number of years on the people of the United States to repay the debt of three billion dollars incurred at the time of the dispute among the American people from 1861 to 1865 over the issue of slavery. In 1866 the government's income amounted to fifty-five crore eighty lakh dollars ($558,000,000) from a combination of taxes and land revenues. Every year from 1861 to 1867 the income only from taxes varied from forty to fifty crore dollars ($400,000,000 to $500,000,000). The per capita tax, which prior to this was one and three-quarters dollars, had to be raised to seventeen dollars. More recently, as the debt has continued to decline, more and more taxes of various kinds have been canceled. In 1883 the income of the United States government was forty crore dollars ($400,000,000). Against this amount, payment of interest on the national debt amounted to five crore dollars ($50,000,000); the pension of the soldiers who fought for the government during the American Civil War was sixty crore sixty lakh dollars ($606,000,000); the expenses of the Army and Navy were sixty crore forty lakh dollars ($604,000,000), out of which one crore dollars ($10,000,000) were spent on repairs to the ports and other waterways, and sixty lakh dollars ($6,000,000) were given toward the subsistence of the American Indians. (No one should think that the United States government gives sixty lakh dollars as simple charity to the American Indians. The very small amount of money that is said to be given to them — but which is actually kept on deposit in the United States Treasury — for the limitless land that was snatched from them by force or by fraud, yields an annual interest of somewhat more than sixty lakh dollars [$6,000,000]. This amount is distributed among their various tribes in small quantities for their subsistence. It is not at all adequate for them.) Six crore eighty lakh dollars ($68,000,000) were spent on public works. (What these public works are will be explained further on.) The salaries of the people who oversee the United States government, namely, the president, the two bodies of the Congress (the House of Representatives and the Senate), and the vice president, amount to a total of twenty lakh fifty-four thousand dollars ($2,054,000). These are the figures for the main expenditures. There are many other additional expenses.

This then is a brief account of the system of government of the United States. Here we have a picture of the star-studded banner of the United States for you to see. George Washington, the first president of this nation, had a battle standard on which stars and red and white stripes were depicted. It was very beautiful. The American people felt that their national flag should look like this battle standard, and in honor of Washington they took the designs from his battle standard for their flag. How can I describe the beauty of this flag? There are white stars on a dark blue field — just like the sky overhead — and beyond that field, red and white stripes. No other country has such a beautiful banner — and who else could have a nation that is such an abode of happiness for its citizens and is run with such beautiful orderliness? Just as the joyful stars move about freely in the clear azure realm of the clouds as a delight to the eyes of the inhabitants of the earth, so do these independent states of America, situated as they are in the midst of the clear, blue waters of the Atlantic and the Pacific oceans, delight all people of proper feeling with their grand and calm splendor. Seeing the flag of the United States must immediately remind you of the nature of the nation's system of government — by means of which all fifty of the states and territories, even while each retains its independence, function in conformity with a single national government in Washington; exactly as Earth, Mercury, Venus, and all the planets, even while each retains its own independent and unique position and motion, remain under the sway of one solar system. The combined area of all these states is two-and-a-half times that of our own Hindusthan, and their wealth is very great. How is it possible to describe the full worthiness of the great power that is this system of government — on the strength of which such a great nation, in such a brief time, overcame every kind of obstacle and adversity and became the most exalted and prosperous of all the nations on the face of the earth? Liberty, the originator of that system of government, the source of all happiness, the true living power of humankind, has a statue standing in the New York harbor, like the Delhi Gate of the United States, that enthralls the heart of the entire world with its calm, holy, and pleasing brightness. She stands with a torch in her one hand to shed the light of freedom upon the entire world and a book in her other hand to eradicate the ignorance of humankind by giving it knowledge. It is no surprise then that the sight of her and the sight[33] of the United States, which is the throne of the Goddess of Liberty and the abode of wisdom and progress, should fill the heart of every high-minded person, which is prostrated by the suffering of servitude, with joy; and that while standing there he should forget his wretched condition for a moment and become as one with the heavenly joy of liberty and should wish from the depths of his heart that all the peoples of all the nations of the earth should receive the gift of such a system of government, of such liberty, of such unity, and of such brotherly love.

33. Trans.: The word Ramabai uses in both cases for "sight" is *darśana:* "Sight or seeing: also looking. 2 A dream or vision. . . . 4 Visiting any idol or sacred shrine" (Molesworth). The religious (and ritualistic) sense of the word is clearly appropriate here in the context of Ramabai's invocation to the "Goddess of Liberty." — *PCE*

CHAPTER 4

Living Conditions

As an aid to the people who are studying in a drawing school, a person or an object is positioned in one place and the class of students is made to gather around and instructed to draw a picture of that object or that person. Some sit in front of the object, some at one side, some behind it, and some at an oblique angle to it as they are drawing so that the object is drawn as it is seen from all these different perspectives. If we see a picture of the right side of the object, this does not mean that it does not have a left side. Or if we see a picture of its front, this does not mean that the object does not have a back. We can conclude from this only that the side of the object we see in the picture is the one the painter could see and that he could not see the other sides of it. It is impossible for anyone to view all the sides of an object simultaneously and draw its picture. It is the same when it comes to describing the living conditions of any country. No one can see all the facets of these living conditions so it cannot be assumed that the opinion of any one person is without error.

When you have read the description of our customs, traditions, and living conditions by the English and American people who have traveled in Hindusthan, it is easy to understand how any foreigner visiting another country must see its people in a very different light. So instead of asserting a rigid theory that the living conditions of the American people are of exactly such and such a kind and of only so many types, my aim in this chapter and in the entire volume is to tell you how I myself thought them to be.

The one aspect of the living conditions of the American people that is seen most clearly everywhere is the *concern for the common good*[1] (i.e., beneficialness for all the people) in the people's way of thinking, in their system of government, and in many other consequential matters. In Hindusthan, in England, or in other older countries, everything is made for and all services are provided to a select class, and these are not available to the mass of ordinary people. Such a thing is extremely rare in the United States. The *public-spiritedness*[2] in the system of government of the United States is the chief reason for the *concern for the common good* in almost all other things. Nobody here thinks of a king as being the guardian and the proprietor of his subjects — nor of the subjects and all other things as being put on this earth solely for the pleasure of the king. Because here it is everyone's belief that the subjects themselves are king and that it is only right to have those things within the state's system of government that are of benefit to all the subjects. In this country, which is *"of the people, governed by the people, and existing only for the people,"* only those things are implemented that are determined to be good by majority vote. The people select whom they want as the leader of the nation, of a state, or of a town and elevate them to their proper place. The people themselves have the laws made that they want to have. There is no opportunity allowed in this country for any self-indulgent person to exercise power capriciously and to govern the subjects exactly as he himself wills, answerable only to the king.

There is fundamentally no division of the society here into superior, mediate, and inferior classes. Although social discrimination and bigotry[3] are more or less prevalent wherever you go, here they are not as rigid and as harmful to the nation as the social discrimination in our country or in other older monarchies. The most important of the many remedies that have been implemented to remove the social discrimination that still exists is the free education all children receive in the schools. The children of all residents of the United States receive a free education. All children here, as members of

1. Trans.: Ramabai uses the term *sarvajaninapana* here, the same term she used in the previous chapter except that here she uses the Marathi abstract noun ending *pana* rather than the expected Sanskrit ending *tva* and creates a rather odd Sanskrit-Marathi hybrid. She follows it in the text with the same parenthetical definition as in Chapter 3. It might be translated literally as "commonwealness." — *PCE*

2. Trans.: Once again Ramabai "Marathifies" a term she used in the previous chapter (here rendered *sarvajanikapana*) by substituting the Marathi abstract noun ending *pana* in place of the expected Sanskrit ending *ta.* — *PCE*

3. Trans.: The words Ramabai uses here are *jatibheda* and *jatimatsara,* which might ordinarily be translated as "casteism" and "caste hatred" respectively. In the American context (not to mention here the Indian), the word "caste" seems highly problematic, and the better equivalents would seem to be "social discrimination" and "bigotry." — *PCE*

one social group *(jata)* and as residents of one nation, learn to treat one another with amity and courtesy. They are not educated to think that one person, by virtue of his social group *(jata)*, is superior within their society while someone else is inherently inferior. They are educated to understand that they are all *human beings* and should treat one another with humanity. Every child has the assurance that although he might be bereft and penniless today, it is entirely possible, if he makes the effort, to become the nation's president tomorrow. He knows perfectly well that it is according to his own fitness that he will attain either a superior or an inferior position in society. A person's *social group (jata)* is not the determining reason for whatever condition or position he may attain. It is the *worthiness* of people that is the principal means of attaining superiority or inferiority.

Everything in the cities and even in the villages, from the streets, meeting halls, and boarding houses to the price of goods, is arranged for the public's convenience. The major streets in the cities are mostly paved with round or square stones or with bricks; and trolley lines made out of iron rails have been laid over them to make it convenient for horse-drawn trolley cars to get around everywhere very cheaply. Those people who travel these streets with a need to display their wealth — paying a five-dollar fare to go by private buggy — have to endure a very bumpy ride. The poor, who pay a fare of only a few pennies to go as far as four or five miles, do not have a bumpy ride at all. This is one example of the sort of thing that is done here — always bearing the convenience of the many in mind. Since streets need to be nice and wide for people to come and go without hindrance, the streets in every city in this country are made to be nice and big. There are masonry sidewalks on both sides of the streets. Underneath these sidewalks or dug beneath the middle of the roads, sewers are built as a drain for the town's wastewater. Because there are sidewalks, people have no need to walk in the middle of the street where carriages come and go; so their own passage to and fro is made safe and easy. This means, of course, that it doesn't take much time either to go to or to come from work. And because the city's drainage system is not open, what is more, you don't have to put up with the stench of sewage.[4]

It has to be understood as the great good fortune of the American people that their municipalities here are not wise and capable like the richly self-

4. In our country men relieve themselves wherever they please along the roads. Nobody does that here. How surprising it is that no one tries to put an end to such a completely disgraceful thing. This reform is as necessary as any other social reform. It is a horrible and very harmful thing for respectable women and children to see such filthy and shameful things as they walk along a road. If people were to insist that the municipalities in our country construct latrines in sufficient number at such places, this could easily be accomplished. — *PRS*

rule-endowed,[5] wisdom-endued municipalities of our land. There, whenever some sahib comes to town the erudite managers of our municipalities spend pots of money on decorating and illuminating the city and, especially where the sahib happens to be staying, on creating a splendid park endowed with every perfection. And that is why they do not have the money to keep the city clean and to put up streetlights and such things at those places that are most frequented by the common people. And so, of course, the common, ordinary people do not receive the benefits of cleanliness and good health or the services to which they are entitled. In the United States it is simply out of the realm of possibility that such a thing should happen. The taxes that people pay on their houses here are used expressly to provide them their own services. If they do not receive these services, they do not stop at merely badmouthing the municipality for its negligence; if the town's managing council does not fulfill its duties even after being notified two or three times, the people simply send them packing. The custom of decorating the city at the cost of the municipality all for the dear sake of any sahib who happens to be passing through simply does not exist in the United States. So the money that is given for the purpose of installing streetlights on public streets and cleaning drains and latrines and such is not wasted on building arches and erecting banners in honor of the sahib.

There is always a health department that is closely connected to the municipality. Without anyone having to tell it to do so, it goes around everywhere and oversees the hygiene of the city. They pay particular attention to inspecting the produce that is sold in the markets, such as vegetables, fish, milk, butter, and so on, to ensure that they are hygienic and edible. Should there be an outbreak of some disease in any part of the city, they are likewise very diligent about seeing that the drains and latrines and such are clean and about searching out the causes of the disease and eradicating them. Throughout the city there are always public parks and places for people to enjoy the outdoors. These parks are not perforce located near the homes of people belonging to one particular class but rather at such places that all the people find convenient to use. If the rich want to, they can spend their own money and have their own private gardens or whatever else might give them pleasure. But municipalities will not inconvenience the common people by spending the money of the poor to beautify the neighborhoods of the rich.

5. Trans.: The word Ramabai uses is *svarajyasampanna.* Her clearly sarcastic use of the term *svarajya* here may well be a subtle dig at the more bellicose, socially conservative nationalists of that time, particularly Vishnushastri Chiplunkar and Bal Gangadhar (Lokmanya) Tilak, who made the word their rallying cry, e.g., Tilak's famous line: *Svarajya ha majha janmasiddha hakka ahe* ("Self-rule is my birthright"). — *PCE*

A person doesn't have to go to a lot of expense and trouble here to obtain any information he might need. Both in the cities and in the smaller towns the police maintain excellent law and order. American policemen have not yet learned the art practiced by the police in our land of taking their own good time arriving at the scene of a robbery or a street-fight — having made sure to give the culprit ample time to flee — and then acting like swashbuckling heroes. If a stranger should need information to find his way around on the streets of a city and asks a policeman for help, he will be told what he needs in the most courteous way possible. At every intersection, crossing, and busy street, in lanes and on street corners, there are policemen on patrol standing at not a very great a distance from each other. Those who drive the public horse-trolleys, the drivers of trains, the ticket collectors, and so on all treat their passengers with the utmost courtesy. (I will say more further on, in the section on trains, about the American system of train travel.)

Of all the services in any town, the most excellent and most important one is the piped water supply. The water that is needed for daily use is kept in storage, whether at some distance from the city or closer by. Since there is plenty of good, fresh water everywhere, there is never a season of drought. The place where they keep the water in storage is called a reservoir. From there the water is pumped through the city's pipes by steam-driven machines. Night or day, the tap water is never shut off. At various places around the city public water troughs and taps are constructed so that draft animals and passersby can have a drink. In the event of a house or a warehouse catching fire, they have water hydrants installed on every street corner at a short distance from each other that they use in putting out the fire.

All the arrangements for fighting house fires are first-rate and well worth bearing in mind. There are fire stations at short distances from each other where brave men who are highly skilled at putting out fires are stationed at all times for this one purpose. They receive excellent wages. In the same way that *our* government spends its money, much more than it can afford, to maintain a martial army, all for the purpose of sacrificing the lives of men at a place of execution called the battlefield, the local governments in the United States prepare and maintain a kind of fire-fighting "army," entirely for the purpose of saving people's lives. Their tactics, their skill at what they do, and their systematic way of doing it are most surprising and exemplary. Even their horses are trained to do their work in an exemplary way. Horses are needed to haul ladders, rubber hoses, picks, spades, axes, and the steam engines that are needed to pump water up through the hoses. This equipment is maintained on the spot ready to go in such a way that no time is lost in loading up the horses. Indeed, the horses are so well-trained that the moment they hear the fire alarm they themselves go over to their equipment and by shaking it cause it to drop down on their backs. You can't help but be amazed when you see their intelligence.

At various places around town at short distances from each other, there are mechanical knobs used to send alarms to the fire stations. They are connected to wires and are made to operate like a telegraph machine by means of electricity. Every house-owner knows their locations. When these knobs are turned or pressed, in accordance with the printed instructions that are posted at various places in alcoves or in boxes, a warning bell goes off, by means of the wires connected to it, in the nearest fire station. The location of the house where the fire has broken out, both the neighborhood and the street, is indicated by the number of strokes of the alarm bell. Thereupon, the firemen in the fire station that is closest to that street get themselves ready to go within five seconds; and, equipped with all the tools and implements needed to fight the fire and their protective clothing, they rush to the aid of those who are in danger. No matter how tall the burning house is or how fierce the fire, they fight it without the smallest sign of fear or laxity.

The people here do not hesitate to go to the aid of someone who is in a jam. If a carriage gets stuck on the road, even well-dressed men will get down in the mud or in the gutter and help pull it free. Respectable men in our own country who find themselves in a situation like this have the idea that it is beneath both the standing of their social group *(jata)* and their position in society to do anything like this and will quietly go on their way.

If you are to see the true character of the living conditions of any nation, it is much better to examine the conditions of the people who live in its villages rather than taking as its pattern the life in a big city like Mumbai or Calcutta. Ever since I came here I have had to spend a good deal of my time staying in the cities, but I also found plenty of opportunity to obtain information about the villages. I would not hesitate to say that states such as Pennsylvania, New York, New Jersey, Connecticut, and Massachusetts are typical of an older pattern of living conditions while states such as Illinois, Iowa, Nebraska, Colorado, and California are typical of a newer pattern.

Almost all the families in the smaller towns and villages live in their own houses, and the land on which they build their houses also belongs to them. Although the landlord-tenant system is not altogether nonexistent in this country, it is very uncommon. Someone who owns a lot of land or who is very wealthy does not attain a position of eminence in society only for that reason. He is one American among thousands — and this is the basis for the respect he enjoys. Laws concerning the purchase and sale of both fixed and liquid assets are extremely simple and convenient. So even though the owner of a house or land is the independent owner of his own property, he is not called a *jagirdār* or *zamindār*.[6] That is because the distinct and separate class of tenants that exists in older countries such as England and Scotland (where the tenants are at all times dependent on their landlords) is nowhere to be seen in this country. Even the owner of a great deal of land works the land himself. His sons or his hired hands help him do the work. The owners of small farms work their own fields and in their own homes and make a little extra money by helping the big farmers in their spare time. This does not mean that the hired hand is considered inferior to the rich farmer. And that is why respectable but poor householders[7] are not ashamed of earning money by hiring themselves out to do whatever work they like.

The wives and daughters of these householders do all the chores within the home. During the harvest season, when there is always a lot of work to be done, a hired housemaid or two may come and work for them for a couple of months. People have the freedom here to do whatever has to be done and at whatever time just as it suits them, whether it be what in our land is thought of as the meanest possible occupation — that of sweeper or latrine cleaner — or the most respected occupations of teacher or religious preceptor; and by doing any particular kind of work they do not think that their dignity is diminished. This work must be of such a nature, of course, that it would not damage a person's reputation.

Even though it is the established practice everywhere for them to do whatever kind of work needs to be done, the people who live in villages here do not present themselves as small-town rubes. People who wear ragged clothes and who look like paupers and beggars are extremely uncommon. But then, nobody pays much attention either to someone who tries to show off by parading about town in fine clothes. If some newcomer to this country were to take pity on the poverty of some person they see walking to work dressed in ordinary, dirty work clothes and pull out a coin or two to give him, it would be taken as a terrible insult.

There does not appear to be much crime in the smaller towns nor, with the exception of drinking liquor and smoking tobacco, much in the way of vices. There is very little fear of theft. Sometimes people will go to sleep in their

6. Ed.: *Jagirdār:* holder of a *jagir* or lands granted by a ruler to a client, notable, or official. *Zamindār* (Persian: lit., "zamin" = "land," plus suffix "*-dār*" = "holder"): holder of lands, usually a large hereditary holding. Both terms migrated into languages of India and are found in standard English dictionaries. As such, they denote status, power, and wealth. — *REF*

7. Trans.: Ramabai uses the common Sanskrit loan *gṛhastha* here, which is nowadays (depending somewhat on context) typically translated as "gentleman." Here the original sense of the word as "householder" seems more pertinent. — *PCE*

houses without latching their doors on the inside — and they won't lock their doors even when they go out. Smaller towns with a population of around a thousand typically have a poorhouse or a shelter where at most five to six elderly people or destitute people who cannot work because of some illness are supported at the expense of the town's residents. Just as it is the established practice among the townspeople to do every variety of work, it is also very clear that they have a great fondness for learning. Towns with a population of around a thousand typically have a public library, and the books in their collections aren't simply fluff. Volumes on science, history, law, and ethics written by important scholars such as Huxley; books (prose and verse) on poetry, sculpture, painting, music, medicine; the best novels; a handful of monthly magazines, weeklies, and daily newspapers that are popular and well-known both in Europe and in this country — all are available for everyone to read.

There is at least one high school and five to six primary schools for younger children in towns like these. It is very rare to find a person who cannot read or write. The person whom you saw in the morning dressed in dirty clothes, carrying his tools on his shoulder, going out to plow his land or spread fertilizer or chop wood, is the same person you will see in the evening dressed in clean clothes, keeping the fireplace warm in his own home, chatting happily with his wife and children, or else reading some magazine like *Century, Atlantic Monthly,* or *North American Review,* or maybe a book. He has a musical instrument in the sitting room of his house; two or three newspapers on the table; and on a reading stand, volumes by famous scholars and poets such as Milton, Tennyson, Longfellow, Gibbon, Macaulay, and others, which are not kept there just for display; they are carefully read and studied by the entire family. There are at least five to six pictures hanging on the walls. The members of the family possess a good bit of information about what is happening in their own country as well as in other countries. We have seen that the housewife and the daughters do the cooking, the washing, the scrubbing, and other such housework in the morning. In the afternoon or in the evening after supper you may see one of them knitting socks or doing some embroidery, someone else playing a sweet-sounding musical instrument or painting beautiful flowers on china cups or on canvases, someone else taking out the Latin grammar book and learning the daily lessons (all for the purpose of passing the entrance examination to study at a major school). Regularly, morning and evening, the master or mistress of the house reads one or two chapters from the Scriptures and prays; and the mother entertains her young children by reading them stories from the Scriptures, from history books, or from other books. When they hear from their own mother's mouth these stories from their past — how their brave ancestors suffered and labored to bequeath them this independent country and how great their courage was; how Lincoln, for example, as a child was so poor but by his hard work and exemplary character became the president of this country; and so on — little children have their hearts awakened to a love for their country, to a desire to make a name for themselves, and to the hope that if they work hard, they (just as Washington, Lincoln, and Garfield) can also reach a successful and exemplary position in life. Nor is it the case that girls, just for being girls, have to suffer nothing but discouragement. They too listen to the biographies of exemplary and famous women and cling to the hope that they will be able to become like them someday. When their mother finds the time to go out to attend the meeting of some society, whether its purpose is the furtherance of learning or of charity or of religion, they go along with her and see for themselves what it is all about, thereby developing a taste for learning and a desire to aid the welfare of others. They do not have to suffer, as girls in our own land do, the pain of separation from their mother and life among uncaring in-laws brought about by the tyranny of the social custom of child marriage. Not to be allowed to do the smallest thing on your own account just because you happen to be a woman; to be required to spend your entire life in a state of dependence; to be simply destined for exclusion from the joys of independence; should your husband die tomorrow, to be insulted by people as a child widow, tormented, starved, forced against your will to work as a drudge, cursed and abused, your hair shaved off by the barber, or despised and belittled simply for not having a place to call your own; to have nobody either in heaven or on earth to act as your protector — this veritable flame of despair and suffering can never burn up the fresh green growth of hope in the heart of an American girl! Nobody humiliates her just because she happens to be a *woman* or a dependent *girl.* In the same way as her brother, she is considered worthy of her parents' love and tenderness. In the same way as her brother, she is given the means to obtain an education and to learn arts and technical skills. And she has the hope that someday she will at least become her own mistress, the owner of her own house, and a self-reliant, independent American citizen. As I am writing this description of the felicitous American family, I see here standing almost tangibly before my eyes the many families I witnessed in that country. It will suffice, as an example, to tell the story of one such family.

A year ago I went to Gilbertville, a small town in the state of New York. In May 1887 I had first made the acquaintance of several of the students at Cornell University, and one of them invited me to come and give a speech in his hometown. During the holidays he returned home and made all the necessary preparations, whereupon his mother sent me a letter of invitation.

When I arrived in Gilbertville, George (that was the boy's name) came to the train in his carriage and took me to his home, which was about a mile from the station. George's mother and sister were waiting for us at the front door. The moment we arrived they came out to the carriage and welcomed me most respectfully and ushered me into the house. George meanwhile took the horses out to graze in a nearby field. In the evening his father and his brother returned home from their work in the fields. Their clothes were very dirty. His mother started cooking supper then, and his sister began to set the table for the meal with plates, bowls, spoons, and so on. When everything was ready, all the members of the family, having already washed their hands and put on clean clothes, sat down on chairs around the table and had their meal. (The people here are altogether ignorant of the custom of men eating first and women eating after them! The master of the house, the mistress, and the children all eat together. If anything is needed during the course of the meal, the daughter or the son or somebody else will get up, go get it, and place it near their mother.) After the meal was over and the other household tasks completed, all the members of the family came into the sitting room. The mother sat down at the writing table to write letters. The father and the son stood behind the daughter, who was playing a musical instrument, joined their voices with her sweet voice, and started to sing. After this we had an extremely enjoyable time chatting about this and that.

The next morning the master of the house, along with George and his brother, went out to the fields to work while George's mother and sister got busy with the household work. Our meeting was to begin after lunch at two o'clock. George's mother was to preside over the meeting. She is the president of the society that has been established there for the furtherance of religion and charitable works. She gave a very nice speech and conducted the meeting in an exemplary way. Anyone who had seen her working in her kitchen would have thought that she must never have done anything else in her life but cook. It became quite evident during the meeting, however, that she was finely educated and thoroughly conversant with good etiquette and social custom. Her husband plows the fields, grazes the cattle, harnesses the horses to the wagons, spreads fertilizer, cuts wood, mows the hay, and supervises the farm. When he is out working in the fields, you would think that this was the only work he knew anything about and that he simply wouldn't be up to speed on any other subject. But when he returns home in the afternoon, this very same farmer talks of philosophical things and discusses subjects such as the pronunciation of Greek words, the close ties between Latin grammar and Greek grammar, the similarity between Arnold's poem "Light of Asia" and the life of Christ, his opinions on Theosophy and its proponents, the difference between the British system of political governance and this country's, and so on. The son, while he is at home, is a farmer through and through. But when the holidays are over, he will return to his studies at the university, will take his final fourth-year exams, and will later on become either a clergyman or a businessman. One of the other sons has completed his education and is employed in an important position in New York City. The third son will remain at home and work the farm. One daughter has completed her education, is married to the man she herself wished to marry, and is running her own home independently. How proud of both her children this loving mother must have felt when she told me, "I would be so glad if my younger daughter would go to Cornell University for her education along with her brother. My Georgie will work for some days to earn the money to cover his expenses and then return to the university to continue his studies. My dearest wish is that my daughter should do the same. She herself is very enthusiastic about going and studying there with Georgie." How can I describe my own gladness when I heard her saying this — that her daughter should go to the university exactly as her son does? When will parents in our land start to say this? When will this evil notion of theirs — that the worthiness and the capabilities of their daughter are somehow inferior to those of their son — disappear?

On the third day it was time for George to go back to school. His mother packed up a bunch of fruit, cookies, and other provisions for him, and his sister accompanied him in the carriage to see him off at the station. Along the way both of them together, sister and brother, began to sing merrily. As I sat watching this happy brother and sister riding through the woods to the train, singing their unsullied and holy songs of gladness, how it reminded me of tales out of our own land of the young children of the holy sages — the rishis — of ancient times. How happy, how joyful the two of them were! Both of them share the hope that their lives will be fruitful; both of them have the same rights, the same worth; and all the paths of advancement are open to both of them. Just because one of them is a girl does not mean she will know, if only just in a dream, the despair that comes from lack of independence. The other one, just because he is a man, does not humiliate his sister by his arrogance, either in word or in deed. Both of them are hardworking and both desire recognition for themselves. Because both of them have the same independence, no matter how hard the work or long the labor, they can earn for themselves the grace both of *Sarasvatī* and of *Lakṣmī*.[8] It is

8. Trans.: *Sarasvatī:* "The wife of Brahma, the goddess of speech and eloquence" (Molesworth). *Lakṣmī:* "The wife of Vishnu and the goddess of wealth, prosperity, splendor, elegance etc." (Molesworth). — *KG*

not very surprising then that the nation where you find this kind of equality between men and women — the equality indeed of all humankind — and where all the people are masters of their own lives, wealth, liberty, and consciences, should be a nation of the greatest eminence and that its inhabitants should be happy. No, not all American families are like the one I have described above. The old Marathi proverb, "Where there's a village, there will always be a Maharwada,"[9] is applicable to America as well. Even in American villages there are people who range anywhere from exemplary to mediocre to inferior. Some are engrossed in cheap luxury and indulge in idle chatter; some are of a serious disposition, hardworking and self-controlled; some are the leaders of society, some the blind followers; some are proud, some humble; some boneheaded, some cunning and deceitful — all these types are to be found in American society. Nevertheless, as a whole, American society is independent, and it is possible to see the signs everywhere in it of the kind of advancement it is possible to attain in human society — by means only of independence.

In the same way that all the qualities of an ocean or a river are present within every drop of water, the virtues that gave birth to a free nation like the United States are present in every American town and corporate body. The exemplary system of government that lies at the root of this nation's advancements is the fruit of the self-governance[10] that is present throughout its towns and throughout its society. It is as if the American populace was fed the rituals of self-governance and of their system of government right along with the pabulum of their infancy. Go wherever you will, to a small village or to a big city, you cannot help but notice their unity of purpose and their orderly way of doing things. If someone decides to do some particular thing, he gathers a few acquaintances together and explains his purpose in doing it; then, whatever they decide is right by majority vote, they do. No matter how small a task might be, an organization[11] has to be formed to do it; and no matter how small that organization might be, there have to be at least three office-bearers

9. Trans.: *Gāṃva āhe tetheṃ mhāravāḍā āhe.* The *mahāravāḍā* was where the Mahars, untouchables, resided — always on the outskirts of the village. The Mahars were required to perform the most degrading tasks in the community, e.g., disposing of the carcasses of dead animals. A. Manwaring, in *Marathi Proverbs* (New Delhi: Asian Educational Service, 1991 [1899]), p. 243, gives as the common sense of the proverb, "Nothing is perfect in life." — *KG and PCE*

10. *Ātmaśāsana* = the kind of thoughtful behavior by which we govern ourselves so that other people's rights are not infringed. — *PRS*

11. Trans.: *Maṇḍaḷī* (lit. "circle"), the all-purpose word Ramabai uses here, she uses elsewhere in the text to render "association," "guild," and "union." This word can also be used in the sense of "committee." — *PCE*

to organize it: the president, the secretary, and the treasurer. These organizations may even consist of no more than two or three members; and yet the system by which the organization's work is to be done is all laid out in a list of rules. We see then that voluntary organizations are formed to do almost everything that is important; in order to keep the organizations focused on doing their work in the proper way, they have rules; in making these rules the opinions of all the members of the organization are consulted; and once the rules are accepted by majority vote they are followed. These are the principal seeds of all self-governance, and they are present virtually everywhere. From out of these seeds sprang a sapling in the form of the local governments. This sapling put forth numerous branches in the form of the system of county government; and they in turn produced fine flowers in the form of the system of state government. And from those flowers came the divine fruit of the national system of government of the United States. It is through their families and through their schools that children receive instruction in this kind of self-governance. At home their parents do each and every thing in an established way. At school the children are taught the habit of deciding by majority vote what games to play during recess and of behaving in an orderly way. Every effort is made to imprint on children's minds that they must do whatever task is appointed to them in whatever way they can according to their ability and that they should not trouble other people over small things or ask for their help in doing them.

The system of government of the United States is of such a kind that the higher level of government in the city of Washington does not interfere at all in the work that ought to be done by the state government. And the state government in turn does not help do the work that is best done by the county. And the county does not interfere in the work that is best accomplished by the local system. This excellent system makes the American people experts in self-governance, and that is why these people have become so self-reliant. The seed of self-reliance must be present in each and every family; and only if it is present there will a nation, which consists of thousands and millions of families joined together, also come to possess the fine virtue of self-reliance. The institution of the American family is like the institution of the nation. The husband doesn't intrude in the work the wife does best, and the parents do not take it upon themselves to do the tasks best done at the hands of their children.

The patriotism and nationalism of the American people are mixed with a great deal of pride. The English have always considered themselves to be the most superior of all communities *(jātī);* and since the ancestors of the Americans were English, it is quite understandable that they, too, should have imbibed the pride of their English ancestors. But this is a new nation, and in keeping with the rule that anything will grow vigorously in fresh soil, their native pride, since it first germinated in this fertile ground, has grown enormously; and by now these people have come to illustrate the Hindi maxim, "The son has surpassed the father."[12] They have developed a veritable habit, when it comes to describing everything belonging to their country, of comparing it with everything belonging to other countries — and then of saying that they and theirs are always best. "Our factory is the biggest"; "Our country is the best"; "Our nation is first and foremost"; "The structures of our intellectual faculties, of our brains, are the most sensitive and well-balanced of all"; and where does this stop? They are famous for this bad habit of theirs of claiming, "Ours is always the best." Go to a church and listen to a sermon, and you will hear the preacher say, "Our religion, our society, our social customs are the best." Read a book written by a military leader such as General Grant, and he will tell you, "Our army is the best-trained of all the armies of all the countries in the world." Go to a public meeting, and you will hear the speaker singing veritable ballads in praise of the customs of "our country" and of "our community *(jata)*." They think nothing of the brilliance of other people compared to their own. One can't help but notice that there is a quite remarkable lack of humility even among the common, ordinary people. Nevertheless, the American people on the whole do not hesitate to show a proper respect for others. And that is because from childhood they have learned the lessons of self-governance, and so the excellent attribute of self-respect is well-developed in them. The person who knows the value of his own reputation and who guards it carefully has a special regard for the reputation of others.

12. Trans.: *Bāpase beṭā savāī:* a Hindi phrase meaning, "The son is excess by a quarter to the father," i.e., the son is more than a match to the father. — *KG*

CHAPTER 5

Domestic Conditions

So much for the general living conditions. Now I must say a few words about domestic conditions in the cities and the villages. Although people everywhere commonly hold that within the house *(gṛha)* it is the housewife *(gṛhiṇī)* who is paramount, within the American house the housewife is considered especially so. The American housewife is in a very real sense a *gṛhaśrī.*[1] (There are of course exceptions to this rule.) Since a house is of course indispensable for a housewife as a place for her to live, it would not be out of place to mention a few things about the houses here before describing her.

The interior arrangement of the houses here, whether in the smallest hamlet or in the city, is pretty much the same; but the exterior construction is of different kinds. In the cities the walls of the houses are generally made of stone and brick. In the villages and in the smaller cities there are a great many houses made of lumber. Because coal is universally used here as fuel and there is a great abundance of trees everywhere, there is a large market for wood, especially for use in house construction. The foundation of a house is usually built out of brick or stone, while the upper part of the house is built out of a combination of wooden boards, beams, and posts. Seen from the outside, the walls of the house look like slatted window shutters. On the inside, thick boards or paper are fixed to the walls; then they are given a coat of plaster; and finally they are overlaid with colorful paper. These paper wall-coverings

1. Trans.: *Śrī* is a common name for *Lakṣmī,* "the goddess of wealth, prosperity, splendor, elegance etc." (Molesworth). *Gṛha,* as we have seen, means "house." So the American housewife is seen here as such a goddess of her home. — *KG*

are very durable, and they leave no place for bedbugs and such to hide. The houses have many windows, through which plentiful light and an abundance of fresh air enter the house and move about freely on all sides. The windows are fitted with large panes of glass so that even in winter when the windows must be closed the house is not dark. During the summer there is a profusion of flies, mosquitoes, and such; so in order to rid themselves of this nuisance, to some extent at least, they put up shutters of fine wire screen — so the air is not prevented from entering the house but the nuisance of flies is reduced. Various sorts of curtains, made either out of lace or out of plain cloth, are hung at the windows as a way of decorating them and also to keep too much light from coming in, and they are arranged so they can be drawn aside whenever you want. Except for the kitchen and the front steps, the floors and stairs in all the rest of the house are covered with carpets or mats. The floor beneath them is fitted and laid with wooden planking. Once or twice a year the carpets and mats are taken up, swept down, and cleaned. In the average house there is one sitting room, a dining room, a kitchen, a guestroom, and a separate room for each person to sleep in. Numerous conveniences are provided such as cupboards for hanging up your clothes, shelves for your books, tables, chairs, and so on. They store things like firewood, vegetables, and milk in the basement.

In the houses in the cities there is always a bathroom — in which there is always a large, oblong, galvanized tank-like vessel called a "bathtub." Two pipes, one for cold and one for hot water, lead to it. The hot water pipe is connected to a larger tubular urn next to the stove in the kitchen. This saves the trouble of having to carry water upstairs and of having a separate stove for heating the water. Most of the houses in the villages do not have a bathroom, which poses a great difficulty for those who are used to taking a daily bath. Generally speaking, nobody here takes a bath every day. They pour a jug of water in a washbasin and wipe their bodies off with a wet washcloth, and only occasionally do they take a full bath. (People in the villages remain content with nothing but "washcloth baths" for months at a time.) During the winter they fire up a large furnace[2] in the basement. In order to convey the heat it produces throughout the house, iron pipes are attached to it and taken then to each of the rooms. The arrangement they provide for opening and closing them according to your need is called a "register."

In most of the cities and even in the smaller towns here they use gas

2. Trans.: The word Ramabai uses here is *āgaṭī:* "A heap of sticks and straws kindled: also a few embers or live coals placed in a vessel, a chafing dish. . . . A hole dug in the ground to hold fuel and fire" (Molesworth). — *PCE*

lamps[3] both in their houses and along the streets. This country has an abundance of combustible natural gas.[4] In the city by the name of Pittsburgh, as in so many other towns, most of the work such as cooking, running machines, heating the houses, lighting the houses and the streets, and so on is done by means of this combustible gas. In the smaller towns that do not have plants to process this combustible gas, they make use of petroleum.[5] Throughout the newly settled cities in the west they use electric lights. In the east and in many of the older cities you can see electric lights being used only in a few places.

The arrangements they have for dining at home are exactly like those they have in Europe. It is customary to wash the white cloths that are used to cover the dining table, the white napkins used to wipe your mouth and hands during a meal, the washcloths needed by the people in each of the rooms to wash themselves, the bedcovers, the pillowcases, and so on, right at home. The cook or the maidservant — or sometimes even the mistress of the house herself — becomes the washerwoman and washes and irons these linens. The cook is usually Negro or Irish. Many poor American women live and work as cooks in people's houses. Not wanting to have a servant is every bit as rare in this country as it is in our country. A thoughtful and intelligent housewife, however, learns to do everything herself. She even helps her servant with her work. But there are also many thoughtless housewives here, and many of them cannot cook; so people have started schools to teach them how to cook. Because it is very expensive to set up housekeeping in the city, many people live there as lodgers. By paying twenty-five or thirty dollars a month (the value of one dollar is approximately three rupees), one can usually have quite a nice lodging arrangement. Lodgers are given one room of their own in the house, and they dine with the members of the family. Respectable people can live as lodgers with well-born families of good character. Many good women here, owing to their poverty, have lodgers staying in their houses and make their living in this way. It is customary even for middle-class, well-to-do families to have lodgers. Not only is it expensive to live in hotels[6] and inns, but you cannot enjoy domestic life there.

3. Trans.: *Dhurāce dive* is Ramabai's usage here, literally "lamps of smoke (or vapor or fumes)." — *KG*

4. Trans.: The word Ramabai uses here is *khanijavāta,* literally "mineral air (or wind)." —*PCE*

5. Trans.: *Khanijatela,* literally "mineral oil," a word that conforms to present-day Marathi usage. — *PCE*

6. Trans.: *Khāṇāvaḷa* is the somewhat old-fashioned Marathi word Ramabai uses here and consistently in what follows in the sense of "hotel." Molesworth defines it: "Common eating (at a public eating house)." — *PCE*

Ed.: Inns, hotels, and restaurants did not exist in India before the nineteenth century. — *REF*

I stayed as a lodger in a certain lady's house for about two years in Philadelphia. She is very good-natured. By no means are all women as good as she is as housewives — or as good-natured or as competent in their housekeeping. Still, it is possible to learn something about the daily routine of most housewives here from the way this lady runs her home. She gets up at around 5:30 or 6:00 A.M., bathes (a sponge bath or only her face and hands), does her hair, dresses, and comes downstairs. (In cities the houses have three or four floors; the kitchen, dining room, and living room are on the bottom floor.) She goes to the kitchen and tells the cook what to prepare for breakfast; sweeps the dining room; sets the table with knives, forks, spoons, napkins, saucers, teacups, and water glasses; puts on a hat that covers her ears; takes a shawl or a wrap to keep warm and a basket in her hand; and goes to the market. There she buys the vegetables and fruit that are needed each day and brings them home. At 7:00 A.M. either the cook or she herself rings a bell, at the sound of which all the people in the house get out of bed, wash or bathe, dress, and get themselves ready. At 7:30, when they hear the bell rung a second time, they all come downstairs for breakfast. At 8:00, when breakfast is over, the cook goes upstairs, sweeps all the rooms, shakes out the bedclothes, and makes the beds. Usually the female lodgers shake out their own bedclothes, make their own beds, and tidy up their own rooms. Male lodgers, whether from the pressure of work or whether from laziness, leave this task to the maidservant. Meanwhile, the housewife washes the dirty plates (which are made of china), and the bowls, glasses, spoons, knives, and whatnot with soap and hot water and wipes them dry. After chopping vegetables for lunch, she checks the household accounts; after which, for a short time, she reads the newspapers; and if there are other tasks to be done, she does them as and when they need to be done. If anything is needed from the market, she goes out and does the marketing. She helps her cook a great deal. The cook does all the household tasks such as washing the clothes, sweeping, scrubbing the dirty dishes, taking out the garbage, washing the steps and cleaning the courtyard, and lighting the stoves and fireplaces. She is paid sixteen dollars (i.e., forty-eight rupees) a month in wages and maintenance. On Mondays and Tuesdays the house is always bustling and busy with the laundry being done. Large tubs are set up in the backyard, and the clothes are soaked for some time in boiling water and soap before being washed. Here in this country they do not beat the clothes on a rock when washing them. Soap is applied to the clothes and they are scrubbed clean on a wooden board — a board that has small, wave-like, parallel furrows about a finger's width apart and overlaid with tin. Then they are rinsed in bluing, wrung out, and put up to dry. The clothes are ironed, either after starching them or without starching them, and then folded. Every house has a laundry of this kind.

Lunch is at one o'clock in the afternoon. On this occasion too a bell is rung to summon the members of the household for lunch. At least in terms of what they are accustomed to, the food is quite good. Boiled potatoes, cabbage, turnips, beets, or other seasonal vegetables; meat or fish; eggs; a green, leafy vegetable called "lettuce" or red radishes as a salad; "tomatoes" (what we know as "English eggplant") and sliced cucumbers, during their season, are placed on the dining room table. They know nothing about seasoning vegetables with spices as they are being cooked the way we do. There is always salt, powdered black pepper, and chili powder on the table for anyone to use as they wish. For the salad there is a little bottle of vinegar from which you take as much as you want. Sometimes they fry the eggplant or the potatoes in lard. Beside this, they usually prepare a kind of delicacy called "cake." This and puddings[7] of many different kinds are served at the end of the meal. Various kinds of fruit are served during their seasons. Anyone who does not enjoy eating meat, fish, eggs, and things cooked in lard has a very difficult time of it here when it comes to meals. Such people have to subsist on little more than milk, bread, and fruit.

In the afternoon or in the morning after breakfast, this lady mends or patches torn clothes or sews new clothes. For the most part, every house has a sewing machine, which is very useful in this cold country. People visit one another either in the morning or in the afternoon. When the household work is done, this lady reads books and newspapers as she finds the time, attends lectures, and also lends a hand in numerous charitable works. They have a home here for fallen women. This lady is the secretary of the board that manages this home. Apart from this, she helps with many other religious and charitable works, donating money and her own labor to the extent she can. Sometimes she goes to the hospital and visits the sick.

In families with children, their mothers take excellent care of them. The American home is a proverbial refuge[8] of happiness, where both the parents and the children are well-behaved and always anxious to fulfill their respective duties. In the evening after supper, the parents gather their children in the living room to sit and warm themselves by the fireplace. They tell them happy and entertaining stories and talk sweetly and gently with them. This is a very happy time for them. When the children address their parents, they call them "dear Mother" or "dear Father." And the parents in turn use endearing terms such as "my darling" or "my child." Love for their children is continually ex-

7. Trans.: The word Ramabai uses is *khirī* (sing. *khīra*), sweet pudding-like dishes typically made of rice or vermicelli boiled in milk and spiced. — *PCE*

8. Trans.: The word Ramabai uses here is *māheraghara*, the maternal home of a married woman, and proverbial as a place of rest, relaxation, peace, and joy. — *KG*

pressed in their conversation. A husband and wife cannot speak to each other without addressing one another as "my dear" or "darling."

In respectable families nobody ever utters bad words or curses. Swearing, cursing, or talking defiantly is considered to be a sin and a sign of vulgarity. Generally if they want to ask somebody for something or want somebody to do something, they ask, "Will you please do it?" or "Please do such and such a thing." And if the person does what has been asked or conveys a message or brings something — or on any other occasion like that — they very politely reply, "Thank you very much." They do not walk between two people who are standing or sitting together; and if there is no avoiding it, they always say, "Excuse me." If it is necessary to get up and leave the table when a number of people are dining together in a house, they ask permission of the master or mistress of the house. If they can't hear what somebody else is saying, they say, "Pardon me, what did you say?" Because children receive an education in this kind of social etiquette right from their childhood, it benefits them greatly.

Both within the family and out in society, people give due honor and respect to both men and women. Men have many ways of showing respect to women. When a man has occasion to speak to a woman, no matter who she is, he removes his hat and addresses her with the term "Madam."[9] Whether at home or out in a public gathering, women are given their seats first. If trains or public carriages are crowded and any women show up, the men get up from their seats and make a place for the women to sit. (Not that all men invariably respect good manners such as these.) Young and healthy women have the same way of showing respect to old and infirm men.

Women who are respectable and discreet do not quarrel with anyone. I have already mentioned the Marathi proverb, "Every village has a Maharwada,"[10] and just as everywhere else, they do have their quarrels here; but they are not shouting matches or occasions for swearing and cursing as in our country. When someone gets angry with somebody else, it is enough simply not to have anything more to do with the person. For a more ordinary quarrel it is enough merely to change the tone of your voice. Instead of saying thank you in a soft, sweet voice, say, "Well then, I am much obliged," in a slightly stern and angry tone. When the fight is between rude and ignorant people, not only is there a torrent of foul words, but sometimes it can even come to the point of fisticuffs.

9. Trans.: *Bāīsāheba* is the word Ramabai uses here. — *PCE*

10. Trans.: *Gāṃva āhe tetheṃ mhāravāḍā āhe.* A. Manwaring, in *Marathi Proverbs* (New Delhi: Asian Educational Service, 1991 [1899]), p. 243, gives as the common sense of the proverb: "Nothing is perfect in life." — *PCE*

When people meet, they clasp their right hands together and shake them; and if you were literally to translate the customary salutation on such an occasion, it would come out as, "How do you do?" — i.e., "How is your health?" It is customary to ask this question every time they meet each other, and the appropriate answer is, "I am fine" — i.e., "My health is excellent." This answer may not always be true, of course; but linguistic usage is so strange it leaves hardly any room to choose between truth and falsehood.

You need something to say when you meet somebody else, so the people here start out by criticizing the prevailing weather. If the day is pleasant and the sky is clear, they praise it by saying, "Oh, what a nice day it is!" But days of the kind that please everyone are very few; and whatever a day might bring, it cannot manage to please everyone at all times. Some people don't like rain; some can't stand the cold; some hate it when it's hot and humid; some eagerly look for the rain to come; and some wait impatiently for when the snow flurries begin, the rivers freeze over, and they can go skating.[11] In short, whatever the day brings, poor thing, it can never please anyone at all. Although on most occasions these people are in the habit of turning up their noses at whatever weather the day brings, they have, to a very high degree, attained an appreciation of natural beauty. Not all people are perceptive judges or connoisseurs of these things, but it is very rare to encounter a person here who does not praise some fine object when he sees it.

It is only natural for people to ask a lot of questions when they first meet some foreign-born or newly arrived person. Here they ask these questions in the most polite way possible. Just as we ask all kinds of strange questions of them when women from here and other Western countries come to visit us, when we come for a visit here, the women here also do not fail to do the same to us.

Fashions and Affectations[12]

If the original meaning of the word *na-khare* is "that which is not true," then there is plenty of *nakhare* to be seen in the dress and finery of women here. They are for the most part very pretty, and many of them are naturally very

11. Trans.: This is almost certainly the first occurrence in Marathi of the verb "to skate" — taken verbatim from English but with the Marathi gerundive ending added. — *PCE*

12. Trans.: The word Ramabai uses here, *nakhare*, is from the Persian: "Feminine airs and blandishments; arts of display; coquetry; . . . swelling, strutting, swaggering, vaunting, vaporing" (Molesworth). Ramabai plays this off against the homonymous Marathi construction *na-khare*, i.e., not true. — *PCE*

beautiful. If you were to see the way they arrange their homes, you would easily understand how much they love natural beauty. The Romans were the first to imitate the Hellenic people's love of natural beauty in ancient times; then they in turn taught it to the English and the other Europeans. The people of this country have followed in their footsteps in every respect, as is obvious from the arrangement and construction of their cities, their ordinary houses, their large public buildings, their churches, and so on. Even so, when it comes to women's clothes and many other things, there is very little beauty to be seen, and every year many changes are made in them. When France was a monarchy the queen of Paris used to set the pattern in dress and finery of every kind for all European and American women. It was the custom for everyone to laud whatever the queen of Paris and other rich, fashionable women in Paris did and to imitate it.

Twenty-five years ago, when my parents were sailing with the entire family from Kumatha to Mumbai, they had to stop and wait for two or three days at Sadashivgad for the next boat. The place where we disembarked was near a newly constructed railway line, on the far side of which there was the platform of a railway station. The afternoon of the day we disembarked three English women came and sat down on a bench in the station. The skirts of each of their dresses bulged out so far that, whether they were standing or sitting, they totally enveloped the space within a diameter of at least one-and-a-half or two yards. Never before this had I seen such strange clothes — or the kind of ruddy-faced[13] women who wore them. I was afraid of them from the moment I saw them. But just then a man came along carrying a small basket that was filled with something and gave it to these women, one of whom immediately got up, took the basket, put it under the bench she was sitting on, and then sat down again. I laugh now when I remember how frightened I was when I saw this and how queasy my stomach felt. But at the time I was convinced that these women must be some sort of *Kaikāḍīṇas*[14] or else female demons who went about stealing people's children and other possessions and then hid them under their bulging skirts. I had not the slightest doubt in my mind that if I ever wandered away out of my mother's or my father's sight, these women would steal me too and put me in that bag under their skirts and carry me off.

These big bulging dresses, of which I had been so frightened as a child,

13. Trans.: The word Ramabai uses here is *tāmramukhī*, literally "coppery-faced." — *PCE*

14. Trans.: The *Kaikāḍīs* (feminine, *Kaikāḍīṇa*) are a wandering community of basket-makers, who were formerly included among the "criminal tribes" — and consequently regarded with much the same kind of animus and fear as the Gypsies were in Europe. — *PCE*

came into existence owing simply to a whim of the queen of Paris; and for some years all the women of Europe, large and small, rich and poor, educated and uneducated, imagined them to be beautiful and wore them. When the empress of Paris was pregnant, she didn't want anyone to notice the change in her figure, so she started to wear skirts that bulged about her. When they saw this, not only did all the fashionable women themselves start to wear this kind of dress as the latest marvelous fashion (never bothering to find out the original reason for it), but they even made young girls dress up in this style of dress. How the queen of Paris must have laughed to herself about that! Some other notable beauty was just a bit too short, so she tried to conceal it by raising the heels of her shoes a couple of inches. When they saw this, other women also raised the heels of their shoes, without ever knowing the original reason for it. The practice of wearing high-heeled shoes continues to this day.

People who seek to enhance their beauty by wearing gold, silver, or other kinds of ornaments or who wear clothes of the latest fashion sometimes trade their own beauty for ugliness. And it isn't just our own country to which this rule applies but also England and the United States, which have reached the very pinnacle of progress. When Chinese women have their feet bound in an attempt to make them smaller, how much pain they have to suffer; and for this the women here pity them greatly. Some say this Chinese custom is a sign of the slavery of women. Others are of the opinion that this is proof of the evil effect Buddhism and Confucianism have had on the Chinese. In the act of criticizing the evil customs of other peoples *(jātī)*, many very strange conjectures fill their heads. But like the man carrying a double packsack in Aesop's fable, it is only natural that they see perfectly well all the things in the front pocket of their own packsack — while being blind to the things they carry in its rear pocket. The women here think that a narrow waist is an important indication of beauty. In order to make their waists narrow, they wear a kind of waistcoat called a "corset," which is a sleeveless jacket that is made of whalebone and straps of steel and that is narrow in the middle and much wider above and below. An ordinary, healthy woman of medium height generally has a waist measurement of thirty-nine or forty finger-widths. By squeezing their waists, the women here reduce them to thirty or even twenty-four finger-widths.[15] When a girl turns twelve or so, she is taught the habit of wearing a corset. Because of this practice, many women find it impossible to breathe properly, and their lungs are damaged. And because of the pressure of the corset, the spleen and the stomach are displaced into the lower abdomen,

15. Trans.: These measurements would be twenty-six or twenty-seven inches and twenty or sixteen inches respectively. — *KG*

and there they put excessive pressure on the uterus. As a consequence, they cannot digest food properly; they cannot breathe deeply; they suffer from diseases of the spleen and lungs; during childbirth they have to suffer a great deal more pain than is normal; and God only knows how many other trials and tribulations they have to endure!

On top of that, they have one more device that is meant to add beauty to their figures and clothes called the "bustle." It is made of heavy wires woven together, and it has two or three different shapes. It is tied to the waist underneath the skirt of a dress and hangs down the back. When a dress is worn on top, it makes it bulge out at the back in the area below the waist. No one but *Saṭavāī*[16] could possibly know what beauty there could be in a bustle. And it certainly would seem that it must have been no one but *Ṣaṣṭhīdevī* who created it *(sṛṣṭi kelelī)* because it certainly never occurred to Mother Nature *(Sṛṣṭidevata)* to fasten a natural bustle to the backsides of European and American women at the time they are born. Around the bustle and underneath the dress they wear two or three very ample petticoats, the weight of which, along with that of the dress and of the bustle, is six or seven *sera*s.[17] All this weight bears directly on the stomach; and needless to say, this does not produce a good effect.

In this cold country it is perfectly fine that feet should have the protection of shoes. But some fashion-crazy women want their feet to be smaller than they are and wear extremely small, tight shoes, owing to which their feet become misshapen and their toes develop large bunions. And because they have high heels on their shoes the weight of the body does not fall evenly on the entire foot when they walk but falls mostly on the forward part — causing damage to the toe nails. Fashions such as these are more popular in the cities than in the smaller towns. When they see the vain and extravagant ways of the rich, poor women imitate them. Both rich and poor women spend vast sums of money on buying items of dress. The leather gloves they wear are so tight it takes a good bit of time just to put them on; and when they are being worn, women's hands look like nothing so much as rolls of paper. If they are preparing to go out somewhere for dinner or for a walk or to meet somebody, even in the summer when it is blazing hot (even if they are sweating from the heat) they have to have their gloves on.

16. Trans.: *Saṭavāī:* "A vulgar name of goddess Durga — or Devi. . . . 2 Applied as a term of reviling to a woman" (Molesworth). From Sanskrit *Ṣaṣṭhi,* a name of Durga. This is one of the *khaḍaka* (harsh) deities, who is propitiated on the sixth day after childbirth because "a distemper incidental to infants [is] considered as a visitation from her" (Molesworth). — *PCE*

17. Trans. and Ed.: A *śera* is an obsolete measure of weight which varied greatly from place to place. From references elsewhere in the text we can calculate that Ramabai's *śera* was slightly less than two pounds. — *PCE* and *REF*

Recently a dress-reform movement has been started in this country. Many knowledgeable women, anatomists among them, are reforming the entire pattern of their dress. This reformed pattern of dress has been designed scientifically;[18] and not only is it pleasing and comfortable to wear but it allows you to do any kind of work you want — i.e., simply wearing it does not in itself present an obstacle to doing any particular kind of work. These women in the dress-reform movement are making wholehearted efforts to dissuade women both in their own country and abroad from wearing bad, fashionable clothes that damage the natural figure and health of their bodies. The progressive people of Japan have avidly taken to imitating not just the good qualities of the Europeans but their bad qualities as well. Japanese women have begun to give up their own clumsy unfashionable clothes in favor of clothes such as European women wear. When I went to the home of Frances*bāī* Willard[19] to say goodbye, she said to me, "Wherever you may go, particularly to Japan, urge the women not to damage their health by wearing silly, fashionable clothes. This is my last message to you. If we intend to be useful to society, all of us will have to bring about a reform in our clothes."

The basic purpose of a hat, which is to protect the head from the cold or from harsh sunlight, has been forgotten by most of the women here. Nowadays hats have turned into a kind of ornament for the head. They decorate their hats with colorful silk cloth, silk and satin ribbons, artificial fabric flowers, and so on. But beyond that, they also have the practice of attaching the feathers of beautiful birds or even the bodies of entire birds that have been killed and stuffed with straw to their hats. A few years ago, in order to attract public attention to herself, a woman of ill repute in Paris fixed an entire bird to her hat and went to the theater. When they saw this even respectable women, thinking this to be the latest fashion (and never asking what started it), took up the practice of attaching beautiful birds to their hats. For the sake of this evil custom, millions of beautiful birds are sacrificed by evil hunters who make their living through this trade; and snobbish women, not thinking what they do, give it their encouragement. Not only do the poor birds lose their lives because of this trade, but they must suffer excruciating pain. To keep the colors of their beautiful feathers from fading, they have to

18. Trans.: *Śāstrīyarītyā:* literally, in the manner of the *sāstras*; but here used in its modern sense of "scientifically." — *PCE*

19. Trans.: Frances Elizabeth Caroline Willard (1839-1898) was one of the founders of the National Women's Christian Temperance Union (WCTU) in 1874 and was elected president of the World's WCTU in 1891. She also worked to reform working conditions in industry and to promote women's suffrage. See also Chapter 8. — *PCE*

be skinned while they are still half alive. Who could even begin to describe this cruelty and the suffering of these poor birds? Two years ago at one shop in London, in a period of three months the skins of 404,464 birds from the West Indies and Brazil and the bodies of 356,389 of our own beautiful Hindusthani birds were sold. There are thousands of such shops in Europe and America; and who can even begin to estimate how many countless millions of dead birds are sold in them every year? And this is not even to speak of the altogether pointless destruction of how many countless nestlings that must take place. No sooner do their parents go out to find food than some reprobate takes their lives; all the while back in the nest the clutch of nestlings, their beaks wide open from hunger, cheep pitifully for their mother, but she is no longer alive to answer them. Because they are not fully fledged, they cannot go out and find food for themselves. After a day or two of fruitless calling and calling, they die of hunger. Oh! It breaks my heart! I cannot help saying it, but if there exists a person with a heart so stony that he does not have tears in his eyes when he thinks about the plight of these birds, he is a blot on the human race. If the women who wear hats that are decorated with birds had only known what a terrible loss it is to the world and how much the birds must suffer, they certainly would have given up this practice. Recently, in Western countries, societies that are called by the name Audubon have been established.[20] Their fundamental purpose is to protect birds. We pray to God that their efforts may be rewarded with all the success they could hope for.

Applying pink tints to cheeks and nails and putting on white powder for the sake of beauty is also one aspect of fashion here. In the case of hair loss because of old age or because of ill health during youth, it is the firmly established custom everywhere to wear a wig made of false hair to improve their looks. To curl their hair, they wet it before going to bed at night, wrap it around rods made of horn or paper rollers, and press the rolls of hair with heated tongs. Some women apply oil and distilled alcohol and fix folds of their hair like upside-down Turkish arches above their foreheads. The practice of replacing teeth that fall out in middle age with false teeth is prevalent even in parts of our own country. Here in this country, fitting artificial teeth in your mouth is about the same as the verse, "after casting away worn-out garments, a man later takes new ones."[21] The expert crafts-

20. Trans.: John James Audubon (1785-1851), American ornithologist noted for his drawings and paintings of birds, was the inspiration for the founding of the Audubon Society. — *PCE*

21. Trans.: *Vāsāṃsi jīrṇāni yathā vihāya/navāni gṛhṇāti naro' parāṇi* (*Bhagavad Gītā* 2.22). The translation is by Winthrop Sargent in *The Bhagavad Gita* (Albany: SUNY Press,

men here have created artificial teeth that are in every respect as good as real teeth. If some pretty, young woman has crooked teeth, she goes to a dentist and has her teeth pulled and replaced with beautiful artificial teeth — all to improve her looks. It wasn't just the occasional odd person who asked me whether *my* teeth were real. In Philadelphia, one old woman simply couldn't believe that my teeth were real until she had opened my mouth and carefully examined the palate and everything else. Whether these people eat too much meat or who knows why, their teeth are intrinsically not very strong, and they fall out very early. Artificial teeth are very useful to them. They add comeliness to the face, but they are also very useful in chewing thick, tough items of food.

Men also have some of their own fashions and affectations, just as women do. But men make every effort to appear, at least on the surface, to be plain and simple. The men who follow the fashions are for the most part very young, or else they have rich parents. Even poor young men, when they see the affectations and the style of dress of rich people and spendthrifts, make a big show of imitating them. Such a lot of things fall into the category of men's affectations: changing their clothes three or four times a day, wearing different styles of clothes, wearing their hats just ever so slightly tilted, stroking their mustaches, carrying a slim cane, strutting about, talking smartly, and so on and so on. Men's dress here is of the European type, uniform in color (usually black or light brown with a hat of the same color) and quite plain. Wearing it does not present the slightest obstacle to doing work. It is extremely serviceable to any hardworking man — to anyone who does any kind of work at any hour. The clothes a clergyman wears are somewhat different from that of ordinary men: their tunics are long enough to reach to their knees. The clothes they wear on festive occasions are made of expensive fabric, and some are attractive in appearance while some are quite ill-looking.

Generally speaking, there are two vices that are widespread among the men of the United States. One is the drinking of liquor and the other is the smoking of cigars.[22] The ancestors of the Anglo-Saxon tribe *(jāta),* from which most of the American people take their origin, used to drink an alcoholic beverage called "beer" from very ancient times. Later on, as ever-new kinds of alcoholic beverages began to be produced, the people's addiction to drink kept growing apace. Ever since the United States became independent,

---

1984), p. 107. Grateful acknowledgements to Gudrun Buhnemann for identifying the quotation. — *PCE*

22. Trans.: The word Ramabai uses here is *cirūṭa* (i.e., cheroot) from Tamil. — *PCE*

people have been coming in a steady stream to settle here from virtually all the ethnic groups *(jātī)* in Europe. Every year hundreds of thousands of people have been coming to the United States to settle. A very large number of them are German, Italian, and Irish. These people are especially famous when it comes to drink. Because of their massive influx into the United States, the original Americans, following the example of the newcomers, have seen their own addiction to drink grow enormously. The addiction to smoking tobacco has also burgeoned in exactly the same way. It is very easy to see the prevalence of these addictions from the following table of the annual national expenditures of the United States. Every year these people spend as follows:[23]

Propagation of religion:	Rs. one crore sixty-five lakh (Rs. 16,500,000)
Clergymen's salaries:	Rs. three crore sixty lakh (Rs. 36,000,000)
Education:	Rs. twenty-eight crore eighty lakh (Rs. 288,000,000)
Tea and coffee:	Rs. forty-three crore fifty lakh (Rs. 435,000,000)
Sugar and molasses:	Rs. forty-six crore fifty lakh (Rs. 465,000,000)
Shoes and socks:	Rs. fifty-nine crore ten lakh (Rs. 591,000,000)
Metals such as iron:	Rs. seventy-eight crore eighty lakh (Rs. 788,000,000)
Meat:	Rs. ninety crore ninety lakh (Rs. 909,000,000)
Bread:	Rs. one hundred sixty-one crore fifty lakh (Rs. 1,615,000,00)
Tobacco:	Rs. one hundred forty-seven crore (Rs. 1,470,000,000)
Alcohol:	Rs. two hundred seventy crore (Rs. 2,700,000,000)

Seeing how damaging drink is to the health of the people and to the country, hundreds of thousands of American women and men have been protesting against it. I do not fear to say that the spread of various kinds of immorality among the American people nowadays has undoubtedly arisen out of the two vices I have mentioned above.

23. Trans.: The following figures are all quoted in rupees. As we have seen, the exchange rate at that time was approximately three rupees to one dollar. — *PCE*

Racial Discrimination and Bigotry[24]

"Wherever the *paḷasa* goes, it has only three leaves."[25] Whatever the place, whatever the circumstances in which humankind may have found itself, there does not appear to have been much change in its intrinsic faults and virtues. It is certainly true that the United States of America is famous for its wealth, its education, and its progress; but racial discrimination and bigotry, the mortal enemies of all progress and virtue, are not nonexistent in this country.

When the ancestors of the American people left England and came here, they brought all the hoary English traditions with them. After their nation became independent, in order to be consistent with the precept of the Declaration of Independence that stated, "All men created by God are equal," they were obliged to make substantial changes in the ancient British practices of social discrimination *(jātibheda)*. Even so, until 1861 this precept did not apply to everyone. Owing to their practice of buying and selling people of the African race *(habaśī jāta)* like cattle, they held the belief that the Negro race[26] was inferior by birth to people of the white race *(jāta)*. While the Negroes were still slaves, it was strictly forbidden to eat with them, to marry them, and so on. And it is the same even today. It is true that the Negroes were emancipated, but the contempt that the whites had conceived for their race *(jāta)* is unchanged even today. I have been to hundreds of places to eat so far, but I have never had occasion to see a Negro dining with a white person. Nor is that all. Even at the time of worship in God's own holy temples, only on extremely rare occasions have I seen a Negro sitting next to a white person. Negroes have their own separate places of worship, and their preachers also belong for the most part to their own race and are scarcely to be seen in the society of whites.

It has not yet been even twenty-five years since the Negroes were emancipated, but when you see the progress their race has made on the strength solely

24. Trans.: *Jātibheda* and *jātimatsara* are the words Ramabai uses here, the same as in Chapter 4, where they were rendered as "social discrimination" and "bigotry." The subject matter of this section of the present chapter makes it quite clear, however, that "racial discrimination" is specifically intended here. — *PCE*

25. Trans.: *Paḷasa koṭheṃ gelā tarī tyālā tīnaca pāneṃ*. A. Manwaring gives a slightly varying version of this "very favorite proverb," which he translates, "Go where you will the Palas is triple-leaved," and of which he gives the common sense, "Man's character is the same everywhere." *Marathi Proverbs*, p. 157. The *paḷasa* tree is the Flame of the Forest or Butea frondosa. — *PCE*

26. Trans.: *Nigro jāta* is Ramabai's usage here. In what follows she alternates between using *nigro jātīceṃ manuṣyeṃ* (people of the Negro race) and simply *nigro* (Negro, Negroes). For simplicity's sake, we shall consistently use "Negro" or "Negroes." — *PCE*

of their own hard work, you cannot help but commend their perseverance and their self-reliance. Less than twenty-five years ago a Negro was forbidden even to read and write. It was their lot to be born like cattle, to grow like cattle, and — after giving everything they had to the service of whoever had bought them — in the end to die like cattle. From the point of view of the law they were not even human beings. They did not have any human rights at all. They did not even have the right, the single most holy right that strengthens social ties in human society, to get married legally. But God bless William Lloyd Garrison, Elizabeth Herrick, Lucretia Mott, Wendell Phillips,[27] and the many other fine, decent people like them who suffered many hard labors, adversities, and adverse public opinion to create in the United States a change in public opinion that favored the emancipation of the Negro race — and thereby put the entire human race under a debt of gratitude that can never be repaid. The American Negro was emancipated in 1865, and from the end of the American Civil War up to the present day, with the help of good, decent people and through his own strength, he has left behind him his status of an animal and has attained the status of a human being. People of that race have now become teachers, preachers, lawyers, doctors, merchants, and even senators in the Congress of the United States. Nowadays there is not a single right that a white citizen of the United States has that a black citizen does not have. And welcome signs are starting to appear that in the near future the existing discrimination between the blacks and the whites (as in not dining together) will disappear.[28]

The ordinary American also has a great hatred for the original inhabitants of America, the Red Indians. The government of the United States made treaties with various tribes *(jātī)* of Indians — but did not keep the terms of those treaties. Violating the promises they had made, the government seized the lands they had set aside for the Indians; then they turned around and made themselves the paragons of virtue and turned the Indian people into the thieves. Nowadays there are some good, decent Americans who are working hard for the advancement of their Red countrymen.[29] In order to save face the United States government has opened a few industrial schools for In-

27. Trans.: William Lloyd Garrison (1805-1879), Lucretia Coffin Mott (1793-1880), and Wendell Phillips (1811-1884) were all prominent abolitionists and members or leaders of the American Anti-Slavery Society, which was founded in 1833. Elizabeth Herrick remains unidentified but must have been a fellow-abolitionist of that era. — *PCE*

28. Trans.: This highly optimistic view of the future of race relations in the United States might have had some warrant more than a decade earlier before the end of Reconstruction in the South. In fact, Ramabai's visit coincided with the transition to the worst of the Jim Crow era when African Americans were systematically segregated and disfranchised. — *PCE*

29. Trans.: *Deśabandhū:* literally, "country-brother." — *KG*

dian children using the Indian people's own money, which is kept on deposit in the government treasury. Some of the best of these schools are the Hampton Institute in Virginia, the Carlisle Indian School in Pennsylvania, and the Lincoln Institute in Philadelphia.[30]

Not only do the Indian people not enjoy any of the rights of American citizenship, they do not even have the right to file a suit against anyone in any ordinary court of the United States. The United States government has allotted certain places, called "Indian reservations," where the various Red Indian tribes are to live. If any Indian should cross the borders of his reservation, he either loses his life to an American hunter's bullet or else he is caught in the clutches of some judge and is punished for leaving his reservation without permission. A deputy of the United States government called an "Indian agent" lives on each reservation to oversee the Indian people. This agent is an absolute, sovereign ruler over the Indian people. The United States government delegates to him the responsibility for supplying the staples of food and drink to the Indian people on the reservation. Whatever this man may choose to do, that is the rule; and whatever he may choose to say, that is the divine truth.[31] There are very few honest Indian agents, and the poor Indians suffer horribly at their hands. Whether because of their ignorance or because of their natural disposition, the Indian people are extremely forbearing. Very rarely do they complain to the government; and even if they did, it is highly unlikely that the government would do anything in response. If from time to time it should happen that public opinion is swayed in favor of the Indians by reports about them made by people who care, the government, as a way of saving face, appoints a commission to study the facts of the case. Generally speaking, there are good and impartial men and women on these commissions. And they have taken great pains to bring to the attention of the American citizens the extent of the tyranny suffered by the Indian people even to this day; and their efforts have succeeded to some extent. A large number of compassionate men and women have joined together to establish a committee, which has branches in many places in the United States, in support of the welfare of the Indian people.

30. Trans.: The Hampton Institute was actually founded in 1868 as a school for African Americans, although for some time at the end of the 1870s a program of industrial training was conducted there (under the supervision of Booker T. Washington) for a relatively small number of Native Americans. The Carlisle Indian School was in operation from 1879 to 1918. The "Lincoln Institute" apparently refers to Lincoln University, Chester County, Pennsylvania, which was chartered in 1854 as the Ashmun Institute and which, like the Hampton Institute, was dedicated to providing higher education to African Americans. — *PCE*

31. Trans.: More literally: "Whatever this man does, that is the East [i.e., inarguable fact]; and whatever he says, that is a Vedic utterance *(vedavākya)*." — *PCE*

It must be said that of all the people who have sought the true welfare of the Indian people, a woman by the name of Helen Hunt was the foremost.[32] Until she informed the American citizens with historical evidence and first-hand experience as to what the real conditions of the Indian people were, nobody knew anything specific about the matter. The United States government appointed Helen Hunt as an Indian Commissioner. She lived for five or six years right out there in the middle of the wilds in the company of these uncivilized *(rānaṭī)* people and described their real conditions in a book she wrote entitled *A Century of Dishonor* [1881], which really opened the eyes of the American people. She also wrote a novel entitled *Ramona* [1884], in which she portrayed the plight of the Indian people. The great efforts she made on behalf of the welfare of the Indian people are now beginning to bear fruit to some extent.

Another woman cut to her measure is Alice Fletcher,[33] who is making tireless efforts on behalf of the welfare of two Indian tribes called the Winnebago and the Omaha. Her efforts, along with those of her friends, have succeeded in getting the United States government to grant these two tribes the right to bring the land on their reservations under cultivation. These people have now begun to farm successfully and have begun to learn other occupations as well. A settlement has been reached whereby, once they learn in a few more years how to read and write and engage in the common occupations and begin to understand such matters and such rules as are essential to human society, they will be given all the rights of American citizenship.

There is a tribe called the Cherokees who live in what is called the Indian Territory. It is surprising indeed to see the progress made by the people of this tribe on the strength of their own intelligence and hard work. On their reservation they have established a system of government based on the pattern of the system of government of the United States and thus brought their little state up to the level of any American state in the United States. A certain

32. Trans.: Helen Hunt Jackson (1830-1885) was a poet, essayist, and novelist, and a lifelong friend of the poet Emily Dickinson. — *PCE*

33. Trans.: Alice Cunningham Fletcher (1838-1923), American anthropologist and founding member of the American Anthropological Association, lived for extended periods among the Omaha, Pawnee, Nez Perce, and other Native American tribes and published widely on the subject of Native American culture. Her zealous promotion of Indian welfare, partly at the behest of the Bureau of Indian Affairs, was instrumental in the passage of the Dawes General Allotment Act in 1887, under which tribal landholdings were broken up into individual holdings. Over the course of the nearly fifty years before the Act was repealed, what had been started with the best of intentions ended with the loss by Native Americans of over two-thirds of their tribal lands. — *PCE*

man from this Indian tribe devised a script for his language and started a method for writing his language. These progressive Cherokee Indian people have put a complete stop to the practice of buying and selling slaves of their own tribe. They have given up all their uncivilized *(rānaṭī)* customs and have given special attention to the spread of education among their own people. If the other tribes of Indian people work as hard to bring about their own advancement as the Cherokees have, their conditions will also rapidly improve.

The American people are not at all troubled when the Japanese immigrate to America and become American citizens. They have nothing but contempt, however, for the Chinese. When the Chinese come to America they do not dispose of their native clothes and dress themselves like Americans the way the Japanese do; they do not shave off their tufts of hair; they do not throw away their wooden shoes and wear American leather shoes; and it is for trivial reasons such as these that the American people hate the Chinese. This is a great blot indeed on the reputation of this freedom-loving race *(jāta)* that likes to call itself civilized.

The Chinese are extremely industrious by nature. They go to distant lands and engage themselves in business and work. They are both temperate and frugal. They do not have the habit of spending money extravagantly the way the Europeans do; and they do not charge four times what it is worth for the work they do. Small-minded Westerners hate them because of this. They say that the Chinese diminish the value of work; that they are of poor character and dirty; that their morals are bad; that they "come here and ruin our morals"; and so forth and so on. Many Westerners think that the Chinese are altogether devoid of virtues; that they are veritable warehouses of malefaction; that their very touch or any social intercourse with them will destroy one's own morals. And because of this, a great many evil-minded people among them hate the Chinese from the bottom of their hearts. They persecute the Chinese in any way they can. Some plunder their houses, some slaughter them, and some busy themselves poisoning the minds of their fellow citizens against the Chinese. Two years ago some narrow-minded people made life perfectly miserable for the Chinese who were living in the northern states — and even killed numbers of them. This doesn't mean, however, that there isn't anyone here who thinks better of it. There are those who espouse the cause of the powerless and harmless Chinese and who work for their welfare to the extent they can. Numbers of seasoned, scholarly writers have written books and essays demonstrating that the Chinese are not the epitome of evil but are possessed of some excellent virtues. Some of these people have established committees for the welfare of the Chinese.

People belonging to the Irish, German, Scandinavian, Italian, and Russian ethnic groups *(jātī)*, who come to the United States to escape the political powers that be or the tyranny or the poverty of their own lands, are also heartily despised by the majority here; but they are not considered as altogether worthless as the Chinese because the color of their skin and their facial features are fairly similar to the ruddy complexion and features of the English. The people of this country also have the same habit of blaming each other for everything. If a riot breaks out in one of their states, somebody is sure to say, "Those Irish are at the bottom of it." When they see a vast upsurge in the use of alcohol or other intoxicants in their state, they say, "Oh, the Germans are to blame. What are they born for but to drink?" If immorality is rampant, all the blame for it is placed on the heads of the poor Chinese. If bad officials are elected, there is a general hue and cry, "The Negroes sold their votes. That's why we're saddled with officials like these." All sorts of different forms of bigotry can be seen manifested everywhere. And the reason for this, plain and simple, is ignorance about each other — and the evil ideas that find their origins in that ignorance.

Having become aware of the presence of this sort of racial discrimination and bigotry among the common people in the United States and having understood how destructive this is to the unity and prosperity of this country, many thoughtful people are working to eradicate these evils. Many good, upright people regard even the most despised groups, such as the Negroes, the Indians, and the Chinese, as human beings exactly as themselves. Not only that, these good people are persuaded that if these others were given the same opportunities that they themselves enjoy, they would be their equals in every respect. But it is not easy to eradicate all at once a custom that has become so firmly rooted. The idea that the nonwhite communities *(jātī)* such as the Negroes are of inferior worth is deeply ingrained. Even so, there can be no fear at all that the racial discrimination and bigotry here in the United States will ever reach the level of caste discrimination *(jātibheda)* in Hindusthan. Day by day, as progress is continuing to be made and as knowledge is continuing to spread among the people, this bigotry, which has its origins in ignorance, is diminishing. Public advocates of morality and education who seek the best interests of their country are giving excellent instruction by word and by deed both to young children in their schools and to adults in their religious communities and are impressing it upon their minds that their own welfare and the welfare of their country lies in treating one another with civility and in regarding everyone as an equal. As a consequence, racial discrimination and bigotry are diminishing day by day, and mutual love, civility, and respect are growing among the people.

Even in the southern states, where the common people regarded the Negro as being on the level of the donkey or even worse, customs and attitudes are changing along with the times. Twenty-five years ago not only did a black and a white person never sit down to eat together, but a Negro was not even permitted to travel with whites in the same train compartment or the same carriage. Now the Negro has begun to travel with white people whether it be in horse trolleys or in trains. An educated white man does not consider it an insult to himself to get up and give his seat to a Negro woman if the train is crowded. Occasionally, if a railway station dining hall is very crowded and there is no other place available, a Negro will even be given a seat at the same table as white people.

Character

As a rule the qualities the American people can be seen to possess are very good and worthy of imitation. By and large these people tell the truth and hold religion in honor, but they are neither fanatically religious nor overscrupulous with the truth. They show great affection toward their children, and they have great love for their parents. A great deal of care and trouble is taken by parents to ensure the welfare and proper development of their offspring. They do not hesitate to give however much money and effort is required to ensure that their children get a useful education. They do not exert more than the necessary authority over their children — and thus do not rob them of their independence. Not that the children are remiss in giving proper respect to their parents either. Sons and especially daughters are ever eager to be of service to their parents and in this way to stay in their good graces. I have seen many instances of daughters refusing to get married even though they had received marriage proposals from prospective husbands who were very well-to-do, educated, and most suitable because they feared that after they got married they would have to leave their aged parents and there would be no one left to look after them. Many refused excellent, well-paying positions; and there are lots of examples of this kind to be seen, especially among women, of self-sacrifice. Men do not hesitate to leave their parents and go far away on account of their jobs; and American parents do not feel it is fair, out of consideration for their own welfare, to hold on to their sons and stand in the way of their progress. (This is something that those parents in Hindusthan who do not let their children go abroad for their education or for other business might do well to bear in mind. The extreme love that makes them not want their children to leave is really not love at all when it stands in the way of their children's advancement — but rather a type of selfishness.) American parents take the finest care of their children when they are young and, after educating them, set them up in some occupation. But when their children are ready to start working, the parents do not spoil them needlessly. The established pattern the American people had twenty years ago for distributing property among their children was rather like that found among uncultivated *(rānaṭī)* people. In those days daughters used to receive an extremely small share of their parents' property. But nowadays the laws in the United States concerning inheritance are being improved to a large extent. The practice of distributing wealth equally among sons and daughters is becoming increasingly common. For the most part the parents' responsibility toward their children extends only as far as educating them well and getting them started in some occupation. After the children have grown up and are able to work on their own, their parents do not worry too much about them.

In recent times an attitude of deference toward women has been growing among the people of the United States. The proof of this lies in the fact that whereas previously men used to appoint some other man as guardian and trustee for the protection of their children and property when they died, only because they thought women to be altogether ignorant and unsuitable for the purpose, nowadays many wealthy and middle-class people have begun to appoint their wives or their sisters as the guardians of their children and property. From what many experienced and knowledgeable American people have told me, I have concluded that the women of America are morally more upright than the men. As a rule women are modest, virtuous, and faithful to their husbands. But I have heard it said that many men are not as faithful to their wives as they ought to be.

The point of what I am saying about them is that on the whole the American people are kind-hearted, courteous, generous, moral, industrious, and intent on advancement.

The Seasons of the Year

Following the custom of the Anglo-Saxons, the American people hold that there are only four seasons in the year. March, April, and May constitute the spring; June, July, and August constitute the summer; September, October, and November constitute the autumn; and December, January, and February constitute the winter. As the condition of the soil, the temperatures, and other such seasonal factors change over the course of the four seasons, corresponding changes can be seen in people's dress, in their festivals, in their household furniture, and in what they eat and drink. At the start of each season shops are well-stocked with goods that are appropriate and necessary to that season. Newspapers, dilapidated walls of old houses, public squares and street corners, and shop windows are filled with all kinds of advertisements. Railway stations and railway lines and even the spaces above carriage windows are swarming with advertisements of every kind. These people have totally mastered both all the arts of advertising and all the tricks for extracting money from people's purses. In order to attract attention to a particular product, they print bits of verse about it, write it up in a nice way, or simply write its name in very large, brightly colored letters and stick it up on a wall some place. They write the name on fence posts, rocks, tiled roofs, trees, and many other places. Although vast amounts of money have to be spent on advertising, it produces plenty of profit too.

The night I arrived in Philadelphia I had occasion to see my first sample of the advertising here. As I was traveling along in a public horse trolley, I noticed a leaflet printed in very large letters pasted in the space just above the window opposite me. Its first line read, "God helps those who help themselves."[34] I told myself, "My goodness! How moral the people of this country must be! They must put up moral slogans of this sort in public places like this so that people can read them wherever they happen to be, even if they are just coming or going in the streets, and so be reminded of good things and even develop a taste for morality." But when I read the second line of the leaflet, I grew a bit suspicious of how true this could be. It read, "*Soapolio* [this was the name of some soap] — a fine way to help yourself!" Witty verses, lovers' dialogues, and all kinds of entertaining things are written in the advertisements in newspapers and in magazines for hundreds of products like Soapolio.[35]

34. *Prayatnīṃ parameśvara* (literally, "Through effort, God") most likely is our own adaptation of this proverb. — *PRS*

Trans.: A. Manwaring lists a slight variant, *prayatnāntīṃ parameśvara,* which he translates, "At the end of effort is God." *Marathi Proverbs,* p. 197. — *PCE*

35. It must be remembered that no one has the freedom here to advertise filthy and obscene things in the newspapers and in public places. It is most lamentable thing that in our own country there are no such regulations. Everyone should be ashamed of the many unspeakable advertisements (take for example the advertisement for semen invigorant) that fill our newspapers. One is surprised and saddened to see that respectable gentlemen, the owners of large and well-reputed newspapers, give space for offensive advertisements such as this one in their newspapers. These newspapers are seen and read by women of respectable families and by children with impressionable minds. Pure-minded men also have occasion to read them. It is difficult even to estimate how many good and decent people's hearts are grieved and how many children's minds are polluted by this. Why don't the morally upright gentlemen of our country do something to regulate this? What are our highly reputed organizations for moral education doing? What a blot it is on the reputations of those gentlemen, such as the owners of these newspapers, who take so much pride in showing themselves to be working for the public welfare and, what is more, who like to call themselves devoutly religious and respectable, that by giving space in their newspapers to advertisements like this they should impress evil things on the minds of immature children,

At the start of each season there is always one great mad rush to make new clothes and to turn upside down and rearrange all the furniture in the house. In all the shops, large and small, there are huge crowds of women buying things. It is only the women here who go out and do the household shopping. Bargaining is not at all customary in the stores; almost all goods are sold at fixed prices. But in place of bargaining they do have another calamitous custom that plagues the shopkeepers here, and that is — comparison shopping. Not that anybody should buy things without first examining them properly. But the need to send the shopkeeper back and forth fifty times for every last little item, then to make him open up thirteen bolts of fabric, and then to go out and make the rounds of seventeen other stores doesn't benefit either party. What is more, it is extremely tiresome and a great waste of time. Indeed, it can be actually harmful to people. The shopkeepers in this country and their salesmen and saleswomen do not sit leaning back on bolsters or against the wall while selling their wares. There are high counters in front of the shelves and cupboards in their shops, behind which the salespeople have to stand to do their work. Many women who work in stores sometimes do not get to sit down for ten hours at a stretch. It doesn't even occur to many people when they go to places like this how wrong and troublesome it is to make these women walk back and forth fifty times for every last little thing.

It is the custom here to present gifts to friends and relatives on holidays and on birthdays. During the holidays all the stores are stocked with especially nice things.

Summer

Spring is considered to be the best of all the seasons. (A brief description of it is given later on.[36]) When I arrived in the United States of America in March 1886, the winter was receding and spring was just beginning so I wasn't able to see then what winter is really like here. Between the last part of March and the end of April it rained frequently and sometimes it would snow. From May to September it is very hot here. Indeed, the mercury sometimes climbs to 110

---

teaching these future bearers of our family lines to listen to, think about, and meditate upon immoral things and so open wide the path of destruction to them! If, before the government itself passes some law and ties their hands, they resolved of their own volition not to give space in their papers to offensive advertisements and unspeakable words and showed themselves to be acting in good faith, there would then be some point to their public sermonizing against petitioning the government for laws regulating each and every matter of concern. — *PRS*

36. Ed.: Unfortunately, this description is never given. — *REF*

degrees Fahrenheit, but such days are very rare. On an average summer day the temperature is between 80 and 85 degrees. Because the houses here and all the amenities in them are designed for winter, the summer here is much more difficult for us to bear than our summers back at home. And because their customs and ways here are so different from ours, it makes it much more difficult for us to adjust.

An interesting thing happened to me in the house of the lady where I lived as a lodger in Philadelphia. It is true that when I was in my own room on the third floor nobody would bother me about anything I did; but I had to be very careful of the way I acted when I went downstairs at mealtimes in the company of other people. One day in June it was terribly hot, and there wasn't so much as a puff of air. It was after 2 P.M., and there wasn't a sound anywhere in the whole house, so, as I did every day without thinking anything of it, I went downstairs to get a glass of water to drink from the kitchen — in my bare feet. By some unhappy happenstance, the one thing that ought not to have happened did happen that day. I was just turning to go upstairs with my glass of water when, out of the blue, there was old Dr. B. standing in front of me on the stairs. Whatever it was that poor old man was thinking when he saw my bare feet, it might be better not to ask. But his face grew very small, and the expression on his face looked like that of somebody who had been either badly frightened or else given a terrible shock of sorrowful surprise at having been made witness to some truly shameless behavior. So of course I didn't look at his face very long, and I fled like a sudden breeze to my room.

Two or three hours later, as I sat reading something and was already starting to forget the incident, somebody came and knocked at my door. As I said, "Yes, come in," a twelve-year-old boy opened the door and came in. He was our old Dr. B's grandson. He handed me a little note and left. I opened the note, and this is what I read:

> I know it is customary in your country for everyone to walk around without wearing shoes and socks. But here in our country, doing so is not considered to be an act of proper modesty. Members of my family have been saddened and surprised to see you walking barefoot. Be so gracious as to wear your shoes and socks when you come downstairs.
>
> Your friend, Mrs. B.[37]

37. After I returned here — that is, to Hindusthan — I received a letter from Mrs. B. She has asked me in it whether I wear shoes here or not. — *PRS*

From that time forth I resolved never to commit the crime again of walking barefoot in front of anyone as long as I was in this country.

Just as in our own country, during the summer there are plagues of flies, mosquitoes, and other winged pests here in America too. The mosquitoes in the state of New Jersey are not in the least degree less worthy than the mosquitoes in Mirzapur or Calcutta. On the shores of Lake Michigan near Chicago there is a summer resort *(grīṣmavihāra)*[38] called Lake Bluff. I had to spend three or four days and nights there. In the daytime and during the first part of the night it was so hot I can't begin to tell you, and there was not the slightest breeze either. On top of that, there was a veritable deluge of mosquitoes. The vision, which I no longer had after I left Assam in 1882, of the hell that is called the *Andhakūpa Naraka*[39] revisited me again on the shores of Lake Michigan in 1887. Here is a description of this hell in chapter five of the *Śrīmadbhāgavata:* "The man who hates insects such as gnats and mosquitoes is cast into the Andhakupa hell; thrown into darkness there, he can never sleep nor does he get any rest. The mosquitoes, lice, flies, bedbugs, and all the other living things he has hated, bite him unceasingly and take their revenge on him."[40] Those wishing to have a true vision of this hell should certainly go to Mirzapur, Calcutta, Assam, and regions such as that. Nor is it the case that our own land of Maharashtra[41] is at all inferior in this respect to the other regions of Hindusthan. I only appreciated the true worthiness of these old kinsmen and friends of ours, however, when I met them after a long, long time in a foreign country like America. Before this I had never understood so clearly the meaning of the verse, "Mosquitoes cause more hurt by humming in the ear than by sucking the blood."[42]

This country may have its ravages in the way of flies and such; but the clever people of America protect themselves by means of such remedies as extermination and many other ingenious devices. When summer is just beginning they put up wire-mesh screens on all the doors and windows of their

38. A place where people go for rest or for a change of air in summer. — *PRS*

39. Trans.: *Andhakūpa,* literally, "blind well," or "a well of which the mouth is hidden" (Sir Monier Monier-Williams, *A Sanskrit-English Dictionary* [Oxford: Oxford University Press, 1982 (1899)]). — *PCE*

40. Trans.: Ramabai quotes this in what is apparently her own Marathi translation from the original Sanskrit. — *PCE*

41. Trans.: *Mahārāṣtra deśa* is Ramabai's very conscious usage here, even though it would be another seventy years before Maharashtra would be officially formed and named as one of the states of the Republic of India. — *PCE*

42. Trans.: *Rudhirādānādadhikaṃ dunoti karṇe kvaṇan maśakaḥ* (from Govardhanacarya, *Āryāsaptaśatī,* verse 59). Our grateful acknowledgements to Gudrun Buhnemann for identifying the quotation. — *PCE*

houses, and to a great extent this keeps the flying pests from coming in. In May people are vastly busy everywhere taking up the rugs, mats, and carpets from the floors and staircases of their houses, washing and sweeping them, repapering the walls, and many other things.

Everyone who is in the field of education has a vacation during the months of June, July, and August. Many government workers also get a few days of vacation during summer. Even the busiest people take a few days of rest during this season. The idle rich, those born into wealth, are on vacation all year long, but even they think they ought to take a few days off and leave their homes to go to some summer resort. During their vacation days everyone who has some money goes, either together with their families or by themselves, to a summer resort, whether nearby or far away, to enjoy themselves for a few days. The main reason for staying at a summer resort is to put aside work and domestic worries for some days and to get some rest and relaxation. I cannot stop myself saying, however, that like so many other customs that were started with the best of intentions, this custom is also, in a certain very real sense, quite oppressive. At these resorts there isn't the smallest sign of anything like rest and relaxation. It would be more accurate to think of them as something more like conventions. During the three months of summer there is always a huge crowd of people at Saratoga, Cape May, Niagara, Chautauqua, Lake Bluff, and other well-known places. Everywhere you see one unceasing rush of people going out for ballroom songs, musical comedies, social chatter, dinner parties, and so on and so forth. There are hotels[43] of every size and description at each of these places for the convenience of travelers.

Anybody would be astonished to see the splendor of the hotels in America; the hotels in Chicago, New York, Philadelphia, Boston, and other cities are like nothing less than the celestial palace of Indra.[44] The cost of building the Palmer House, a very famous hotel in Chicago, with all of its gold and silver and decorative fittings, was more than sixty lakh rupees (Rs. 6,000,000). It accommodates fifteen or sixteen hundred paying guests, apart from the five or six hundred men and women who are employed as attendants. There is a carriage house[45] adjacent to the hotel. If you count up the four or five hundred horses, the two hundred or two hundred and fifty carriages and buggies

43. Trans.: *Khāṇāvaḷī* (literally, "boarding houses") is the old-fashioned word Ramabai uses here, as in what follows and elsewhere (as we have seen), in the sense of "hotels." — *PCE*

44. Trans.: *Indra:* "The name of the deity presiding over Swarga (the Hindu paradise) and the secondary divinities" (Molesworth). — *KG*

45. Trans.: *Gāḍīkhānā* is the word Ramabai uses here. Literally, a place to keep carriages, horses, and accessories. — *KG*

that are kept there, as well as all the coachmen, ostlers, and guards, along with what they are paid in wages, you can't help but be struck with amazement. And there are many such hotels in this country. Both the rich as well as plenty of middle-class people stay in these hotels. Not that anybody can find much happiness or rest and relaxation in living there all the time. But many people will spend well beyond their means to stay for at least a week in some famous hotel for no better reason than to get their names in the newspapers one way or another. How blessed are . . . the great ambitions of man! The minimum charge for one person to stay in the kind of hotel[46] described above is three or four dollars a day. For a mid-level room the rate is five or six dollars, and a deluxe room costs ten dollars. On top of this, the charges for laundry, carriages, and so on are all extra.

One of my friends from Chicago insisted that I come and stay in Saratoga with her for a week. So in August 1887 I went there with her. Saratoga truly is a beautiful spot, and the landscape all around it is superb. Many wealthy people have mansions and beautiful parks there. Every afternoon they have bands playing sweetly in the gardens to entertain the people who have come there to visit. Thousands of men, women, and pretty children dress up in fine clothes and go out to enjoy the air and have a good time.

Saratoga has quite a number of remarkable springs. The taste of their water, which is mixed with various minerals, is quite strange — rather like soda water. They say that the water from these springs is extremely salubrious. The ailment does not exist — whether it be indigestion, tuberculosis, asthma, or anything else — that cannot be cured by water from these springs! They tell of a wealthy man in our own country who had made it a rule never to drink any water but what came from the Ganga. It is widely reported that he employed hundreds of Brahman servants to fetch him the Ganga water he needed from a distance of many hundreds of miles. The rich and fashionable people of America have spring water brought to them for their use from places like Saratoga over distances of hundreds of miles. But just as a man who lives on the banks of the Ganga itself will treat that river lightly and go on a lengthy pilgrimage to bathe in some other sacred river, the fashionable people who live around Saratoga don't think much of the superiority of the spring water that comes from there and drink instead the highly reputed water imported for them from distant countries like Germany. It cannot be said that the person who drinks the Saratoga spring water never falls prey to ailments such as indigestion, tuberculosis, or diseases of the blood; but if one person or another just

46. Trans.: Here Ramabai switches to the obsolete word of Persian origin *sarāya* (i.e., sarai or caravansary). — *PCE*

happens to talk something up a bit, multitudes will soon start following in procession behind him, playing their harps[47] and singing its praises to the skies. In short, the compulsion to imitate is to be found everywhere.

During our stay in Saratoga my friend from Chicago took me out to one of the gardens to take the air one morning before breakfast. It was a very quiet and pleasant day, and in the morning there was a slight chill, so wherever we turned the garden was full of delight. As we were strolling about in the garden we came to the edge of one of the springs. A brick wall had been built around it to a height of about a yard, and a boy was sitting at the gate. He charged us a few pennies each to enter. A lot of men, women, and children were already there, paying a few pennies each for small tumblers of the spring water, and they were drinking it — and belching — with the greatest enthusiasm. My friend drank two tumblers of the water and told me to drink it too. But when I declined, she was very surprised and said, "You mean to say you won't drink this salubrious water? It will purify your blood and put an end to all your digestive problems." I replied, "Yes, my friend, that may be true, but the moment it struck me that people are drinking this water from tumblers that hundreds of others have previously put to their lips and sanctified with their saliva without ever bothering to wash them clean and that I myself would have a share of this kind of holy water, all my digestive problems instantly disappeared. So now I no longer have any need to imbibe this sacred libation."[48]

Autumn

The United States is so full of beauty that its beauty does not diminish during any of its seasons. Through its characteristic endowments each season adorns nature with some special ornament. But when autumn arrives, a season that has neither the extreme cold of winter nor the extreme heat of summer and that offers nothing but delight to the human race, the beauty of this golden land of the United States is filled with an even more beguiling and ethereal radiance. The

47. Trans.: *Tuṇatuṇeṃ* is the word Ramabai uses here. This is the one-stringed lute commonly played by pilgrims in Maharashtra as they process in their thousands each year to Pandharpur. *Tuṇatuṇeṃ lāvaṇeṃ* is the equivalent Marathi idiom for the English "to harp upon (something)" (Molesworth). — *PCE*

48. *Tīrtha* is the word Ramabai uses here to sharpen the sarcasm: "A holy stream, or water brought from one; water in which a Brahman, Sanyasi etc. has dipped his foot; which has been poured over an idol etc.; holy water" (Molesworth). To imbibe or even touch the saliva (or bodily fluids) of another, especially of lower birth, is to be polluted and to lose caste (purity). — *PCE* and *REF*

leaves everywhere change their colors in this season. At the beginning of winter the trees shed all their leaves; but just before this, during the last days of autumn, if any lover of natural beauty were to come and roam the forests of the United States, he would realize the full truth of the words I have just written.

The leaves of the silver maple, which is just one of the many species *(jati)* of trees here that are called maples, turn deep red in the autumn. There are many other trees like it too, but I don't know their names. There are also many species of a tree called the oak. Its leaves change into many different, very beautiful colors. The beauty of the forests in the Adirondack Mountains in the state of New York and in the Allegheny Mountains in Pennsylvania during the fall is indescribable. Many enthusiastic people travel through these mountains for no other reason than to enjoy the autumn beauty. I also had occasion to travel through this beautiful region by train on account of some work. A river called the Susquehanna flows through the Allegheny Mountains. The path this river takes is very serpentine, and on both of its banks there are many maples and other kinds of trees. From Manankchank to Water Gap[49] and some miles further along, the beauty of the forest is quite simply unsurpassable.

Using the technique of photography it is possible to reproduce an exact image of a person's form. If only there had been the same kind of device to reproduce the *colors* of the sky and of the woods, it might have been possible to convey to those who have never been there some idea at least of just how beautiful the autumn is in that region. Imagine us, if you will, traveling slowly through this region aboard a train, more like a palace on wheels, sitting in seats covered with beautiful velvet cushions. It is a fine day and the sky is clear, yet one or two clouds can be seen from time to time roaming about the open sky. Up ahead of us, on both sides of us, and behind us, wherever you look, tall mountain peaks stand with their heads touching the sky; and the pines of various species that grow on them cover the mountains with the sapphire blue of their foliage as if with a mantle of dark blue clouds; while, scattered everywhere among them like so many jewels, the birches, maples, oaks, and many other trees and vines and shrubs dapple the woodland with the myriad hues — red, yellow, green, purple, and auburn — of their leaves. To one side a crystal clear river is rippling its way through the heart of the mountain range at the very foot of the slopes; and here and there the sun shining off it gives the impression of molten silver. When we look upon this scene, it is very easy to imagine that we have entered the celestial

49. Manankchank and Water Gap are two railway stations. — *PRS*

Trans.: *Manāṅkacaṅka* is the regular transliteration of Ramabai's devanagari version of the first name. What the original spelling might have been remains a mystery. Neither Water Gap nor Manankchank appear on current maps. — *PCE*

Nandana[50] or *Caitraratha*[51] groves on Mount Meru[52] as they are described in the Puranas. The inhabitants of the United States, old and young, are ever eager to enjoy this kind of seasonal beauty.

In addition to the beauty of the woods in this season, there is one other thing that adds to the people's joy, and that is the harvesting of the crops and the gathering in of the fruit. This is a time of the greatest happiness in the homes of all farmers. When fruit of every kind — such as the kind called "apple" — begins to ripen in great heaps everywhere, the children are simply transported by delight.

At the end of November they celebrate the festival of Thanksgiving here. On that day they decorate every part of their churches with freshly harvested ears of corn and with vegetables, flowers, and fruit; and large and small they sing praises to God in sweet voices and thank him reverently for the abundant crops he has bestowed. And indeed this is an altogether delightful and agreeable scene to behold.

It rains a lot in the United States in November, the last month of autumn, and in December, the first month of winter. It would not be far wrong to call this the rainy season of the United States. There are intermittent showers in winter, spring, and autumn as well.

Winter

Ha ha ha! Hoo hoo hoo! Oo! Hoo! Legs and arms shiver from the cold, teeth chatter, and words tend to emerge in a strange lisp; people start to walk on *top* of the river water without a second thought; cutting butter even with a good sharp knife takes a good bit of strength; and instead of drinking milk, you sometimes have to chew bits and pieces of it! Such is the great power of the cold. In a big country like the United States, everything is bigger than life. On summer days you sometimes get just about desperate from the heat — sometimes you feel like a sesame seed *pāpaḍa*[53] roasting in the sun, sometimes you

50. Trans.: The pleasure ground of Indra, the deity presiding over *svarga*, or heavenly paradise. — *KG*

51. Trans.: The grove of Kubera, lord of wealth, that is cultivated by Citraratha, king of the Gandharvas, who are the celestial musicians of Indra's court. — *PCE*

52. Trans.: The sacred mythical and golden mountain representing the center point of the universe; abode or meeting place of the gods, generally associated with some peak in the Himalayas, from whence the Ganges flows. — *KG* and *REF*

53. Trans.: "Papadam," the familiar rendering of this in English, is a thin, rolled-out wafer made from various lentils or rice flour and set out to dry in the hot sun. — *PCE*

sweat so much you wonder if your body is going to melt away. But let winter come and you would think that nobody here could possibly know what summer is. Clothes made of plain, thin, white fabrics vanish like phantasms in a dream, and in their place you start to see all around you thick woolen coats and jackets, wraps, thick shoes with double linings, leather shirts, long coats lined with fur, caps with ear muffs, socks, gloves, and many other kinds of cold-weather wear. Anyone who has not come to this country and lived in the northern regions and seen the power of winter will never be able even to imagine the cold here. On really cold days sometimes the mercury in the thermometers drops to ten or twenty degrees below zero Fahrenheit. Rivers, springs, and lakes all freeze over completely, and their water turns as hard as rock.

It is difficult even to guess the amount of ice that city-dwellers and even a lot of people living in towns and villages make use of in place of drinking water. In winter when the rivers and lakes freeze over, they put ice away in storage for people to use in summer. Storehouses for ice have been built on the banks of all the big rivers and lakes where there isn't much human traffic. These storehouses are shaped like square bungalows and do not have doors. There are no more than two or three windows high up in the wooden walls near the eaves, with ladders leading up to them. Then, at the proper time, they cut blocks of ice from the frozen surface of the river, approximately two feet by two feet square and one or one-and-a-half feet thick, and very cleverly bring them up to the storehouse and put them in storage. To keep the ice from melting from the heat of the sun, they bury the blocks in sawdust and arrange to keep them well-removed from sun and wind. In summer they remove the ice from the storehouses, load up hundreds and thousands of carts, and sell it to the people in the cities. Every morning ice merchants bring their carts around and leave the proper allotment of ice at every house. In some homes they require just one block of ice; in some, two or more; some take half or a quarter or even just an eighth of a block. In every house they have a large container just for drinking water, which they fill with clean tap water and then ad large chunks of ice. In this way everyone has cool water to drink in summer. Although this cool water is very pleasant on the tongue, it can be extremely harmful if not drunk in moderation and with all due caution. People who come in from the heat gulp it down thirstily; and although it is true that it cools their stomachs and quenches their thirst, the melting of this very cold ice has a very bad effect on their overheated intestines. For this reason it is better if at all possible not to drink ice-cold water; and if that is too difficult to avoid, at least you can drink it a sip at a time and hold it in your mouth to make it less cold before you swallow it. There is little fear then of any ill effects from it.

In the months of January and February a simple walk out on the streets can be a big problem. Anyone who doesn't know about this will be happy to see how sparkling and clean the sidewalk is when he leaves the house; but the moment he takes a step or two, his feet slide out from him and down he goes! If anyone else happens to be around when this happens, she inquires most solicitously, "Oh, my goodness, did you hurt yourself when you slipped and fell?" But even though he is bruised and in pain from landing on the pavement, he will reply, a little confusedly and with an expression on his face as if nothing were amiss, "No, no, not at all!" During the winter you see many startling things like this in the streets. So many people have this strange way of feeling embarrassed when they slip and fall. There is nothing to be ashamed of in this, of course, but habits are very strong. The moment they fall down they jump back up, and not looking to see if anybody is laughing at them, they hurry away. The expression on their faces then looks very strange indeed.

In March this year (i.e., 1888) I went from Philadelphia to New York. The sky that day was clear, the sun was shining brightly, and it felt quite warm and humid. (The previous day the weather had changed slightly, and it had rained a little.) That afternoon, at the invitation of the Reverend Dr. Heber Newton, I spoke in his big church, where a huge crowd of men and women had gathered. My plan was to speak at two more places in New York (for the purpose of securing help for the project I had started) and establish two associations, then leave for Boston for some urgent work on Wednesday morning. The next morning when I woke up I noticed that the windowpanes in my room looked very strange. They were coated with a thick layer of some white stuff, and it looked as if somebody had worked an extremely beautiful and intricate floral design in it. When I went to the window to see what this remarkable thing could be, I saw that everything — the street, the housetops, the windows, the doors — was covered up with snow, snow that was whiter and brighter than the stars. The New York I was seeing had been completely changed from the New York I had seen just the day before. I could scarcely believe that these two cities were one and the same. Beautiful, broad streets like Madison Avenue and Fifth Avenue were filled with snow and seemed to have become quite narrow. Maybe its only purpose was to make it snow harder, who knows, but that day a tremendous wind was blowing, and the mercury in the thermometer dropped to four degrees. The cold was like everything I have been saying. The tap water was just about ready to freeze. That morning at breakfast when the cook gave me a glass of milk to drink as she did every day, I had to chew it like lumps of sugar before I could swallow it. The cold made even the warmth of the fire seem to fade away. The falling snow put a stop to all traffic in the streets. And none of the shops in the city were open. If any unlucky person or animal had been caught out in this terrible snowstorm, there would have been some doubt whether she would have made it home alive. The trams, buggies, and elevated trains that perpetually move about the city were all shut down!

Snow does not make the slightest sound as it falls. It comes down without anyone even being aware of it — as if somebody were to stand and sift fine white flour so that it fell ever so lightly to the ground, never making a sound. When snowflakes come down from the sky, these tiniest of things look as lovely as the delicate white petals of jasmine flowers, dancing and gamboling, flying and falling, swirling and racing, like so many merry pixies. If you catch snowflakes on a piece of dark cloth, you can see that their shapes are very beautiful and strange. But it is impossible to describe to anyone who hasn't seen it for himself how beautiful and startling the ground, the trees, and shrubs, the open fields, the roads, and the housetops look when they are covered up with sparkling white snow. Only a Kalidasa or a Shakespeare or Sarasvatidevi herself[54] would know how to describe a scene this beautiful. For a person as feeble-minded as myself to begin such a description would be the height of folly.

Although snow may fall to the earth looking so white and beautiful and, like a shy woman, not make the slightest sound or commotion to make anyone even aware of its presence, no one who has witnessed its dreadful power will ever forget it. Suppose a snowflake were to fall on the palm of your hand. It looks no bigger than the very smallest lentil, and it isn't even a quarter as thick as the very thinnest petal of a mustard flower. And the instant the snowflake touches your palm it melts away from the heat of your body — so you don't need to move so much as a finger to destroy it. How light and delicate a thing it is! But let these tiniest of flakes fall together as a shower of snow, and it won't take you very long to realize just what these common little ordinary snowflakes when gathered in great numbers can do. And this is how they came to visit a vast deluge on New York City and all the surrounding area. They fell in drifts everywhere in the streets like sand dunes in a desert. They left the superior intellect of the American people, who have made the very deities of fire, water, thunderbolt, and wind their humble servants, stunned and stupefied. They stopped in their tracks the fiery, high-velocity iron horses that pull their trains. They killed man and beast alike along the roads they traveled, falling on them and suffocating them under their weight. They destroyed trains and bridges. And it is impos-

54. Trans.: The goddess of wisdom, learning, eloquence, and literature. — *KG*

sible even to estimate the extent of everything else they did. The deluge of snow within the city was such that there was no way left to get essential commodities like milk or coal. The railway line between New York and Boston was closed down, and even the telegraph poles collapsed and the wires broke so that nobody knew what was happening in these two cities. On Monday, news of this blizzard in New York reached England via telegraph lines under the sea, and from there, using the same roundabout way,[55] returned by telegraph to Boston! Fifty trains that were en route between Boston and New York were stranded on the line for two or three days because their locomotives could not make their way through the snowdrifts on the tracks. Quite a few of these trains derailed and crashed, and many people died. There were lots of people who paid a fare of fifty dollars (approximately 150 rupees) per vehicle to get from Pennsylvania Station to the center of the city. That Wednesday I had a meeting to go to. The venue was maybe a quarter of a mile from where I was lodging; and I had to pay a fare of ten dollars (approximately 30 rupees) to get there. On Thursday when I went and inquired at Grand Central Station, I learned that the railway line to Boston had not yet been cleared. That same day I was supposed to meet the manager of our association for some very urgent work. When I saw that there was no way I could go by train, I tried to find out if there were still boats going around to Boston by sea. But it turned out that even that route was closed so I decided to go back to Philadelphia.

The distance between New York and Philadelphia is a hundred miles, and a fast train takes two-and-a-quarter hours to get there. But from Monday all the way up to Thursday morning that line had also been closed because of the blizzard, and there had been many accidents on it. Our train left New York at 11:00 A.M. but did not reach Philadelphia until 8:00 P.M. The railway track before us and all the surrounding region were covered with snow; and the sunlight falling on it blinded everyone on the train. The train faced many obstacles as it moved onward. Thousands of men were busy shoveling the snow from off the track. Our own train had two large locomotives pulling it; and there were at least thirty other trains, which had been stranded, that passed right in front of us on their way to New York, each one of them with two or three locomotives to pull them. But it was no easy task to pull a train through that vast desert of snow. There were huge drifts on both sides of the railway

55. Trans.: *Drāviḍī prāṇāyāma karūṇa* (literally, "having made a Dravidian *prāṇāyāma*") is the striking idiom Ramabai uses here: "A circuitous or devious mode of speaking or acting. . . . 2 A roundabout way to a place; also a long, tedious and pointless journey . . ." (Molesworth). — *PCE*

line. Sometimes, as the train moved forward pushing the snow from off the track, half of it would disappear into a snowdrift. In some places where the wind had been especially strong, the snowdrifts were piled ten feet high in all the region around, and the houses, farms, and orchards were completely covered by them.

Two or three days after this all took place, following my arrival in Philadelphia, I received a letter from a friend. She wrote to say that this kind of storm is extremely rare in the eastern part of the country and that compared to the snowstorms they get out in the west and in the north the storm we had gone through was nothing! Out there the mercury in the thermometers drops to sixty degrees below zero, and the snow drifts are as much as twenty-five or thirty feet high. In a disastrous situation like that, millions of cattle with no place to take shelter out on the wide open plains in the west find themselves left to the tender mercies of this awful cold and die. Last year and the year before last eighty lakh (8,000,000) cattle died in this way from the cold. My hair stands on end when I try to imagine the horrible suffering these poor animals had to endure. And what is worse, no one can possibly know how many thousands of people and other animals and birds die out there every year from the cold.

We have seen that even though the winter here is very severe, people can profit from it. When the rivers freeze over some people make a business of putting the ice in storage and selling it. You also find millions of both men and women enjoying the sports that are called skating[56] and tobogganing.[57] In quite a few cold regions, especially in Canada, there are perky people who cut big blocks and bricks of ice and build large castles. They make the bricks out of the ice they find at some good site on the banks of a river or a lake and build the walls using water in place of mortar, that is, after placing bricks one on top of the other they pour water over them, and because the water freezes hard from the cold, the ice-brick walls become very strong. They build huge ice castles of this kind and then illuminate them beautifully with lights. Then some people will dress themselves up as the soldiers of two warring parties

56. Skating is a sport in which people put special wooden shoes on their feet called "skates" and go out sliding, with many different maneuvers, on the frozen surface of a river or a lake. Skates have flat, sharp, iron blades attached to them down the center of the sole from the heel to the middle toe. When you put on skates you cannot remain standing in one place. — *PRS*

57. Tobogganing is a sport that came from the original people of America, the Indians. When it has snowed a lot, it is great fun to come sliding down a slope from some high place. This is called a toboggan slide. The toboggan itself is made from wood. It has no wheels, and it looks like a flat-bottomed boat. — *PRS*

and put on a mock battle. They use quite wonderful fireworks in this battle instead of gunpowder and bullets. The display of the lights at night in these ice palaces along with the fireworks is really very beautiful and quite indescribable. Thousands of men, women, and children come, some from distant places, and gather to watch the fun. St. Paul and Montreal are two cities that are famous for their ice palaces.

During the last part of January 1888, I went from Philadelphia to Indianapolis, the capital city of the state of Indiana. This city is twelve or thirteen hundred miles to the west of Philadelphia. The route that takes you there is very beautiful. After leaving Philadelphia you go for hundreds of miles through the Allegheny Mountains. Like the foothills of the Himalayas, the Alleghenies are extremely beautiful and quite grand. They are covered with tall pines, oaks, birches, and many other trees. You see forests and woodlands everywhere in a vigorous condition of natural beauty. The large Susquehanna River follows a serpentine course through the middle of the mountains; and the railway line mostly follows the bank of the river itself — so anyone who travels this route gets to see all the ample beauty of the earth. I myself have traveled this route two or three times. Once it was in winter, and snow had fallen everywhere you looked. So both the Allegheny mountain peaks and their foothills had been turned a dazzling white. Anyone who has looked upon this heart-stirring scene of snow-covered mountains that are whiter than moonlight and that dazzle you in the sunlight surely cannot help but feel that their eyes have found fulfillment.

At the beginning of February I went to visit a girls' school in the village of Farmington, near the city of Hartford, Connecticut. This village is quite far away from the railway line. On this occasion there was no four-wheeled cart or carriage for us to ride in, but there was a special kind of wheel-less vehicle called a sleigh. I climbed in and headed off for Farmington with a friend. When it has snowed the ground is somewhat like the loose sand in a desert, and horses have a hard time pulling any vehicle that has wheels; but pulling a wheel-less sleigh is much easier. Actually, it is great fun to ride in a sleigh. The people here, young and old, are always ready and eager to enjoy a sleigh ride. On the road to Farmington we found everything around us lying deep in snow. It was as if all the surrounding hills, the bushes and trees, and the housetops had settled down to sleep, muffled with a covering of white snow against the cold.

On the whole, the winters here are very pleasant for a healthy person.

National Festivals

The national festivals of the United States are considered to be New Year's Day, Washington's birthday, the anniversary of Christ's death,[58] Decoration Day, Independence Day, Thanksgiving Day, and the anniversary of Christ's birth.[59] On these days all shops, offices, factories, and schools are closed, and everyone gets a holiday. New Year's Day[60] is celebrated on the first day of January. This is an ancient nonreligious festival that the American people have inherited from their ancestors. Easter, i.e., Christ's memorial day *(punyatithi)*, and Christmas are regarded as holy in honor of the founder of Christianity. February 22 is George Washington's birthday. During the last century the American people declared their independence as a nation and severed their ties with England. So of course there was a war between the English and them in which Washington defeated the English and brought victory to his nation. The American people were so grateful for this that they made Washington the first president of their country, and thereafter everyone came to regard him as the Father of the Nation. All the people here honor him on his birthday by celebrating it in whatever way they think best; and speeches are made in public meetings in praise of him. Decoration Day, the day when graves are decorated, will be described later on.[61]

Independence Day comes on the Fourth of July. On July 4, 1776, the thirteen former American colonies became thirteen independent states and declared that they no longer had any connection with English rule. And they did not stop at merely saying that their nation was independent, they *made* themselves independent by fighting a war against a strong country like England and defeating it. The day of this national festival is very important. The people in every city, town, and village in this country celebrate it with great pride. In public assembly halls the greatness of the nation and the success of the country are sung, and patriotic speeches are given. Everywhere you look you see the star-spangled national flag of the United States put out on display.

58. Trans.: *Puṇyatithi,* the anniversary day of a person's death on which the eldest son performs the commemorative *śrāddha* ceremony, is the word Ramabai uses here. Strictly speaking this should be taken to refer to Good Friday, not Easter, but the latter is what Ramabai clearly intends. It is interesting to note that Ramabai refrains from using the common Marathi equivalent for Easter. — *KG*

59. Trans.: *Khristajayantī* is the word Ramabai uses here in the sense of Christmas. Again she refrains from using the common Marathi equivalent. — *PCE*

60. Trans.: *Varṣapratipadā* is the word Ramabai uses even though in Marathi it refers to the first day of the lunar month *Caitra* (March-April). — *PCE*

61. Unfortunately, Ramabai never provides this description. — *REF*

All the public places and markets are decorated with lights, and fireworks are set off. Children have a grand time, what with all the good things they get to eat and the fireworks. It would not be far wrong to say that the Fourth of July is the *Divāḷī* festival[62] of this country. It would seem that everyone in our own country has forgotten the true meaning of Divali. At one time Divali was considered a political festival because on the fourteenth day of the dark half of the lunar month *Kārtika*,[63] Krishna slew the demon king Narakasura and conquered and subdued his kingdom of Pragjyotishpur. Now Divali falls more in the category of a religious festival. Even if Divali were taken as a political festival, there would still be a difference as great as night and day between it and the Fourth of July. On the day of Divali an independent king was killed, and his son and heir was turned into just another vassal king and robbed of his independence. On the Fourth of July a small country resolved not to remain in vassalage to a tyrannical and greedy nation and made itself independent. And it pledged (at least in word if not entirely in deed) to give that independence to anyone who might come to live in this nation.

During my stay in Philadelphia I had a chance to experience all the hustle and bustle of this festival. Several good speakers gave excellent patriotic speeches in that city's Independence Hall, which is the birthplace of the goddess of liberty. Star-spangled flags were waving all around the city. The entrances of large stores and the vestibules of buildings in the major business districts were decorated with red, white, and blue bunting, medallions, swags, and so on. At night everything was lit up, and on the bridge over the Schuylkill River, there was a varied and wonderful display of fireworks. Men and women came from near and far and brought their children with them to watch all the fun from a public park called Fair Mount Park. In that crowd of thousands of people the thing that was most evident was their joy, enthusiasm, and delight.

The festival of Thanksgiving Day comes in the month of November. During this month all the crops are harvested and there is an abundance of grain, vegetables, and fruit. After picking a convenient date in the month of November, the president of the country publishes a proclamation (not a decree!) to the citizens of America: "On such and such a date, celebrate Thanksgiving Day with me and pray, thanking God with utmost humility for the grace he has bestowed

62. Trans.: The biggest and most important Hindu festival, *Divāḷī* (also *dīpāvali*, i.e., a row of lamps) takes place over four days straddling the end of the lunar month *Āśvina* and the beginning of the lunar month *Kārtika* at the end of the harvest season. It is India's "Festival of Lights." — *PCE*

63. Trans.: An apparent slip of Ramabai's pen, this should be the lunar month of *Āśvina*. — *PCE*

upon our country this year and for giving us abundant crops." Then, on the appointed day, all the shops and all the offices are closed. Men and women, old and young, they all go to their temples and churches to worship God. On that day a great deal of charity is given to the poor and needy. For the most part nobody invites guests into their homes to eat with them on these festival days, although sometimes they may invite their friends or relatives over for a meal. The way they celebrate their festivals is for the members of each family to make their own special dishes in their own homes, then to go out and see the public festivities and spend the day in merriment.

There are many other festivals besides these public festivals. The people belonging to different creeds celebrate their own festivals according to their own ideas. Among the Roman Catholics the death and birth anniversaries of their saints are regarded as holy. Millions of Irish people, sick of British oppression, have left their homeland and come to settle in this independent country, and they celebrate the festivals of their own ethnic group *(svajāta)* and their church in a grand way. On the birthday of their patron deity *(kuladeva)* St. Patrick, they raise green banners on their housetops. All the other numerous ethnic groups *(jātī)* that have immigrated from Europe, such as the Germans, the Scandinavians, the Italians, the French, and the Russians, celebrate their own festivals in much the same way.

Just as we prepare delicacies like *lāḍū* and *jilébī*[64] during our festivals, here in the United States they make a great to-do over the preparation of their own kinds of special dishes. One thing, though, is that on their festival days there is a great deal of animal slaughter. In the same way that we grow vegetables in our gardens and on our farms and keep them for special occasions, here the people "cultivate" turkeys and chickens. They regard the flesh of the turkey as very delicious. If they have a guest in their home, they roast one or two whole turkeys and provide their guest with a nice feast.[65]

64. Trans.: These are two kinds of sweets that are typically served on festive occasions. — *KG*

65. About two thousand years ago even the Brahmans in our country were eaters of meat. It was customary for a *śrotriya* Brahman [a Brahman versed in the study of the Vedas and a maintainer of the sacred fire] to slaughter a fat, healthy, young cow or a male or female calf to prepare a feast for a visiting son-in-law or a king. There are verses in the *Manusmṛti* that say that if on the occasion of a death anniversary *(śrāddha)* Brahmans are given fish and other kinds of meat to eat, one's forebears will be gratified for a certain number of years. In northern Hindusthan most of the Brahmans belonging to the *pañcagauḍa* community *(jāta)* slaughter a female or male goat in honor of their guests. Bengali Brahmans eat fish, goats, and other unforbidden kinds of meat. Although animal slaughter has stopped to a large extent in our country, owing to the teaching of the Buddha, many people even today don't hesitate to eat meat if they can get it. — *PRS*

Because the eating of meat is the common practice wherever you go here, there is a vast amount of animal slaughter. In the middle part of the country, to the west of the states of Illinois, Ohio, and Missouri, there are vast plains where there isn't very much human settlement. Some ambitious businessmen out there have set up huge "plantations" and "farms" for the cultivation of cattle and pigs, and they supply this moving, breathing, fresh produce to cities thousands of miles away. These heartless butchers are too caught up in making profits to pay the slightest attention to the weal or woe of their cattle. Millions of cattle out on these plains in the middle of the country suffer horribly and die, panting with thirst out in the scorching sun, being drenched by rain, or freezing in the snow. They are not provided any shelter in which they can lie down or even stand.

In the states of New York and Massachusetts where the principal "Humane Societies"[66] are located, they are working hard, each in their own way, to reduce the cruelty that is inflicted on these animals. From information they have provided, information supported by documented proof, we learn that during the last two years more than eighty lakh (8,000,000) head of cattle died during the winter from the snow and the cold because they were left out in the open on these western plains. I shudder whenever I remember the distressing state of the livestock I saw the summer I was traveling through the states of Iowa and Nebraska. Hundreds of cattle were out grazing on the open plains where there wasn't a tree to be seen anywhere; around two o'clock in the afternoon the sun was terrifically hot and bright, and the poor cattle had been provided no place to lie down in the shade. If there happened to be an occasional pond filled with rainwater, bunches of cattle would go and stand in it. Tiny newborn calves, unable to bear the heat of the sun, would go and lie somewhere beside a fence, poking their heads into the spotty and wholly inadequate shade cast by the two- or three-inch wide horizontal fence rails. Ten or twenty head of cattle might be seen standing around some little bush poking their heads into the bit of shade it cast. Elsewhere, because there was no fence or trees or bushes or ponds, these poor helpless cattle were lying about on the grass showing all the signs of their distress. But when you remember the even worse plight that awaits them, you cannot help but think that their present deprivation is truly a bit of paradise. These hundreds and thousands

66. Trans.: *Bhūtadayecyā maṇḍaḷyā* (literally, "committees of compassion for all animal life") is the phrase Ramabai uses here and in what follows. It is evident from the context that she is referring to branches of the Society for the Prevention of Cruelty to Animals, the first of which (the ASPCA) was established in the state of New York in 1866. As the more generic "Humane Society" is somewhat closer to Ramabai's own usage, we will use it consistently in what follows. — *PCE*

and millions of cattle you see out grazing in the pastures are all destined for one thing: to quench the flame in human stomachs! These pastures are, simply put, the vegetable farms of the American people. Here cattle, sheep, and pigs are bred; and at the appointed time, these moving, breathing vegetables are packed in railway cars and transported thousands of miles away. Sometimes these animals are kept confined without food or water for five or six days. At journey's end they are given a little food to eat — then handed over to the butcher. I have never seen these slaughterhouses, nor do I have any desire to see them. But from the descriptions I have read of them it seems to me they are, in very truth and deed, hells; and the butchers and those who earn their livelihood through this cruel trade must belong to some class *(varga)* of beings that is altogether different from either humans or demons *(rākṣasa)*, i.e., that class of *"ke te na jānīmahe."*[67]

If you take them as a whole, the people of this country are very warm-hearted and kind; but whether because of this carnivorous habit of theirs or who knows what other reason, they seem not to have much concern for the weal or woe of nonhuman animals. I remember reading a beautiful essay a couple of years ago in the magazine called *Bālabodha Mevā*, which is run by the American Marathi Mission in Mumbai.[68] There was an illustration accompanying the essay in which a woman and her children were shown caressing a cow and feeding it handfuls of feed. In the essay itself, the author wrote one particular sentence with a great feeling of pride. What it said in essence was that the people of Hindusthan treat cattle and other animals with great cruelty whereas in America they treat them with much affection. There is certainly some truth to this, but it is a truth that won't find substantiation everywhere. It is true that in our country the poor bullocks and horses have to suffer a great deal, but it simply is not the case that nobody shows them affection. In our villages and even in some places in our cities, in those families that keep milking cows in their homes, the women and children show as much affection toward their cows and calves as they do toward members of their own family. The cruelty that merchants, milkmen, and butchers inflict

67. Who they are we do not know. — *PRS*

Trans.: The quotation is from Bhartrihari, *Nītiśataka*, verse 46 in some editions. Our grateful acknowledgements to Gudrun Buhnemann for identifying the quotation. — *PCE*

68. Trans.: *Bālabodha Mevā* (Fruit for a Child's Understanding) was established in 1872, as the first magazine in Marathi designed specifically for children, by the American Marathi Mission. This was one of the first overseas missions commissioned by the Congregationalist American Board of Commissioners for Foreign Missions. It began its work in Mumbai in 1813 and over the course of the nineteenth century remained the flagship Protestant mission in the Bombay Presidency. — *PCE*

on cows is certainly bad — and everyone must strive to eradicate it. But to say that this sort of cruelty does not exist in America is quite simply not true. At least no one who has seen the plight of the horses belonging to the cruel cartmen in the city markets and industrial towns here is going to believe that the practice of being cruel to animals is absent in America.

Twenty-five years ago, a kind-hearted gentleman from New York by the name of Henry Bergh[69] began to espouse the cause of dumb animals. Nobody could begin to describe the cruelty with which people treated dumb animals in those days. When Henry Bergh began to speak out on behalf of animals, almost everyone ridiculed him. Some said he was insane. Some devout people said, "This heretic contradicts Scripture, which clearly says that God gave man authority over all animals and that therefore they have been created solely for the benefit of man." With scriptural authority such as this, what more did they need? And everyone began to persecute this advocate of the cause of animals, Henry Bergh. Hundreds of times as he was walking about in the streets of New York people hit him with stones and advanced their own opinions by throwing garbage, mud, and worse at him. But Henry Bergh was a man of extraordinary integrity and determination. Although he had to overcome thousands of obstacles, he did not give up the humane task he had taken upon himself. After years of hard work, he was able to see a law passed that prohibited cruelty to animals.

There came a time one evening when it seemed as if the city of New York suddenly woke up. Five hundred cabs that were traveling about the streets of New York were stopped and the horses that were harnessed to them were examined. All the horses that were sick, lame, or extremely weak were untied and taken away without so much as a by-your-leave to the owners. After this everyone came to know who Henry Bergh was; and they also knew that owners no longer had the right to mistreat dumb animals in any way they pleased. Henry Bergh's labors bore this fruit. Recently public opinion has swung very much in favor of animals. The humane society of Massachusetts is working very diligently for this cause. Although George T. Angell,[70] the president of this organization, is quite an old man, he labors night and day for the welfare of animals. As a result of his labors and those of many other good-hearted men and women, humane societies have been established in all the

69. Trans.: Henry Bergh (b. 1813) founded the American Society for the Prevention of Cruelty to Animals (ASPCA) in New York in 1866. This was the first humane organization in the Western Hemisphere. — *PCE*

70. Trans.: George T. Angell (d. 1909) founded the Massachusetts Society for the Prevention of Cruelty to Animals (MSPCA) in Boston in 1868. In 1890 he published the first American edition of Anna Sewell's humane classic, *Black Beauty.* — *PCE*

major cities of the country. Many laws have been passed prohibiting cruelty to animals and birds. In order to spread humane feeling among children, "Bands of Mercy" have been established. More than six thousand of these groups have been created so far, and at present the work of the humane societies is being carried forward through their hands. We have a dire need of such groups in our own country. It is essential to teach children right from childhood the meaning of benevolent action, humaneness, and the proper way in which to use all things.

Although good-hearted people have been working everywhere in this way for the welfare of animals, there is still much cruelty being inflicted on nonhuman creatures. Fashion-crazy women sacrifice countless beautiful birds every year to decorate their hats. You find plenty of people in this country who point to scriptural authority when they say, "If animals and birds were created for the benefit of man, then why shouldn't we use them in any way we want?" It is evident that people simply don't understand what a chicken suffers when after being purchased in the market it is brought alive to be cooked at home, with its legs tied together with a string and held upside down by its feet with its head dangling. One day I was standing in the street in Philadelphia waiting for a ride when I saw a boy of thirteen or fourteen standing some distance away holding a live chicken by its feet with its head dangling toward the ground. I went up to him and said, "Brother, why don't you hold the chicken with its head up?" He smiled a bit and said, "It's more convenient to carry them by their feet." "Oh, is that so? I don't think you would be so happy if somebody carried you around by your feet with your head hanging down. Am I right or am I wrong?" The boy laughed when he heard this, and to humor me he held the chicken with its head up for a few moments. That evening when I told this story at the place where I was lodging, one young woman teacher said, "It is simply our custom to carry a chicken upside down, and that is the right way to do it." But I remained slightly skeptical about this. After all, we have never bothered to ask chickens their opinion about whether it is right or wrong to carry them around hanging upside down. (It goes without saying, of course, that in our own country we have the same cruel practice of hanging chickens and other animals upside down.)

Sometimes, instead of hanging pictures on the walls of their dining rooms, the people here have stuffed peacocks or stuffed pigeons hanging upside down on display. They also have the practice of painting and displaying on their walls pictures of freshly caught fish hung from a hook and all covered with blood, of rabbits killed in the hunt, and of other such things. It should not have to be said that this is not a good custom. It is through seeing cruel pictures like these that children's minds are rendered cruel.

Sometimes children's sports, and those that adults also play, are extremely cruel. Beautiful young women, tender children, young men, and even educated gentlemen of middle age go fishing as an entertainment. They tie a length of line to a long thin rod; then they attach pieces of meat to the iron hook at the other end of the line, and they lower this into the water. When the poor, hungry fish come along hoping to eat the meat, they swallow the hook along with the meat, the hook gets stuck in their throats, and they lose their lives. "Oh, look!" these heartless people then say, "I've got a fish on my line!" And they pull the fish out of the water and feast their eyes on its death agonies. When you see these practices of theirs, you can't help but feel that it would be a very good thing indeed if the compassionate missionaries of the Lord Buddha were to come here and turn their hearts around![71]

The American people have many forms of entertainment. They are for the most part an extremely industrious and hardworking people so it is only right that they should entertain themselves a bit when their work is done. A sport called lawn tennis is very popular with women and men in this country. This sport provides good exercise for them during winter and spring. Men play a game called baseball; they also wrestle and row boats. Women also sometimes row boats during the summer. In winter it is a common practice to go out skating on frozen rivers and lakes. It is also customary for men and women to sing and dance together during festivals and holidays. It is an altogether excellent thing that men and women should take delight in the priceless, God-given gift of music; but the way they have here of dancing is not a good thing. They have theaters everywhere in the cities and even in the small

71. Hindusthan and America are on opposites sides of the earth, so it is only natural for the American people to imagine that we walk around upside down, i.e., with our heads down and our feet up — and for us to imagine, in exactly the same way, that the American people walk around upside down. *Mutatis mutandis,* the way we have of being humane in our country is the exact opposite of the way the American people have. They inflict pain on nonhuman creatures, while we make asylums for them, establish cow-refuges, with the greatest of compassion give bedbugs, lice, mosquitoes, and ants human blood to sustain them, feed the snake with milk and worship it — but we think nothing of human life. If somebody dies in a neighboring house, we lock ourselves in our own house. When there is an outbreak of cholera or some other disease and our neighbors are hard hit, we find it difficult to see to their wants and needs. Our women die of various diseases, but unless and until the English take us to task, we do not open hospitals for them. We regard the cow as equal to our own mother and fall at her feet, but we beat our wives, the mothers of our children, almost to the point of death. Our princes and rajahs spend hundreds of thousands of rupees in hosting feasts for children of the English, who are already well fed and happy, and for English officials; but it does not occur to them to open orphanages for poor orphan children and industrial schools for the benefit of the poor of our country! Compared to the American people, we truly do have a greater store of humaneness! — *PRS*

towns. People are crazy about going to see plays. From time to time they also hold music concerts in concert halls, where everything is superbly ordered and arranged; and many respectable men and women go and listen to vocal and instrumental music. In the evening or at other leisure times, they go, young and old, man and woman, to public parks to enjoy the fresh air. Although it is true that the American people have a passion for going to see plays and other games and sports, they do not fritter away their money and their time in doing nothing but going to plays — unlike so many idle people in our own country. When their work is done and it is time for rest and relaxation, they engage in sports and games for entertainment; and when it is time to work, they work their fingers to the bone.

CHAPTER 6

The Pursuit of Learning

China has the most ancient system of self-rule *(svarājya)* of all the states in the five continents of Asia, Europe, Africa, America, and Australia. It has survived for four thousand years right up to the present day. Ancient kingdoms such as Egypt, Greece, Rome, and Hindusthan have all been destroyed. Some of them are even now being trampled under the feet of foreign enemies; some have quietly submitted themselves to powerful foreign states; and of some no sign remains except their names. But China is still independent, and it still governs itself. Even though it occasionally must bend its head before a powerful Western enemy, it possesses the strength to uplift both itself and its subjects and to empower itself to compete with the Western countries — and indeed it is reforming itself in such a way. Let the Americans, the English, and the other European people disrespect, mock, or show contempt for the Chinese people as much as they want — but the fact is they remain afraid of them. By any current measure, China has no reason to fear foreign invasion. It is quite clear that if China now institutes some changes that are consistent with the new times and the new conditions of life and strengthens itself as a nation from within, it will not be injured by the perils attacking her from outside.

What could explain why this nation has attained such strength, stability, and importance? The Chinese people's guru, *Confucius,* said, "Where there is learning, there can no longer be any social discrimination *(jātibheda)*." In accordance with this teaching of his, the Chinese people never believed in the superiority of any one special social group *(jāta)* but believed rather that the real reasons for a person's superiority are his learning and his good morals; and instead of placing the administration of the state into the hands of noblemen and particular social groups *(jātī)*, they established the practice of giving the proper degree of authority to any particular person in accordance with the degree of his learning and the excellence of his behavior. Consequently, even a Chinese man born into a poor, unknown, and humble family has the hope of climbing to a position of great worth on the strength of his learning and his moral uprightness. Learning has the highest priority among Chinese men. Even ordinary day laborers can read and write. The man who cannot read and write is very rare. Why wouldn't that country be strong in which the administration of the state has been founded upon learning in this manner? It is hardly surprising that a country whose citizens forever go diligently about their work and business, do not coddle lazy beggars, and have a love of learning should continue to govern itself. It would be surprising indeed if this were not the case.

A scholar by the name of Plutarch has said, "The beautiful building of law and justice built by Numa[1] collapsed because it was not built on the foundation of learning." What other reason could there be for the retrogression of a state in which all other things were good? What more compelling reason could there be for its ruin and fall than that its polity did not have the support of a firm foundation of learning? You would have to call it quite marvelous indeed if a nation was not destroyed where only a very few people are educated — and people belonging to one or two select social groups *(jātī)* at that — and where all the rest of the thousands and millions of inhabitants are enveloped by the darkness of ignorance and have no room even to hope to attain a higher position.

As in China, the political leaders and moral teachers of the United States have realized the importance of education. They know full well that unless all the citizens of the nation know at least how to read and write, their self-rule *(svarājya)* cannot last. And recently, what is more, they have begun to understand how essential it is that education be made accessible to women as well. In this respect they have surpassed China. Gradually all nations, including China, will realize how important women's education is. The strength of the United States lies not in its standing army, its cannons, and its swords, but in the love of learning and the industriousness of its citizens.

Ever since the people of the Puritan sect, seeing that they were not able to practice their religion freely in their own country, crossed the Atlantic Ocean and came to settle in America, they have understood that their children had to have an education, and they established schools for them accordingly. Martin

1. Trans.: Numa Pompilius, the legendary second king and lawgiver of Rome (715-672 BCE), was the subject (along with Lycurgus) of one of Plutarch's *Parallel Lives*. — *PCE*

Luther first tried to free Christians from their slavery to the Roman Catholic priests; and ever since that time the idea of how necessary it is for common people to receive a certain amount of education has started to be accepted in Europe. Luther understood that the reason the false priests could deceive millions of naive people and bind them with the chains of false doctrine was ignorance. So he translated the Bible into a language everybody understood and preached that everybody should read it and practice their faith independently and thoughtfully. Speaking from the belief that a teacher's place was more important than a preacher's, Luther said, "Had I not been a preacher, I would have certainly become a teacher." In order to practice religion with true independence of thought, people must have the power to read the Scriptures; and in order to conduct themselves lawfully, they must have the power to understand the whys and wherefores of the laws of their country.

A few years after the Puritans settled in America, they made it their policy that every village in their colony that had fifty or more families should have one teacher for every fifty families. They passed a law requiring the teacher to teach all the children and the servants of these families to read and write and requiring the townspeople to provide the teacher the means to live on. Some years later the settlers in the other colonies, following the example set by the people of Massachusetts, made similar laws in their own colonies. In 1665 the people of Massachusetts established free schools everywhere in their state and made it mandatory for all the residents there to send their children and dependents to study in those schools. The same kind of laws were made later on in the other colonies of New England. But the situation in the southern state of Virginia was very different. There they had neither free schools nor printing presses. The lack of learning among the populace — and likewise in the other southern states — had terrible consequences, as history has made abundantly clear.

Although the public system of education[2] in the United States is a governmental function, it has no connection with the federal government. The responsibility belongs to each of the state governments to provide education to its own citizens and their children; and in whatever way is most convenient, it establishes schools, higher institutions of learning, and such, and bears their expenses. Hence, all the states and territories have their own separate systems of education. Of the thirty-eight states, twenty-eight have large

2. Trans.: *Vidyākhātem̦*, the term Ramabai introduces here and uses consistently throughout the rest of the chapter, would normally be translated "education department"; but given the decentralized "system of education" she proceeds to describe, we have chosen the latter phrase as, in this context, the less awkward translation equivalent. — *PCE*

training colleges for teachers — for a total of ninety-eight altogether. The male and female teachers who are trained in them teach the children in all the nation's schools, public or private.[3] Realizing how necessary it was that its citizens and their children receive an education and that the responsibility for bearing the cost of education should belong to the government, the government of the United States, at the very founding of this democratic nation, passed laws that encouraged education. In 1785 — that is, as soon as their war with England to gain independence was over — the Continental Congress of the United States made it mandatory for each state to set aside one-sixteenth of its public lands to provide for the costs of its system of education. In 1848 the nation's Congress passed a new bill that allotted 68,000,000 additional acres of public land to the then twenty-seven states to give further encouragement to education. And this is not even to mention the vast tracts of public land the government has allotted for the establishment of the numerous state universities. In 1862 a great deal more land was allotted for the establishment of agricultural and industrial schools in all the states. The total amount of land given by the federal government to the states and territories up to 1886 for the use of their systems of education was 78,000,000 acres — which is greater than the total area of the three countries of England, Scotland, and Ireland combined.

Germany is foremost among all the nations of Europe in providing education to its people. They spend 103,500,000 rupees every year there on education. The United Kingdom is a close second to Germany. Their annual expenditure for education is about 100,275,000 rupees. The government of the United States spends anywhere from 279,000,000 to 288,000,000 rupees annually to educate its citizens. The annual expenditure of the Department of the Army of this same government is on the average 141,000,000 rupees. It is reported that the Department of the Army of the United Kingdom requires an annual expenditure of 433,500,000 rupees. We can see from this that the British government spends three times as much for the army of the United Kingdom as the government of the United States spends for its army, and that the government of the United States spends two-and-a-half to two-and-three-quarters times as much to educate its people as the government of Great Britain does. The only reason for such a night and day difference is that the very life of the monarchies of Europe resides in their armies, whereas the strength and life breath of the democracy of the United States resides in edu-

3. Trans.: The words Ramabai consistently uses throughout this chapter — translated consistently here as "public" and "private" — are *sarkārī* (governmental) and *svatantra* (independent), the first from Persian and the second from Sanskrit. — *PCE*

cation. There is only one nation in the entire world that spends more on its system of education than on its department of war — and that is none other than this democratic nation.

It is forbidden to teach religion — i.e., the particular tenets of various religious denominations — in public schools. Every morning before the start of the school day, the headmaster or headmistress of the school reads a small portion from the Bible but does not make either comment or commentary on it. This practice is approved by one and all. Except for the strictest followers of the Roman Catholic Church *(pantha)*, all the rest of the people expect that their own children and the rest of the common people should receive an education. The Roman Catholic priests have been afraid of education right from the beginning because they knew full well that educated people would not accept their teaching blindly. But even the ordinary Roman Catholics of the United States have recently begun to show their support for education, and even they send their children to the public schools — and there nobody bothers them about their beliefs. Although the Roman Catholic pope issued edicts to his disciples ordering them not to accept this kind of secular public education, these edicts are proving futile. When a plate filled with the ambrosial delicacies of learning is set before a hungry man and somebody tells him, "Don't eat a single one of them," how will these words by themselves persuade the hungry man?

I have already reported above that the government of the United States spends its own money to provide education to its people; but this government is a democratically elected governing body and the money it has to spend in this task comes from the taxes received from its citizens. In our own country, which is under British rule, the subjects also pay taxes to support the cost of the education department *(vidyākhātem̩)*. But not only does the government not consult its subjects' opinions about how this money is spent, it collects the taxes that are levied from its subjects and then turns around and also charges them a monthly fee *(gurudakṣiṇā)* for educating their children. In 1880 four-fifths of the cost of the public system of education in the United States was paid by tax revenues and the remaining one-fifth was paid by the money received from the sale or rental of lands connected to the schools. The citizens of the United States gladly pay the taxes required to support the cost of their system of education. It is abundantly clear from this just how great their love of learning is.

Apart from the public schools there are also thousands of superior schools[4] that are mostly independent and have been privately founded. They

4. Trans.: *Variṣtha śāḷā* (alternating with *variṣṭha vidyālaya*) is Ramabai's ambiguous us-

are financed by fees collected from their pupils and by donations from generous people. Quite a number of them also receive some aid from the government. Because most of the superior schools have been authorized by the government, their managing boards are able to award appropriate degrees to their own students. There is a great deal of disparity in the ranking of these superior schools. The kind of school that is given the name of "university" in one place falls into the category of a superior school in another place. Many schools, such as Harvard, Columbia, Cornell, Princeton, Michigan, and Oberlin, call themselves superior-level universities. Other universities do not have the same rank they do. Apart from the primary-level public schools in this country, there are 3,550 superior-level schools, colleges,[5] and universities, in which about 500,000 students are studying. Of these schools 364 are superior colleges and universities, in which the total number of male and female students is 59,594.

We learn from the last census that in 1880 to 1881 there were 180,750 public and private schools in the United States, in which there were as many as 273,000 actively teaching. Out of this total 154,375 were women! (Detailed information about women's educational attainments in this country is given in the chapter "The Condition of Women.") The war-fighting army of the United States numbers no more than twenty-five or thirty thousand; but this army of teachers, which battles ignorance and which toils night and day to overcome it, numbers about 275,000; so how could the fortunes of this country do anything but flourish? It can come as no surprise then that the nation whose glory and the people *(jāta)* whose independence this vast army stands perpetually ready to defend should, out of all the nations of the earth, sparkle like the very finest gem.

When I arrived in Philadelphia at the beginning of 1886 I intended to stay in America only for two or three months. But when, as circumstances would have it, I went to see the public schools in that city, I was so delighted by what I saw of their management, their manner of teaching, the competence of their teachers, and so on, that I decided to stay in this country somewhat longer and learn about their system of education and their method of instruction. And this is how it came about that I stayed here. Over the course of the past two years and nine months, wherever I have had to go I have made it a point to visit their primary and superior schools and learn about their

---

age here and throughout the next two or three paragraphs. The way in which she uses the terms seems to include — without much if any distinction between them — both secondary and post-secondary institutions of learning. — *PCE*

5. Trans.: Although *vidyālayeṃ* (literally "schools") is the term used here, it appears from the context that Ramabai must mean "colleges." — *PCE*

methods of instruction. The mode of higher education in the large countries of Europe, such as Germany and England, may be extremely good, but it would not be wrong to say that in the field of general public education the United States ranks the highest.

I think that on the whole American teachers are excellent. The women teachers here are for the most part modest, humble, self-restrained, diligent, firm but affectionate, and capable of maintaining excellent order and discipline in the schools. They are proud of their position and of their schools, and they strive night and day to enhance the standing of their schools. They believe that there is far more honor in gaining their students' love, in giving them a superior education, and in earning their parents' respect than in making their students fear them and forcing them to show respect. Ever since women first entered the profession of teaching, the practice of giving harsh punishments to children has come to an end in most of the schools here. Educated women are able to get children to do superior work and to be obedient without beating them. The women teachers of this country know absolutely nothing of such cruel punishments as "riding the mare,"[6] the "restraining stick,"[7] beatings with a cane, repeated standing up and sitting down, pinching, twisting ears, slapping, and the "chair."[8] In a few places where I went to see a school, I had occasion to see a stubborn child or two being punished. Their punishment was, generally speaking, nothing more than to remain sitting silently on a tall chair for a quarter of an hour or half an hour. The worst punishment is to make a child stand in a corner for some length of time. The method the teachers use of teaching the lessons is so exemplary and so interesting that the children become very enthusiastic about learning. I had occasion to hear many children exclaiming, "When will vacation be over and school begin?" So it isn't so surprising that the children should think it a terrible punishment to be made to stop learning their lessons — when their teachers make their instruction so interesting for the students — and to go sit in some prominent spot with their arms and legs folded and nothing to do. Almost all naughty children will come around if only out of the simple fear that they will have to stop learning one of their lessons and have to sit somewhere with nothing to do while all the other children in the school point their

6. Trans.: *Ghoḍīvara deṇeṃ* (literally, "to give on the mare"): the *ghoḍī* in this case was "the loop or cord from which offending schoolboys are suspended by the hands" (Molesworth). — *PCE*

7. Trans.: *Koladāṇḍī:* "A stick or bar fastened to the neck of a surly dog. 2 A mode of intervolving the arms and legs, and thus pinning them by driving in a long stick: — as in securing criminals" (Molesworth). — *PCE*

8. Trans.: *Khuracī:* no description is to be found in the standard references. — *PCE*

fingers at them and have a quiet laugh at their expense. But it should not be forgotten either that even in America there are some churlish teachers and some incorrigible students!

In ordinary primary schools they teach all the following subjects: writing, reading, English grammar, the history of the United States, arithmetic, geography, the drawing of maps and pictures, sewing, physical exercise, and hygiene. In some places, depending on the teachers' discretion, they also teach some science subjects. The subjects that are taught in their superior schools are the same as the subjects taught in our own English-medium high schools and colleges.[9] But here they have none of the kind of rote learning we have in our own country. In women's schools, in addition to these subjects, they commonly teach vocal and instrumental music, needlework, calligraphy, and other useful things.

In public primary schools, girls and boys study together in one place. The same rule applies in most of their superior schools as well; but in some places they do have separate schools for girls and boys. In the best universities it is also becoming the established practice to offer the same instruction to men and women together. Women study alongside men at Oberlin, Michigan, Cornell, and many other universities; and this not only produces great benefits for the students, it also fosters the spread of moral conduct within society. Ever since women were first admitted to the schools where previously only men were taught, the student bodies have been demonstrating increasing modesty, and every kind of indecent conduct has either disappeared or is in the process of disappearing. After many years of experience in this matter, the principal teachers, leading scholars, and presidents of the major schools in this country have by now expressed themselves as in favor of women students. The presidents and professors of schools such as Michigan, Cornell, and Oberlin are promoters of this idea. In 1884, while writing his historical account of the Hawaiian Islands, General Armstrong,[10] the famous president of the excellent industrial school, Hampton Institute, said,

> The only way to strengthen those who are morally weak is constantly to keep testing them — in the same way you would make re-

9. Trans.: Here Ramabai borrows, in transliterated form, the English words "high schools" and "colleges." "English-medium" schools are elite schools in India, as opposed to those that use the vernacular language. — *PCE*

10. Trans.: Samuel Chapman Armstrong (1839-1893), born in Hawaii, was commissioned colonel of a black regiment of the Union Army during the Civil War; in 1868 he founded the Hampton Normal and Agricultural Institute (now Hampton Institute) for the education of African Americans. — *PCE*

peated trial of any object under favorable conditions. It is essential to eliminate the prejudices that people of two different communities *(jātī)* carry in their minds about their relations with each other, to replace them with proper understandings, and to teach them proper ways and habits. And that can be done not merely by telling them things in theory and by preaching to them. Only if you teach them by practical demonstration will it be of any use. If two social groups *(jātī)* — men and women, say — are kept away from each other and later on the occasion arises where they have to interact with one another, they won't be very adept at it. Doing that is like keeping a child away from water and trying to teach him how to swim. If anybody can claim to have actual experience that, in spite of the very best arrangements, it is morally questionable to teach boys and girls of one community *(jāta)* together in one school, it would be better for them to give up all hope of any progress for that community and to believe that it is the predetermined fate of this community to fall into immorality and to perish. It is certainly true that in order to teach men and women together it is essential to have morally upright and excellent teachers and expensive school buildings; but if our object is to see that some particular human community *(jāta)* survives by growing strong in body, mind, and morals, it is possible to achieve this only by combining the practice of civility, religion, and interrelationships modeled on that of family members toward one another — and by no other means. The one place where women and men receive equal rights and equal opportunities to show their individual worth is the coeducational school; and that is the place which provides a superior way for them to make each other's acquaintance and to recognize each other's worth. Our experience at Hampton has offered us occasion to think deeply about the many different kinds of relations that pertain between up-and-coming young men and women; and with every passing day we think it to be a better thing that men and women should be educated together in one place, interacting with one another as if belonging to one morally upright family.

Some years ago only men used to be on the managing boards of both public and private schools; but now, in some few institutions, women and men of understanding and foresight have made well-educated women the managers and superintendents — after coming to the realization that in the task of educating children, women have the greatest usefulness; that indeed it is the mothers of children who have a far greater concern for such things as whether their children are receiving a moral education, whether it is the kind it ought to be or not, whether the teachers are morally upright or not, and so on. And these women superintendents are bringing about great improvements in the system of education. It does begin to appear that this understanding is everywhere gaining strength and will soon start to be fully implemented: that is, if women are allowed to work as full equals to men in the system of education — as in all other fields — and if they are allowed to express their opinions about how things should best be organized, every single field will be improved, and the entire country will benefit. May the good Lord bring this to pass. Because it should be obvious that the welfare of the country does not lie in having one wheel of the societal cart going in one direction and the other wheel going off God only knows where — but in having both wheels going together in one and the same direction. It is quite simply mistaken to think that it is only men who are sufficiently wise in all matters and that it is only men who have a superior knowledge of all things.

Some years ago the people of one of the tribes *(jātī)* of the original inhabitants of America called the Conestogas — with whom the *Mahātmā* William Penn made a treaty of friendship that was to last as long as the sun and moon shall last — used to appoint women as well as men as their representatives to speak in council. The English men of that time found this practice very surprising. When they asked the Conestogas, "Why do you allow women to speak in public meetings?" the Conestogas replied, "Some women are wiser than some men." This truth that an "uncivilized" tribe *(rānaṭī jāta)* two or three hundred years ago understood as plainly as the sun at noonday[11] has only now just barely begun to be understood by the Americans, a tribe *(jāta)* that is the brightest ornament of civilization. But the Americans have still to realize the full importance of this truth. The reason that day by day the system of education here, and so many other things, are showing improvement and attaining excellence is largely that night and day educated, disciplined women are making the most strenuous efforts with the most heartfelt concern to bring about improvements in these fields. Impartial, farsighted men in this country are supporters of this view.

The number of white inhabitants of this country who do not know at least how to read and write is very small. Ninety-three percent of men and

11. Trans.: *Karatalāmalakavat* (literally, "as plain as a myrobalan in the palm of the hand"): "used of anything on which, from the clearness and cogency of the evidence it bears, dispute seems impossible. Corresponding to 'Like the sun at noonday'" (Molesworth). A myrobalan is the prunelike fruit of certain tropical plants used in tanning and dyeing. — *PCE*

eighty-nine percent of women can read and write. That the number of literate women is slightly lower than the number of men is certainly not because their intellect or their brains are inferior but because it has not yet been sixty years since they were given access to even an ordinary education, and it has not yet been even thirty-six years since they could enter higher education; whereas education has been available to men for hundreds of years even before this nation was founded. In such a short time (within fifty or sixty years) and even though they had to endure numerous hardships and struggled against popular sentiment and thousands of obstacles, women have reached the stage in education where they are on a level with men. It is quite clear from this just how solid and genuine their virtues — their mental acuity, their patient industriousness, and their immovable courage — are. By 1870, 175 schools had been established to provide women a secondary[12] and higher education. This rose to 227 in 1880; and in the past eight years hundreds of superior schools have been established for women. It is easy to see from this just how enthusiastic women are about learning when given the chance. Who can ever calculate how much brilliance and maturity this fine growth in women's education brings and will continue to bring to this democratic nation of the United States?

What follows are some details about the people who were studying in the various branches of knowledge in the schools here as of 1880. Out of the entire population of this country, one person in 5 was going to school to get a primary or general education. One in every 455 was receiving a secondary-level education.[13] Out of every 842 people, one was receiving a higher education in a college or university.[14] Out of every 1,848 people, one was being educated in business and commerce. Out of every 4,321 people, one was receiving an education in science. One in every 9,568 was being taught theology. And one in every 16,001 was being educated in law. From this it is abundantly clear what a passion the American people have for education and how firmly rooted in their minds is the understanding that the advancement (or the reversal) of their country will be commensurate with the regard they have for education!

For some years past numerous farsighted men and women have understood that education does not consist solely of making children literate — but

12. Trans.: *Madhyama* (literally "middle") is the word Ramabai uses here, in clear distinction to *variṣṭha* ("superior" or "higher"). — *PCE*

13. Trans.: *Dusryā pratīceṃ śikṣaṇa* (literally "second-level education") is the phrase Ramabai uses here. — *PCE*

14. Trans.: Once again Ramabai borrows, in transliterated form, the English words "college" and "university." — *PCE*

that for students to realize the full fruits of their education they must be given occupational training along with their book learning, and that only then will the millions of rupees spent in the field of education and the labor of hundreds of thousands of people be fruitful; and they have accordingly begun to provide occupational training in ordinary schools. The great erudite professors of Germany were of the same opinion. According to Froebel, the famous teacher and creator of the educational method called "kindergarten," a person should receive an education from earliest childhood, and this should be of such a kind that his hands, feet, intellect, sight, hearing, and speech — that is to say his entire body and mind — will all be equally brought into play and will all grow strong in equal measure. As soon as an infant begins to recognize objects, his parents should pay attention to encouraging good character and good habits and, as they are talking and playing with him, to teaching both his body and his mind. Only if a person receives such a superior all-around education right from his earliest childhood will he develop fully. Froebel says that the education of children is altogether dependent upon their mothers. As long as their mothers do not receive an education and moral instruction, it is vain to hope that their children will develop in a normal, balanced, and comely way.

The people in this country call the famous Miss Elizabeth Peabody,[15] a highly honored and elderly woman from the state of Massachusetts, the "mother of child education." This saintly lady endured countless hardships, struggled against numerous obstacles and unfavorable public opinion, and worked patiently for many years to propagate Froebel's kindergarten method of education in this country. About two years ago I met this lady. She is now almost eighty-six years old and is physically quite feeble. Although old age may have made her body infirm, her mind and her intellect are still young. Her face brightens whenever she talks about education. She told me about her own experience as a child. Her mother was a highly virtuous, thoughtful, and loving woman. She educated her daughter for the most part at home. It is all due to the grace of her loving mother that Elizabeth has risen today to such eminence and is counted among the principal people who built the edifice of education in this country. While she was talking about her mother, old Peabody*bāī*'s face blossomed with happiness, and for a moment her old age was forgotten and she looked as pretty as a child again! When Elizabeth turned fifteen or sixteen and was obliged to earn her own livelihood, she began by teaching children.

15. Trans.: Elizabeth Palmer Peabody (1804-1894) was a Unitarian and a prominent member of the transcendental movement in nineteenth-century Boston. In 1860 she opened the first kindergarten in the United States. — *PCE*

Later on, after a few years of saving up her money, she made a particular study of education, then went to Europe where she learned about their excellent methods of education. After going to Germany and studying Froebel's method, she became convinced that this method was most suitable for instilling the best habits and character in children from their earliest years and, based on these, for establishing a firm foundation for their morals, their general education, and their overall development. Without these things empty book learning by itself can have no real benefit. After she returned to her own country she lectured on this subject in hundreds of places. She taught thousands of women the kindergarten method, and she herself taught children in this way. Now all her labors are reaching fruition; and how it gladdens our hearts that she has the satisfaction of seeing during her own lifetime the people of her own country being able to enjoy the immortal fruit of her labors. There are very few people in this world, indeed, who have the great good fortune of being allowed to see their labors reach fruition.

The kindergarten method has been introduced in the public education systems of renowned seats of learning[16] such as St. Louis, Philadelphia, and Boston. And it appears that very soon it will also be introduced in other cities. It has been twelve years now since this method was adopted in St. Louis, and their public schools are superior now to all the rest of the public schools in this country. The national conference of teachers that met in Chicago in 1887 and in San Francisco this year (i.e., 1888) organized an exhibition of things made by schoolchildren, such as school workbooks, pictures, and maps, in which the schools of St. Louis won first place and a trophy. Everyone realized from this that the Froebel method is a superior one and that it provides a good foundation for all branches of learning. Although this method has not spread in public schools to the same extent it has in private schools, it is safe to conclude that it soon will.

Following in Miss Peabody's footsteps, teachers such as Professor Adler[17] and Colonel Parker[18] have begun to corroborate the importance of providing occupational training along with book learning. Dr. Adler has es-

16. Trans.: *Vidyāpīṭha* (literally, "seat of learning") has more recently assumed the sense of "university"; but in this context the original sense seems to be the intended one. — *PCE*

17. Trans.: Felix Adler (1851-1933) was a German-born American educator and the founder, in 1876, of the New York Society for Ethical Culture. He was professor of political and social ethics at Columbia from 1902 to 1918. — *PCE*

18. Trans.: Francis Wayland Parker (1837-1902), a student of Froebel's method in Germany in the 1870s, was an American leader of progressive education who served as superintendent of schools in Quincy, Massachusetts; in Boston; and in Cook County, Illinois. In 1899 he founded the Chicago Institute, which became the University of Chicago's school of education. — *PCE*

tablished an excellent school in the city of New York where children receive both kinds of education, and what is more they enjoy this a great deal. Colonel Parker, who is the principal of the Cook County Normal School near Chicago, teaches thousands of men and women teachers how children should be given occupational training. His method is most praiseworthy.

The occupational training that I have mentioned here should not be mistaken for vocational training in the trades such as carpentry and blacksmithing. Many private and public schools have been established to teach these kinds of trades. What I mean by occupational training is different: at the same time that children are being taught to read and write, it is important to teach them how to work with their hands, to draw pictures or mold clay models freehand of various figures from merely looking at them, to use various tools and implements, and much, much more, all in order to strengthen the muscles of their arms and legs along with their brains. Not only are children's muscles strengthened by doing this but they also have fun; moreover, because it helps to establish what kind of learning they are most interested in, it is easier to know the proper place to send them for the field of studies or the trade they want to enter. This sort of education is very helpful in establishing which child is slow in mathematics but might perhaps excel in learning to be an artist or an artisan, which child can't draw but might perhaps be able to read fine books, and so on. In cities such as Boston, Philadelphia, New York, Chicago, and St. Louis, independent schools have been established to provide this sort of education. There is a very large school in a town in the state of Massachusetts called Quincy where the superior educational method they use truly does help children, large or small, to acquire practical knowledge along with book learning and to develop a taste for hard work. This method has come to be known as the "Quincy Method."

In the town of Hampton, Virginia, an agricultural school has been established through the efforts of General Armstrong, in which boys and girls from the tribes *(jātī)* of uncivilized *(rānaṭī)* Indians and of the half-civilized *(arddhavaṭa rānaṭī)* Negroes just recently emancipated from slavery receive occupational training along with their book learning. It is true that the Hampton school is an "agricultural" school, but it also offers instruction in other useful trades. The children who have been educated there leave behind them their uncivilized *(rānaṭī)* condition and, as if reborn, become well-mannered and industrious — and they are prepared to go out and live in any kind of polite society. This goes to show just how great the combined power of book learning accompanied by occupational training is.

It simply is not true that going to school for some years in and of itself is sufficient to make children adept in the business of life. Their school education merely points them in the direction of their future responsibilities. In the same way that the very first elementary school lessons make it possible for a student to read and write and thereby open the door to all the treasures of knowledge for, say, a student of philosophy, a school education is the means for opening the door to every kind of practical and scientific knowledge. But these gems of knowledge, which a person must remain diligently engaged in finding even after he has passed through that door, can be obtained only through a great variety of different agencies, among which two of the principal ones are the reading of newspapers and the careful study of both modern and ancient books. Just as the people here are provided with the means for receiving a school education, they have also been provided with numerous means, even after they leave school, for obtaining wide-ranging and useful knowledge through the reading of books.

As soon as the Puritans settled here they established the universal practice of reading newspapers. They were by nature politically inclined, and they had a strong urge to learn about affairs of state and all the latest things. Later on, at the time the government was changed here, the men and women and even the children of New England would wait expectantly to learn about the events that were taking place in their country: who had won or who had lost a battle, who said what in the Continental Congress in Philadelphia, and so on. At first they had handwritten newspapers in this country; then somewhat later they began to have printed journals. In a democratic nation — a nation in which every person has the firm conviction *that this nation belongs to him*, that he has the closest connection with both the nation's welfare and its losses, and that he has a hand in making both the current laws of the nation and all such new things as make the nation prosper — it is altogether fitting that the people should have the strongest desire to know what is happening in their nation and then to decide what their duty is accordingly. There is no more excellent means for them to learn these essential things than the newspapers.

This country has never had a "Press Act" — that is, a law prohibiting people from openly expressing their opinions in the newspapers — such as they have under the Tsar of Russia or in Hindusthan under the rule of sahibs like Lord Lytton.[19] And as long as there is a democracy here, they will never have this kind of prohibition here. If not the people themselves, who should express their opinions openly about those things that are most closely con-

19. Trans.: Lord Lytton, Governor-General and Viceroy of India from 1876-1880, presided over the enactment of the highly unpopular and repressive "Vernacular Press Act" of 1878. — *PCE*

nected to the weal and woe of the people? It is only those who coerce a show of respect from the people, those who seek to fill their own begging bowls by stamping their feet on the bellies of their subjects, who feel any necessity for detestable laws like the Press Act. In this country anyone and everyone can express their opinions openly. If President Cleveland should feel that he ought to cancel the tariffs on imported goods but a street-sweeper or a shoemaker does not like this, he does not fear to correct the president, and he does not hesitate to point out his faults just because Mr. Cleveland happens to be the president! Wherever you look, in every home, in every street, in shops, in lanes and alleys, in the mansions of the rich and in the hovels of the poor, you see people holding newspapers in their hands — large or little, dailies, weeklies, bi-weeklies, or monthlies. If a coachman has to park his carriage and wait for somebody, he immediately pulls a newspaper from his pocket and starts to read it. Women cooks, women laborers, laundrymen, tailors, street-sweepers, coal-sellers, chimney sweeps, and more — all the people read newspapers in their spare time. Morning or evening, when people come home for breakfast or dinner, they hold a newspaper in one hand and read it while they are eating. Something happens, be it in the morning or in the evening, three thousand miles away; and by means of the telegraph news of it goes from one coast of this vast country to the other, is immediately printed in the newspapers, and within twelve or fifteen hours all the people are able to read about it. It is hard to find a town or a village here that doesn't have some sort of local newspaper. The price of these newspapers is also extremely modest, ranging from one *paisā* to two *āṇās*.[20] The total number of newspapers and magazines published in this country in 1880 was 11,314, out of which, as I have learned, four-fifths published stories of political, social, and practical import, and one-fifth were monthly or weekly papers related to commerce and business and various branches of science. In the eight years since then, hundreds of additional newspapers and magazines must have emerged.

It is worth bearing in mind that out of these more than 11,000 papers, 10,515 newspapers and magazines are published in English. In order to keep the country united and to make it possible for the people from one area of the country to understand the thoughts of the people from another area, it is quite necessary to have unity of language. The French, Scandinavians, Spanish, Dutch, Italians, Welsh, Bohemians, Polish, Portuguese, and all the other European ethnic groups *(jātī)* that immigrate to this country speak their own

20. Trans.: In the old monetary system in India there were sixteen *āṇās* ("annas") to a rupee and six *paisās* to an *āṇā*. So this would translate respectively to less than a penny and to about a nickel in the American currency of that time. — *PCE*

languages within their own families and publish altogether about a thousand papers in their own languages. But they have to interact almost everywhere with people who speak English. In the public schools they teach only English, the political administration is conducted in English, and the work of business and commerce, accounting, and everything else has to be done in English; so they cannot get along without learning English. And when you hear nothing but this language being spoken everywhere, it doesn't take a lot of effort to learn it. There are approximately ten crore (100,000,000) people, settled in all parts of the world, who are English by birth and who speak English as their native language. Extrapolating from this, people who take particular pride in this language have begun to say that English will become the language of all the people of the world. It is impossible to say how true this will turn out to be; but it certainly is true that the growth and spread of this language is something quite amazing.

Now why should not our own people give this matter some thought? When our Indian National Congress[21] meets in Calcutta, Madras, Mumbai, or the Panjab, the people who come from one region of Hindusthan do not understand the language of speakers who come from another region. So they hammer away at their grand speeches in English — and what use can these speeches possibly have for common, ordinary people? To eliminate all the languages of our country and to replace them with English would be tantamount to sinking the land of Hindusthan in the sea and placing the English Isles in its place. If our most learned, intelligent, and thoughtful people really are trying to raise up their own country and their own race *(svajāta)*, how can it be that they haven't realized the necessity of having one language that everyone in their country understands — and that is, what is more, a *native* language? What if English has become by now the language of ten crore (100,000,000) people? There is a language of the same rank in our own land. Hindi is understood by almost all the people of Hindusthan. Be it Braj or Mathuri, Avadhi, Panjabi, or Madhya Deshi, they are all dialects of Hindi; and the small differences among them are as minor as the differences between the Marathi spoken in Pune and the Marathi spoken on the Konkan coast or up on the plateau of the Desh. When you include all the dialects mentioned above, Hindi is at the present time the mother tongue of ten or twelve crore (120,000,000) of the people of Hindusthan. The language of our neighbors,

21. Trans.: *Rāṣṭrīya sabhā* is the Marathi equivalent Ramabai uses for the Indian National Congress, which had just been established in 1885 as the organizational vehicle for India's budding nationalist movement and which had convened its first annual meeting that same year in Mumbai. — *PCE*

the Gujaratis, is half-Hindi and half-Marathi. So what would be so difficult about making a great language like Hindi our national language? When the Muslims were in power, they made Urdu the common language of all public interaction; and Urdu is not a separate language in itself; it contains in it a mixture of words from other languages, half from Hindi and the rest from Arabic, Persian, Marathi, Kannada, and so on. Now, it doesn't take much effort to learn Hindi either. Just as in English, all the languages of the world can be included in Hindi, so there is no real obstacle to its growth. And Hindi grammar is very easy. Words from Arabic, Persian, Sanskrit, English, and even *Rākṣasi*[22] can be taken into Hindi and be given the forms of Hindi. When such a priceless and beautiful language is available to us and when it would be so easy to make it the national language, will our most learned brothers take a moment to explain why they use English, a language that has come from beyond the seven seas and that is as incomprehensible to ordinary people as Egyptian hieroglyphics, to conduct their discussions of public issues? If our national and public assemblies take this matter seriously, all farsighted well-wishers of our country will strive each in their own way to spread the use of Hindi, from Kanyakumari to the Himalayas and from the junction of the Indus and the sea in the west to the borders of Manipur in the east. This will come as a great incentive to both journalists and writers of books. When Madrasi brothers meet Panjabi brothers, they will have no difficulty talking to each other. And how many languages do you suppose there are in this world that cannot be written in our own Devanagari — known also as the "child-simple"[23] — script? The sounds needed for all the languages in our nation are present already in this script. So even if we take words from all these languages and make a true *koḍaboḷeṃ*[24] of eighteen different kinds of grain out of Hindi, it will still be able to be written in Devanagari characters. It is my humble request that during its next meeting our Indian National Congress give this matter due consideration.

I certainly don't mean to suggest that all newspapers in the United States are good and that all the subject matter appearing in them is the best. Wherever people have the freedom to express their opinions in public, there will be a blend of both the good and the bad. But if anyone investigates this matter carefully, they will see that it is the good that predominates. The whole

22. Trans.: The rude and corrupted Sanskrit given to the demon and fiend characters in mythological plays. — *KG*

23. Trans.: *Bālabodha:* "Teachable or explainable to children, i.e. simple" (Molesworth). — *PCE*

24. Trans.: A treat made out of a paste of mixed pulses that is shaped like a coil and fried. — *KG*

object of newspaper publishing, which is to educate ordinary people in an easy and inexpensive way about subjects of religious, practical, and scientific interest, has been achieved here. The biggest and most influential newspaper publishers are not satisfied by reporting only those matters that relate to their own country. The owner of the paper called *The New York Herald* provided enough money and other assistance to make possible the travels of the famous explorer Henry Stanley, who explored many different regions of the distant and unknown continent of Africa and won immortal fame for himself. Since that time many other newspaper publishers have also sent their reporters to many faraway lands to explore new things and have put the entire world in their debt.

American magazines such as *Century* and *Harper's Magazine* actually surpass all the European magazines when it comes to such things as their abundance of subject matter, their depth of coverage, their illustrations, and their quality of printing. It is said that Austria has the finest quality of printing in all of Europe; but it was the owners of the finest printing presses in Austria who commended the owner of the American magazine *Century* for the excellent quality of his printing and of his illustrations and who requested him to teach them the techniques for achieving such quality in printing. The articles that appear in magazines like *Century* are extremely good. The owners of these magazines pay their writers a hundred or two hundred dollars or even more — i.e., three hundred to six hundred rupees — per article. It costs hundreds of rupees just to create one of the etchings needed to print the excellent illustrations that appear in them. So it is clear that capital worth hundreds of thousands of rupees is needed to run such monthly and weekly magazines. But even after bearing such enormous costs, the owners still make huge profits; and if you ask why, the reason quite simply is public patronage. The number of people who buy a magazine like *Century* is not less than one or one-and-a-quarter lakhs (125,000).[25] The actual printing is done with the

25. Magazines like *Century* are meant for adults; but the people here have a great concern for the proper development of young children. A famous magazine like *St. Nicholas Magazine* is published just for children. Its publisher, Mrs. Mary Mapes Dodge, is a fine scholar and through her sharpness and skill is keeping abreast with the most eminent and learned journalists of this country. It is said that even in England there is no magazine as handsome, well-illustrated, entertaining, of such excellent quality, that makes the mysteries of science so accessible to children as *St. Nicholas Magazine.* There are many other popular magazines besides it that are being published just for children, such as *Harper's Young People* and *Youth's Companion.* All of them have more than one lakh (100,000) subscribers each. And here the subscribers make sure to send in their subscriptions in a timely way. A certain hardworking person has calculated that the amount of paper used annually to publish newspapers and magazines here is around one lakh

aid of steam power. At the beginning of each month these magazines are ready for sale in every city in the United States and in all the big cities of Europe. When you travel anywhere in trains or public carriages, there are always newspaper boys who bring these magazines and the local newspapers around for sale. There are hundreds of thousands of people who buy the newspapers that come out every day in a city like New York — such is the level of public patronage for them here. The reasons for this abundant public support are that there is a commonly shared language, almost everyone can read and write, and everyone has the greatest concern for their country. It is not surprising that the publishers of books and newspapers are highly motivated and that they fulfill their duties zealously; nor is it surprising that people everywhere appreciate the solid quality of their work and that the people give them such generous patronage. But in order for all these things to happen, it is necessary first that people have freedom of thought and the courage to express their opinions — and that they have pride in their country alive and well in their hearts.

Just as is the case with newspapers, new books are being published here all the time. Older English books, books written by modern writers, translations of the best books in foreign languages, and so on, are constantly coming out in a great variety of editions. And they are not priced beyond the capacity of people to buy them. The same book is published in several different editions, some very expensive and some cheap, some large in size, some small, and some of medium size. This allows all different kinds of people, from the very poorest to millionaires, to read these books. Nor is this limited only to smaller books. Even enormous tomes such as the *Encyclopaedia Britannica* are printed and sold at very reasonable prices given their size. The *Encyclopaedia Britannica* is the largest encyclopedia in the world. It is very costly in England, but in America it is available for 200 or 225 rupees. As a result, many editions of it have been published here, and fifty or sixty thousand copies of it have been sold. According to one knowledgeable gentleman, four times as many copies of the *Encyclopaedia Britannica* have been sold in America as in England. A publisher with the name of Appleton has edited and published the *American Encyclopedia,* which also costs somewhat more than 200 rupees. Around one lakh (100,000) copies of it have been sold.

The books that are written and published first in England are sold in America — and the books from here are sold in England — at reduced prices.

---

seven thousand (107,000) tons — i.e., twenty-nine lakh ninety-six thousand (2,996,000) maunds [an obsolete measure approximately one thirtieth of a ton]. In the United Kingdom of Great Britain 94,000 tons of paper are required for the same purpose. — *PRS*

The reason for this is that the books registered with the government of each country are like so many wares thrown onto the streets of the other country. As yet these two governments have not signed a treaty to respect the rights of their respective authors in each other's countries and to protect their property from being stolen. As a consequence, the publishers in both England and America are going around filling their begging bowls by brazenly stealing their neighbor's printed goods in broad daylight. Ethical people in both these countries are agitating against this kind of daylight robbery, but the booksellers of neither of these countries show any inclination toward legal regulation of their trade.

The authors here are not dependent on royal patronage for the recognition of their books. The patronage of the public here is greater than even a thousand royal patrons. Books are given recognition according to the worth of their authors. These people are voracious readers of books. Every year $90,000,000 — which, based on the current price of silver, is about 270,000,000 rupees — are spent here on nothing more than the purchase of books and newspapers. Every family, large or small, has some books, whether a few or a lot depending on what they can afford. Even ordinary coachmen, farmers, and laborers have collections of books in their homes. In the homes of middle-class people and wealthy people there is invariably at least a small library of books. There is moreover a profusion of public reading rooms and libraries everywhere. If you go out of your way to search out a village that does not have at least a tiny public library, you may be just lucky enough to find it.[26] As for the big cities, they have many very large libraries. The men and women who value learning are always working with the greatest zeal and concern to improve the libraries of their own towns. They take the greatest pride in thinking that their town, just like their country, is the very best place in the whole world. I understand that at the present, just within the schools in the United States, there are 23,000 libraries that hold 45,000,000 volumes altogether. Besides this there are another 3,500,000 volumes in institutions of higher learning. And this is not to mention the tens of millions of books in such enormous libraries as the Philadelphia Library, the Boston City Library, the Astor Library, and the Library of Congress. It is said that the number of books in these libraries exceeds 50,000,000. It hardly needs to be said that the number of men and women who borrow books from these libraries is also very large. Not that everyone everywhere reads only the best books written about the most impor-

26. *Auṣadhāpurteṃ koṭheṃ sāmpaḍaleṃ tara sāmpaḍela:* "You just might find enough somewhere to serve as medicine — i.e., the minutest amount." See V. V. Bhide, ed., *Marāṭhī bhāṣece vākpracāra va mhaṇī* (Pune: Chitrashala Prakashan, 1959 [1918]), p. 109. — *PCE*

tant subjects. People read good books or bad books depending on their level of education and their own tastes. Those who must spend their days doing hard work or else who yawn away the time with nothing much to do have an inordinate fondness for novels — and this sometimes even assumes the character of a real vice. There are also those who adorn their intellects with gems from the treasury of knowledge by reading books of the best or of middling quality. Many people also go to great lengths to prevent the publication of bad and obscene books or articles; and their efforts are even succeeding to a large extent.

As a whole, the American people have a great fondness for education; and as long as the sun of knowledge — although sometimes it appears only after having been covered over by clouds of ignorance or of injurious knowledge — showers its bright rays in every direction within the United States and continues the work of destroying the darkness of ignorance, we need have no fear that the minds and bodies of its people will ever be brought under subjugation.

CHAPTER 7

Religious Creeds and Charity

In England the religious creed called the "Church of England" and the authority of the Crown have become inseparable. The king or queen of England must belong to that creed, and their subjects must bear the cost of supporting the priests[1] of that creed. Whether what they believe is in agreement with this aforementioned creed or not, the government squeezes the taxes out of them and enriches the priests and the acolytes of "The Church." It is certainly very strange that in an advanced country like England the people are forced to make such a show of respect. It is even said that the bishops and other priests of the English church who have gone out to our land to perform the duties of state-appointed priests receive large salaries from the treasury of Hindusthan. What the truth of the matter is I do not know. If it *is* true, then this too is a very strange thing.

In the United States there is no shared identity between its democratic polity and any particular religious creed. So the people here all follow whatever religious creed seems right to each one of them, and they willingly and gladly give money to support the cost of the clergy, the churches,[2] and so on

1. Trans.: *Mahanta* (as in the present case), *purohita, upādhyāya, upādhyā, ācārya,* and *dharmādhikārī* are all terms that Ramabai uses quite interchangeably throughout this chapter in the sense of "priest" or "clergyman." Except where "priest" is clearly indicated by the context (as in the present case), we have opted in the translation consistently to use "clergyman" or "clergy" throughout this chapter. — *PCE*

2. Trans.: For "church" Ramabai uses, in the present case and elsewhere throughout the chapter, *deūḷa* (literally "temple"), as well as the words (used quite interchangeably with *deūḷa*) *mandīra, bhajanālaya, bhajanamandīra, īśvaraprārthanāmandīra,* or simply "church"

of those creeds. The government does not collect a separate tax from them in the name of a Department of Religion; and yet the practice of religion isn't the slightest bit less prevalent here than it is in England. Only the creed of the "English church" is honored and respected in England for the reason that it alone has royal sanction. People who profess this creed look down upon those belonging to other creeds as "Dissenters" — i.e., as belonging to an opposing creed. In the independent states of America, by popular custom nobody privileges one creed more and one creed less, because here it is simply out of the question that any one particular creed would be specially chosen as fit for royal favor.

Many people in England say that if the government does not organize religion, the people will all become irreligious. But this belief of theirs is obviously false because, while there are only 144 churches for every 100,000 people in England, in the United States there are 181 churches for the same number of people. From this we can see how clearly untrue it is that in the United States, where religion is not supported by the government, the religious disposition *(dharmabuddhi)* of the people is in any way inferior.

In 1880 there were 92,000 churches in the United States. Somewhat more than 80,000 of these had been built by followers of the Protestant creed, and the rest belonged to those of the Roman Catholic persuasion *(pantha)*. The total fixed and liquid assets of all these churches taken together comes to $350,000,000, which is wealth of approximately one billion *(abja)* rupees or more. There are altogether 77,000 clergymen belonging to all the different creeds. A hundred or a hundred and fifty years ago there were terrible differences in this country over the question of beliefs. The Puritans of Massachusetts used to treat the followers of other creeds with the greatest malice. They badly persecuted a large number of the followers of the Quaker creed. They accused many women of other creeds of being witches and burnt them alive at the stake. Some people they hanged, some they put in prison, some they beat like cattle in the streets with whips, and some they banished after confiscating their property. In 1705 the rulers of the state of Virginia passed a law that anyone who did not profess to believe that there are three persons in one God existing in perfect unity and that the Bible is composed by God should be punished with three years in prison; and that if he denied these things again, he should be subject to numerous obstacles to public employment and such.

In the latter part of the eighteenth century, when the American people were busy severing their political ties to England and becoming independent,

---

in transliteration *(carca)*. In the translation we have opted consistently to use the word "church." — *PCE*

they put these differences of belief aside and established unity among themselves. Fearing that if they did not act with one accord on this occasion, their country would go on bearing the stamp of the British monarchy and of "The Church," the American people cast behind them all differences over matters of belief, united themselves, rallied against England, and won their independence. Even now, for the same reason, they set aside their conflicts over matters of belief and act in unity — and they certainly will continue to do so in the future.

Not that there is no prejudice with regard to what people believe in this country. But everyone here has the same freedom of thought concerning religion, so they maintain active relations with one another without inquiring about or arguing too much over one another's beliefs. That is why the number of examples you will find in this country of people belonging to opposing religious creeds but remaining friends in daily life is far greater than you will find in England. When there is a meeting somewhere dedicated to religious concerns, its members will even invite their friends who hold opposing beliefs. Out of consideration for their friendship these friends cannot then decline the invitation. In this way people of opposing beliefs mingle together socially, and as a matter of course they get the chance to understand one another's beliefs; and the antipathy toward people who hold opposing beliefs, which is born solely out of ignorance, to a very large extent disappears. This is a matter of the greatest importance — and worthy of everyone's closest attention. One of the major reasons for hostility and quarrels between human beings is ignorance about each other. Another reason is the habit of always finding fault. Here the people have to a large extent begun to let go of the habit of finding fault with the beliefs of the many different people who belong to their country and who belong to their religion.

Almost all of the people in the United States are Christians, of which there are two principal creeds, Roman Catholic and Protestant — and within these, numerous sub-creeds as well. Although there are differences of belief among them, there is no fundamental difference in the religion they espouse. These differences of belief do not stand in the way of anything that concerns the welfare of the country.[3] In one and the same family you can find the hus-

3. The people of our own country should certainly give this matter some thought. Even though the creeds and the religions we espouse as a people are all so different, it is possible — it is essential — that we should unite ourselves in working for the welfare of our country and for the welfare of our people. Even if we hold to the notion that by following some particular religion or creed we will go in the afterlife to a most select and special place while our neighbors who belong to opposing creeds and to different religions will go to a very different place, let this notion be restricted to the afterlife alone. In this present life at least, we have no choice but to

band and the wife or the children and their parents holding different religious beliefs, but this in no way diminishes the natural love they have for each other.

From the founding of the United States as a nation up to the present day, no religious creed of any kind has been granted special patronage by the national government — nor will it ever be. The government has the same degree of connection to religious creeds (and no more) that it does to medicine, agriculture, or general commerce and business. But if outsiders seek to interfere in the religious beliefs of some person or of some community *(samāja)* and if that person or that community suffers from this, the government will intervene even in a religious matter to prevent this from happening. Similarly, if a particular religion's teachings stand in violation of the nation's laws, the government will not allow people to practice these teachings. The Mormon church *(pantha)*, for example, teaches (among other things) that one man should be married to several wives at the same time. This is a violation of the national laws of the United States so the federal government has decided not to allow this or one or two similar teachings to be practiced.

Within the creed in England called the "English Church," it is the custom that a priest buy and sell the office he holds. It is common knowledge that people there sell commissions in the army and in quite a number of other fields in the very same way. This auctioning off of church offices is most harmful both to the country and to the religious disposition of the people. Whoever pays the highest price gets the office — no matter how worthy or unworthy the man who wins the auction may be. When a large benefice is put up for sale, some wealthy man buys it, appoints a couple of priests under his control, and then sits back and enjoys life. It wouldn't be wrong to say that this is very much like the highhandedness of the temples and monasteries in our own country. Because of this practice there are many unworthy priests in the parishes of England. By this I do not mean to say that all the priests there are like that. My point is only that there are people there who practice the

---

live together in one country and upon one earth. And at least within the limits of this present life, we have not had occasion to experience that God's excellent gifts — of sunshine, rain, wind, earth, and so much more — are enjoyed only by us and not by the people of other creeds. When we can clearly see that the mercy God bestows upon us he bestows in no smaller measure upon our brothers and sisters who follow other religions and creeds, why should we not act with affection, civility, and love toward them? Why should we not unite ourselves in working for the welfare of the country and of the people? Hindu, Muslim, Christian, Shaiva, Vaishnava, *Gāṇapatya*, Shia and Sunni, Episcopalian, Presbyterian, Methodist, Unitarian, Trinitarian, and polytheist — all must put aside their bigotry over creeds, unite themselves, and render service to the country. — *PRS*

priesthood after buying it at auction. If the people who live in a village should by some chance get a good religious teacher *(dharmopadeśaka)*, they must be considered highly fortunate!

In America the offices of the clergy are not bought and sold in this way. Here the clergy are chosen by popular vote. As a consequence, the clergy for the most part are elected only when they are seen to be learned, responsible men of good conduct. By this it should not be understood that every last clergyman here is a paragon of all virtues. If the people feel that a clergyman is bad, they dismiss him. Because the clergy here are learned and good and decent, people take a special interest in religion. The management of the churches here, like the management of everything else in the country, runs smoothly. Every place of worship has a managing board that conducts all the business of the church. Go anywhere in the United States and observe how they conduct any of their business — people are appointed to their positions by democratic vote. There is no difference when it comes to making religious appointments.

Another calamitous thing in England is that every church there gets a great deal of its income from landed property — that is to say, the land that is leased out in the name of the church is handed over to people to be put to productive use. Then let the tenant commit whatever sins he will on that consecrated land, all that matters is that revenue is produced for the church. There are numerous liquor distilleries and taverns on these lands. How astonishing it is that the money which is to be used for people's salvation should be obtained through the killing of people! Here in America the land attached to churches is very small. Some years ago even in this country they had the practice just as in England of renting out space in their churches to anyone who wanted it. In one Methodist church people used to worship God upstairs while in the basement of the same church space was rented out for the purpose of storing liquor. Another very strange thing was that during the days of the slave trade in this country people were not ashamed to use money acquired through the sale of slaves for such worthy things as church expenses and propagating their faith. They firmly believed that God had created the black people of Africa for them to make use of just as they pleased like so many cattle — so what could be so wrong about using the money obtained through their sale for religious purposes? The three upper castes[4] in our own country — not just the Brahmans — also believed that God created the peo-

4. Trans.: *Varṇa* (lit. "color") is the word Ramabai uses here, invoking the classical Hindu *caturvarṇavyavasthā* ("four-caste system"), of which the three upper ("twice-born") *varṇas* are *brāhmaṇa, kṣatrīya,* and *vaiśya.* — *PCE*

ple of the Shudra caste *(śudra jāta)* for the sole purpose of serving them and, what is more, that the very act of serving them — and this alone — was the Shudras' means of salvation *(muktisādhana)*. When people exist in an uncivilized *(rānaṭī)* state, they hold evil beliefs such as these. To make people serve you until their dying breath and then not only to give them nothing for their labor but to hold that you are doing them a great favor by letting them serve you and are thereby opening the path of salvation to them — if this isn't barbarism *(rānaṭīpaṇā)*, then what is it? In the same way exactly, the horrible demonic practice of selling human blood and using the proceeds to cover the costs of the work of preaching your religion for the salvation of other people is nothing if not barbaric *(rānaṭī)*. It is a matter of great joy that as of now these practices have been stopped in the United States.

Here in America the expense of supporting clergymen — just as the other church expenses — is covered by the people's charitable giving.[5] In churches having congregations of at least five hundred people, the clergyman receives an average of two hundred dollars a month in salary. Besides this, those who are appointed to look after the upkeep of the church also have to be paid a considerable salary. It also costs a lot for the chairs, benches, lamps, mats, carpets, and so on that are used in the church building. (The churches here are always very well appointed.) To meet all these expenses the people who attend each church make voluntary contributions. Every Sunday morning and evening when the worship service is over, it is the custom for men appointed by the managing board of the church to bring small flat plates around to the people who have come to church and for them to put money in those plates, each according to his ability, to be used for the work of the church. They have another method of raising money that I must describe here even though I do not like it. The pews and chairs closest to the front of the church are rented. They are reserved for whoever pays the rent for them. That this sort of business dealing should be conducted in the Lord's house of prayer and that it should be the rich who are thus allowed to hear the sermon at their greater convenience is quite simply wrong. The churches make a good deal of money this way. It would not be far wrong to say that this belongs to the same category as the absurd belief at Gaya and our other pilgrimage places *(kṣetreṃ)* that the ancestors of anyone who pays more money to the attending priest will be promoted to a higher position. It should not be taken for granted that those who buy their seats and sit at the front of the church

5. Trans.: *Dānadharma:* "A comprehensive term for charitable acts and works" (Molesworth). This or simply *dāna* ("gift") is used through the rest of this chapter for "charity." *Dharma* is the concept that comes closest to the English term "religion." — *PCE*

are all devout. There are plenty of hypocrites among those who spend their money to sit up front. Going to church every Sunday with your children and the rest of the household is thought to be a sign of good breeding — that is, of true decorum. So there are plenty of people who go to church even though they have no love for God *(bhakti)* in their hearts. There are also lots of people here who do charity solely to make a name for themselves. Although they do not receive lengthy titles of honor from the government for making major charitable donations — in the manner they do at the behest of the government in our country, in the form of the G.C.S.I., the C.S.I., the C.I.E., and so on — they do get a lot of publicity through the newspapers.

Even given all these measures church expenses are not likely to be completely met. So the women here come up with a variety of ways to collect large amounts of money to support the cost of religious works. Two-thirds of the people who go to church are women. More than half the money needed for church expenses is received from these women. In my opinion it is a matter of considerable doubt that these religious congregations could function without women. Men do not have as great a concern as women do for the preacher's[6] maintenance. When the women in our country go to hear a recitation of the Puranas[7] or to worship at the temple *(devadarśana)*, they never go empty-handed. They offer money, a betelnut, a flower, a piece of fruit, or at least a handful of rice to the *purāṇīka.* (When men go to the temple they usually satisfy themselves with just ringing the bell with an empty hand.) And yet, even though virtually all the priests *(bhaṭa)* and *purāṇīka*s are maintained in this way through the charity of women, the pious Vedanta-espousing *purāṇīka*s are forever telling the people, "Women are inherently wicked. Whatever there is of wickedness in Creation, that has been put by the Creator into the creation of women. They are the fetters about the feet of men; they are the reason for the ruination of religion; those men who wish to attain salvation *(muktī)* should not look upon their faces; they should not have the right to study the scriptures; they should not read the *Vedas;* they should not preach; if there is one specific reason for the ruination of men in this world, it is women." This really has to be called the absolute height of gratitude thus shown in the conduct and in the preaching of these *purāṇīka*s! Previously the men in this country had the very same kind of evil and strange ideas about

6. Trans.: The word Ramabai uses here is *purānīka:* literally, "A Brahmin well read in the Puranas. 2 A public expounder of them" (Molesworth). — *KG*

7. Trans.: *Purāṇa:* "A [category of] sacred and poetical text. There are eighteen. They comprise the whole body of Hindu theology. Each should treat of five topics especially[:] the creation, the destruction and the renovation of worlds, the genealogy of gods and heroes, the reigns of the Manus, and the transactions of their descendants" (Molesworth). — *PCE*

women. They used to say that women should never be allowed to preach. Quite a number of people even went to the extent of believing that women should not even sing the litany. Although this idea has not yet completely disappeared, its force has greatly diminished. Of the 77,000 members of the clergy in the United States, 165 are women. Twenty years ago there were not even four or five. In those days they used to consider it a monstrous thing that women should preach.

Just as the Christians in all other countries, these people regard Sunday as a holy day. Business and trade stop virtually everywhere on Sundays. In those states where business doesn't stop on Sundays, there are many devout people who are agitating to have it stopped. On Sunday all government offices, public and private schools, and factories are closed. On this holy day devout men and women go to church, worship God, and listen to sermons. They believe that the propagation of their faith is an intrinsic part of their religion. They invite one and all to come to their churches. Although there is no religious instruction in the schools, most of the people instruct their own children about religion every day in their own homes. They also gather the children together in church, read some verses from the Bible, and give them religious teaching. The schools that meet every Sunday in the churches for the religious instruction of children and adults are called "Sunday schools." The devout people of this country pay a lot of attention also to giving religious instruction to the immigrants who come to this country and to setting them on a righteous path. The committees that propagate their faith in this manner are called "Home Missions." The number of women and men who propagate their faith with heart and mind, laboring night and day, is very large. They believe that a person cannot gain salvation outside the Christian religion so they spend a great deal of money to propagate their faith in foreign lands. Hundreds of men and women from this country have left their homes and families and all their comforts and conveniences and have gone, all for the sake of their faith, to distant places to seek the welfare of the people in foreign lands. About a hundred years ago a few missionaries from America came to our country.[8] At that time the East India Company would not allow them to preach their religion within its domains. In Bengal and in Madras their pleas fell on deaf ears. Many of them had wives who died, and they suffered other terrible misfortunes. They then came to Mumbai, where the government did

8. Trans.: The American Board of Commissioners for Foreign Missions (ABCFM) was founded by the Congregationalists in 1810 as the first foreign missions board in the United States. Its first overseas mission left in 1812 for India and began its work in Mumbai as the American Marathi Mission in 1813. — *PCE*

not want them to stay either. But in the end, out of shame for what people would call them if they expelled from their domains such inoffensive people who had come with the sole purpose of spreading their faith, the English government allowed them to stay in Mumbai.[9] The climate in Mumbai did not agree with them; the government also showed them no favors; and the people who lived there met them with hostility and persecution. In that foreign land there was nobody to provide them protection, and they had left their own land far behind them. The means to travel to and from their own land were also not as plentiful and easily available then as they are now. In spite of all these difficulties, they went on with their work, and at present they have thirty or thirty-five churches in Hindusthan. "Go forth to every part of the world and proclaim the good news to the whole creation" — such is Christ's command. These strenuous efforts of theirs have all been made in obedience to that command.

If anyone were to think that those who provide financial support for this work of propagating their faith are all rich, they would be sorely mistaken. It is the poor who provide the greatest help in this work. The wealthy are not that greatly concerned about religion here. There are zealous ones among them too — but they are very few. In New York there is an enormous theater called the Italian Opera House, which was built by seventy of the wealthiest people there. It cost $9,800,000, and each one of those seventy people contributed $140,000. They spend their money for their own enjoyment. But what support there is for the work of propagating their faith comes from the poor. Although the American people firmly believe that non-Christians will go to eternal hell, they spend a total of only $5,500,000 for the purpose of propagating their faith. In the United States today there are at the very least 10,000,000 people who listen to religious teaching in the churches, and all of them are followers of one or another of the Christian denominations *(sampradāya).* Their wealth is growing every year by about $310,000,000; and one-fifth of this nation's entire wealth, $8,728,400,000 — i.e., 26,185,200,000 rupees — is in their hands. So wealthy as they are, they spend, however, a total of only 16,500,000 rupees annually for the work of propagating their faith. This religious expenditure represents no more than a one hundred fifty-ninth part of their total wealth. That is extraordinarily little when compared to the remarkable wealth of the people of this country; and the portion of this that comes from the poor and especially from poor women is greater than that

9. Trans.: In fact the East India Company had little choice but to grant the ABCFM missionaries permission to stay following the inclusion of the "missionary clause" in the Company's charter as a condition of its renewal by Parliament in July 1813. — *PCE*

which comes from the wealthy. It is the women here who take upon themselves the enormous work of collecting this money. There are 10,000,000 people in this country who drink alcoholic beverages every year to the tune of $900,000,000 — that is, 2,700,000,000 rupees — and who smoke tobacco every year worth 1,470,000,000 rupees. From this it is quite evident that tobacco and liquor have far greater prominence in this country than religion. And what an extremely unfortunate and lamentable matter that is. The prohibitionist and decency societies are working very hard to eliminate both of these vices from this country. May the Lord grant them success and free this fair country from the clutches of the demon of alcohol, the fiend of tobacco, and immorality — such is my prayer to God.

The devout people of our own land give to anyone who cares to ask. Giving to an orphan is certainly only for the good; but the necessity of determining who is worthy and who is not worthy of charity goes unheeded in our land — and as a consequence beggary has spread enormously wherever you look. "To give charity to the unworthy is not only useless — it is accounted as sin," such is the teaching even of our own upright ancestors. But who gives any thought to that? Imagine a fat, immaculate holy man.[10] Somebody gives him money, and what does he do but go right out and buy ganja and smoke it. Not only does he ruin himself by his addiction to ganja, but this vice is passed along to children and to other people as well — because there are a lot of people who pattern their behavior on such saints and sages! And so it is that from charity that is bestowed in this way upon those who are undeserving, laziness and evil vices run rampant in our country, and the country itself reaches a most deplorable state. I have visited a great number of pilgrimage sites, and I have seen the kind of charity that is bestowed in these places. The offerings that are made there to the presiding priests[11] go only to those who do not deserve them. These priests reduce their patrons to beggars. The one who plunders his patron the most by working upon his religious and other fears is given the title "Most Learned of Hierophants"[12] — and he is said to know what's what and to do what's smart.

10. Trans.: *Laṭṭha, nirañjana bairāgī* is Ramabai's sarcastic phrase here. *Nirañjana:* "Void of imperfection, darkness, error" (Molesworth). *Bairāgī:* "An individual of a class of mendicants who renounce the world and practise austerities. They are devotees of *Viṣṇu*" (Molesworth). — *PCE*

11. Trans.: *Paṇḍyā* is Ramabai's term: "A title of Hindustani Brahmans . . . of the *pañcagauḍa* division" (Molesworth). They are retained by pilgrims to perform the rituals at Hindu sacred places. — *KG*

12. Trans.: *Tīrthopādhyāya vidvān* is Ramabai's clearly sarcastic term here: *vidvān* (one deeply learned in the *śāstras*) would be thought an oxymoron in the context of *tīrthopādhyāya* (a high-sounding name for a priest who works a holy place). — *PCE*

The way in which people do their charitable giving here is very different from the way we do it there. Nobody goes about the streets here begging. Public opinion and the nation's laws prohibit begging in public. If somebody comes to the door and begs, they are refused any handouts. Occasionally you will see blind, lame, feeble, or aged people sitting by the roadside selling trifles such as matchboxes, twine, or mirrors. Some pious soul will buy one or two things from them and pay them a little extra. But do not assume that these people are heartless because they do not give to just anyone who begs from them. These people are most careful about giving charity only to the deserving. Whether it be in a village or in a big city, the people collect through voluntary donations the money needed for the care of the orphans, the disabled, and those too feeble to work who live within their own communities; and the small tax, moreover, that the residents of a town are obliged to pay for works of charity, they pay most willingly. This money is given to the charge of a managing committee for charitable works in each community. These committees are called "Boards of Charities." The men and women who manage these boards are elected by a public vote; and they are extremely respectable, honest, and devout — people who do their work attentively and with the greatest of zeal. The regulation of these boards of charity is exactly the same as for all other organizations. Half the money needed for all the charity that is done in this nation comes from people's private giving and half from the government. All of this money is spent exclusively for the sake of those who are truly disabled and unable to earn their own livelihood.

There are many people in our land of the sort who would never even consider moving away from their homes. It is an altogether different matter with the people here. In many instances they go about from town to town in search of business and work. It may happen that, after they go to another town or another region, they are reduced to poverty. There is also a great deal of poverty among the people who come to settle here from Europe. They do not always find work immediately. There are many people of this kind — trapped in poverty, traveling all about the country — and many sorts of beggars too. Where these people stay, what they do, what their conditions are, and so on, are questions being addressed by numerous devoutly religious people here (and even among these, women are a majority). But even though these worthy people do this work out of wholly selfless motives and without pay, occasionally the work is badly organized; but that cannot be avoided. Mistakes are bound to happen no matter what the task may be — whether it be right at the start or after things have progressed some ways. To err is, after all, only human. Anyone who works at doing something will make mistakes. Most of the people in our land will not undertake to do anything on their own initiative; but if somebody else starts something, how ready and eager they are to point out all his faults. The American people don't waste their time like that sitting around finding fault. If they run into disorganization somewhere, they apply remedies to correct it; and they give whole-hearted encouragement to those individuals who do anything for the public good. There are two ways of providing for the poor in this country: first, giving refuge to the destitute — that is, giving food, clothing, and so on to those who do not have them; and second, inquiring into the conditions of those who, even though they do work, do not get adequate food and clothing and then arranging for their needs — that is, inquiring into who is oppressing them, what their own rights are, and so on, and then protecting them from their oppressors.

In our own land the number of beggars has vastly increased because charity is thoughtlessly handed out to holy men who have grown utterly slothful through their complete addiction to the vices of ganja and tobacco and to many others like them who have the strength to work but do not do so. This being the case, we ought not to give charity to such as these — thereby extending an enabling hand to evil vices and pulling sin down on our own heads. Anyone who has even a little extra strength to work will not receive the smallest bit of charity in the United States. One of the fundamental precepts of their creed is, "He who would eat must work." Don't even ask about the extent of the laziness in our country, where just about anybody can sit around being idle and yet get food to eat. All they have to do is rub their bodies with sacred ashes, let their hair grow matted and long, wear beads about their necks, or dress in saffron robes — and the people will treat them as saints and sages and feed them free of charge. Our people consider begging and giving charity to anyone who asks it of them to be an intrinsic part of their religion. If the occasion should arise that allows somebody to enter a good position with a large salary, all kinds of people claiming to be his relations and seeking only for a place to fill their bellies will immediately fill his house. But let him fall on hard times and presto, the very same people will not hesitate to turn on him. Here it is not like that. Everybody works to the extent he is able. Even very young poor boys go around selling newspapers, shouting the headlines of the day. During winter some of them shovel snow from the roads. Even widows who have no one left to whom to turn earn their own keep by working. And their young children work in a variety of ways to be of help to their mothers. Here in the United States, in fact, begging is itself given the character of an occupation. There are people called Gypsies here who, like the *Kaikāḍīs*[13] in our land, make their living by begging — but the Gypsies play

13. Trans.: The *Kaikāḍīs* are a wandering community of basket makers, who were for-

musical instruments and such as a way to entertain people. Many beggars also entertain people with dancing monkeys and some with dancing bears. To provide shelter for old people and children who have nobody to care for them, there are asylums. Even in these homes there are always appropriate kinds of work for these people to do.

There are a great many people with tuberculosis in this country. Although the consumption of liquor and tobacco is among the primary causes of this disease, the people here will not rid themselves of these twin vices! Meanwhile our own people are also picking up these vices with great gusto and growing more and more feeble by the day. What reason could there be but liquor for the delicate state of Raosaheb's[14] health and for everybody having to be told that he cannot be seen because of his aching head! All on account of this one vice there is chaos inside the home, ill-repute outside, and an utter wasting away of money; and all too soon the summons comes and you have to answer to Yamaji Bhaskar[15] himself. And even so, our people are being engulfed by this evil addiction. Blessed indeed is our need to imitate! Here in the United States there are many people who have fallen ill from these twin vices. Some tell you their spleen is ruined, some say they can't digest their food! Some complain about feeling weak. And so it is that the bodies of the many who have become addicted to alcohol and tobacco now shelter any number of diseases — and most especially tuberculosis. Cases such as these are sent off to asylums. Having to go to an asylum here is considered to be a terribly shameful thing. There are lots of people in this country who exclaim, "I would rather die than go to an asylum," and who act accordingly. You meet people here who say they would take a pistol and shoot themselves rather than live as the ward of an asylum. And even the patients in these places are made to do light work (such as watering the potted plants).

Here self-respect can be seen thriving everywhere. They feel from the bottom of their hearts that no one should eat what others have earned. No one in this country would give money to anyone else without a very good reason — nor would anyone accept it. Most people in our land wouldn't even know what manner of thing self-respect and self-pride are. If they get something free from somebody else, they accept it gladly and then turn around and announce that now they have enough to manage for at least another four

---

merly included among the "criminal tribes" — and consequently regarded with much the same kind of attitude as the Gypsies were in Europe and America. — *PCE*

14. Trans.: *Raosaheb* is a title of honor reserved for gentlemen. Here Ramabai uses the title as a term of sarcasm. — *KG*

15. *Yamājībhāskara:* "[One of the] familiar names for Yama, the Minos or Judge of departed spirits." — *PCE*

months! They borrow money, and if they can't repay it, they say they will do so in their next life; but it doesn't worry them in the least that they will have to take a new birth to pay off their old debt!

In the United States the incidence of beggars who come from other countries is very high. One seventh of the inhabitants here are foreigners, but 30 percent of the criminals are foreigners. There are many reasons for this, but the chief one is that because foreigners do not find work quickly, they get involved in dealings that land them in the "rent-free house."[16] There are not that many handicapped people for whom assistance and refuge must be provided by the public, the reason being that unless the people who come and settle in a foreign country are fit and strong, they will not leave their own land in the first place. In the United Kingdom of Great Britain and Ireland, thirty-three people out of every thousand require public assistance. In the United States out of the same number of people only five have to be given public assistance — in other words, one person out of every two hundred or half a person out of every one hundred. It can be rapidly deduced from this how small the incidence of begging is here and how large the degree of employment. I should think the incidence of beggars in our country must be 150 percent! In the United States right now a lot of the people have come from outside, which means that they really and truly have an enormous diversity of social groups *(jātī)* here.[17] There are also a good many settlements of Negroes, whom they used to sell here as slaves. Among the Negroes the number of people who require public assistance, as also of beggars, is extremely small. This is a fine example of how hardworking a people can become once they have gotten the freedom they previously lacked. There is a host of hardworking people among the Negroes; some as lawyers, some as barristers, some as businessmen, some as this, and some as that; they are all devoted to hard work. It has not yet been a full twenty-five years since the emancipation of the slaves, and yet they have come to match other people in every type of work. This is a living, breathing example of just what advantages accrue from people being given their freedom. Those people who favored the slave trade used to argue that as soon as the Negroes were emancipated grievous calamities would befall the land, the country would be destroyed, begging would run rampant, theft and robbery would vastly in-

16. Trans.: *Binabhāḍyācem̩ ghara,* i.e., prison. — *KG*

17. Trans.: *Atharāpagaḍa jātī* (literally, "castes of eighteen turbans") is the idiom Ramabai uses here. V. V. Bhide, in *Marāṭhī bhāṣece vākpracāra va mhaṇī* (Pune: Chitrashala Prakashan, 1959 [1918]), explicates it thus: "The Hindu people's style of tying a turban is different in every caste *(jāta)*. There are as many styles of turban as there are castes *(jātī)*. Hence *aṭharāpagaḍa jātī* means all the castes *(jātī);* the people of all the castes" (p. 294). — *PCE*

crease, the peace would founder; but I am very happy to see that not a single one of these things has happened.

Believing it to be their task to put people to work who are able-bodied but do not know how to work, the churches here provide these people with training of one kind or another. In the United States the amount spent on beggars is $18,000,000 — that is, only one third of the amount spent on beggars in England. This figure goes to show just how small the incidence of begging is here. Here are some of the reasons for the small number of beggars in the United States: it is only people who are willing to work hard who go and settle in a new land; there is as much land available here for cultivation as anyone could need; there is plenty of work; and those who are willing to work hard need never fear that they will die of starvation wherever they might go. Those who are lazy find no respect in the United States. The person who adopts an attitude of sanctified sloth, in keeping with the saying, "If only God is with me, I'll have everything provided for me right here in my bed,"[18] will simply not get any food to eat.

In the past they used to ship criminals from Austria, Germany, and England to the United States, but now the national government has passed many rigorous laws concerning beggars and immigrants, which prohibit entry into the country to this sort of criminal, lazy, and idle people and to beggars. When I was inquiring about the specific laws concerning the immigrants who come and settle here, people would ask me, "What do you mean to do with the information you are gathering? We do not want to have the beggars and drones of your country coming here." It is only too evident from this that the sound of the drum announcing our poverty and sloth has reached even these shores! They say, "It wouldn't worry us if the people who came here from your land were hardworking people." I in turn reassured them, "It will turn out exactly as you say. How will the lazy ones ever manage even to come here?" The moment these people see that some lazy drone has arrived here from a foreign land, that he doesn't have the strength to work and earn his own living, and that he doesn't want to work, they make him pack up his bags and return to his own land.

I have mentioned above that the number of people with disabilities, i.e., the blind, the mute, the lame, the infirm, etc., is very small. One person in every 2,720 is blind, and one person in every 2,094 is mute. It is certainly a good

18. Trans.: *Asela mājhā harī tara deīla khāṭalyāvarī.* Manwaring, in *Marathi Proverbs* (New Delhi: Asian Educational Service, 1991 [1899]), lists a variant, *dere harī bājevarī,* which he renders, "O Hari! give to me on my cot, i.e., God will supply our wants even if we sit still and do nothing" (p. 217). — *PCE*

thing to give charity to the blind, but were they to receive an education and to begin to do some work in keeping with their abilities, not only would the country benefit but poverty would be reduced. There are numerous schools for the blind here. Every state has at least two or three schools for the blind, the expenses of which are borne by the local government. In these schools the blind are taught through the medium of touch. The blind have very acute senses of hearing and of touch, and their entire understanding is concentrated in these senses. Their intelligence is very penetrating. The blind can weave and do many other kinds of work. I have in my possession some things made by the blind. They are even taught geography. Special globes and maps are made for them so that they can learn about geography through touch. They are also taught mathematics. The kindergarten method of education accomplishes marvels in the education of the blind! There are many singers among the blind and many who play musical instruments. I have heard a blind person playing a musical instrument in church very sweetly. (Here in America parents take a great deal of care of their children's eyes. Mothers in our country put oil in their children's eyes and apply lampblack[19] to their eyelids, but that is not done here.)

There are also many schools for the deaf and the mute. The ingenious people here have also gone to great lengths to educate them! There is one school for them in New York where there are five hundred students. I was vastly astonished when I saw how they were being educated. In this school there was a deaf-mute boy who was also blind. The person who was showing me around introduced me to this handicapped boy. Touching the boy's hand with his fingers, he told him that there was a certain woman from Hindusthan who had come to see him and that if he wished to say anything to her, he should speak — and within moments he had written two or three sentences about me on a piece of paper with the help of a machine called a "typewriter" and brought them to us. My guide allowed me to keep that piece of paper, which I have carefully saved ever since. On it the boy had written my name, the name of my country, and the purpose of my visit to this country and had expressed his joy at my coming here. I was overcome by amazement when I saw this; and I felt at that moment that if miracles do happen in this world, this surely was one!

Besides this there are numerous orphanages and industrial schools here in the United States, and there are schools for mentally disabled children as well. For those who are infirm, orphaned, and such, there are 430 homes in

19. Trans.: *Kājaḷa:* "Lamp-black. It is considered as a collyrium, and is applied medicinally and ornamentally" (Molesworth). — *PCE*

all. There are 56 schools for the blind and the deaf-mute and 30 for mentally disabled children. On the whole, the teachers in these schools teach their pupils with the greatest of care and ingenuity.

The people here believe that it is a matter of religious sanction that they work hard for the better management of prisons, inquire after the health of the prisoners, give them moral instruction, and so on. In our own land, not only do people believe that there can be not the slightest connection between prison inmates and themselves, apparently they also think that having any connection at all with them is utterly demeaning and contemptible. That is why no one ever visits the prisons even in the spirit of inquiring after the health of the prisoners. Now, it cannot be said that everyone who goes to prison is an absolute criminal. (And even if that were the case, does that matter? Why indeed should we not visit the prisons at least to inquire after the well-being of the inmates?) The occasion can even arise when an innocent man is sent to prison. So who can say with absolute certainty that he will never have to go to prison? I have not yet seen a prison in Hindusthan. Previously I knew nothing about the prisons there, but I got some idea of them from reading *One Hundred and One Days in the Dongari Prison* by Gopalrao Agarkar after the incident that took place in Kolhapur.[20] Fifty years ago the situation of prison inmates in the United States was terrible. In most places they were locked up in tunnels and mines. With chains around their necks and fetters about their hands and feet, even children were subjected to every kind of misery. In brief, there used to be a vast amount of disorder and anguish everywhere in the prisons. But nowadays, ever since devout and virtuous men and women have begun to visit the prisons, they have turned into something more like the purdah apartments[21] in our own land. I have seen the prisons here.

20. Trans.: Gopal Ganesh Agarkar (1856-1895) was one of the preeminent intellectuals and social reformers of nineteenth-century Maharashtra. He was one of the founders, along with Bal Gangadhar (Lokmanya) Tilak, of the highly influential newspapers *Kesarī* and *Mahratta;* later (after parting ways with Tilak) the influential editor of the social reformist journal *Sudhāraka;* and at the end of his life the principal of Fergusson College, Pune. He wrote the book *Doṅgarīcyā turuṅgāta ekaśe eka divasa* in 1882. Then, along with Tilak, he was sent to prison on charges of defamation under the Vernacular Press Act. Their conviction stemmed from their editorial denunciation of M. V. Barve, the dewan of the princely state of Kolhapur, whose ruler, a descendant of Shivaji, "commanded a patriotic following throughout Maharashtra" (Richard Tucker, *Ranade and the Roots of Indian Nationalism* [Chicago: University of Chicago Press, 1972], pp. 188-89), and against whom there was evidence (published by Agarkar and Tilak) that Barve had instigated a plot for his removal. Agarkar's book offers an account of the deplorable plight of the prison inmates in the Dongari prison. — *PCE*

21. Trans.: *Janānakhānā* is the word Ramabai uses: "The female apartments; gyneceum, seraglio, harem" (Molesworth). — *PCE*

They are very clean, and precautions have been taken to eliminate any fear of fires. The inmates are given sound moral instruction. They are instructed in how to behave themselves properly when they leave prison. There are even libraries for them in the prisons — and even pots of flowering plants and such. Every Sunday they have time off, which they spend in saying prayers. Goodhearted people show compassion for the inmates out of their belief that it is a lack of proper parental instruction that has brought them to the point of having to go to prison. There are numerous associations of these good people. There are also numerous reformatories for children. The first such home was established in 1824. By 1874 there were thirty-four such homes, and $8,000,000 were being spent for their operation. During these past fifty years a total of 91,402 children were reformed, and some 70,000 turned out to be hardworking and respectable. In these homes the children are given moral instruction. Great care is taken that the children do not adopt one another's bad behavior. Prison inmates here are not given very much corporal punishment, but they do still wear chains. In many states they execute people by means of electricity instead of by hanging. When an inmate completes his term of punishment and is released from prison, he receives all the rights of citizenship.

There are many special hospitals here for people having particular illnesses — just as there are many hospitals for ordinary patients. The government bears the cost of running them, although there are also many hospitals that operate on the fees that people are charged. People of genuine piety attend to the well-being of patients in a variety of ways. There might be women who sing pleasant songs and hymns and who read the Scriptures for the patients to hear. Others might tell stories and the news of the day or read newspapers or play musical instruments. Some might distribute sweets or fragrant flowers. Giving flowers to the sick has indeed become an established custom here. The group that is most responsible for the giving of flowers is called the "Flower Mission." I have met the devout woman who first came up with the idea of giving flowers to the sick. Even though a paralytic stroke some eight or ten years ago left her a complete invalid, she continues to do many acts of charity such as this. There is genuine compassion to be found here in the United States. In our land nobody as yet understands this kind of genuine compassion. We have plenty of sick people, and more and more hospitals are being provided for them. What a fine thing it would be if somebody were to visit the sick in these hospitals, talk kindly to them, inquire after their health, give them flowers, and so on. We imitate the American and other Western people with the greatest of zeal when it comes to drinking liquor, smoking tobacco, and talking like atheists. How much it would benefit both us and our country if instead of that we just as zealously imitated their best qualities and customs!

CHAPTER 8

The Condition of Women

Just as every other child, I too loved to listen to fantastic tales when I was small. Who doesn't take pleasure from hearing the folk tales that are so prevalent in our land or the astonishing stories out of the Puranas and the epics — the *Mahābhārata*, the *Bhāgavata Purāṇa*, the *Rāmāyaṇa*, the *Adbhuta Rāmāyaṇa*,[1] the *Jaiminī Aśvamedha*,[2] and more? Who hasn't felt a thrill listening to these stories? And who hasn't entertained the thought that they too might have the strength to accomplish mighty deeds of the same kind? But you will find that there are extremely few children (or adults) who have not become discouraged when they have been reminded of their own frailty, general ignorance, and absence of means and when they have realized that they will never have what it takes to accomplish mighty deeds like these — and that in fact these stories are themselves nothing more than fabricated fictions. We take such pleasure from and are so enthusiastic about reading imaginary fictions and amazing tales; so why shouldn't we be just as enthusiastic about reading accounts of things that really happened? Seven years ago it had never

1. Trans.: The *Adbhuta Rāmāyaṇa* ("Amazing Ramayana"), in keeping with its name, gives a heroic character to Sita, who upstages even Rama. Portrayed as an incarnation of Durga, she possesses the power to slay demons. So when the ten-headed Ravana is killed and another appears with a hundred heads whom Rama cannot face, it is Sita who must slay him. See A. K. Ramanujan, "Three Hundred *Rāmāyaṇas*," in *Many Rāmāyaṇas: The Diversity of a Narrative Tradition in South Asia*, ed. Paula Richman (Delhi: Oxford University Press, 1992), 43-44. — *PCE*

2. Trans.: The *Jaiminī Aśvamedha*, commonly attributed to the popular early-eighteenth-century Marathi poet Shridhar, is a retelling of the Pandavas' triumphal horse-sacrifice in the fourteenth *parva* of the *Mahābhārata*. — *PCE*

even occurred to me that I would actually be given an opportunity to see the kind of power that, like the supernatural strength of a Haihayarjuna,[3] can block up the flow of a mighty river — or to see even Sita Devi herself, who can slay invincible demons (like the hundred-headed or thousand-headed Ravanas) that are possessed of that same kind of supernatural strength. But in due course of time I did witness these amazing things, and I am happy indeed that I am the first one to be given the opportunity to write an account of them, however brief, to present to the brothers and sisters of my homeland.

Some months ago I came across a book written by the famous English scholar Harriet Martineau on the subject *Society in America.*[4] She wrote this book after returning home from her visit in 1840 to America where she had observed the conditions of society here. While describing in her book the condition of women in this country, this English woman states:

> They [the women in this country] do not receive any higher education, and all access to it is also closed to them. A bit of singing, the playing of musical instruments, enough reading and writing just to get along, and sewing — that is the total extent of their learning. They do not have social or political liberties of any sort. If by some chance they become widows or fall into penury, they have no choice but to earn their living by working as a seamstress, working as a cook, doing menial service (in gentlemen's homes), and other such work; or to get married again and to marry against their wishes. The existence of women is quite simply not recognized in the laws

3. Trans.: *Haihayārjuna,* also known by the names Kartavirya and Sahasrarjuna, is told about in late recensions of the *Mahābhārata* and in the *Agni* and *Mārkaṇḍeya Purāṇas.* As a boon from Dattatreya, he was given a thousand arms, conquest of the earth, and invincibility in battle. The story of how he stopped the flow of one of India's mighty rivers *(mahānadī),* the Narmada, is as follows: "Once while Kartavirya was playing in the waters of the Narmada with his queens, Ravana the king of Lanka came there and after worshipping the river descended into it to bathe with his thousands of demon followers. Naturally the calm waters were disturbed, and this made Sahasrarjuna angry. With his thousand arms he held back the flow of the Narmada from above. Seeing this, Ravana grew enraged, and he challenged Sahasrarjuna to do battle with him. Thereupon a terrific fight ensued between the two. In the end Ravana was defeated and had to withdraw, and Sahasrajuna released the flow of the Narmada, which he had blocked" (*Bhāratīya Saṃskṛtikośa,* vol. 4, ed. Mahadevshastri Joshi [Pune: Bharatiya Sanskriti-kosha Mandal, 1987], p. 700). — *PCE*

4. Trans.: Harriet Martineau (1802-1876) was a well-known English writer of her times (best known for a series of educational works mostly in the field of political economy) and a friend of Thomas Malthus, George Eliot, Thomas Carlyle, and other distinguished Victorians. She actually made her visit to America in 1834-1836. *Society in America* was first published in 1837. — *PCE*

> of this country. *Like the other slaves who are openly bought and sold, they are nothing but men's chattels.* There is no exception to this, whether in matters of politics or in the eyes of the law. You may find an occasional exception or two out in society, but that too is very rare.

Harriet Martineau has written many such things in her book, all of which are very important, but I cannot quote them here owing to lack of space and time. "Like the other slaves who are openly bought and sold, they are nothing but men's chattels" — this one sentence reflects so well the lamentable and terrible condition of women in this country no more than fifty or sixty years ago.

To describe the courage, patient toil, and prolonged labors of those who made the effort to raise themselves out of this condition, an avatar of Sarasvati[5] herself would need to descend upon this earth; a person of such feeble understanding as myself could never do it justice. Of all the great deeds that have been accomplished up to the present day in the face of the greatest difficulties by benevolent and compassionate people (the emancipation of the slaves, the spreading of the temperance movement,[6] etc.), the most difficult one by far has been the emancipation of women. After all, it is perfectly clear that buying slaves like so many cattle, making them work without pay, and impeding not just their material but their spiritual advancement are actions *(karma)* that are both extremely despicable and cruel. Everyone can also see what damage is inflicted on both the physical and mental well-being of humankind by the vice of drinking alcoholic beverages and the like. The evils that emanate from these things are all perfectly manifest; but the evils arising from the servitude of women are almost never even noticed. After the manner of latent diseases of the heart, while they may not be apparent on the surface, deep within they are continually eating away the very heart of humankind. For the most part everyone feels that women do not live in servitude and that their condition is exactly as it ought to be. The belief that women are not oppressed and that their condition should not be different from what it is now has so firmly established itself in everyone's minds it seems quite impossible that even the idea of its wrongness could suggest itself to anyone. What need is there to exaggerate when women themselves believe that their condi-

5. Trans.: The Hindu goddess of wisdom and learning. — *KG*

6. Trans.: *Madyapānaniṣedhakamata* (literally, "creed of the prohibition of the consumption of alcoholic beverages") is Ramabai's usage here and consistently throughout the rest of the chapter. For ease of usage and since it is the "temperance movement" to which she is referring, we have chosen consistently to use this in the translation. — *PCE*

tion is just as it ought to be? In the past when the people of Africa were held in slavery in America, many of them had exactly the same frame of mind: "We may be held in slavery, but that in itself constitutes our happiness; we may be the lowest of the low, and the man in whose keeping we find ourselves may kill us or deliver us, but we have no alternative to him; and no matter how he may degrade us, we can do nothing but quietly bear it." When human beings have reached this state, it can only be called the final stage of their servitude. How can you even begin to calculate the evils of that servitude by which the two most precious God-given gifts to humankind, proper self-respect and the will to freedom, are thus destroyed?

In the opinion of numerous knowledgeable Western scholars, "The importance of any community *(jāta)* and the worthiness of any religion *(dharma)* should be tested by the condition of the women belonging to that community or to that religion." This is true. Women are constitutionally less strong than men and by disposition more forbearing, which makes it extremely easy for men to usurp their natural rights and to keep them in any condition that suits them; but if you take the ethical view of the matter, brute strength is not true strength: it is not a sign of superior character to usurp the rights of your neighbor just because he is weak. Whether speaking of ancient or of modern times, it is clear that the use of brute force has been largely predominant among half-civilized *(ardhavaṭa rānaṭī)* and completely uncivilized people. "The strong man will twist your ear"[7] — such is the sum total of their morality. And when someone who possesses the needed strength follows this morality without any concern for justice and usurps somebody else's kingdom, he himself then becomes the king. It is in this sort of morality that the custom that prevailed in ancient times (and that still prevails today) of honoring brave warriors as if they were gods has its origin. The glorifiers of this morality have a far greater taste for war than for peace. They believe that whatever might be decided by means of weapons and physical strength, that alone is the truth and that alone is justice. But no matter what the country, to the degree that knowledge and civility increase, the glorification of brute force will decrease, the people will begin to believe that strength of mind is superior to physical might, and they will assign a higher position to those things that accord with civility and that are endowed with art and skill than to the lardaceous and sophistical maxims of hayseed pundits. Such people do not call it justice when the property and the rights of others are usurped just because they happen to be weaker. To protect the weak, to forgive someone who has

7. Trans.: *Baḷī to kāna piḷī.* See A. Manwaring, *Marathi Proverbs* (New Delhi: Asian Educational Service, 1991 [1899]), p. 60. — *PCE*

wronged you instead of returning them evil; although strong yourself, to act with humility and not with overbearing pride — these are the things they start to call justice. From this it quite naturally follows that as knowledge continues to increase and as people continue to progress, civility and moral rectitude will also continue to grow. It is for this reason that the doctrine by which unquestioned authority must be exercised over women just because they are constitutionally less strong than men is uncivilized *(rānaṭī);* and that as men continue to grow wiser and continue to improve themselves, they do not look at women's lack of physical strength but increasingly honor women's virtues and raise them to a position of esteem. Along with everything else, their base opinion of women also changes, and their hearts are filled with an attitude of reverent respect. That is why the advancement of any country can be easily tested by the condition of the women in that country.

The people of this country have a way of saying that the social conditions in England, as also of the American people who have come here from that land, are superior to all others because their women receive honorable treatment everywhere and because women and men in these countries are regarded as equals. And those who take pride in Christianity say that it is because of Christianity that women have attained superior status — since women do not receive any respect whatsoever among the people belonging to other religions. Although there might be a good bit of truth in both of these claims, there is also a large portion of untruth, as you will realize after thinking it through. It is not as if the condition of women in all the communities *(jātī)* that call themselves Christian is of one unvarying kind. The Russian, Italian, Greek, French, Swiss, Finnish, English, and American people are all Christians, but there are large differences in the condition of women in these communities. To call oneself a follower of a certain religion and actually to practice that religion are two altogether different things. Just about all of the people in these countries call themselves Christians, but all of them do not act according to the teachings of Christ. In the religion that Christ taught and in the customs that he promulgated, he did not make any distinction between women as one and men as another; but that kind of impartiality is not acceptable to all people here. When it comes to their acknowledgment of the worthiness of women and to their treatment of them, some demonstrate through their actions that they are loyal to the creed of Christ, some to that of St. Paul or of Moses or even of Satan; but all of them will insist that they remain loyal to the Christian creed. The Christianity of Christ himself and that of St. Paul who followed in conformity with him says that in Christ there is no distinction of man and woman, that indeed all people are the children of God. But nowadays in most of the creeds that are prevalent in this country, women are regarded as lower than men. They do not have the right to stand at the pulpit and expound the Scriptures as men do nor to perform the sacraments and other religious rites and rituals. At the time of their marriage they have to take the vow, "I will obey my husband's commands." The teaching given by the clergy(men) is that the husband is to stand as the head of his wife. So the claim of all those who call themselves Christians, that the independence, high position, and honor that women have attained in England and in this country are all due to their religion, is false. It would be more fitting if that religion by means of which women have attained this superior position were called "true religion" or "Christ's religion" (not that which prevails as "Christianity") — and without the adjective "our" attached to it by the people of all these different creeds. The prevailing Christianity of the day keeps changing every so often in conformity with the leanings of public opinion. From the very beginning, the custom has come down to us of all the various clergymen of all the various creeds pressing, pounding, and kneading it like a ball of wax and shaping it to their own liking and to that of public opinion. Just how many different shapes these clergymen have given Christianity and how its meaning has continued to change can be clearly seen in the histories of the slaves and of the women of this country.

About two hundred years ago there arose a sect called the Quakers who, amongst their own people, did not discriminate — at least in matters of religion — between men and women. According to them God's love is exactly the same for both women and men. Whether they be women or whether they be men, God inspires them according to who possesses what degree of worthiness. That is why they believe that anyone, be it man or woman, who is inspired by God should preach. But in other matters even the Quakers used to believe that women were of lesser worthiness than men. In 1840, when the World Anti-Slavery Convention convened in London, Lucretia Mott[8] and many other prominent women went from America as delegates of the American Anti-Slavery Society. Many Quakers attended this convention, and one well-known Quaker gentleman by the name of Joseph Sreerge served as its president. Even so, even at a conference that had been convened to discuss a movement of such benevolence, he refused to give representation to these women — women who had consecrated themselves, body, mind, and substance, to the service of the Anti-Slavery Society, and who had even put their

8. Trans.: Lucretia Coffin Mott (1793-1880) was a prominent Quaker, abolitionist, and women's rights advocate, a founder of the Anti-Slavery Convention of American Women in 1837 and an organizer, with Elizabeth Cady Stanton, of the Seneca Falls Convention for women's rights in 1848. See also Chapter 5. — *PCE*

own lives at risk. When they asked why they were being refused, they received the answer, "It is our British custom."

Recently (in May 1888), a conference of Methodist clergymen and gentlemen was convened in New York City. Methodist churches from many places each sent their own delegates to this grand conference. Among those sent were five eminent women. But they were not accorded the place that was their due at this conference. The fact that they were *women* was the only reason for this. One thing that is worth bearing in mind here is that two-thirds of the members of the Methodist denomination are women, and it is entirely on the strength of their exertions that the support of the clergymen in virtually all their churches as well as all their charitable acts can continue. The same is true of the churches belonging to other denominations. Whenever charity or benevolent acts are to be undertaken, the task of raising money for them almost always falls on the shoulders of women. First they do their own housework or the work they do to earn a living; then in whatever time they can find they sew clothes, do embroidery, create the most surprisingly beautiful things, go from house to house and win people over to their cause; and doing however many other such things may be required, they gather money and gifts in kind for charity and benevolent acts to the tune of many crores of rupees [i.e., millions of dollars]. Then, when the time comes to decide how the money should be dispersed, it is the men who do so; and president, vice president, and so on of whatever committee is formed to oversee these charitable acts are all men. The ones who do the secretarial and other vexatious, monotonous jobs are all, of course, women. How really fine this act of justice rendered by the Methodist church looks in the bright sunlight of progress of this nineteenth century of ours! Except for such denominations as the Congregationalists, the Quakers, the Unitarians, the Universalists, and a progressive branch of the Methodists, the Christian churches of other denominations do not allow women the liberty to expound the Scriptures in their churches — for no other reason than that they are women! At one place in his letters to the Corinthians, St. Paul has written, "Your women should maintain silence in church."[9] Women may be as pure as anybody could wish, they may be learned, they may be eloquent and talented, they may be a hundred times superior to male preachers, but their one and only failing is that they are women; and so even if they receive divine inspiration to expound the Scriptures, men give them the command, "Sit silent and keep your mouth shut."

9. Trans.: 1 Corinthians 14:34 (as rendered in *The New English Bible*): "As in all congregations of God's people, women should not address the meeting. They have no licence to speak, but should keep their place as the law directs." — *PCE*

It has not yet been sixty years since the dawning of the improvement of the condition of women in this country, but in this short time they have begun to obtain many of the fine fruits of their hard labor and prolonged efforts. Even at the time when Harriet Martineau wrote about the women here, "Like the other slaves who are openly bought and sold, they are nothing but men's chattels," there were a few women here who saw the insult being inflicted on their kind *(jāta)* and who tried to alert American society to the injustice of this. A hundred years ago the sister of the famous Robert Lee in the state of Virginia and the wife of John Adams in the state of Massachusetts told officials of the government in no uncertain terms that since women did not have the right to vote in political matters they would not pay their taxes. But nobody paid much attention to this at that time. Later on, when the anti-slavery opinion first began to manifest itself after 1830, the question of improving the condition of women also began to take shape. In 1832 William Lloyd Garrison established the first anti-slavery society.[10] He, along with Wendell Phillips and many other prominent speakers, gave speeches in hundreds and thousands of meetings on the subject of the wrongfulness of the enslavement of African men and women. The very same arguments they made against the slavery of the African people were directly applicable to the condition of women's servitude as well. When they realized this fact, some very brave, very daring women started a campaign of speaking in public meetings espousing the cause of their own kind *(jāta)* along with that of the African slaves.

The year 1832 must be called a golden year — during which the chains of slavery that bound the slaves suffered a major blow and began to break, and, in a similar way, the root cause of women's servitude and mean condition, which is ignorance, also became infected with "wasting disease."[11] This was the wonderful year in which the highly renowned school by the name of Oberlin College was established in Oberlin, Ohio.[12] The founders of this college made it the rule in deciding the fitness of a person for higher education that no distinction be made on the basis of the color of their skins — whether black, white, yellow, or other — or on the basis of female or male genders *(jātī);* but that whoever had a passion for learning should be taught in full

10. Trans.: It was in fact in 1833 that William Lloyd Garrison (1805-1879) took the lead in organizing the American Anti-Slavery Society. — *PCE*

11. Trans.: *Kṣayaroga* (a literal rendering of the obsolete English term "wasting disease") is the Marathi word for pulmonary tuberculosis. — *PCE*

12. Trans.: Once again, it was in fact in 1833 that Oberlin College was founded. And it wasn't until two years later that Oberlin became the first college in the United States to admit students without consideration of race. — *PCE*

generosity of spirit. It has not been very many years as yet since better times began to dawn for the women of this country, but now day by day the sun of their good fortune is starting to shine ever more brightly. Signs are starting to appear that henceforth in a very few years they will receive all the same rights as men and this nation of the United Sates will finally become a completely democratic dominion. Women are steadily moving forward day by day in all areas of social and political life. The subject I propose to address in this chapter is an account of the various fields in which women have made progress during the last fifty or sixty years, of the benefits that society has gained from this, and of women's present condition.

Education

The mainspring of progress is education. It has been sixty years now since the women of this country began to receive some degree of education. It has been just barely a hundred years since the English woman Mary Wollstonecraft publicly declared that women in England should receive education.[13] In 1789 this woman openly argued that the biggest obstacle to the progress of women in England was their lack of education and that it was reprehensible to prevent women from obtaining an education. In 1799 a woman by the name of Hannah More[14] wrote a number of books and made public her opinion that it is only fitting and right that women receive an education. In 1809 a gentleman by the name of Sydney Smith[15] brought before society in the form of a book his own opinion in support of women's education. The two decades from 1789 to 1809 might well be called the prologue to the history of Western women's education. During those twenty years a desire sprouted in the hearts of many women and men to see a beginning everywhere to women's education, and day by day it grew only stronger.

In 1819 an American woman by the name of Emma Willard[16] for the

13. Trans.: Mary Wollstonecraft (1759-1797) published her *A Vindication of the Rights of Woman* in 1792. — *PCE*

14. Trans.: Hannah More (1745-1833) was an English writer, dramatist, and philanthropist, close associate of such luminaries as Samuel Johnson, Samuel Richardson, and Horace Walpole, and hostess of the first Blue Stocking Club, where intellectual women could discuss the issues of the day. — *PCE*

15. Trans.: Sydney Smith (1771-1845), an English clergyman and writer and one of the founders of the *Edinburgh Review*, had a large reputation in his time as a lecturer on moral philosophy. — *PCE*

16. Trans.: Emma Willard (1787-1870), largely self-educated, published her *Plan for Im-*

first time tried to secure the means to provide education to her fellow countrywomen. That year she applied to the legislative assembly of the state of New York requesting that this assembly establish a school for women; and it could be said that from that day the history of higher education for American women began — not that women actually did begin to receive higher education from that time, however. Up until 1831 almost all the proponents of women's education were of a mind to say that women ought to receive only a basic education; that not only would they not benefit from higher education, but it would cause them to lose their characteristic humility, beauty, and usefulness to society, and they would become arrogant, uncaring, and thoughtless. In 1832 a facility for women to receive higher education on an equal footing with men was created at Oberlin College in the state of Ohio.[17] The founders of Oberlin College threw aside the prevailing uncivilized *(rānaṭī)* beliefs about the inferior worthiness of women and set a superlative example for the world. Boston, the capital of the state of Massachusetts, is held in repute as being the oldest seat of learning in the United States. People have the idea that Boston's scholars are superior, that they are always a step ahead of everyone else in matters related to progress, public welfare, and so on. But before 1878 not a single higher-level school had been opened for girls in the city of Boston. One hundred and twenty-five years after Harvard College (in Cambridge, Massachusetts), which calls itself the jewel in the crown of the best universities in America, was established for men and had attained its pride of place, permission was finally granted to the girls of Massachusetts to enter the lowest-level schools. Bearing this in mind when you analyze the history (begun so very recently) of women's education in this country, you can't help but be astonished by the prodigious achievements of women in the field of education in such a short period of time.

When we see how much progress has been made, however, no one should take this to mean that it all happened in the absence of any obstacle. No sooner would women pick up some new book to read or declare their wish publicly to study some new branch of knowledge than from every side — from the newspapers, from clergymen's pulpits, from the mouths of public orators, in the doctrinal statements of religious organizations, from the upturned noses and eyes and sharp tongues of their neighbors — they would be assaulted (and continue to be assaulted even now) with a shower of abuse, con-

---

proving Female Education in 1818, the following year opened the first school in the United States to offer a college-level education for women, and in 1821 founded the Troy Female Seminary (now the Emma Willard School) in Troy, New York. — *PCE*

17. Trans.: The year was actually 1833. For the first four years women studied at Oberlin in the specially designated "Women's Department." — *PCE*

tempt, criticism, condescension, hostile looks, and more. Only something that is inherently pure and that has the support of undying truth could possibly hope to endure such a thunderous outpouring of hostility and still survive to this day. During these fifty years every possible kind of clergyman, physician, scientist, philosopher, male teacher, college principal, journalist, and shaper of public opinion (however humble or however great) has considered women's education from every possible angle and put to the test the questions of whether or not it would accord with theology, physiology, philosophy, popular custom, economics, etc.; and whether, once it had begun, it would benefit or harm the country. Now they have begun to find it increasingly difficult to contest the truth, so most of them have reluctantly come around to saying, "There is nothing to be alarmed about if women get a little education."

In the western part of the United States there is a state called Colorado where from an eternity past there have lain across the earth tall ranges of unmovable mountains, vast and constituted of pure stone, called the "Rockies." It would seem like quite an impossible thing to break these mountain ranges, to find a route and dig a way through them — so how could some insignificant little stream have the strength to do so? But just see now what a surprising thing this is! When the Arkansas River set out ever so quietly to find a way through the Rocky Mountains, the seas and the lakes and all the other rivers that flow through the plains must have felt surprised and saddened to see this fey determination of hers;[18] and those skyscraping stony piles, the Rockies, must have pitied her. The smaller mountains probably scoffed at her and called her names when they saw her foolhardiness. But the Arkansas River paid no attention to what anyone said. She may have been a small, narrow, frail river, but her determination was strong enough to pick up even the mountains that stood before her and toss them aside. With prolonged exertions and the strength of her own determination she conquered even the Rocky Mountains. Simply by beating against that endless and impenetrable stony pile, the tiny Arkansas broke right through the ranges of the Rocky Mountains and made a passage for herself exactly as it suited her. Well done, Arkansas River! And well done, American women! Like this little river they may have lacked strength and they may not have had the support of weapons, money, public opinion, or religious affiliations; but on the strength of nothing more than their own prolonged exertions and sheer determination, they beat against the thousands of obstacles they faced — obstacles that were a hundred times more vast, difficult, insurmountable, and impenetrable than the Rocky Mountains — dug

18. Trans.: The feminine gender of "river" *(nadī)* in Marathi is crucial to the personification Ramabai uses here and the comparison to it she develops a bit further on. — *PCE*

passages right through them, and made a way for themselves exactly as it suited their purpose. I say it one more time: Well done, American women!

The arguments against women's education that could be heard flowing from everyone's mouth and that were universally accepted as true not just twenty-five but even ten years ago have, to a very large extent, begun to recede now. Their objections then — that women would become arrogant after becoming educated; that they would neglect their housework and the care of their children; that they would not know how to cook; that they did not possess enough physical, mental, or spiritual strength to study hard and pass the college examinations and yet carry their health intact across the vast sea of their studies; that if they did finish their education and start to work, men would have to sit at home; that men's employment would plunge; that the world would be overwhelmed by disaster; and so on and so on — have now begun to die out, and their corpses are being buried in deep graves. From time to time one or another of the ghosts of these objections might appear before society and frighten the cowardly; but because of their total absence of bones, marrow, brains, or life, they immediately dissolve into nothing and disappear.

At present (1888), of all the provisions that have been made in the United States for women to receive a higher as well as a general education, it is the colleges that are the principal and the best provision. Educational conferences, established lecture series, correspondence schools, and the examinations set by certain universities are four of the secondary provisions. Details about the schools in which women were receiving both higher education and practical training in 1886 are as follows:

Colleges established for women only	266
Colleges where men and women receive the same kind of higher education as equals	207
Engineering and agricultural schools established for men but where women may also study	17
Science institutes	3
Medical schools	36
Total number of schools	529

Women students studying in colleges established for women only	27,143
Women students studying along with men	8,833
Combined total of women students in higher education and science	35,976

Besides this, girls can study to be teachers in most of the public training schools that provide a secondary-level education. These are as follows:

Public teachers' colleges	117
Independent (privately funded) teachers' colleges	36
Total number of women students in these colleges	27,185

In public schools at the primary and common levels and in almost all public high schools, boys and girls study together and receive the same education.[19] Seventy years ago there were no primary schools for girls, whereas all the doors to education were open to men. Men had not only primary schools but also the best provisions for gaining knowledge and learning professions in colleges, universities, science institutes, and so on. In spite of the opposition of public opinion to women's education and so many other obstacles, as of

19. It was in 1818 that primary schools for girls, just like those for boys, were established in the United States. During the seventy years from that time up to the present, the women of this country have been making steady progress in education so that now there are thousands of well-educated and intelligent women in this country who shine like jewels with the brilliance of their merits; but this by itself should not lead us to think that all women have the same provisions for receiving an education as all men nor that women's schools receive the same generous support from the public as schools created for men. Following are some details about men's colleges existing in 1886:

Total number of universities and colleges	346
Science institutes	90
Theological institutes	142
Law schools	49
Schools for medicine, dentistry, pharmacology, etc.	175
Total	802
Number of students in these colleges	78,185

The assessed value of men's schools, the land belonging to them, and the equipment needed in the schools is $62,356,638, i.e., 187,069,914 rupees. The money kept in investments for the upkeep of these colleges is $57,782,303, i.e., 173,346,909 rupees, from which the annual income is $3,271,991, i.e., 9,815,973 rupees.

When you compare this amount with the money spent for women's education you will see what a large difference there is between them. Altogether there are 529 schools where women receive higher education. The assessed value of their buildings, lands, teaching-related equipment, etc., is $9,635,282, i.e., 28,905,846 rupees. The amount invested for the operation of these colleges, the value of their fixed assets, etc., altogether comes to $2,376,619, i.e., 7,129,857 rupees; and their annual income is $136,809, i.e., 410,427 rupees.

In 1886 the local, state, and national governments of the United States appropriated $1,690,275, i.e., 5,070,825 rupees, in support of men's higher education; but to encourage women's higher education they gave not so much as a single broken cowry shell! — *PRS*

today the women of the United States are looking to achieve equality with men in education. This is a matter of no small surprise. We learn from the census of 1880 that in that year 8 percent of white American men (the Negro race excluded) were illiterate and that 11 percent of white women could not read or write. This proves that in general education women were not far behind men.

When that noble-minded woman, Mrs. Emma Willard, applied to the state government of New York for a small grant to aid the setting up of a mid-level women's school (established in 1821, by the name of Troy Seminary) the government refused to give money for this good cause. In an essay expressing her distress, she said, "If the welcome occasion had ever arisen for me to die in the fires of sacrifice for this cause [of women's education], I would have blessed that pyre and embraced the burning brands with joy." Hundreds of noble-minded women who like Willard*bāī* had a passion for education, when they saw that the government and popular opinion did not support them, said, "Even though I die for this cause, it is better — dying for something like this is immortality." They expended body, mind, and substance for the betterment of their own kind *(svajata)*. The strong current of their determination, like that of the Arkansas River, broke through impenetrable and insurmountable piles of vast stone obstacles, like those of the Rocky Mountains, and left the road to women's education open and free of danger. Nowadays in numerous schools such as Oberlin College, Vassar College, the University of Michigan, Smith College, Wellesley College, Harvard Annex, Ingham University, Bryn Mawr College, and Cornell University,[20] women are receiving an excellent education that is equal to men's. All this progress that has been made in women's education in the United States was brought about not by indulging in mere storytelling, empty daydreams, and fruitless arguments, nor by sitting on soft mattresses and leaning against feather bolsters. The women here who have a passion for education, as well as some liberal-hearted men, brought about this golden age for the women of this country by braving all the nay-saying of public censure, bearing endless stress and strain, and engaging in ceaseless labor.

In the past many people felt deeply concerned about whether women were capable of doing the hard studying required for an education the way men do. In 1858, an American gentleman by the name of Matthew Vassar was

20. Oberlin, Michigan, and Cornell are schools in which women and men are educated together. — *PRS*

Trans.: Harvard Annex would later become Radcliffe College. Ingham University, founded in 1837 in LeRoy, New York, as the LeRoy Female Seminary and in 1857 chartered as Ingham University, was closed in 1892. — *PCE*

planning to open a college for women, and he asked for advice about this project from the famous philanthropic scholar William Chambers of Edinburgh, Scotland. Mr. Chambers expressed his surprise and distress over Mr. Vassar's intentions and gave him the following excellent advice: "Don't let yourself get bogged down in opening a college for women. If you insist on doing so, there can be no doubt you will end up having to hang your head in shame, a victim of your own folly. Instead of opening a college for women, it would be far better for you to open a school for the blind, the deaf, and the mute or else a couple of asylums for the mentally disabled." Nowadays the number of skeptical scholars like Mr. Chambers is steadily decreasing. When it became known that women were receiving as rigorous and superior an education as men at the University of Michigan, a number of organizations from various parts of Europe and South America sent representatives to the United States to examine carefully and to see for themselves whether this plan was harmful or beneficial, whether it was conducive to women's health to obtain an education in the company of men and on a par with men, and whether the rigorous education given to men is accessible to women's intelligence or not — and they came away convinced. Broadminded men and women who have given serious thought to this matter have not the slightest doubt anymore about the benefits of women's education or of higher education for women. Exactly what benefits the United States as a nation is receiving and how much progress this society is making through women's education will be discussed later on. Before I conclude this part, I will quote two statements here to show what a difference there is between what public opinion about women's education was forty years ago and what it is now. In 1850 men who were leaders and shapers of public opinion were saying, "Women's education should never assume the form of higher learning. Only headstrong women of unnatural dispositions will allow room in their hearts for the ambition of pursuing higher learning. But no matter how hard they might try, nothing could ever come of it anyway because everyone knows that women do not have as much mental (intellectual) strength as men." In 1880 the shapers of public opinion were saying, "The future condition of our very society is being shaped by the fact that provisions are being made for women to pursue an education on a par with men in schools where previously only men received an education. Women are not mere inanimate dolls to be made to dance as men would make them dance; they themselves have the power to understand what benefits them and what does not. It is altogether in keeping with our own native customs that women should have the freedom to express what they want for themselves."

Fifty years ago in the United States there did not exist even four or five higher-level schools for women. Nowadays it is doubtful whether there are even four or five of the best colleges and universities in the entire country where women are not allowed to study on a par with men. Even at a time when absurd beliefs reigned supreme over everyone's mind — "Women's education is a dreadful and calamitous thing that will destroy society; women will become unnatural and arrogant and the joys of hearth and home will disappear from off the face of the earth" — there were some few farsighted, impartial men and women of wisdom who had dared to plunge the tiny boat of their own beliefs into the vast flow of the river of public opinion and sail it against the current by saying, "It will be extremely difficult for people who belong to a human society that has taken shape during a period that has produced a Mrs. [Mary] Summerwell and a Mrs. [Elizabeth Barrett] Browning to say that women do not have the strength to obtain a first-class education. If women are provided the means to obtain the same liberal, inspiring, and genuine education our young men do in our colleges, our society will be enormously benefited."[21]

More recently, ever since more numerous provisions have been made for woman to obtain a first-class education, people have been realizing the truth of this just-quoted prediction. No one but semi-literates or total know-nothings can dare to say that women's intelligence is not equal to men's. Columbia and Johns Hopkins Universities, two of America's best universities, which transgressed the boundaries of old custom and allowed women to cross their thresholds, whether out of generosity or because they had no choice, wrought an amazing and unprecedented miracle by conferring the highest degrees they can bestow on two excellent postgraduate women scholars. When Harvard University, which is located in the new Cambridge in the state of Massachusetts, slavishly followed the pattern set by the old Cambridge,[22] and refused to offer women the immortalizing fruits of knowledge[23]

21. Thus did the famous scholar and president of the University of Michigan, James B. Angell, publicly express his opinion many years ago. — *PRS*

22. Some years ago there was absolutely no provision made for women to study at Cambridge University in England. Now they receive an excellent education there at two colleges, Newnham and Girton, that have been opened for women. Nowadays women do have the right to study and to write examinations on an equal footing with the men in Cambridge University. But the directors of this university still have some remnants of their ancestors' uncivilized *(rānaṭī)* nature left in them. They may permit women to study there and to write examinations, but they refuse to confer on women who have passed their examinations the degrees that they have rightfully earned through many years of labor! Truly the liberality and the courtesy of the highly advanced English and of the Cambridge scholars no less are unparalleled! — *PRS*

23. Trans.: *Jñānāmṛtaphaḷa:* "[The] fabled fruit [of *jñāna*, i.e., knowledge] of which he that eats becomes immortal" (Molesworth). — *KG*

that are constantly being offered men within its walls from out of the inexhaustible stores of Sarasvati Devi, some hardworking women opened an independent school, if not within Harvard, then just outside its gates, in an effort to obtain those immortalizing fruits from the same inexhaustible stores; and they made a success of it.

In the eastern states women have entered the very best schools such as Michigan and Cornell; and women's colleges such as Wellesley, Smith, Vassar, and Bryn Mawr, which compete with the just-mentioned universities, have been and continue to be established. In virtually all the colleges and universities out in the western states, provision has been made for women to study along with men, so the very need to establish separate schools for women no longer exists. Nowhere can it be said that higher education has caused any loss to women's physical health or beauty. We need not even speak of the smaller and mid-level schools. In Cornell, Vassar, Wellesley, Smith, Bryn Mawr, and schools like them, there are thousands of young women getting a higher education. I have been to every one of these places and stayed for a few days, and I have carefully examined this matter, as also others. I have learned from this experience that there can be not the slightest doubt that higher education agrees extremely well with women. Their beauty does not suffer any loss from it. Their gentle, modest character does not change, and they do not turn into something unnatural. Many women who have obtained degrees from these schools have gotten married and are now running their homes very capably. Just because they are educated does not mean they slight their children and their housework. Nor is it the case that, just because they are educated, their husbands have reason to suffer distress or grow wearied of them — to the ruination of their homes. I have visited the homes of many women who studied at the schools I named above and seen how their households are run, and I have inquired into their husbands' well-being. So I was happy to hear their husbands time and again express the view that women should receive a good education.

Two years ago Miss Alice Freeman[24] was the president of Wellesley College. Before she took this position, it was the universal belief that a woman would never be able to become the president even of a small school and manage it properly — let alone a major college. But Alice Freeman astonished the world by taking over the presidency of a prestigious college where six hun-

24. Trans.: Alice Elvira Freeman Palmer (1855-1902), educated at the University of Michigan, was president of Wellesley from 1882 to 1887, and from 1892 to 1895 was dean of women at the University of Chicago. She married the philosopher George Herbert Palmer of Harvard in 1887. — *PCE*

dred aspiring young women were receiving a higher education and handling her responsibilities in a first-rate way. The trustees of Columbia University (after giving her an examination) honored Alice Freeman's scholarship in the fit and proper way by conferring a Ph.D. on her. (This is the highest degree that universities can bestow on a person.) A certain doubting soul felt this concern for her: "Because this president of a major college has had to devote her entire life (thirty years) to her studies, she must have not the slightest knowledge of housework. And it must be a matter of serious doubt that she will ever find a husband. Granted, she can manage a college and major assemblies in an exemplary way, she can teach, she can take up a scientific subject and go head-to-head in debate with the most distinguished scholars, but what is the use of it all? What is the fruit of all her studies if she, being a woman, cannot run a home for her husband?" But please, dear fellows, try to show some restraint! Even a woman scholar like Alice Freeman has every likelihood of finding a husband — and indeed, to speak only of her, she has. And he himself is not just some ordinary run-of-the-mill scholar, either! Alice Freeman, who holds a prestigious Ph.D., is now running her home in a most exemplary way. Just as when it came to all matters related to a major college, she has an intimate knowledge of the smallest household affairs as well. Who could have even the smallest doubt that she can manage the care of her home every bit as well as she did a college with six hundred women students? But enough of that. If you ask what, in the end, became of our friend above (who was so eager to find fault), this is all I can say as I conclude this part: "The doubting soul perishes. For the doubting soul there is neither this world nor the world beyond, nor any happiness."[25]

Employment

The history of women's education for half a century from 1828 to 1888 is altogether astonishing, fascinating, and instructive. I have already mentioned above that somewhat less than sixty years ago Mrs. Emma Willard applied to the legislative assembly of the state of New York requesting aid from the government for women's schools. In her petition Willard*bāī* made it very clear that, in keeping with the prevailing beliefs of that time, there was no need for

25. Trans.: *Saṃśayātma vinaśyati/nāyaṃ loko'sti na paro na sukhaṃ saṃśayātmanaḥ* (*Bhāgavad Gītā* 4.40, lines 2-4). The present translation is a slight adaptation of S. Radhakrishnan's in *A Sourcebook of Indian Philosophy,* ed. S. Radhakrishnan and Charles A. Moore (Princeton: Princeton University Press, 1957), p. 119. — *PCE*

women to be given higher education, but that it was altogether necessary for them to have a general education. Even this very modest request from her did not meet the approval of the learned legislators of New York. They refused to give the smallest encouragement even to general education for women. One great scholar, a statesman who immortalized his fame as a nonentity by uttering the following bit of perspicuity, actually said, "It is a most terrible thing for women to have an education. The moment they are educated they will begin to look down on housework. So women's education is a terrible threat to society and nation alike."

It was the opinion of some that women's brains would be harmed by studying mathematics and law and that they would fall deathly ill. Studying scientific subjects would make them lose their faith in religion. If they studied Greek, their femininity would disappear, and they would become rude and rowdy like men. Some said, "Whatever else you say, if women are educated, men will lose their employment. They will have to sit at home rocking babies on their laps and singing lullabies or doing the cooking. And why? Because educated women will usurp men's jobs." Some especially thoughtful men said, "No, no, there's no need to fear that women will take away our jobs. Women fundamentally don't have the brains it takes to make use of their education or the scientific knowledge they might acquire. You only have to fear a headache if you have a head in the first place. Only if women had the brains in their heads to get a first-rate education would you have to worry about their becoming scholars. But where will they get the brains to put in their heads in the first place?"[26] Other intelligent, worldly-wise gentlemen said, "Well, but where will women find the time to get themselves educated? And anyway, even if we suppose for a moment they do, once they are educated what use will women be able to make of their education?"

There is no point now to sitting around discussing how true or how imaginary all these misgivings were. A hundred years ago in the United States women could not even work as teachers in the public schools because men thought that women did not have the strength to keep boisterous boys under

26. Fifty years ago nobody must have even imagined the present state of women's education in the United States. I have already reported, in the previous part, that nowhere is it to be seen or heard that by studying mathematics, law, the principles of science, Greek, etc., women become ill, mad, or rowdy, that their feminine nature is turned topsy-turvy, or that among educated women there is a total absence of love for home and children. It is true that because women have become educated they have now begun to engage in hundreds of kinds of employment, but men's jobs have not disappeared as a consequence; quite to the contrary, during the past fifty years business and industry have increased a hundredfold in the United States and produced great prosperity. This I have shown in the chapter entitled "Trade and Business." — *PRS*

control and give them the proper training. But in 1789 the all-male legislative assembly of Massachusetts passed a new law — whether as an idle test of whether women really could teach in the schools or because they only wanted to get the job done by paying lower wages — which allowed women to teach general education in the public schools of local governments. At that time women were not allowed to teach anything but the most basic levels of reading, writing, and arithmetic, the reason being that, out of fear that women's health would break down if they had to study too hard, all those learned, thoughtful, and compassionate men, with the greatest of care, put together a special "women's curriculum." It cannot be said with any certainty that those who studied this curriculum were ever able to pen even the shortest letter using grammatically correct language — much less prepare boys for a higher education or teach it themselves. With the passage of time, oppressed by fear of the mountainous obstacles and the Great Wall of China of negative public opinion they faced, but unwilling just to sit idle, women educated themselves even as they remained at home. When people finally began to recognize the worthiness and substance of women teachers and how useful they were in teaching general education, wiser heads began to think that women teachers ought to receive a higher level of education than the "women's curriculum" afforded them, so they could do their work as teachers better.

Still later, even after women began to receive higher education, the way was still not open to them to be appointed to positions as teachers at any of the colleges. But it was the University of Michigan that opened the golden gates of its temple of Sarasvati and invited women to come and sit (along with men) at her throne and worship her. Since that time women have begun to find opportunities to prove what the extent of their competence and intelligence is by their excellent work and by their appointments (in accordance with their merits) to positions (previously reserved exclusively for men) as teachers, professors, presidents of schools, and so on. Nobody now doubts the ability of women to manage a school or to train children properly. Indeed, the performance of women met the approval of all three levels of government (local, state, and national) in the United States to such an extent that they have turned over almost all the primary and middle education of children to women. And now women teachers have even begun to take higher education into their own hands. There are altogether 273,000 teachers who are teaching in the nation's schools (i.e., schools of the superior, middle, and lower grades and the universities), out of which 154,375 are women teachers. Apart from this, women have become teachers in numerous private and public superior-level schools, where they teach such difficult scientific and philosophical subjects as mathematics, chemistry, botany, astronomy, physiology, optics, and physics; and their performance in these jobs is excellent. Some women have become presidents or vice presidents of schools or superintendents of all the schools in one city; some have become senior teachers, deans, or chaplains.[27] Some women have written comprehensible books on difficult subjects such as political science, philosophy, history, procedural law, and science. Some woman scholars have been studying not only in the United States but also in the ancient universities of Europe and have received commendations from the great scholars there. In the same manner as the woman scholar Caroline Herschel,[28] Professor Maria Mitchell,[29] who is professor of astronomy at Vassar College, became highly accomplished in the field of astronomy, discovered new stars and planets, and received a commendation and a prize from the government of Russia. She has made her name immortal in the circles of Western astronomers. Professor Jane M. Bancroft has written a book entitled *Parliaments of Paris,* describing the politics of France. In the opinion of the great scholars at Johns Hopkins, Cornell, and other universities, it has turned out to be one of the very best books on the subject of politics. The renowned Professor Louisa Reed Stowell of the University of Michigan has become so accomplished in her knowledge of microscopy that the members of the very important Royal Microscopical Society of London have made her a member of their society. Nowadays women scholars are gaining membership on equal terms with male scholars in all the most renowned and important scientific societies in America. Sixty years ago had anyone predicted to the learned — if somewhat feeble-visioned — legislative assembly of New York such things as that during the next half century women would enter the field of education and achieve all these prodigious things, that more than half the work of educating millions of their sons and providing them moral instruction would be handed over to women, it would have sounded as improbable as a rabbit having horns, not only to the statesmen of New York but to the entire world.

It is impossible to say enough when describing and praising the state of advancement educated women have brought to education in the United States ever since they entered the system of education here. Women alone can

27. Trans.: *Nītyupadeśaka* (literally, "expounder of morals") is Ramabai's rather odd coinage here, but the context suggests what she might intend by it. — *PCE*

28. Trans.: Caroline Lucretia Herschel (1750-1848), German-born British astronomer, was the first woman to make significant astronomical discoveries. She received the gold medal of the Royal Astronomical Society in 1828. — *PCE*

29. Trans.: Maria Mitchell (1818-1889), privately educated, became (in 1848) the first woman to be elected to the American Academy of Arts and Sciences, a distinction she earned for her discoveries in astronomy. She was professor of astronomy at Vassar from 1865 to 1888. — *PCE*

take the credit for starting (but only after a great struggle) the kindergarten method of education, which has been such a boon to thousands and indeed hundreds of thousands of children and thanks to which the disciplining of tender children by spanking them on their backs, hands, and faces has disappeared. Elizabeth Peabody[30] and her disciples taught the kindergarten method to thousands of women, while wealthy women such as Mrs. Quincy Show and Mrs. Elizabeth Thompson, by giving financial support to women teachers such as Elizabeth Peabody, provided the needed resources for bringing the kindergarten method into general use. When the local government of Boston would not allow a place nor provide the funds for kindergarten education in their system of public education, one of Boston's wealthy philanthropic women, Mrs. Quincy Show, took it upon herself to help bring the system of kindergarten education into use in her own city. Out of her own private charity she established numerous kindergarten schools in Boston, and she has continued the practice over the past twelve years of spending $36,000 — i.e., approximately 108,000 rupees — annually for their development. Now, after finally recognizing just how worthwhile this curriculum is, the government has given its permission to implement the kindergarten method in its public schools. The famous woman philanthropist of New York, Mrs. Elizabeth Thompson, spends 200,000 rupees on children's education and on occupational education every year. Almost all her income is being spent on the education of children while she herself just manages to get by, almost as austerely as a nun.[31] It is only because educated women such as Elizabeth Peabody, Mrs. Show, and Mrs. Thompson have devoted themselves, body, mind, and substance, to this just cause that the system of education in the United States has attained such an advanced state.

The educated women of the United States perform the work of teachers in two ways. The first is by actually teaching in the schools while the other is by providing moral instruction to society at large and by elevating people's minds through the medium of the newspapers. About twenty-five years have passed since women first entered the profession of journalism. Before that time it was the common practice that anybody could write whatever they wanted in the newspapers, and there weren't very many restrictions on the use of obscene language. Educated women objected to this because even young boys and girls would read these newspapers. So they began to

30. Trans.: Elizabeth Palmer Peabody (1804-1894) opened the first English-language kindergarten in the United States in Boston in 1860. See also Chapter 6. — *PCE*

31. Trans.: *Sannyāsinī*, feminine form of *sannyāsī* (m): "One that has cast off all worldly possessions and carnal or natural affections, an ascetic" (Molesworth). — *PCE*

take over various sections of the newspapers, one after the other. This practice is still continuing today and is producing many benefits. In those newspapers that have women's sections, great care is taken not to publish improper stories that malign women or articles that defy morality. What is more, these newspapers gain in interest and attraction because of the felicitous language and style of writing women use. Weighty newspapers such as the *New York Herald,* the *Philadelphia Ledger,* the *Boston Transcript,* the *Boston Herald,* and the *Chicago Inter-Ocean* enjoy great support from women writers. Every well-known newspaper invariably has a women's section, and for the most part nowadays obscene language does not appear in the newspapers. Women can discuss through the newspapers such matters as what things they and their children lack; what needs to be done for the welfare of children and of society; what customs need to be changed; what manner of curriculum should be taught in the schools; and what sorts of laws are needed to ensure that men and women receive equal justice. The realization is now dawning that women's mouths, which from the beginning of creation powerful men (grown oblivious to any sense of duty in the unrestrained indulgence of their superior physical strength) had forcibly kept shut, are now being opened, not to the detriment of society but to its benefit. Nowadays women are no longer content with having just a section of a big newspaper; they have begun to open independent newspapers of their own. There are hundreds of newspapers that are being run entirely by women. Many newspapers and magazines such as the *Boston Women's Journal,* the *Chicago Justicia,* the *Union Signal,* the *Beatrice Women's Tribune, Women's Work for Women, Children's Work for Children, Saint Nicholas,* and the *Women's Magazine* are proving themselves to be very useful in the task of improving the way in which social and political affairs and public education are conducted. The weekly newspaper called the *Union Signal* grew in the most remarkable manner. Six or seven years ago, some five or six women opened this newspaper with an investment of $2,500. At that time the prohibition of alcohol did not have much public favor — and it still does not. It seemed very doubtful that this paper, which was started by leaders of the Women's Temperance Union, would succeed. But now it appears to have become quite popular. It now has a capital investment of $50,000, and it has more than 40,000 subscribers. The circle of women who run this newspaper has started four or five other newspapers in furtherance of the temperance movement. In 1888 this circle published 52,000,000 pages of printed matter and greatly aided the cause of prohibition in the United States. Just this year they made $93,000 related to their printing work. It was also a matter of the most serious concern whether the *Boston Women's Journal* could run successfully because it is an advocate of the opinion that women should receive political rights exactly the same as men. In the same way that, thirty years ago, the people of the United States were opposed to women's education, today they are opposed to women receiving political rights. But in the same way that, through their tireless efforts, women changed public opinion about education, they are now determined to change public opinion in this matter as well; and signs are beginning to appear that they will accomplish this. Here and there within the business of journalism it can be plainly seen that women are better fit for it than men. There is no longer any need now for pure-minded men and women or children to read filthy newspapers only because there are no others.

Among the benefits that have accrued since women entered the various occupations, the benefit of having women physicians is a very important one. Unenlightened women cannot properly take care of their own health or the health of their children. The human race suffers untold injury from this ignorance of theirs. That is why it is so necessary that women gain a knowledge of medicine. But the people of the United States had very strange ideas about this. Thirty or thirty-five years ago, a medical school for women was established in Philadelphia. At the time people hounded its founders unsparingly. People thought that by studying medicine women would be corrupted, their natural delicacy would disappear, and they would no longer be fit for housework. When people have no knowledge of something they draw the strangest conclusions about it. At least half the people in the world are always rushing to express their opinion about some matter without ever bothering to inform themselves about it first, and as a consequence the remaining people develop doubts about it too. But if they were to inform themselves first and then express their opinion for or against the matter, the untold injury the world must suffer when hundreds of new ways of doing things are not adopted and new things are not put into use would be avoided. Now that thirty years have passed since the first women's medical school was established, the people of the United States are beginning to realize just how useful women doctors are to society. At the present time here in the United States, there are more than a thousand women registered as doctors. Their net annual income ranges from $100 to $50,000. Nowadays women doctors are sought after everywhere. People have had the unassailable experience that men are not as skillful as women are in caring for the sick.

While on this subject, I shall give one example here of how completely public opinion has changed. Some twenty years ago the renowned society of male doctors called the Philadelphia County Medical Association placed a ban on women doctors and even resolved not to entertain so much as the sight of their faces. The reasons they gave for this were that (1) the purity of women's minds would be so sullied by studying medicine they would start to act in ways unbecoming of women and that (2) because women's brains weigh less than men's, they could never have the degree of competence they would need in a subject as difficult as medicine — which made it likely that many lives would be lost at their hands. It would appear that, before these fine brothers of ours adopted the second of these excuses for placing their ban on women doctors, they conveniently forgot the fact that they themselves are the elder brothers of *Yamarāja.*[32] It is simply unheard of that the number of people dying at the hands of a *Yamī*[33] are as great as the number dying at the hands of these elder brethren of Yama. In 1888 signs were beginning to appear that the murky brains of the County Medical Association must have cleared up a good deal. Not only did they lift their ban on women doctors, they actually pleaded with them on bended knee to become members of their renowned association. Twenty-five years ago there was not so much as a single reputable medical association in which women doctors were members. Now you are not likely to find so much as a single first-rate medical society that does not have women doctors as members. Whether inferior-brained women do indeed have what it takes to study a subject as difficult as medicine should become clear from the following story. There is one especially prestigious medical society in the United States. Doctors write the finest quality essays for this society on subjects the society assigns them, and they win large prizes for these essays. On one occasion the subject assigned for the essays happened to be "The Necessity for Women to Rest during Menstruation."[34] When it came time to judge the essays, out of the four or five submitted by the competitors one turned out to be of clearly superior quality, and the decision was made to give its author the award of $500. This essayist had in fact practiced a small subterfuge: instead of writing her entire name on the essay in the place designated for a signature, she wrote only her initials. Now it so happened that this society regarded women doctors with a great deal of hostility; and they could not even imagine that they would ever receive essays of such profundity from women. But when they came to know, only after the prize had been awarded, that a woman (a resident of New York City), the renowned Dr. Mary Putnam

32. Trans.: *Yamarāja* or *Yama:* "[T]he deity that judges the dead. . . . Hence applied to a fierce, savage, pitiless man" (Molesworth). — *KG*

33. Trans.: Another example of Ramabai's word play, *Yamī* is at one level clearly to be read as the feminine of *Yama,* hence as an analogue for women doctors; at the same time it carries its proper sense as given by Molesworth: "That controls or restrains. 2 That practises *yamaniyama* [acts of self-restraint] . . . that has subdued his senses and passions." — *PCE*

34. Trans.: *Asparśasamayīṃ:* literally, "during the not-to-be-touched time." — *PCE*

Jacobi,[35] had written the essay, this poor partisan medical society found itself in quite a spot, having to admit that it was a woman who had written such an essay and that it was they who had chosen her to win the prize. But what could they do, poor things? By announcing the prize they had already let the cat out of the bag, so they had no choice but to let the prize be given to Dr. Jacobi.

There is a medical school in the city of New York called the New York Infirmary that is considered to be among the best public and private medical schools in the United States. Its founder is a woman doctor, and needless to say she is counted among the best doctors in the United States. When Dr. Elizabeth Blackwell,[36] the founder of the New York Infirmary, returned from Europe to her homeland around 1850 after completing her medical studies and acquiring much experience, it came to her notice that there was a dire need for the establishment of hospitals for women. In the large public hospitals that were under the supervision of highly reputed male doctors, women, who were deemed to have inferior brains, were not allowed admission to study such things as patient care and surgery. So in 1857, this hardworking woman along with her sister established not only their renowned hospital but a medical school that was attached to it.[37] Hardworking and philanthropic women just like her started to give her their aid and support. And following her example, the women of Boston opened a hospital in 1862 called the New England Hospital for Women and Children. Exactly as in the case of the New York Infirmary, women who have just finished their medical studies come here to this hospital as well to obtain priceless experience in such things as patient care and surgery through direct application or through observation. Our beloved compatriot Dr. Anandibai Joshi stayed in this same New England Hospital to gain experience after she finished her course of medical studies in Philadelphia. Taking their cue from Boston, the women of Philadelphia opened a hospital for women and children that is connected to the Women's Medical Col-

35. Trans.: Mary Corinna Putnam Jacobi (1842-1906), graduate of the Woman's Medical College of Pennsylvania (1864) and of the Ecole de Medecine in Paris (1871), had a distinguished career in New York City as a physician, professor of medicine (at the Woman's Medical College of the New York Infirmary for Women and Children), and writer. She won the Boylston Prize from Harvard in 1876 for one of her essays. — *PCE*

36. Trans.: Elizabeth Blackwell (1821-1910) was the first woman to receive a medical degree (in 1849) in the United States but because of prejudice was unable to practice medicine for several years. The New York Infirmary for Women and Children started out as a one-room dispensary in 1853. — *PCE*

37. Trans.: The Women's Medical College of the New York Infirmary was established in 1868. — *PCE*

lege in Philadelphia. There too provision has been made to give practical training to women who have completed their medical education. Based on the same pattern as the three hospitals I have already mentioned, there are the Chicago Hospital for Women and Children in the city of Chicago, the Pacific Hospital for Women and Children in the city of San Francisco, the Ohio Hospital in the city of Cincinnati, and the Northwestern Hospital in the city of Minneapolis. This makes a total of seven first-rate hospitals and training schools established and run by women that shine with an unfading brilliance across the northern states of the United States — like the seven bright stars of the Seven Sages[38] that shine their splendor across the northern skies — delighting the society of both men and women who have their eyes fixed on them with hope and enthusiasm. It is a matter of true joy that, following the example set by the women of the United States, the women of England are also establishing the same kind of hospitals and training colleges.

At the present time in this country there are thirty-six medical schools established for women only, in which the responsibility for teaching is almost entirely given to women. Even in mixed colleges many women doctors are working as teachers. From all this it is evident that the belief of the people of the United States that women would be corrupted if they studied medicine has changed. From the time women began to study medicine, knowledgeable people in this field have begun to regard the human body and the subject of anatomy as pure and sacred things. The foulness and indecency that used to accompany the teaching of anatomy at the medical schools before women came there to study have now been completely stopped. Faced with the modest and praiseworthy moral conduct of the women students, the male teachers and students who had made such a foul thing of anatomy began to feel ashamed of their actions. Nowadays, on account of these women, the manner and the language used in teaching anatomy have changed so much for the better that people are manifesting the hope that it be taught even to very young, eight- or ten-year-old children.

One more extremely useful profession that women have entered is the practice of law in the courts. In 1868 Washington University in the city of St. Louis allowed women to be taught law. Then, in 1869, for the first time in the United States, a woman, Arabella Mansfield,[39] was admitted to the bar and

38. Trans.: *Saptarṣi*, i.e., *saptaṛṣi:* "The seven saints of the Brahmarshi order . . . Kaśyapa, Atri, Bharadvāja, Viśvāmitra, Gautama, Jagadagni, Vaśiṣṭha. . . . These form, in astronomy, the asterism of Ursa Major" (Molesworth). — *PCE*

39. Trans.: Arabella Mansfield (1846-1911) was admitted to the Iowa bar in 1869 but pursued an academic career at Iowa Wesleyan and DePauw University instead of practicing law. — *PCE*

started her practice as a lawyer. Since that time almost all the major universities have given women permission to study law in their schools. Many people had doubts that women would be able to study a subject as difficult as law, but now these doubts have all but vanished. After witnessing the excellence of their work in the courts, their way of arguing cases in strict compliance with the law, their constitutional fitness to perform as equals with all the major male lawyers, and best of all their modest and decent conduct, little doubt remains now in people's minds about the worthiness of women as lawyers. There are hundreds of women who have been admitted to the bar in the United States. Just as the male lawyers here do, they set up small separate law firms to do their work. There are twenty-one law firms of this sort belonging to married couples in which both the husband and the wife are lawyers.

There used to be many people who had doubts about how women would be able to preserve their respectability and their modesty if they began to practice law in the courts where all kinds of cases, good and bad, make their appearance. But these skeptics ought to have borne one thing in mind: it is not only cases involving men that appear in the courts but also cases involving women. You will not find as many individuals who commit crimes among womankind as among men — and this is a matter for congratulation and a great adornment to womankind — but there are certainly a few of them who are women. And men simply cannot understand their problems the way that lawyers of their own kind *(svajātīya)* can. It isn't especially hard for a thoughtful person to understand just how awkward it can be for women when they enter a place where they are surrounded by men and there isn't even a single woman present. Indeed, there should be no grounds for objection to respectable women entering any place where there are respectable men — and it is imperative that in the courts of law the appointed officials such as the judges and the lawyers be respectable. Ever since women have started to become lawyers, the likelihood has greatly increased that women who have committed crimes will receive proper justice. But enough of that.

Experience has shown then that there is nothing lacking to be found in the natural modesty of the women lawyers of the United States or in the honor and respect they are shown. Not only do all men maintain a proper respect for women lawyers in the courtrooms where they are present, but from the time women entered the courts the common rules prohibiting unseemly conduct such as smoking tobacco and using foul language in the courtroom have been more strictly enforced. If anyone wants to see just how accomplished women are in the field of law, they aren't likely to really grasp this unless they go see for themselves how women perform in the Supreme Court of the United States and in other courts of law. Men have been practicing law in the United States for hundreds of years while it has been barely twenty years now since women have won the right to take the bar exams. In this short period of time these brave women have attained parity with male law firms that have enjoyed a superior position of respect for hundreds of years. As of yet they have not produced lawyers of such renown as O'Fannel, Curren, Webster, and Coates. But where is it written that they won't? And who would want to say that all *male* lawyers are of that caliber?

The monthly legal review called the *Legal News* has been published in Chicago since 1868. It is published by Myra Bradwell.[40] This woman is president of the largest association in the United States of its kind that publishes law-related books. The impressive volume entitled *Bradwell Appellate Court Reports,* which was prepared under her supervision, is famous everywhere, and almost all lawyers make use of it. Another woman by the name of Caroline White publishes a bimonthly review called the *Chicago Law Times,* which is also highly regarded in legal circles for its excellence.

In 1886 the women law graduates and the women law students of the University of Michigan founded a committee called the Equity Club. Its object is to establish relations of friendship among women not only in the United States but in all those countries where women have won the right to practice law, to provide support to one another, and to help bring about the progress of womankind. Men may have been practicing law for thousands of years, but nobody has ever heard of them establishing committees like the Equity Club for the welfare of common *man*kind — all without making any distinctions based on social groups *(jātī)* or nationalities. This is an excellent example of how educated women make good use of any right that they receive.

The fourth important profession that women have entered is that of the clergy. For some years after the founding of Christianity, Christian women had the right to expound the Scriptures just the same as men. At that time it was the rule that only an individual authorized by God — someone to whom God had given his holy power and appointed to the task of expounding the Scriptures, whether man or woman — should do so. The Christianity preached by Christ is very simple, and its rules are equally applicable to both men and women. The Supreme Being,[41] Christ's God, gives his Holy Spirit in exactly the same way to women and to men without making any distinction *(jātibheda)* between them. He shows no partiality such as humans do and

40. Trans.: Myra Bradwell (1831-1894), founder (in 1868) as well as publisher and editor of the *Chicago Legal News,* passed her bar exam in 1869 with honors but was not admitted to the bar in Illinois until 1892. — *PCE*

41. Trans.: *Parameśvara:* "The Supreme Being; the Lord of the Universe" (Molesworth). — *PCE*

does not commit the task of expounding the Scriptures to the charge solely of men. He gives the appropriate gifts to the appropriate persons. He gives these gifts to many different men and many different women in unique and different ways. There is no rule that certain gifts — goodness of character, artistic skill, scholarship, the power of healing — should be received only by womankind and certain of them only by men. But when Christianity came under the control of people like the Romans, who regarded womankind as inferior, they introduced their own good and evil notions to the Christian religion. The Roman Catholic priests and monks used to regard women as an enemy in the same way they did Satan.[42] They and others just like them seized from women the right to expound the Scriptures. Even though given God's own inspiration to expound the Scriptures, women have had to bear silence even to this day and listen without demur to whatever men might say because of this prohibition by partisan men. But now in this nineteenth century of ours, owing to the light of knowledge, men have begun to see their mistakes. Numbers of impartial clergymen coming from most of the Christian countries have begun to say that women should have the right to expound the Scriptures. There are currently 165 women in the United States who are ordained ministers within various denominations. The people of this country have begun to see as a matter of experience that on numerous occasions the work of propagating the faith is not carried out in as straightforward and natural a manner by the male clergy as it is by the female clergy. For this and other reasons, the desire to have more women clergy in their country is taking firm root among the mass of the people.

Stenography, i.e., shorthand, is another occupation that women have entered. They have become so accomplished at stenography that in recent times in the United States the most important and renowned journalists and lawyers, with the greatest of respect for them, are giving tasks of major responsibility in their offices to women stenographers. Women who have entered this occupation earn much more than the average woman teacher. They study stenography for a year or a year and a half; and after doing a short apprenticeship, they take down verbatim the speeches in the Supreme Court and in other such places where the most prominent public speakers give their speeches. They earn from five to twenty dollars an hour for this work.

When the English scholar Harriet Martineau came to the United States in 1840, women were at liberty to enter only seven menial occupations, namely, (1) teaching children the alphabet and handwriting; (2) sewing; (3) running a

42. Trans.: *Saitāna*, literally, "Satan, the devil" (Molesworth), is an Arabic loan word. — *PCE*

boarding house; (4) working as a servant in somebody else's home; (5) composing type in a printing press; (6) folding and stitching the pages of books at a bindery; and (7) doing the most menial jobs in factories. But now those days are gone forever. Now that women have become educated, those who have the capacity to enter occupations that are superior to those mentioned above will not be satisfied with doing nothing but those occupations. Even though they do not receive much assistance and encouragement from the national government or the state governments of the United States, with the help of their own keen intelligence, determination, and perseverance they are developing their God-given powers of creativity. From the census of 1880 we learn that in the United States women were engaged in 300 different kinds of work. In the single state of Massachusetts there were 251,158 women engaged in 284 different occupations. Their annual income ranges from $150 to $3,000.

It is commonly said that women are not creative because they have limited brains — and that only because women lacked all creativity did it have to be left to men to come up with all the new ideas there have ever been. My response is that women did not come up with new ideas not because of the inferiority of their brains but because no one ever gave them the opportunity or the encouragement to develop their creative powers. Here and there we can indeed find cases where women came up with new ideas but because of their inherent generosity they let them be published under the names of men. For example, the sister of the famous European musician and instrumentalist Beethoven composed many very fine and surpassingly melodious musical compositions,[43] but she let them be published under her brother's name. It was on the strength of these musical compositions that Beethoven's fame has become immortal, but very few people must have known that they were composed by his sister.[44] In a similar case, Caroline Herschel, the sister of the astronomer William Herschel, made the discovery of several heavenly bodies. During the course of his astronomical studies she assisted him in an essential way with her surpassing abilities in mathematics. But although William Herschel earned the greatest of fame owing to the selfless assistance and untiring labor of Caroline Herschel, the world did not assign her any share in his success. One reason that women such as Beethoven's sister allowed their ideas and discoveries to be published under the name of their male relatives or male

43. Trans.: Ramabai uses here the terms *rāga* and *rāgiṇī* of classical Indian music. *Rāga:* "A mode of song or music. There are six. . . . They are personified in poetry and mythology, and have each six . . . feminine modifications . . . termed *rāgiṇī*. . . . the popular enumeration of the *rāga* amounts to some dozens" (Molesworth). — *PCE*

44. Trans.: What Ramabai's source was for this apocryphal story is unknown. She may have had Felix Mendelssohn and his sister Fanny in mind. — *PCE*

acquaintances was the inherent generosity of their characters. Another is that in times past people from almost all countries had the barbarous *(rānaṭī)* belief (which is still prevalent in our own land) that it was a most horribly disgraceful thing for women to discover new things or to achieve any other kind of accomplishment for which they would gain worldly fame.

Nowadays discoveries that women have made are gradually starting to receive encouragement in the United States. Up until just very recently women have registered a total of 1,935 patents with the government of the United States for new ideas and inventions they have developed. And these are not just trivial ideas either. They clearly exhibit the knowledge these women had of the most difficult subjects of science. For example, in 1845 one woman invented an underwater telescope. Another woman invented life jackets and life rafts for people who sail the seas. Another one built a machine for producing steam. Still another one made improvements to the steam mechanism used in steam locomotives. One invented a device for reducing the noise made by trains running through cities. One discovered a means for preventing soil erosion during floods. Still another one invented a non-inductive electric cable.[45] Women have also invented a great many very useful machines such as a mechanism for loading grain onto ships, a machine for threshing grain, and a machine for harvesting crops. This clearly leaves no room for anyone to say that women are not creative.

Many of you must know that in China and in some places in Hindusthan there are women navigators. In the United States it is not normally the custom for women to work as navigators on boats. But it does begin to appear that henceforth the women here will start to enter this occupation as well. On many of the steamboats that sail the two major rivers called the Hudson and the Mississippi, women who are experts in navigation are captains of boats, and they perform their duties with great skill and on a solid scientific basis. Nowadays you will not find many occupations in the United States that women have not entered. Over the past forty years, ever since they got the freedom to enter a variety of occupations, their employment has been steadily on the rise. Seven percent of the farmers in the United States now are women who operate their own farms, and 16 percent of the people who make their living from manufacturing[46] are women. More than 600,000 women make their living from manufacturing. Besides this, there are over sixty thou-

45. Trans.: Ramabai invents a Marathi equivalent here — *apravartaka vijecā śeṇḍā* — but also provides the English in parentheses. — *PCE*

46. Trans.: *Śilpakalā:* although the word is nowadays used to mean "sculpture," Ramabai consistently uses it (see especially Chapter 9) in the sense of "manual/mechanical arts," i.e., "manufacturing." — *PCE*

sand who run their own businesses or who are sales agents for store owners. There are thousands of women who work for the telegraph service, who sell train tickets, and who work for the postal service. Women who work as cooks and maidservants in other people's homes number 1,360,000.

Legal Rights

It is cause for surprise and distress then that even though there has been so much progress in all areas in the United States, the law has given women very few rights. Almost all of the social regulations have been derived from ancient English laws — which have as their foundation the laws of Moses and Roman law. When you bear this in mind, the puzzle of why women are regarded as so inferior — looked at from the perspective of current American laws — can be solved. In the newly formed states of the western region, there have been many changes made in the laws pertaining to women. In these states it is the law that the house in which a married man resides conjugally with his wife is to be considered not his alone but also his wife's house. But in almost all of the eastern states, after the death of her husband, a widow does not have the right to stay in his house for more than forty days without paying rent! The kind-hearted, learned men in the state of Maine took pity on the poor, grief-stricken widow and allowed for the provision that that she be allowed to stay for ninety days in the house of her late husband without paying rent! Recently, in quite a number of states, married women have been given the right to make use in whatever way they see fit of the property they themselves have acquired. According to the law, if they remain at home and earn money by sewing other people's clothes, drawing pictures, and so on, they have no rights to what they earn; only if they earn money by working outside the home can they claim it as their own. In quite a number of states, a married woman has complete rights over the fixed and liquid assets given her by her father or her brother, and after her husband's death over one third of his liquid assets. But in many states married women have no rights over any property given them by their fathers or over what they themselves have earned, and they do not receive any share whatsoever from their husbands' assets.

In New York and several other states, a mother cannot claim any rights over her own underage children. If a father, either while he is living or after he dies through his will, hands over custody of his children to whomever he wishes, he is not punished for it. A husband has the right, against his own wife's wishes, to give away to others the children born to her. But if he is insane and has not made out a will regarding his children, the mother can keep her own underage children with her. The children of men and women who are respectably and legally married are called the father's children from the point of view of the law, and their mother has not the slightest right over them. Only the children of unmarried women or of prostitutes are understood to be their mother's children. Two or three years ago the heartless husband of a respectable woman attempted to give her tender babies away to somebody else against her wishes. The poor mother could not bear to be separated from her own children; so in order to be allowed to keep her little ones with her, she had no alternative but to cast aside all modesty and respectability, lie under oath in a court of law, and say, "These children are not by my lawfully wedded husband." Only then did she get her children back. So just see how the laws in countries that call themselves genteel trample underfoot women's modesty, their maternal love, and their own natural God-given rights! The men who make such laws as these can belong neither to the human nor to the demon realm but, it would seem, must belong to that class of "Who they are we do not know."[47] In the states of Kansas, New Jersey, and Iowa, however, mothers can claim rights over their own children.

Some years ago in Massachusetts and other states, women did not have the right as wives to have their bodies buried next to the bodies of their husbands, but now this law has been changed. The moment they are married, women become their husbands' chattel. The clergy have them take a vow: "I will obey my husband's commands." Whatever fixed or liquid assets their father or brother has given them, the very jewelry that they wear, and more, all goes into their husbands' hands.[48] Some years ago wives did not even have

47. Trans.: *Te ke na jānīmahe:* The quotation is from Bhartrihari, *Nītiśataka,* verse 46 (in some editions). Our grateful acknowledgements to Gudrun Buhnemann for help in identifying the quotation. — *PCE*

48. Of all the signs that still exist in American society of their formerly uncivilized *(rānaṭī)* condition, it would not be wrong to say that the extreme subjection of married women is the preeminent one. American men, exactly like the men in our own land, are shameless. They say, "We labor all day, support our families by the sweat of our brow, and provide our wives with food and drink." Men work for eight or ten hours a day, or at the very most twelve hours; but women have to break their backs working sixteen or seventeen hours a day in serving their men, in taking care of their children, in doing the housework, and so on. Not to mention the wives of men who are laborers or farmers or who do other occupations of that sort — who take care of their housework and their children, then work alongside their husbands assisting the men in doing their various occupations, in spite of which the wife does not have any rights over the family income. If she needs a bit of money to pay her expenses, she has to win over her husband, provide convincing answers to his thousands of questions, and beg for it from him. If he refuses to give her the money, not only can she not claim any right over her own hard-earned property (before either the law or the community), but her husband, to the contrary, makes sure to tell her what great favors he has bestowed on her. And the community (the community of men) says, "Men work so

any rights over the clothes that they wore; but at least now the law prohibits husbands from selling or pawning their wives' clothes and other personal effects in order to line their own pockets.

The laws concerning marriage and divorce are different in all the different states of the United States. This makes for a lot of confusion in the social order. Upright people in this country and particularly the Women's Temperance Union and its supporters have begun a long-term effort to make the marriage laws uniform and just everywhere in the country.

It is the law that citizens of the United States should receive justice in the courts from twelve jurors who are their equals.[49] But women do not have the right to receive justice from jurors who are either their equals or of their own kind *(svajātīya)*. In the process of making national and state laws, men — whether they be a hundred times more foolish or given over to vice or whatever else than women — do not allow a law-making assembly to make a peep without first consulting the opinions of men. But women — no matter how learned, intelligent, thoughtful, and morally upright they might be — do not have the right to give their opinion about any of the political arrangements, whether at the national or the local level. It is for this reason, from the point of view at least of the law, that men are far superior to women; so that if they sit as jurors to settle women's judicial cases, the justice rendered by them ipso facto cannot be the same as that rendered by jurors who are the true equals of the female plaintiff. Currently, with the single exception of the Territory of Wyoming, there is not one place in the United States where this most important right of the common American citizen is given to women — for no other reason than that they are women. Nevertheless, the hardworking women here are making an effort to acquire political rights for themselves, and signs are appearing everywhere that their efforts will bear fruit in the course of time.

---

hard to earn money and provide food and clothing for their wives!" Really and truly! What great favors men do bestow on women! If there is no wife in a house, at least two to three servants have to be hired to do all the work that she does. And they have to be paid. Servants don't get their bread to eat free of any cost to the master; and it certainly cannot be said the master does this for them as a favor. But even when a wife does the work of ten servants and her husband gives her food to eat, it is nothing but his favor bestowed on her! — *PRS*

49. Trans.: Rather oddly, in speaking of the American system of justice, Ramabai here resorts to words of Arabic origin: *adālata* ("court of justice") and *insāpha* ("justice"). For "jurors," she uses the Sanskritic *pañca:* "The member of an assembly of arbitration. Used *pl* it signifies the assembly, as this usually consists of five members. 2 A jury" (Molesworth). — *PCE*

Unified Efforts[50] — National Organizations

When the democratic nation of the United States was established, Benjamin Franklin suggested that the motto *e pluribus unum,* i.e., many come together as one, should be inscribed on the nation's seal. Not only do you see this motto inscribed on the national seal wherever you may go in the country, you but can see, hear, and experience this motto at every moment in the actions of the people of this nation. The strength of the United States lies not in its stores of artillery, in its arsenals, or in a vast army. It lies in the educational attainments of the people of this country and in the truth that is expressed in the motto, "Many come together as one." When women were uneducated and lacked all common experience of public life, they did not know about this truth — which is why they had no hand in performing major works of public welfare. The more educated and broad-visioned they became, the higher did this timeless truth rise like the sun in their hearts and begin to grow brighter day by day.

Fifty years ago in the United States, a nation that has become famous all over the world for its progressiveness, there wasn't a single women's association of note. Women used to sit in their own homes or gather together in small groups of three or four at a neighbor's house and chat or do needlework in aid of the churches, the clergy, or the poor. It had never even occurred to anyone that women would be able to do anything more important than this. Not even to speak of men, women themselves had no idea of how great the worthiness, the power, and the intelligence of womankind is. Fifty years ago when an association of women who had a passion for education called the Blue Stocking Club was established in England with the objective of encouraging general educational progress, the entire world laughed to hear of it. The words "Blue Stocking" everywhere became an object of ridicule. Women who called themselves respectable, when they heard the name of this women's association and heard that women attended it to discuss questions of educational progress, were reduced to exclaiming with Sita Devi, "O Mother Earth, receive me into thy bosom."[51] That women should attend a women's associa-

50. Trans.: *Saṃhata prayatna:* Efforts made by many people gathered together in one spirit. *Samhata* = brought into unison, unified. — *KG*

51. Trans.: *De māya dharaṇī ṭhāya.* A. Manwaring, in *Marathi Proverbs,* p. 152, renders it: "O mother (earth)! give me a place." Molesworth gives the slight variant, *De māya dharaṇī ṭhāva,* which he renders, "O mother Earth, receive me into thy bosom." Both variants are cited by Y. R. Date and C. G. Karve, eds., *Mahārāṣṭra vāksampradāya kośa,* vol. 2 (Pune: Varada Books, 1988 [1947]), p. 48. They render the sense as follows: "O Mother Earth! Give me refuge in your belly. (Sita says this when, after Rama had freed her from Ravana and brought her back, he re-

tion or, worse, speak at these associations used to be felt by everyone as nothing short of wicked.

But faced with the radiance of this progressive century of ours, the darkness of the society of which we have spoken here did not last long. The American Sarasvati, Frances Willard, has said somewhere, "During this much acclaimed nineteenth century many amazing (scientific) discoveries have been made; but by far the most amazing of them all is that woman discovered herself." The evidence of this is clear when you analyze the history of the large and small associations American women have created over the past forty years and the unified efforts they have made through them for their own welfare and that of their society and of their nation. In 1848 five or ten courageous, progressive, and highly educated women, Lucretia Mott, Elizabeth Cady Stanton, and others, for the first time established a significant women's organization and began to work toward obtaining for women the rights to have an education and employment on equal terms with men as well as political rights.[52] You might say it was from this time that the unified efforts of American women began. Up until 1869 there might have been other small, miscellaneous women's associations established from time to time — but nobody has heard that these accomplished anything truly important or that assumed the form of a national organization. Through 1858, no "National Women's Organization" had ever come into existence, in the United States or even anywhere else in the world. Until this time the idea had never even occurred to anyone that women were capable not only of establishing a national organization but also of doing everything in proper order that was needed to make it work. Around about 1860 signs began to appear that a terrible war was about to break out in the United States. A dispute arose between the people of the Southern and the Northern states over the enslavement of the African people, because of which feelings of hostility began to smolder on both sides. From 1860 and 1861, when the Southern states issued a vociferous call to battle against their compatriots in the North, up until 1865, the fires of war blazed in both parts of the country, producing general lamentation in American families everywhere. It may be true that the first thing this civil war produced was the terrible poison of sorrow, penury, and pain; but immediately following this it produced two great gems, miraculous and sparkling, like the nectar of immortality and

jected her.) A person says this when he has been gravely afflicted. To reach a state of 'enough is enough; no more.'" — *PCE*

52. Trans.: The Seneca Falls Convention, the first women's rights assembly in America, was organized by Lucretia Mott and Elizabeth Cady Stanton and convened in July 1848. — *PCE*

the wish-fulfilling jewel that emerged from the ocean when it was churned by the gods.[53]

When President Lincoln became the leader of the Northern states he made the enslavement of Africans a capital offense and called upon strong, able-bodied American fighting men to join the army as volunteers in order to break the revolt of the South and save the country's honor. Till then the Northern states had not made any preparations for war. When the brave Northern men respected President Lincoln's call to arms and marched off to battle, they did not even have standard-colored uniforms (trousers, shirts, socks, etc.) to wear. There weren't even any organizations in place to supply these or other war materials. The moment they heard that the soldiers needed clothes to wear when the war began, women from almost all the towns in the Northern states gathered together in their churches and started sewing clothes. To begin with, they supplied enough clothes sewn by them to last the soldiers for three months. This was the occasion when women began to realize just how significant something could be when many people joined together to do it and just how great a benefit could accrue from it, both to society and to the nation.

As time went by and the American Civil War grew more terrible and spread in all directions, an organization called the "Christian Commission" was established in the Northern states. The purpose of this organization was to send clergymen out to the sites of battle to give religious instruction to the soldiers who were fighting on the battlefields and, at the time of death, lead their souls onto the path of salvation — and in this way provide spiritual succor to the soldiers. It fell to the lot of women to raise the money to pay for the expenses of this association, while men assumed the positions in the organization of president, vice president, and so on. The crores of rupees that women raised, through any number of toilsome ways, and offered up to this organization were taken and used by this religious organization to send hundreds of clergymen to the sites of battle to give religious instruction to the soldiers. There can be no doubt that the objective of the organization was

53. Trans.: Ramabai alludes in this sentence to the account in the Purāṇas of the churning of the ocean of milk by the gods, at the behest of Vishnu, in order to retrieve the *amṛta* ("The drink of the immortals, nectar" — Molesworth) that would reinstate the good fortune they had lost in their battle with the *asuras*. During the churning, the ocean first produced the terrible *hālāhala* poison, which was swallowed by Shiva to protect the world from it. Then followed other miraculous things such as the *cintāmaṇi* ("A gem of *svarga* supposed to yield to its possessor every thing wanted" — Molesworth) and finally the *amrta* itself. See *Classical Hindu Mythology: A Reader in the Sanskrit Puranas*, ed. and trans. Cornelia Dimmitt and J. A. B. van Buitenen (Philadelphia: Temple University Press, 1978), p. 74. — *PCE*

most praiseworthy; but the soldiers, wounded on the battlefield, dying of hunger and thirst, and suffering agonizing pain, weren't very interested in listening to sermons. The clergymen, who had gone there to give spiritual succor to their souls, didn't have any knowledge, however, of how to relieve the agonies suffered by the soldiers' "transitory" bodies — and thus to offer them physical succor. It could hardly be held against him if a soldier, wounded in his arm or leg and in this difficult moment needing physical succor, had no use for the pratings of a priest, who instead of offering the wounded soldier what he needed set out to give him a sermon. When they realized the truth of this, many people, women and men, felt that it was necessary to establish an independent organization to offer material aid to suffering, weary, and wounded soldiers and that this organization should appoint women to assist the wounded men on the battlefields and to look after them. So they established an organization called the "Sanitary Commission."

The very existence of this organization as well as the important work it initiated and carried to completion was certainly surprising; but what struck the whole world with surprise was to see the triumphs of the American women who supported this organization, who from first to last collected all the materials and equipment that it needed, and who managed its operation. This organization sent not hundreds but thousands of women and men as nurses to the front. They made the necessary arrangements to provide food and water on time to wounded soldiers on the friendly side (and also to some left behind from the enemy side); set up field hospitals; buried the dead soldiers; and gave all necessary relief to the friendless and destitute. But from where was to come the vast amounts of money and supplies this organization needed to carry out its innumerable tasks? There was no money left in the government treasury; and no one individual had money sufficient to meet the huge expenses of this organization — and even if they did, no one had so much generosity as to donate it all at once. This was the situation when the leading women of the executive committee of this organization had a real brainstorm. Mary A. Livermore[54] together with one or two other women decided to put this idea to work. They wrote petitions to a large number of people in Illinois and other states informing them of their objective and of the means they had in mind to accomplish it. In a very short time words such as these were being published in newspapers throughout the Northern states:

54. Trans.: Mary Ashton Rice Livermore (1820-1905) of Boston was a lifelong proponent of the temperance cause and activist in the women's suffrage movement. During the war she herself worked as a nurse for the Union Army and thereafter organized the Chicago Woman Suffrage Convention in 1868 and founded and edited (from 1868 to 1872) the feminist journals *The Agitator* and *The Women's Journal*. — *PCE*

"In Chicago some enterprising women have come together to organize a charity bazaar. Items sent by benefactors of the bazaar will be sold at a good price and the proceeds sent by these women to defray the costs of the Sanitary Commission. Those philanthropic men and women who wish to assist this good cause should send useful items, as they have the means, to the address of such and such a woman in Chicago."

The women who organized this bazaar estimated that if they could bring it off without a hitch, they would see a profit of at least twenty-five thousand dollars from it. When they heard this, knowledgeable gentlemen and respectable journalists laughed outright. They said it was too far-fetched even to think of women having the brains to make a profit of twenty-five thousand dollars; it would suffice if they didn't make a fiasco of the bazaar once they began it. Some, with expressions of utter contempt, laughed and said that on the stipulated date in Chicago, the potatoes would take out a wedding procession.[55] But these brave, hardworking women paid no heed to people's scorn and contempt. Doing whatever each one of them could wherever they happened to live, they set to work, laboring night and day, to accomplish their objective. Women from Illinois and several other states sent off to Chicago hundreds of items such as clothes they had sewn, curios, preserves of various kinds, pickles, sweets, and so on. And on the appointed day the bazaar opened. Some farmers living near Chicago who were rather too full of themselves — who knows whether as a reward to those who had ridiculed these philanthropic women or what — loaded up their carts with vegetables, flowers, potatoes, and such, and with the greatest of fanfare delivered them to the bazaar. The intelligent women who managed the bazaar had organized it superbly. Thousands of onlookers went to see the bazaar with very mixed intentions, but once they arrived they were most pleasantly surprised to see the superb organization of the bazaar and the politeness of those who had created it, and they purchased some item or other. After the bazaar ended it came to be known to the community of people there that, after subtracting the cost of organizing the bazaar, the proceeds from the sale of the items in it came to more than five times the amount its creators had estimated. The hardworking women of the Sanitary Commission made a profit of about $125,000, i.e., about 375,000 rupees, which they sent to the Commission to use in its work. After this there were bazaars of this kind organized in many other places as a way to help the Sanitary Commission. The last two of these were held in New York and Philadelphia, in the first of which they made a profit of $1,000,000,

55. Trans.: *Baṭāṭyāṃcī varāta:* literally, wedding procession of potatoes. Metaphorically, a ridiculous attempt of foolish people to accomplish something impossible. — *KG*

i.e., 3,000,000 rupees, and in the $1,200,000, i.e., 3,600,000 rupees. It was women who came up with the idea of these bazaars; it was they who organized everything from beginning to end; and it was thousands, hundreds of thousands, of women who made and sent almost all of the items, large and small, that were sold in them. When men — those men who had always taken pride in saying, "We alone are possessed of all public virtues," and who were always going on about women not having the brains to manage practical occupations in public life — saw displayed in women this kind of competence, this methodicalness, this political astuteness, farsightedness, and perseverance, they could only rub their eyes; while those decent-hearted men who recognized the true worthiness of women did not hesitate to congratulate them.

This Sanitary Commission was one kind of national philanthropic organization in which for the first time women had occasion to fill positions of public trust, large and small, and to work as the equals of men. As a result of the countless profits earned by the festivals and bazaars that were organized in aid of this organization and the extraordinary things that were taken from beginning to successful completion, women came to an excellent understanding of the truth that if many people work together straightforwardly, methodically, and with one mind, doing bit by bit as they can, the most exalted objectives can be achieved. And the world came to realize what great things women can accomplish if they receive an education, independence, and the freedom to work. The famous philanthropist from England, Florence Nightingale, put aside the purdah-like constraints[56] of English custom and went out to the war in Crimea where she nursed the wounded soldiers, arranged for the proper care of the sick at the site of the conflict, and set a sterling example for all women of compassion around the world. A reading of the five or six years of American history from 1860 to 1866 will show clearly just how well the women of America followed Nightingale*bāī*'s example. From the outbreak of the American Civil War up to the time that it ended, not only did the women of the Northern states continue to look after their own households, but they also took responsibility for men's employments and other work; and not only did they collect and donate innumerable goods and crores of rupees needed by philanthropic associations such as the Christian Commission and the Sanitary Commission, but many hundreds and thousands of these altruistic

56. Trans.: *Paḍadapośīpaṇā*, made by adding the abstract noun ending *pana* to the Persian loan *padadaposi:* "Privacy, privateness, shelter from observation: also a retired and concealed place" (Molesworth); hence, the purdah system of female seclusion — a common target of many Westerners' criticism of Indian society. So its evocation here in the context of restrictive English custom seems at least to hint at sarcasm. — *PCE*

women went out to the battlefields and took care of the exhausted, worn-out, wounded, and dying soldiers, toiling night and day in their service to them. In the middle of the afternoon or in the middle of the night or at any time at all, ignoring hunger and thirst, physical discomfort, and much worse, with fierce battles raging around them or on any other occasion, wherever anyone needed help, they went themselves and helped one and all in a timely way. Hundreds of the most wealthy women left their homes — homes of great comfort and privilege — and took a life of wandering and deprivation[57] upon themselves to allay the suffering of their compatriots who had gone to the battlefields; and there, putting their own lives at risk, they expended their physical health and strength, their wealth, and even their precious lives in doing every act of kindness. Blessed be those saintly, benevolent mothers of mercy!

From 1865 up to the present time a great many women's societies have been established in the United States — and they will certainly continue to be established. Not only in the United States but in England, France, Germany, Finland, Norway, Italy, and other countries, both local and national women's organizations have been established, organizations that have many different kinds of objectives. If you ask why these national women's organizations have been created, the answer is simply that through their work in organizations such as the Sanitary Commission during the time of the Civil War in the United States, women's inherent competence was revealed to the world; and women themselves came to understand how great their own worthiness and power were, as well as what extraordinary deeds could be accomplished by unified efforts through which many people come together and with one mind do one particular thing. So women then began to put this newly made scientific *(śāstrīya)* discovery about themselves to good use. During these past twenty or twenty-five years, at the very least thirty or forty national women's organizations have been established; and their work has been going on in an orderly and superior way. When the Sanitary Commission was dissolved at the end of the American Civil War, hundreds, indeed thousands, of women's associations, large and small, came into existence in the United States. The word that fifty years ago women used to feel ashamed to utter has today become common usage everywhere. Nowadays, any town with a population of a thousand or twelve hundred that doesn't have some sort of a women's association is very rare. Wherever you go, in small towns or in large cities, there are hundreds of different women's associations — for "Promotion of Education,"

57. Trans.: *Vanavāsa:* "Dwelling in a forest or wood. 2 A wild, wandering, unsettled manner of life" (Molesworth). — *KG*

for "Mutual Edification," for "Assistance to the Poor," for "Temperance," for "Propagation of Morality," for "Promotion of Friendship," for "Protection of Orphans," for "Protection of Children," for "Protection of Prisoners," for "Upliftment of Fallen Women," for "Promotion of Music," for "Philanthropy," for "Protection of Religion," for "Prevention of Cruelty," for "Reform of Education," for "Friendship in Travel," for "Supervision of Working Women," for "Reform of Children's Education," for "Demanding Political Rights," for "Social Progress," for "Women's Progress," for "Propagation of Religion," for "Promotion of Purity," and many more — working body and soul at their worthy tasks and completely focused on the work of seeking their society's and their nation's advancement. Fifty years ago, because women were unschooled they did not understand how worthwhile a unified effort could be; so they went about doing their religious and charitable work separately and alone wherever they happened to live and in whatever way they thought best — which is why no great task was ever accomplished by them. Now that reign of ignorance is over and the age of knowledge has begun. Women have come to the realization that if many of them come together, take one another's advice, and with one common spirit make a unified effort, they can reap many large benefits. Now women are becoming equal partners with men in the great task of promoting the national advancement of the United States. Although, owing to constraints of space, I cannot describe very many of the women's associations here, we shall briefly consider the nature and the outstanding accomplishments of a few of them.[58]

Go to just about any country and you will realize that it is women who are the guardians of religion and morality. Women of all countries and all communities *(jātī)* have been protecting their own religions through their holy and pious conduct, their charity, their devotion to God, and their sacrifice of all things for the protection of their religion. Recently, during the past forty years, these priceless virtues of women belonging to the Christian countries have been discovered, and they have found an opportunity to do religious work independently, following their own conscience. The world has

58. Although all of the organizations that are briefly described here are independent and were started with different objectives, the relations between them are so close that it is very rare to find an example of one association successfully completing some important task on its agenda in which other women's associations have not directly or indirectly given it help. So it cannot be said with any certainty that any one of them should get all the credit for any one of its accomplishments. Not only does an American women's association not feel jealous toward other organizations when it doesn't get all the credit for the success of some work, they are forever ready to aid one another, and it is to them an ornament that they take the greatest of delight in each other's victories and accomplishments. — *PRS*

reaped great benefits from this. Around twenty-five years ago the first women's missionary organization (for the propagation of religion) was established in this country. Now women's missionary organizations have been established in almost all the Christian denominations. Altogether these organizations have around 1,500,000 women as members, and they make donations every year of more than $2,000,000, i.e., 6,000,000 rupees, which they use, through their representatives and organization presidents, for propagating religion and for helping those in need. All these women's mission organizations together print 125,000 copies of religious newspapers and magazines and distribute them everywhere for people to read. They also print crores of small religious leaflets and hand them out wherever they go. The women in these organizations organize 500,000 meetings every year where they give religious talks, read essays, and arrange lectures by important scholars and renowned speakers. All the office-holders of these organizations — their presidents, vice presidents, secretaries, managers, speakers, expositors, treasurers, journalists, magazine publishers, and so on — are women, and women do all the different kinds of work. And they do not rest at doing this kind of religious work themselves but take their young boys and girls with them from a very young age to those associations that are working for the propagation of religion; and often they organize associations of children for children alone to develop in them a taste for doing religious and philanthropic work. Along with this they impress on their children's pure, tender hearts these truths: how effective any work they might do can be if many of them join together with one mind to do it and how happy they can be if they act in this manner out of friendship for each other and if they treat one another with respect. In describing the work of women's missionary organizations, one highly respected American woman scholar once said, "Twenty-five years ago the women of our country would have found it easier to make a trip to the moon than to do such things as speaking in meetings, reading essays, presiding over meetings, preaching, or running newspapers."

Ever since this huge society of women devoted to the propagation of religion came into existence, women have come increasingly to realize how great their own worthiness and power are. In the past it was only clergy*men* who were appointed as representatives of the missionary societies to go to other countries to spread their faith. If they were married, their wives could of course accompany them. But their wives did not themselves have either the permission or the time to teach their faith. In those days it was everyone's belief that women were fundamentally unable to teach their faith, so it was simply out of the question that they should go by themselves to distant lands and spread their faith. Nowadays, even though none of the stricter Christian churches allows the ordination of women as clergy, hundreds of educated, devout women belonging to these churches, both unmarried and widowed, go out, sometimes even on their own, to places within their own country or to countries thousands of miles away; and they commit themselves zealously to the good work of freeing women, whether from poor homes or rich, from the hobbles of falsehood and ignorance. The women's missionary societies in their own land bear the expenses of these women missionaries. They bear the expense and support the continuing work of the schools for boys and girls established by these women, and they send all the equipment and aid that is needed for them.

Women's Clubs

As women's societies for the propagation of their faith were starting to be established in this way, many farsighted, highly educated women began to feel an intense need to form women's clubs. Although associations and clubs are to a large degree similar, there is one important difference. A society or association is an organization established with some particular, overriding objective; only those individuals holding the same opinion who desire to achieve that objective can become members of that organization. There need be no single objective of this kind when it comes to establishing a club. Many different people holding many different opinions can belong to a club, and any one club can do many different kinds of things. Because its members hold different opinions and have different ways of thinking, each one of the members is in a position to hear several opinions expressed by several different people on whatever matters they discuss in the club — and thus is given multiple perspectives on them. Understanding how necessary it was that women be given these kinds of multiple perspectives, twenty years ago some hardworking women established the first American women's club called "Sorosis."[59] Sorosis is a Greek word that means "an aggregate" or "a fusing together of many." When the Sorosis Club was created, most people wondered what use it could have. Women's missionary societies already existed so what was the need for clubs? There was not a single club before this time whose example this club could follow. Although the creators of Sorosis did not tell anyone very clearly what the purpose of the club was, they did intend to accomplish

59. Trans.: Sorosis was established in 1868, one of the first of many women's clubs established after the Civil War — most of them devoted to social service and to promoting the interests of business and professional women. — *PCE*

at least one important thing through the club. In those days women did not have a knowledge of practical affairs such as men did; and because there was no interchange between women holding different opinions, they remained isolated from each other; and, like frogs in a narrow well, they were narrow-minded, dogmatic, and only too apt to criticize people and point out their faults. The creators of Sorosis knew the truth that only a knowledge of various opinions obtained through wide-ranging interaction could make this dogmatism, which was born out of ignorance, disappear; and women would be able to act more in accord with one another and more easily accomplish a variety of important things.

After Sorosis had been established, everyone realized the many benefits that a club could have. Sorosis very quickly assumed a quite formidable, broad-ranging array of aspects to its profile through such activities as the promotion of knowledge, the promotion of friendship, philanthropy, the protection of orphans, and so on. This club investigated the conditions of orphaned and abandoned children in the city of New York and the conditions of the orphanages established for them and published a report on them. This same club can take credit for reforming the existing orphanages and for getting two new orphanages for infants established. It was this club too that investigated the conditions of women working in the factories of New York City; and it provided a great service to these women by alerting the wider community to the way certain factory owners treated their female workers and to the things that needed to be done to improve the conditions of these working women. And this was the club that for the first time sent an application to the trustees of New York University and Columbia University requesting them to give women the right to study at those schools in the same way as men. Owing to constraints of space I cannot describe the hundreds of extremely important and publicly beneficial things that this club has done. Three subjects — religious creeds, political affairs, and women's political rights — are not allowed to be discussed in Sorosis. The reason for this lies in the purpose for which this club was established — to impart knowledge to respectable women of every kind and to engage in philanthropy — from which follows the proviso that the members should not be allowed any occasion to fall out with each other while speaking of religious controversies and such. But it should not be thought that the members of Sorosis have no interest in the three subjects mentioned above. Not only are these subjects given careful consideration in the New England Women's Club, the New Century Club, and many other such clubs that are the offspring of Sorosis, but these clubs have taken a solemn pledge to invite into their societies women of every creed and persuasion; to present their views with full impartiality and educate one another about their creeds; and, without ill-will toward anyone, to spread progressive opinions everywhere.

Some are certain to say that these women's societies and clubs are nothing but an imitation of what men do; but I myself have seen many women's societies and clubs in the United States with which men have no connection at all. It is women alone who were, and who continue to be, responsible for the origins and the growth of women's missionary societies, temperance unions, and clubs. Men's clubs are typically formed for no better purpose than to discuss political affairs or as a means to entertain themselves with dried-out idle chatter or with juvenile games[60] or with other similar things. They are not at all inclined toward such things as philanthropy, the improvement of education, the protection of orphans, aid to the needy and suffering, and so on. I have heard many people say that, because women are not allowed to enter these men's clubs, they are a veritable spree of harmful vices such as drinking liquor and indecent speech. If this is true, I am very pleased and proud to say that in the women's clubs there isn't a trace to be seen of anything imitated from the men's clubs.

Shortly after the creation of Sorosis another very important and well-known club was founded. This was named the Woman's Congress. It goes to great lengths to advance the cause of education for women; which is why it is also called the Association for the Advancement of Women. The most highly educated, farsighted, and experienced women from many places in the United States, women who are passionate about education, are members of this club. This club has managing boards in many different places, and once a year at an appointed place the entire association gathers for a meeting where women scholars read mature and thoughtful essays they have written for the occasion and deliver lectures on a variety of demanding subjects such as politics, social reformation, social conditions, education, art, science, poetry, and history. Owing to the reputation, scholarship, and prominence of its members, this club has a very great reputation within the United States. There is another renowned women's club in Boston called the New England Woman's Club. Its purpose, like that of the Woman's Congress, is the advancement of education. These clubs that promote education do not stop at formal book learning either; at their very founding their members resolved to learn to take cognizance of one another's thoughts about what things are still needed by women today and what measures should be taken to fill those needs — and then to do something practical about it. They learned business management

60. Trans.: *Āṭyāpāṭyā* and *ceṇḍuphaḷī:* traditional children's games corresponding roughly with "tag" and "catch" — and here clearly mentioned with sarcastic intent. — *PCE*

and the procedures for running associations and societies, and they used this knowledge — and have made an ongoing process of using it — to improve the conditions and to alleviate the suffering of women from their own country who are laboring in a variety of occupations. The women's club in the city of Philadelphia, called the New Century Club, is highly renowned for its priceless endowments of progressive and philanthropic ideals. Through this club's efforts an organization called the Working Women's Guild has been established, in which more than seven hundred women who are working in various occupations are members. Only women who earn their own living by working in factories, stores, and so on can become members of this organization. For one or two hours every evening instruction is given in various subjects in the organization's assembly hall. Every day six to seven classes are provided for hundreds of women to study the subjects of their choice. All of them have at least some interest in learning such things as cooking, tailoring, embroidery, weaving, and physical fitness. But the subjects in which many members of the organization take a special interest are poetry, history, and languages. There is a special class in this organization called the "Processes of Thought." When the women in this class listen to and reflect upon the most abstract subjects (starting with philosophy) and then proceed to discuss them, an educated audience can't help but be amazed at the power of their abstract thought and the depth of their intelligence. It was all because a club of hardworking, altruistic women such as those in the New Century Club decided to establish this kind of an organization that women who must work to feed themselves were provided the means to obtain an education, connections to good society, and a place of refuge during difficult times. Recently, respectable, educated women in many other places have followed the example of the New Century Club and established numerous organizations like the Working Women's Guild for the advancement of working women, for the welfare of orphaned, uninformed young women, and for the protection of morality. No one can overestimate the benefits, both to working women and to society, of what these organizations do.

In the city of Boston there is a committee called the Woman's Educational and Industrial Union, i.e., the women's committee for the promotion of education and industry. Experienced and educated women from respectable families are the managers of this committee, and they take turns coming to the committee's office and supervising its work. As of now this committee has four departments; but in the future, if it is felt to be necessary, as many more departments can be added as are needed.

The woman who is manager of the Hospitality Department invites its members, friends, and well-wishers to its assembly hall once a week and provides them hospitality. Everyone is free to come there on this occasion even without having an invitation. Apart from the regular members of the managing board, many knowledgeable and respectable women assist this committee to the extent they can by investigating the difficulties of women who come to them asking for the committee's support and help. In the Business Department, items that are made by women who are poor but who want to do some sort of business are sold at a good price, and there is an arrangement to give each woman her share of the profits. There are more than seven hundred women who make items of one kind or another and bring them there for sale. Last year around twenty-six thousand dollars, i.e., seventy-eight thousand rupees, worth of goods were sold through this department. In the Employment Department, arrangements have been made to find and provide appropriate employment for poor women who wish to work on a salaried basis or for daily wages or for women who wish to work as teachers. There is a branch of this department called the "Snack Room" from which items can be purchased to eat and drink at extremely reasonable prices. If employers do not pay their women employees or women day workers the proper amount for the work they do, these women can bring their complaint before this committee's Advocacy Department, which seeks justice for these women. Not only is the Advocacy Department of this committee widely known all across the city of Boston, but people who play unfairly stand in the greatest fear of it. Out of altruism the most learned and renowned of lawyers represent the cases of poor women in the courts free of charge on behalf of this department. If an unfair employer who doesn't pay for work that has been done is informed that a complaint will be filed against him before the Advocacy Department of this women's committee, that's all it takes. The most high-handed individuals are brought to heel at once.

There are many more organizations that have modeled themselves on this organization in hundreds of places in the United States. They are called "Women's Exchanges." Women manage all of them, and their purpose is to sell at a good price products that women have made for them and to assist women who are poor, who must work to earn their own living, and who have no place of shelter. In some places they have "homes" attached to these exchanges where women who come from other towns to work in the city can rent a place to live. These "homes" are under the supervision of respectable, influential women of each town. Their management is entirely the responsibility of the women's organizations. They are of tremendous help to the working women of the United States.

There is an excellent Christian philanthropic organization in this country for young women called the Young Women's Christian Association. It has branches in almost all the cities, and hundreds of thousands of young women are members. This association was created for several praiseworthy and important purposes such as discussion and propagation of Christianity among young women; religious instruction for untaught women to get them going on the right path; provision of places to live at a nominal rent in good locations for women who must work to earn their own living; and provision of instruction for those who wish to acquaint themselves with some knowledge of languages and science and business. These objectives are being met in an exemplary way.

I mentioned previously that in 1848 several hardworking women gathered together in Seneca Falls in the state of New York and established an organization to give special attention to the political rights of women. This was the very first organization of its kind, established specifically to uphold women's rights. Every other women's association that has come into existence has done so with a debt of gratitude to and in imitation of this one particular organization. When it was founded, the entire world ridiculed its founders. The women who went out to speak on its behalf were pelted with filth and verbally abused and cursed by people who called themselves respectable; the jeering newspapers drew hideous caricatures of them in order to make the world laugh at them; the leaders of society and creators of public opinion scorned and ostracized them; the clergy honored these women with invective and curses that actually better suited their own kind of respectability, calling them apostates, heretics, evildoers, witches, agents of Satan, women of bad character, and so on. But even though the times and public opinion were so hostile to them, these women did not give up their resolve. Ever so many of them went forward with the long labor of women's emancipation, sacrificing the joys of domestic life as well as body, mind, and wealth, enduring even harassment from those very women for whom they had so selflessly sacrificed themselves.

Now this organization has assumed the form of a national-level society and has branches in hundreds of places in the United States.[61] Its headquarters are in Boston. Weekly, biweekly, and monthly magazines as well as books are being published in many places on behalf of this organization. This national organization for women's political rights publishes a famous weekly called the *Women's Journal* from the city of Boston.[62] Following the example

61. Trans.: The National Woman Suffrage Association, led by Elizabeth Cady Stanton and Susan B. Anthony, was founded in 1869. — *PCE*

62. Trans.: The *Women's Journal* (founded 1870) was in fact being published at that time by the American Woman Suffrage Association, which was also founded in 1869 under the leadership of Lucy Stone (1818-1893) and Julia Ward Howe (1819-1910). The two suffragist organizations would unite to form the National American Woman Suffrage Association in 1890, about two years after Ramabai wrote the above. — *PCE*

of this organization, women in England, Canada, Australia, France, Denmark, Finland, etc., have established similar organizations. Owing to the efforts of the National Woman Suffrage Association of the United States, many changes and improvements are being made in the various laws relating to women in this country. In the state of Kansas women have received all the important political rights related to municipal government. In the territory of Wyoming women have received all the same political rights that men enjoy, and the good effects this is having are evident everywhere. (In the countries of Canada, British-ruled Australia, and England, unmarried women and widows have also received rights related to municipal government.) The efforts of these organizations have to a large extent been fruitful, and signs are beginning to appear that in a very short time they will achieve complete success.

The important women's organization that was established forty years ago in Seneca Falls undermined and toppled a very small portion of the wall of the fortress of impenetrable social custom (built by society at large to surround the society of women) that had kept women in captivity and obstructed their advancement at every step; and it opened a narrow path for women to come out of that terrible stronghold. Now, by way of that narrow path, thousands of women are emerging from that stronghold, brigade by brigade, and being emancipated — as they will continue to be.

This Association has now assumed an international status. At the end of March 1888, women from ten or twelve civilized[63] nations were invited by the American Woman Suffrage Association to the city of Washington. At the International Council of Women the Association had organized for this occasion, it was resolved that branches of the Association would be opened in every nation; and this has been implemented in some places. This International Council of Women was not established solely for the purpose of winning political rights for women. It has been given its present form with the view of attaining several important and praiseworthy objectives: that wherever women's societies may be and whatever they may do, they should all maintain relations of friendship among themselves; that they should communicate their ideas with each other and when the occasion demands it come to each other's aid; that they should encourage one another; and that they should establish relations of friendship among the women of all nations. More information about this council is given later on in the book so I won't say more about it here. There are many other women's associations of great importance in this country; but if I tried to give information about all of them, this book would grow far too big so I shall refrain. This essay would be incomplete,

63. Trans.: *Sabhya:* "Polite, well-bred, fit for good company" (Molesworth). — *PCE*

however, if I didn't give at least a little information about the Women's Temperance Union in this country.

In November last year (1887), in the town called Nashville in the state of Tennessee, the fourteenth annual celebration of the Women's National Temperance Union of the United States took place. The president of this organization had invited me to come and attend this event.[64] I went perhaps a thousand miles to Nashville expressly to witness this great celebration and this gathering of leading women from all the states. Huge crowds of women gathered in that town for an entire week. In addition to the three hundred or so leading women who had come there as representatives of women's temperance unions from all the states of this nation, many other women and men had come to witness the ceremonial event.

The state of Tennessee falls in the southern region of this country, and you do not find among the women of that region the same degree of independence, learning, and industriousness as in the North. Some years ago nobody in that part of the country approved of women speaking in a public meeting; and the words "women's organization" had never so much as entered anybody's dreams. Even now women as a group haven't flourished there as much as they might have; nor do they have available to them any means for obtaining a higher education.

On my way to Nashville I had occasion to stay in a city called Louisville in the state of Kentucky and, owing to the insistence of the people there, to speak at a public meeting. The clergyman at the church where I was to give my speech insisted that I sit up on the platform. It was my wish that several of the prominent women of that town should come up and sit on the platform with me, but they said, "In our entire lifetime we've never done anything like that! How can we possibly do so now?" I said, "My dear ladies, you may never have sat on the platform before, but what objection could there be to your doing so now? Come and sit up there with me just this once, that's all I ask. If you come to any harm, you won't ever have to do it again. What do you say?" After some dithering yes or no, five or six of the women agreed to sit on the platform. And although they sat there until my speech was over, they suffered not the slightest harm, needless to say! Even if women in the South do not live under purdah, very few of them possess the independence and self-confidence in public that they should.

64. Trans.: Frances Elizabeth Caroline Willard (1839-1898) was one of the founders of the National Women's Christian Temperance Union (WCTU) in 1874 and was elected president in 1879. Under her leadership the WCTU became the largest women's organization in the United States, and one of the most effective. — *PCE*

When they heard that the annual celebration of the Women's National Temperance Union of the United States was taking place in Nashville (as I mentioned above), many of the people there came to the strangest conclusions about it. Nobody had a very clear idea of what this organization was or what it did. Many of them thought that it must be in the nature of some kind of wild children's game, a comical caricature of an idea lacking all substance conceived by half-mad, half-clever women. The clergymen in several of the churches denied these women permission to organize their meeting in their churches, with the words, "This is an irreligious act. These women are transgressing a biblical command and are committing acts that are wholly unsuitable for womankind." In the end it was decided that this women's meeting should convene in the assembly hall of a public library. The local Women's Temperance Union of Nashville, after Herculean efforts, persuaded the women of the town to give them their help for the celebration. These generous local women invited the women who were coming from distant places to stay in their homes, and they showed them every token of honor and respect.

On the morning of November 16 this amazing celebration began. Seven hundred chairs had been arranged in the assembly hall in rows in a semicircle. There was no room left in the hall to set up any more chairs. The walls of the hall had been decorated with the flags of the various states and with multicolored banners covered with embroidery bearing the mottoes of the women's temperance unions of every state. The platform, where the president and other leading women were to sit, and the area all around it had been decorated with the star-spangled banner of the United States, fragrant flowers, and arches made from the leaves of various trees.

Around nine o'clock in the morning the Women's Union had completely filled the assembly hall. There were also a lot of men in the audience. Then the president, Frances E. Willard, called for everyone's attention and started the proceedings. It would have required the presence there of a great poet adequately to describe the very fine, heart-moving prayers that some of the leading women gave on this occasion, the melodious songs they sang, the heart-stirring sermons they preached, and the matchless, vital, heart-moving, deeply meaningful, and altogether beautiful speech that Frances*bāī* herself gave.

Even before the conclusion of this first meeting on the very first day, many of the clergymen from that town had changed their minds; and they sent invitations to this unprecedented Women's Union, asking them with great insistence, "Please do us the great favor of coming to our churches to organize meetings and to speak." The men who were in the audience stopped their mockery and began to demonstrate their respect and admiration for the union. During the remaining days of that week the leading women of this union would visit as many as six or seven places a day and, morning, afternoon, and evening, give speeches and preach sermons — and yet the people there could not get enough. Even the British Parliament and the Congress of the United States would have had no choice but to feel envious of this temperance union, had they seen its altogether beautiful and superior handling of the resolutions that were passed within the society during the course of that week and the reading of the reports of all that had been accomplished over the preceding year, as well as its unexampled manner of conducting its proceedings that was displayed to one and all. Those who witnessed the public erudition, the power of leadership, the parliamentary skills, the adeptness at maintaining order, and the extraordinary knowledge of the ancient rules of parliamentary order possessed by Frances E. Willard must surely have been convinced that she was a composite image of the three goddesses — of Speech, of Polity, and of Governing Power.[65] There are plenty of proud men who no doubt think that women are simply unable to do anything in an orderly, methodical manner; but anyone who witnessed the society of this women's organization assembled in Nashville and their orderly proceedings must surely have also been convinced — bearing in mind the confusion and disorder that all too often take place in Congress and in Parliament — that it might not be such a bad thing if these two world-famous political institutions were to adopt the example of this women's organization.

On the evening of November 24 the grand celebration was brought to its conclusion. On this occasion, as the leading men and clergymen of Nashville were bidding farewell to the women's society that had been their guest, they praised the organization fervently, saying how totally their opinions about women had been changed and how surprised and pleased they were when they saw the way its meetings were conducted, as well as its excellent organization, its fine objectives, and its ethics of universal benevolence; and they bade farewell to the National Women's Temperance Union of the United States with profound respect and honor, insisting that the following year the Union should come back there again.

In summation, this celebration was an occasion of great joy for everyone. I had never witnessed such an amazing, heart-stirring, and grand spectacle in my entire life. Seeing it was, I felt, a life-fulfillment. Except for the International Council of Women that gathered the end of last March in the city of Washington, no other organization or celebration could match this grand celebration and this grand society.

65. Trans.: *Sarasvatī, Rājanīti,* and *Śāsanaśakti:* the first is the familiar "goddess of speech and eloquence" and wife of Brahma; the other two are personified abstractions. — *PCE*

The Woman's Crusade[66]

The succubus Alcohol and her brother Tobacco have forced their way into people's homes and have wreaked utter havoc there. Men everywhere came up with every sort of fanciful excuse for themselves: "I'm a man, why should I worry about anything I do?"; "Drinking is a good way to overcome fatigue, and chewing or smoking tobacco relaxes the nerves"; "What's there to worry about in drinking a little alcohol as a tonic or as an aid to digestion?"; "It is authorized by the Scriptures"; and so on. Then they proceeded to drink as much alcohol as they wished or consumed other intoxicating substances and squandered whatever money they had. The wide open doors of hell and the roots of a man's utter ruination, the saloons,[67] began to flourish everywhere. Men saw their colorful glass windows and their beautifully decorated doors, and they lost their heads. The saloon keepers, who line their own pockets by ruining people, lured young and old, ignorant and educated, in a great variety of ways and discovered thousands of methods to increase their business. Day by day more and more men were falling victim to their scheming and losing everything they possessed — their happiness, their respectability, their very lives. And through them their poor wives and their tender young children were being reduced to wretchedness. How many thousands of faithful wives were grieving to themselves as they watched their husbands sinking into utter ruin through this evil vice? The hearts of how many hundreds of thousands of mothers were burning with anguish as they watched their sons, whom they loved more then their own lives, forsaking religion, morals, and happiness in this world and the next, following the siren call of liquor, and going to eternal hell? And yet, here were all these poor women bearing their torment in silence, and why? The two great rulers of human society, theology and social custom, have issued their edict to women, "Stay at home and accept everything you hear in silence"; and women humbly submitted to this without so much as a murmur and to this very day have continued to endure endless, intolerable torment and anguish.

But there is a limit to everything in this world. A time comes when even an earthworm, seeing itself afflicted with extreme oppression, prepares itself to fight its enemy in self-defense; so it is not so very surprising that a time invariably comes when human beings — and most especially women, who are ac-

66. Trans.: Here Ramabai uses the English word "crusade" in transliteration. — *PCE*

67. Trans.: As in the case of "priest" and of "church," Ramabai uses a number of interchangeable words in the sense of "saloon": the rather pedantic *śauṇḍikālaya* (as in the present case); *guttā,* the English word "bar" in transliteration; and even *piṭhā* (Bombay slang of that day). We have chosen to render them all as "saloon." — *PCE*

customed to enduring oppression with the greatest fortitude — cannot help but resist oppression if it reaches a certain limit. When the women from the state of Ohio were faced with such a situation, they put aside their purdah restraints and their silence and resolved to fight the saloon keepers, who had pitilessly seized their husbands and sons through their wiles, and to defend their young children and their loved ones. Hundreds of women of good families, slow to anger and full of the best virtues, girded their loins and offered their services to the crusade that had been started against the saloon keepers; and they pledged that they would not retire from the battlefield until they had defeated the enemy and defended their sons and their homes. In this war of theirs they did not cut anybody's throat; they did not deprive anyone of his livelihood through deceit; they did not shed anyone's blood; they did not tear open anyone's heart by speaking harsh words; they did not threaten anyone by taking up guns, swords, cannons, and other deadly weapons; and yet at the mere mention of their name the evil saloon keepers, who inflict such pain on others and then help themselves to their wealth, along with their supporters, began to tremble; Satan himself began to quake when he saw the flag they bore that signifies peace; and at the sound of their sweet, reasonable, edifying words, the very foundations of Satan's fortresses tottered and the fortresses began to fall.

The Crusades[68] of the eleventh and twelfth centuries pale before this amazing, unprecedented, and peaceful crusade of women in the nineteenth century. There can never be any equivalence between this crusade and those. The purpose of those men's Crusades during that past age of barbarism *(rānaṭīpaṇā)* was to tarnish the name of religion by cutting people's throats and washing the entire earth with human blood. The aim of the women's crusade of the nineteenth century was to save people's lives, to draw them forth out of hell itself, and to establish happiness, peace, and joy everywhere within their homes. The men's Crusades of the eleventh and twelfth centuries left hundreds of thousands of people dead through slaughter, whereas the women's crusade of the nineteenth century implemented remedies to draw tens of millions of people from out of the jaws of death. Those barbaric *(rānaṭī)* Crusades defiled the religion of Christ, the Prince of Peace; whereas this modern crusade made this holy religion shine like burnished gold.

This amazing crusade came into being on December 24, 1873, in the town of Hillsboro in the state of Ohio. There, on the evening of December 24, a gen-

68. Crusade = A war fought in the name of the Cross. "The Crusades" is the name given to the wars that people who took pride in Christianity fought in defense of their religion against the Muslims when, at the end of the eleventh century, the Muslims had captured Jerusalem and were planning to capture Spain and other Christian countries. They continued until the thirteenth century of the Christian era. — *PRS*

tleman named Dio Lewis had come to give a lecture, speaking on the subject "Our Girls" before the debating society in Washington Court House.[69] On this occasion he spoke about the great harm caused to humankind by the use of alcohol and other intoxicating drinks and by tobacco and other such substances and then told a story from his own personal experience. His mother was extremely devout and took pride in proper conduct. She was terribly saddened to see what harm was being done to the world by evil habits. Dio's father had lost everything through his addiction to alcohol. Seeing her happiness and her home utterly ruined, Mrs. Lewis decided to rescue her husband, and in the process she discovered a new method for freeing the people of her town from the grip of these evil habits. She herself, along with some of her friends, went to the shops where liquor and other intoxicants were sold, and there she prayed, preached, and pleaded with the saloon keepers to quit a business that was so base and harmful. After some time she succeeded in her good work, and the saloon keepers of that town closed all their shops. After he had told this story, Dio Lewis addressed the women in the meeting: "Ladies, if you will only do the same thing here, your good work cannot fail to succeed. I feel confident that within one week all the saloons here will be closed. If you really want to do this work, those women who will assume the leadership should give their consent to it here and now." The moment they heard Lewis's words fifty women in the meeting stood up to show that they agreed to do this work. Then Lewis turned to the men sitting around him who were temperance supporters and said, "Now that these women have taken the responsibility for this task, tell me how many of you will help them." Immediately sixty or seventy men stood up. After it had been decided in this way to take this task in hand, it was resolved that a meeting would be held in furtherance of this great work on Christmas morning, December 25.

In keeping with the resolution made the previous evening, at ten o'clock in the morning on Christmas Day, a large crowd of people gathered in the Presbyterian church. After they had sung a hymn and offered a prayer, Dio Lewis told the story of his mother once more and spoke for about an hour about what great things women have the power to accomplish and what great resources they possess, in the form of their patience, perseverance, and loving

69. Trans.: Diocletian Lewis (1823-1886) was a popular reform lecturer and author of the postbellum period, a promoter of homeopathy, physical education, and dress reform (among numerous other interests). His temperance lectures in the towns of Hillsboro and Washington County Courthouse, Ohio, during the winter of 1873-1874 inspired the "Woman's Crusade" that led, by the end of 1874, to the founding of the National Woman's Christian Temperance Union (http://www.wctu.com/earlyhistory.html). In her account Ramabai has conflated the two separate towns and occasions as one. — *PCE*

nature, for accomplishing those great things. By the time he had finished speaking, the entire congregation that was assembled there was strongly in favor of his proposal, and that same morning the "Woman's Crusade" began.

For the crusade's organization they adopted the same rules as any other organization and appointed a president, a vice president, a secretary, and a treasurer — and it should not need to be said that these were all women. One brigade of this woman's society was directly sent off to battle. The fifty-two women in this brigade accepted a warrior's challenge — and thereby created a new class of "do or die soldiers."[70] It was decided that this special class of "do or die" soldiers would visit every liquor shop, pray to the Almighty, preach, and persuade the saloon keepers through their pleading to quit the evil business of selling liquor and take up some other more wholesome business. To assist the "do or die" brigade, a committee of responsible people was set up. Thirty-seven men came together to form this committee and accepted the responsibility for providing whatever monetary or other aid the women of the crusade would need. After everything had been properly arranged in this way, this committee appointed a subcommittee and requested it to write up a petition, which they decided would be sent to the vendors of liquor and other intoxicating beverages.

The "do or die" committee appointed Mrs. E. J. Thompson of Hillsboro as its commander and decided on a plan of attack against the enemy. Thompson*bāī* herself has written an account of this first battle as follows:

> On the morning of December 25, 1873, with fear and trembling, our brigade approached a "first-class" saloon belonging to a saloon keeper called Robert Ward. This saloon was famous all over town, and the moment they saw it, the mouths of some of our numbers went dry, and several of them began indeed to tremble. Robert Ward must have heard that we were coming to visit his shop, but it also seems that he had learned what our purpose was in coming there. With the greatest of courtesy he opened the door of his saloon and welcomed us, and with a pleasant smile on his face he held the door open until we had all come inside. Then he closed the door and went around and stood in his usual place behind the "bar" (the raised countertop for dispensing liquor). Then the leader of our brigade [Thompson*bāī* herself] addressed him with these words:

70. Trans.: *Saṃśaptaka:* "a soldier or warrior sworn with others not to fly or give up fighting" (Sir Monier Monier-Williams, *A Sanskrit-English Dictionary* [Oxford: Oxford University Press, 1982 (1899)]). — *PCE*

> "Well, Mr. Ward, I'm sure you must think that this large gathering here is very strange. Let that be as it may, but you certainly must know what our purpose is in coming here." Already in this short time Robert Ward had begun to break out in a sweat. He said, "I would like to talk to Dio Lewis about a couple of things." Mrs. Thompson said, "No, no, Dio Lewis has no connection with our reason for being here. If you will only look carefully at the faces, withered by sorrow and anxiety, of so many of the women among those of us who have gathered here, you will see what effect your unholy trade has had, and you will not be surprised that we have come here today. Our purpose in coming is not to threaten you or to curse you. We have come here in the name of our dear departed friends and of our Savior (and inspired by his example) to forgive you and to pray that God may also forgive you your wrongdoing — if only you will give up this business of yours that causes such harm to our hearts and to our homes."

When he heard this, poor Robert Ward was utterly bewildered. Seeing that it was a good opportunity, Thompson*bāī* turned to her friends and said, "Let us pray" — whereupon all the women immediately knelt down and started to pray. Robert himself, in the company of this holy brigade, began to pray to God. Then all the women joined together to sing a hymn. These poor wives whose husbands and these mothers whose sons had been ruined on account of this saloon, whose happiness had been utterly destroyed, and who for that reason could not bear even the passing thought of this saloon — these very same women had come to this place with love in their hearts and were praying that God should bring this brother who had gone astray back to the path of virtue and that he himself should accept as his own the Savior of the world. It is truly no falsehood that "God is love." Nothing can suffice to describe the greatness of that extraordinary love and the importance of forgiveness. Dio Lewis's prophecy came true. Through the unceasing efforts of these "do or die soldiers," within a week all the saloons in Hillsboro were closed down!

When they heard the news of the crusade in Hillsboro, women from many other places in the United States started to follow the example set by the women of Hillsboro. But crusades of this kind were not a permanent solution, so a number of farsighted women got together and gave thought to making a more unified effort. In 1874 some of the women who had won victories in the "Woman's Crusade" gathered together in the summer resort at Chautauqua. With the stated purpose of making ongoing efforts to destroy the vice of liquor consumption, they founded the Women's Christian Temperance Union. Through the labor of the hardworking, upright, and virtuous women of this country, this very soon assumed the form of a national-level organization and after a short time assumed the name of the National Women's Temperance Union of the United States.[71]

The system of government of this union is a replica of the national system of government of the United States. This is manifested in a superb way at four levels: the local union, the county unions, the state unions, and the national union. The local union is divided according to several functions: the president, the vice president, the secretary, the treasurer, the managing board, and various subcommittees that are appointed to perform special tasks for the organization. Every year when the local organization holds its annual celebration, the union's officeholders are elected and begin their terms in office. In the same way, when all of the unions within a county hold their annual celebration, the county union's officeholders are elected by popular vote. And this is the same way, by popular vote, in which the officeholders are elected to the state and national unions every year. There are more than ten thousand branches of this union in the United States, and it has around two and a half lakh (250,000) women as its members. Although the local union is independent in its own domain, it has to surrender some significant authority to the chief union of the county in order to strengthen itself and to maintain unity and friendship with other local unions; and in the same way the county unions have to surrender some authority to the state unions, and the state unions in turn have to surrender several significant rights to the national union. This enables them to retain their independence and their unity at the same time and thus to be strengthened. The system of government of this union, its smooth and orderly manner of functioning, and its conformity with the law are all most praiseworthy and, in the same way exactly as the national system of government of the United States, remarkable. The multifarious powers that womankind possesses, which had been scattered about among different individuals and which had been as unregulated and ineffective as steam is when it is diffused in the open air, have become as manifoldly effective as steam is when it is brought to bear within a steam engine. Through this union the virtues of proper self-respect, governing acumen, executive disposition, and leadership, which at one time were unknown to women, have been growing among the women of

71. Trans.: The National WCTU was officially established at its first national convention in November 1874 in Cleveland, Ohio. Oddly enough, whether by oversight or by design, in the present case and in all but three places in the text Ramabai excludes the word "Christian" whenever she renders the name of the WCTU. — *PCE*

the United States in an extraordinary and surprising manner. Thanks to the union, the harmful differences of opinion and the bigotry that existed among women of different creeds and different social groups *(jātī)* are disappearing, and undissimulating friendship and sisterly love are continuing to grow in their place.

I feel no embarrassment in saying that, out of all the many unions that exist in the developed countries, this union is the best and the greatest. It would have to be the rarest worthy cause in all the world that this union has not taken upon itself; there is probably not a single example of anyone who has not been the recipient of the loving-kindness flowing from its motherly heart of love; and except for God, no one but this union could have possessed to such a perfect degree the virtues of boldness, seriousness of purpose, courage, and forgiveness. The women's missionary societies that exist in this country and in many other countries are by no means insignificant. They have spent crores of rupees, have eschewed every kind of selfishness, and have labored to bring foreign peoples to the path of righteousness. You cannot praise these societies enough; but, because of the numerous differences of creed and opinion in these societies, they do not have the unity among themselves that they should and do not accomplish as many good things as the temperance union has taken upon itself to do. In the Women's Christian Association only those who call themselves "Evangelicals" are included. People of other creeds do not receive help from them. However many other societies there may be that promote education and philanthropy (and they certainly are excellent and beneficial to the public in their own right), they cannot be compared with the temperance union because their numbers are small and their objectives are limited — whereas the objectives of the Women's Temperance Union are many in number and of great importance. And it has no contentions between creeds within it. Women of all creeds, all social groups *(jātī)*, and all types join together and work as one within the union. When you pause and consider its graduated structure of local, state, national, and international branches; its excellent rules, simple but firm, acceptable to all and able to be followed by all; its extraordinary and outstanding organization, which is superior to every kind of political system and which binds everyone together, you cannot help but say that this union is the crown of all the amazing miracles in God's creation in this age. At present this union has between forty and forty-five departments. The causes for which this union has taken responsibility are listed as follows:

1. To set up temperance unions at various places by sending women speakers as representatives of the union;

2. To send representatives to every nation to establish international women's temperance unions or to do this by means of correspondence;
3. To propagate the creed of temperance among foreign peoples who come to the United States to settle;
4. To propagate the creed of temperance, education, and morality among the people of African race *(jāta)* who were recently emancipated and who are living in both the southern and the northern states;
5. To propagate righteousness and the creed of temperance among young women;
6. To uplift young children by teaching them morality and the creed of temperance;
7. To persuade people of the harm incurred as a matter of course by the offspring of those who consume liquor and other intoxicants;
8. By teaching people the principles of maintaining good health to persuade them of the close connection between health and abstinence from alcohol;
9. To give thought to what changes need to be made in education, and to work toward providing all children in the nation's public schools scientific instruction about the calamities wrought by the consumption of alcohol and other intoxicants;
10. To work toward providing the same kind of instruction in colleges and universities and to propagate the creed of temperance among the young men and women who are studying in these schools;
11. To establish kindergarten schools for young children so as to give them the best children's education and good personal habits;
12. To seek the advancement and growth of Sunday schools (i.e., those schools established to give religious instruction to children and to adults each Sunday) and to propagate the creed of temperance in them;
13. To print and publish books, newspapers, monthly magazines, and large and small pamphlets that propagate the creed of abstinence from alcohol;
14. To work toward the prevention of the publication of books, newspapers, booklets, and so on that are bad, obscene, and immoral and that encourage the consumption of intoxicants;
15. To persuade hardworking people who must labor to earn a living of the benefits of abstinence from alcohol;
16. To teach the customary ways of establishing associations, committees, and large organizations modeled on the rules of parliamentary order and to explain to women as well as to children what general and special rules are used in governing associations;

17. To establish temperance unions of both men and women, to organize them, and to teach how to work effectively through them;
18. To persuade people of the calamitous effects of consuming tobacco, opium, hemp, and other such intoxicants, and of their ill effects on the human body;
19. To work toward preventing the use of liquid medicines containing alcohol and to prove with evidence from scientific and chemical experiments that there is no need to administer medicines containing alcohol;
20. To propagate godliness everywhere;
21. To read religious books for people to hear in many different places and to convince them that the consumption of alcohol is forbidden by the Scriptures;
22. To inquire after the well-being of prisoners in penitentiaries, large and small; to educate them about religion, morality, and the benefits of abstinence from alcohol; to inquire after the well-being of prisoners being held in jails and police stations and people living in orphanages; and to give them aid;
23. To visit the laborers and workmen who work on trains and at railway stations and such places to inform them about the creed of temperance; and by teaching them religion and morality, to bring about their spiritual upliftment;
24. To educate sailors, seamen in the navy, and soldiers in the army about religion and morality and to persuade them of the benefits of abstinence from alcohol;
25. To work toward keeping grape juice containing alcohol from being used in churches during the sacrament called the Lord's Supper;
26. To work toward getting all Christian churches to pray for the work of the prohibitionist organizations to prosper during one special day during the week set aside for special prayers in Christian churches;
27. To work toward the growth of moral purity among the public;
28. To propagate morality, religion, and the creed of temperance among the women of the Mormon church;
29. To work toward getting the people of the United States to abstain from doing business or wrongful acts on Sunday, to consider it a holy day, and to spend it in worshipping God;
30. To visit the homes of respectable women and through numerous small committees to propagate the creed of temperance among them;
31. To present flowers and other things that would bring joy to the sick, the suffering, and the aged in hospitals, nursing homes, and wherever else they may be;

32. To propagate the creed of temperance at fares and festivals and to try by all means to keep liquor from being bought and sold there;
33. To petition the various state governments of the United States as a means to working toward the closure of the liquor trade in the nation;
34. As an aid to the work of propagating morality and temperance, to work toward obtaining for women the political rights to make laws, etc.;
35. To uplift fallen women, give them some sort of vocational training, and set them on the path of righteousness; to protect forsaken, unprotected women who work if they are being oppressed by someone or if their life is in danger of being ruined; to work toward keeping obscene and indecent books and pictures from being published; and to implement various remedies through which social purity will be universally spread;
36. To implement remedies to enhance the utility and growth of the hospital and nursing home established in Chicago by the Women's National Temperance Union, and to train women doctors there, teaching them medical science that advocates abstinence from alcohol;
37. To work toward persuading the presidents of the various nations to let peace be established among all nations and, in the event of any dispute or disagreement between any of them, not to go to war with each other but to end their quarrel on terms to be decided by neutral nations — and thereby put an end to the cruel and demonic custom of making war;
38. To assist philanthropic organizations in various cities and towns.

These are the thirty-eight principal causes, and although there are in addition to these five or six miscellaneous causes for which the Women's Temperance Union has taken responsibility, I shall not mention them here.

In order to carry out the work of the union's forty or forty-five departments, subcommittees have been appointed in different places, and each of these has a superintendent to supervise it. Every year these superintendents have to write summary reports about what things have been done in relation to these departments in every state and territory and submit them to the chief superintendent of the Women's National Temperance Union. Various kinds of information of this sort are published in the annual report of the plenary assembly. The rule is that each member must pay half a dollar, i.e., about one and a half rupees, as an annual membership fee to help cover the expenses the union incurs in so many different places. Apart from this, there are many generous women and gentlemen who make numerous large donations to the union.

If I were to provide information even in summary form of all the things this union has undertaken to do and everything they have accomplished in each of its branches, I would have to write a whole separate book; so I will not let myself get carried away. Every one of the things the union does is very important, but I must mention here one of them that is of supreme importance. I have already mentioned previously that in the United States even young children are taught, exactly the same way as adults, to join together, the many as one, and work in unity. And it is customary even among the young children of the United States to set up associations, exactly like those for adults, through which they undertake to do certain special things. There are thousands of children's organizations in this country such as those for kindness to animals, for advancement of education, for benevolent action, and for propagation of religion, and the hundreds of thousands of girls and boys belonging to them are doing a great variety of worthy things. The children's temperance unions established through the efforts of the National Women's Christian Temperance Union number around fifteen hundred, and around 150,000 children, girls and boys together, are members of them! With the help of their mothers or teachers they are running these splendid unions in fine fashion; and they have all taken a pledge that they will never drink liquor. The Women's Temperance Unions are making unceasing efforts to inculcate the strength and determination in their hearts to keep this pledge. Through the efforts of these women, children are being taught about temperance in Sunday schools (i.e., schools for religious instruction); and thirty-four thousand children from these schools have taken a vow that they will never touch alcohol. These exceptionally diligent women have also worked unremittingly for seven years to get laws passed and enforced by the governments in all thirty-seven states of the United States requiring that scientific instruction about temperance be taught to children in public schools. The children in public schools in all these states who receive scientific instruction about temperance now number more than 6,500,000. The information, complete with examples about the terrible effects of the consumption of alcohol and other intoxicants, which these hundreds of thousands of children are receiving in this scientific manner, will certainly produce at least some long-term effect for good on their minds. Knowing that not much good can come from preaching to those adults who are sunk up to their ears in addiction to alcohol, these smart, farsighted women have turned their efforts to making sure that the education children get is good, all for the sake of improving future generations.

For many years now the state governments of Maine and Iowa have had prohibition laws that prohibit the production and sale of alcohol; but this governmental remedy hasn't worked at all in the face of the underhanded dealings of the liquor sellers, and the liquor trade continues to operate there on the quiet. When the women in the state of Kansas received important political rights related to municipal government about two years ago, the first important task for which they used these rights was totally to shut down the liquor trade in that state. More than half of these women were members of the temperance union. They also busied themselves to see that the liquor trade was not being carried on anywhere on the quiet. The task that the men of the state of Maine have not been able to accomplish for twenty-five or twenty-six years now has been mostly completed within the space of two years by the people of Kansas through the united power of women and men. The senator who has gone to represent Kansas in the Senate of the United States (Senator Ingalls) says, "In Kansas a man lying around drunk from liquor has become a matter for surprise, it happens so very rarely. Liquor stores and taverns are something to be known now only to the archaeologists — those who search the ancient ruins of buildings."[72] When the women in Kansas received a fair number of political rights, some mischief-mongering men in one town in that state (in order to demonstrate by example that giving women political rights is not right and that they would not be able to do work of any political importance) made a respectable woman, who was the mother of children, their mayor.[73] (A "mayor" is the chief officer in any city who runs the town's administration by implementing the laws of the state there.) The men who made this woman mayor realized on the second day of her assuming office that their prediction that women would not be able to run the government and implement the laws was mistaken. As soon as this woman took charge as mayor, she searched out all the places in the town where liquor was sold, the gambling joints, and other such places where illegal activities went

72. PROHIBITION IN KANSAS. — Senator Ingalls, in the *Forum* for August, thus speaks of "Prohibition in Kansas": "Kansas has abolished the saloon. The open dram-shop traffic is as extinct as the sale of indulgences. A drunkard is a phenomenon. The bar-keeper has joined the troubadour, the crusader, and the mound-builder. The brewery, the distillery, and the bonded warehouse are known only to the archaeologist. It seems incredible that among a population of 1,700,000 people, extending from the Missouri River to Colorado, and from Nebraska to Oklahoma, there is not a place which the thirsty or hilarious wayfarer can enter, and, laying down a coin, demand his glass of beer. This does not imply that absolute drouth prevails everywhere, or that 'social irrigation' has entirely disappeared. But the habit of drinking is dying out. Temptation being removed from the young and the infirm, they have been fortified and redeemed. The liquor-seller, being proscribed, is an outlaw, and his vocation disreputable. Drinking, being stigmatized, is out of fashion, and the consumption of intoxicants has enormously decreased. Intelligent and conservative observers estimate the reduction at 90 percent: it cannot be less than 75." — *Original footnote entirely quoted in English by PRS*

73. Trans.: This was Susanna Madora Salter, who was elected in 1887 as the first woman mayor in the United States in the town of Argonia, Kansas. — *PCE*

on and shut them down. The women of the town and the upright men gave her a great deal of help in locating these secret places. Her administration has gained the general approval of the people of that town, and she is exercising her authority in a most orderly and excellent way. Some years ago the members of the National Women's Christian Temperance Union of the United States used to think that there was no need for women to have political rights. But now they have learned through experience that the reason for the failure of the enormous efforts they have made over the past fifteen years to produce the results they should have, is nothing less than their lack of political rights. Almost all of those who carry on the liquor trade are men. They have invested crores of dollars in this business. And they have followers too in a very large number of men. All of them have political rights, and they vote in such a way that this effort by women to get temperance laws passed is stymied. Wherever there is a majority vote, that is where the force of the law lies. In the matter of making laws, the women's side scores zero; while the men's side (most especially the liquor sellers and the drunks) has all the rights to make the laws, and it also has the backing of money. Many men and women have begun to feel that unless women receive at least some of those rights, they will not be able to defeat this demon of liquor. So they are now working tirelessly for women to receive political rights.

On the strength of the innovative executive abilities of the highly respected and honored president of the National Women's Temperance Union of the United States, Miss Frances E. Willard, and with the aid of her friends, an International Women's Temperance Union has now been established. Willard*bāī* developed the idea of it in 1883. Then, in 1884, when all the plans concerning this union had been settled and all the ideas about how it should be made to work had reached maturity, the World's Women's Temperance Union was established. A brave, forceful, and very determined woman, Mrs. Mary Clement Leavitt,[74] became the ambassador of this union and, with the object of establishing temperance unions everywhere she went, set out to circumambulate the earth. She went first to the Hawaiian Islands, then to Australia, Japan, China, Ceylon, Hindusthan, Madagascar, Africa, and other countries, and established hundreds of temperance unions. Now she is going to visit all the countries in Europe. When this single, solitary, unprotected woman left for this great undertaking, she did not have any money or anyone to accompany her; but she does have her almighty God and her own steadfast

74. Trans.: Mary Greenleaf Clement Leavitt (1813-1912) left at the very end of 1884 as the self-styled first "world missionary" for what turned into an eight-year tour around the globe. — *PCE*

determination to accomplish her great task to accompany her. Wherever she goes she receives just the right assistance. Now in almost all the civilized countries, women's temperance unions are beginning to be established. Seeing the enthusiasm and diligence of the women of the United States, the women of England have also been inspired. They have established a national women's temperance union called the British Women's Temperance Association, and many good things are being accomplished through it. In Canada, too, there is a National Women's Temperance Union, which has been making determined efforts to prevent the purchase and sale of liquor in that country. Even in countries such as Australia, the Hawaiian Islands, Madagascar, and Africa, there are associations of this kind. So, my Hindusthani sisters, why are you lagging behind? We really must have a national union of this kind in our country. A massive petition will be sent to the rulers of all nations from the World's Women's Temperance Union. Women from every nation are going to petition their rulers to shut down the purchase and sale of liquor and intoxicants each in their own country. Every woman from Hindusthan ought to sign this petition, and everyone should work to carry the petition to all corners of the land and have it signed. We pray to Providence that there may not be even one mean-spirited person in our Hindusthan who would not support this great undertaking, directly or indirectly. At the present the president of this World's Women's Temperance Union is Miss Frances E. Willard. Today, under her presidency, at the very least 1,000,000 women are working hard for temperance all across the globe. This temperance union is nothing less that the *United Democratic Nation* of the women of all lands. These women, with the help of the holy band of their white ribbon,[75] this sign of peace and love, are binding the entire earth in the bonds of friendship and making it one. They are spreading the priceless store of all happiness, the triple virtues of peace, love, and friendship, among the women of all nations. The great work, which for many thousands of years past could not be accomplished by men or by kings or by great scholars (all those who carry weapons in their hands, who have physical strength, and who are the driving force and rulers of society), was accomplished by women who were scorned as ignorant and weak. Blessed are you, O God! You use the very people this world has scorned as your instruments to vanquish the arrogance of the proud. In your hands even a blade of grass becomes as supremely powerful as a thunderbolt!

75. Trans.: Women belonging to the Women's Christian Temperance Union of the United States and the World's WCTU wear a white ribbon at their breast as a sign of their membership in the union, their sincerity in their work, and their heartfelt love for the entire human race. — *KG*

CHAPTER 9

Trade and Business

If we were to pick a subject that is next in importance and worthiness of consideration only to the governing system of the United States and the condition of its women, it would certainly have to be the industries and businesses here. The eminence the United States has achieved today has mostly been in relation to its industries and businesses. Before describing the nature of these industries and businesses, we shall first consider the numerous things that encourage them.

The concern for the common good[1] in almost all things here is the principal instrument for making them prosper. I have already spoken earlier about the essential things, such as city streets, means of transport (i.e., vehicles), the manner of selling things in stores, schools, newspapers, libraries, and information bureaus, being made to be exceedingly simple and easy for everyone to use.

Government Services for the Public's Convenience

When you take a look at the nature of the national system of government of the United States, it is immediately apparent how much the convenience of the people has been taken into account in creating it. It is certainly true that

1. Trans.: *Sārvajanīnatva,* the word Pandita Ramabai uses here (in the sense of concern for, attention to, the public good) is the same one she uses and defines for the first time in Chapter 3. — *PCE*

with the smooth operation of a nation's government, peace is established within the state, the people are happy, and every kind of business runs well. But it is not as if a government's responsibilities end with merely providing a nation's governance. The government of the United States, understanding that it also has an obligation to provide services for the public's convenience by means of which all the people can reap enhanced benefits, has undertaken to do things of this kind. I shall mention only briefly here which are the principal ones.

The Department of Agriculture

There are about ten thousand people working under this department, most of whom work without being paid. Its headquarters are in the city of Washington. The duty of those who work for the department without pay is to send in news from wherever they live and from the nearby regions about such things as the condition of the farms there; what it costs to export goods to other towns and other countries; the value of goods kept stored on the farms and market gardens and the market price of the same goods when brought to the cities; and details of the commodities used in each place and from what places they come. After receiving this news, the Department of Agriculture publishes it in the form of a report every month, and it is then distributed to the businessmen's associations, newspaper publishers, and so on, in all the principal places, where it greatly benefits the businessmen and most especially the farmers. (The farmers in this country are not enemies of literacy[2] like the farmers in our own Hindusthan. They know how to write; and by reading books, newspapers, and reports like the ones just mentioned, they can inform themselves about how to improve their farms and just what things are required to do this.) When they have absorbed this information, the businessmen and the farmers can take into account such things as the value of the goods they have to sell, the price of what they have to buy, and the cost of labor in various places; and they can carry on their work without a hitch. Many varieties of seed are distributed all over the country through the Department of Agriculture of the United States. They are planted in all sorts of places, and information is painstakingly gathered and published about which types of grain planted in what soils and using what practices will increase productivity by how much, which soils have what characteristics, and so on. In very much the same way, experts in biology, agricultural science, and

2. Trans.: *Akṣaraśatrū:* "An enemy of letters or learning" (Molesworth). — *KG*

chemistry conduct research on the generation, conditions, and eradication of insects and birds that destroy crops in the different regions. This information is printed and distributed to the local farmers' unions. In Washington, on the piece of land that has been given to this department for its own use, the seeds of various grains, fruits and vegetables, onions, and so on, which are produced in every country and in every climate, are tested to see whether they grow in this country or not. Then they determine in which parts of the country they will do best, and they are cultivated there. In this way a great variety of fruits, vegetables, flowers, and grains, which were imported from foreign countries, are now produced here, and they are enhancing the prosperity of the United States. Take for example the oranges that were imported from Bahia. Some years ago these oranges were brought to southern California and planted. Now they are considered to be the best fruit of that region. Those who own orchards there are becoming enormously wealthy through this business. This was the department through which people came to know that foreign commodities such as sugarcane and tea could be produced in this country, and now the entire country has been greatly benefited by their production. Nor are the officials of this department content merely to import seed from foreign lands and cultivate it in their own land; they conduct intensive research and publish the results about a great number of things: what the characteristics are of each type of seed grain; what nutritional value it has; what kinds of diseases it is prone to have and the remedies for those diseases; how many varieties of trees there are in the country, and the wood of which tree is most suited to which uses; etc. Likewise, this department is benefiting the nation tremendously by informing people in every part of the country about the dispositions and the different varieties *(jātī)* of cattle, horses, sheep, hogs, and other useful animals; what hybrids can be produced through the breeding of these varieties; the causes of and remedies for their diseases; etc.

Weather Bureau[3]

Just as with the Department of Agriculture, the government of the United States has established a Weather Bureau as an aid to the general public and to the nation's commerce. In this vast three-thousand-mile-wide and two-thousand-mile-long nation, the Weather Bureau has 150 stations. Its head-

3. Trans.: *Antarikṣavidyāvibhāga:* literally, something closer to "Department of Meteorology." The United States Weather Bureau was created in 1870 and was renamed the National Weather Service in 1970. — *PCE*

quarters are in the city of Washington. There news is received twice a day from each of the 150 stations about the weather and other changes in the atmosphere. The very best experts in astronomy and meteorology, appointed by the government of the United States to this department to develop information about meteorology, record all the changes in the weather at those 150 locations and then send out information that is of practical use to every part of the nation. This information is sent by means of the telegraph. It is arranged to have this information made readily available to the entire public by posting it in the offices, no matter how small, of the thousands of businessmen's and farmers' associations of every kind in cities and towns both large and small, at railway stations, and at all ports and harbors. This enables businessmen, train engineers, travelers, the crews of ships, as well as farmers, grocers, traders, and others to know how the weather is likely to change in what parts of the nation and at what times — and what relation these changes might have with what they do. So there need be neither laxity nor delay in organizing measures to avoid sustaining damage caused by these changes in the weather. These stations that produce information about the daily course of the weather have been set up at all the principal harbors along the seacoast and on the banks of rivers. Information about any changes in the weather is sent from them to Washington where it is put into a form that can be put to practical use before the Chief of Naval Operations of the United States Navy sends it out to all the harbors. Similarly, at dangerous places near the seacoast, on the shores of the Great Lakes, and on the rivers where there is the possibility of shipwreck and loss of human life, lifesaving stations have been set up where small lifesaving boats are kept along with all the equipment needed to help people on sinking ships; and men who are not afraid even to jump into the sea in the middle of a storm and who are intelligent, brave, and experienced are employed with very good pay to go to the aid of people who are on sinking ships.

There is another very useful department run at the government's expense that, in the same way as the Life Saving Service, has been the means of saving the lives of hundreds of thousands of people who have been caught in storms, and it is doing an excellent job. It is called the Lighthouse Service. The United States government had built nine hundred lighthouses on dangerous rocks in the sea by 1880 and had constructed beacons at one thousand locations on the banks of rivers; and their cost is borne by the national treasury. "Light Ships" are also anchored at various places on the sea, wherever ships are in danger of being wrecked. The lamps on all these ships are lit at night or when visibility is reduced because of fog or some other reason. Their light travels a long way so when those who are steering ships see it, they know there is a dangerous rock at that place and steer their ships away.

And this is how thousands of ships are saved from shipwreck and hundreds of thousands of people are saved from drowning. Every single day the weather and the sky are studied, and all the information, such as where a storm will strike and where not, is supplied to every harbor and port. If it is thought that a storm will break near some particular port and that the boats approaching it are in danger, signal flags indicating a storm are raised, and the captains are warned to keep their ships away from that port or harbor. The Commandant of the United States Navy is in charge of communicating information about weather changes and such that are occurring at sea or on rivers and lakes. The Army and Navy Departments of the United States have been given charge of the work of constructing towers for beacons on the rivers, of keeping the river routes in good shape and seeing to their improvement, of improving boat docks on lakes and rivers as well as the ocean harbors and putting them to public use, etc. It is not the custom of the United States government to keep the soldiers and officers of its small standing army fed while they sit around doing nothing. They must work hard for the food they eat. The Army and Navy have very few occasions when they must go to war with anyone and kill people. So they are mostly put to use performing services for the public convenience and saving people's lives — which is certainly a matter for joy and a source of honor and pride for the Republic of the United States.

Other National Services

The department established by the government of the United States to survey the rivers, lakes, and seacoasts is also very important to commerce.[4] The officers of this department and their assistants rigorously inspect the seacoasts, gulfs, bays, inlets, lakes, rivers, harbors, and so on for their merits and their limitations and give detailed information about which of these places are favorable for commerce; out of these, which are of the best, the intermediate, and the poorest quality; what can be done to make any particular harbor or place useful for commerce; and so on. The officers of this department discovered a method for determining latitude; and they researched the phenomenon of high and low tides in the Gulf of Mexico and determined why they happen only once a day there. They have given a great boost to maritime commerce by discovering measures for rescuing ships from the grip of strong

4. Trans.: The Survey of the Coast was established in 1807 as an agency of the Department of the Treasury and renamed the Coast and Geodetic Survey in 1878. — *PCE*

ocean currents and whirlpools, for taking advantage of them for maritime traffic, and so on.

In the city of Washington there is an office of the national government that grants patents and trademarks.[5] Samples and models of the new inventions, new devices, and new products and tools that demonstrate a variety of mechanical arts, dating from the creation of the nation up to the very present, are kept on display there; and those who created them have been — and continue to be — given patents and trademarks for them by this office. In granting these patents the government is not aiming at filling its own coffers; by granting them at a reasonable rate, it protects the rights of craftsmen and encourages craftsmanship. The one place that is most worth visiting in the city of Washington is this Patent Office. When you have gone there and seen the sample models of the inventions about which I have spoken above, you cannot help but feel how incredibly blessed the people of the United States are with craftsmanship and ingenuity. After this nation won its independence, it took about fifty years for proper order to be established, to make up for the losses incurred by the war, and so on. During those years the power of ingenuity among the people here did not develop very much; but from 1836 to 1880 it grew very rapidly. During those forty-four years people received patents from the Patent Office for over 300,000 new devices, designs, machines, and so on. Forty years ago, not more than five or six hundred patents were received from this office every year. Now patents are being given annually for twenty-four to twenty-five thousand designs.

Brochures containing information about various inventions and information of many different kinds are printed at the government's cost and given away free to anyone who asks; and they are sent to every significant association, library, and office in the country. Each year 4,140,000 rupees are spent just on the salaries of the people who work in the government printing press in Washington. In this printing press there are 400 compositors, 50 proofreaders, and 150 printers who work night and day throughout the year. They require 100,000 reams of paper, and a minimum of 750,000,000 pages of printed matter are printed every year. More than 300,000 copies of the Department of Agriculture's informational book are printed at this press and distributed free every year. And there are numerous other offices like this that give out information such as the Geological Survey,[6] the Coast Survey, the

5. Trans.: The United States Patent and Trademark Office was established in 1836 as an agency of the Department of Commerce. — *PCE*

6. Trans.: *Bhūgarbhavidyāvibhāga:* literally, "department of geology." The United States Geological Survey was established in 1879 as an agency of the Department of the Interior. — *PCE*

Bureau of Ethnology,[7] the Fish Commission,[8] the National Museum,[9] and so on. This is, however, nothing more than a cursory guide to the public services of the government of the United States. If I were to do no more than name them all and give the barest information about them, I would have to write any number of books; so it would be better not to let myself get carried away.

Underlying Causes for Greatness

There can be no doubt that the system of government in this country and the government's public services have been greatly instrumental in making the people of the United States supreme in trade and business; but the principal agents of their superiority are actually something quite different. The supreme root causes of greatness and advancement of every kind — *love of industry, self-reliance, self-discipline, and unified efforts* — are universally to be seen in these people. These alone are the principal agents of their preeminence. When this nation achieved independence and the history of its independent citizens' government began, the United States was almost entirely a wilderness. Whatever small human settlement there was, existed along the Atlantic seacoast. And even within that, there was not the extent of trade or traffic there needed to be. There were no good roads on which to travel from one town or from one state to another. The people of our land used to have the idea that travel is the root of all sorrows and that a happy man is one who never has to travel. And what could be the chief reason for this if not the discomforts of travel?[10] When

7. Trans.: *Manujajātividyāvibhāga:* literally, "department of the science of human kind." This probably refers to the U.S. Bureau of Ethnology, established in 1879, the same year as the Geological Survey, to coordinate the study of and make a record of the cultures of the native peoples of the United States. — *PCE*

8. Trans.: *Matsyādijalacaraprāṇividyāvibhāga:* literally, "department of the science of fish and other aquatic creatures." The Office of the Commissioner of Fish and Fisheries (the "Fish Commission"), established by an act of Congress in 1871, might be what Ramabai is referring to here. — *PCE*

9. Trans.: *Rāṣṭrīyapadārthasaṅgrahālaya:* literally, "national collection of material things." One or all of the museums administered by the Smithsonian Institution might be what Ramabai is referring to here. The National Museum of American Art, for example, had its beginnings in 1829. — *PCE*

10. *Pañcame'hani ṣaṣṭhe vā śākaṃ pacati sve gṛhe/anṛṇī cāpravāsī ca sa vāricara modate// Mahābhārata, Vanaparvan* [32.61]. — *PRS*

Trans.: "O amphibious creature, a man who cooketh in his own house, on the fifth or sixth part of the day, with scanty vegetables, but who is not in debt and who stirreth not from home, is truly happy." Grateful acknowledgements to Gudrun Buhnemann. — *KG* and *PCE*

rivers do not have bridges over them and the streams and rivers are in flood, there is nothing to be done but to stay put for up to eight or ten days at a time on the near side, getting drenched by the rain, freezing in the cold, and rotting in the mud. Carts and carriages face the same sort of predicament on the roads: either getting buried in the mud somewhere, smashing against rocks, getting stuck in the desert sands, or worse. On top of that, there is always the fear of wild animals, robbers, and forest fires. So, you survive all these obstacles, as well as the harassments inflicted by cartman and the porter, but that is not the end of it. Further on, every town you come to, there is the exciseman sitting at the gate both as you enter it and as you leave it waiting to accost you. Then what is there left to say? Bundles opened, then tied back up again; every rag, box, and parcel ransacked; bundles stranded, goods lost, and more troubles without end! The poor traveler is left feeling he would be quite pleased to meet the angel of death[11] — but *please* not the exciseman! It is not terribly surprising then that in places where all these obstacles to travel exist, people should feel, "Happy is the man who does not travel!"

But the people here, through their extraordinary industriousness, have done away with all these obstacles. The greater the obstacles they faced, the greater their never-abated enthusiasm grew — a hundred times over indeed. By 1833 they had constructed 115,000 miles of roads, providing for the passage to and fro of people and goods in all the areas that were under human settlement in those days; and they had dug two thousand miles of canals. Such was their industry in those days, but all the services and conveniences were not as yet everywhere available the way they are at present. The state of the municipalities was very poor. Even after an official had issued a notice, a simple house tax could not be collected unless a policeman was sent for it. The job of removing filth and of cleaning up the streets of a town was largely assigned to the pigs. Nor was it customary for a town to have many streetlights. The provisions for drinking water were exactly like those in most of the towns in our own land — with the exception of cities such as Mumbai, Calcutta, Madras, and Pune. They used to make do with water from wells and ponds and with rainwater stored in tanks in their houses. The reason for there being such unremarkable civic amenities was certainly not any lack of industry on their part but rather the obstacles they faced, obstacles of such a kind that nobody in a country like ours, which is densely settled everywhere, would ever have reason to know. The land had to be brought under cultivation, the towns had to be settled, society had to be established, the forests had to be cleared, roads had to be constructed, waterways and land routes for trade and traffic had to

11. Trans.: *Yamadūta:* literally, "messenger of death." — *KG*

be worked out, and because they had few people to do the work, machines had to be invented to make up for this lack. Owing to all these unavoidable obstacles, the work of developing the country proceeded very slowly.

After 1830, when the obstacles mentioned above had been in some measure overcome, the work of development began to move rapidly. Now that all these obstacles have been overcome, the industries and businesses of the American people have begun to assume a quite stupendous — indeed, monstrous — complexion. Machines have now begun to do the work of men and of beasts of burden such as elephants, horses, oxen, and camels. In the same way that machines are used in fighting fires, in supplying water through pipes to entire cities, in printing newspapers, in weaving cloth, and so on, all sorts of machines are also used even in ordinary households. These people have become famous for creating machines by means of which a few people can do a lot of work in a short time. They have become completely accustomed to doing just about every kind of work with the help of machines. Clothes are sewn by machine; shoes are stitched and books bound by machine; nails, pins, pot and pans, tools, medical instruments, and the like are made by machine; lamps are lit by machine; cloth, socks, shirts, and the like are woven by machine; flour is ground, fields sown, grain harvested, hay baled, grain bundled, rice and wheat and other such grains threshed, corn meal sifted into flour, grit, and bran, lumber sawn into planks, and on and on; everything is done with the help of machines. It is impossible even to say how far this practice of theirs of doing their work with machines will go. Nowadays everyone is witness to things being done by machine that some years ago everyone thought would be impossible to do by any other means than human hands. It is not an exaggeration to say that in the very largest stores a machine is used even to convey to the cashier the price of goods that have been sold. With the aid of steam machines the eggs of chickens and of other birds can be kept warm and hatched as living chicks. By this means chicken "cultivation" can be done in many different places. One industrious person has calculated that the mechanical power used in the United States in manufacturing goods is equivalent to the power of 3,410,896 horses, out of which 64 percent is steam power and 35 percent is water power. These two principal kinds of power have remained the life breath of the machines used in the United States, and they are performing the work of crores of people.

It is a matter of common experience that the very earth, water, fire, wind, and sky — what are called the five basic elements[12] in our ancient

12. Trans.: *Pañcamahābhuteṃ:* "The five gross or solid elements, — *pṛthvī, udaka, teja, vāyu, ākāsa*" (Molesworth). — *KG*

texts — have all been put to work in the service of the American people. But even given the great number of machines here, the cost of human labor is not low. Not only that, it is growing very rapidly day by day. Even a common laborer here earns, at the very least, one-and-a-half to two rupees a day. If a person realizes that he cannot make a living in one occupation, there is nothing to prevent him from taking up any other kind of occupation. I have already said earlier that there is no caste discrimination *(jātibheda)* or class discrimination *(vargabheda)* in this country. Since there is no rule that a clergyman's son must become a clergyman, a carpenter's son must become a carpenter, and a blacksmith's son must become a blacksmith, each person has the freedom to enter whatever occupation appeals to him; and so, as it turns out, the person who is most fit to do a particular job is the one who ends up doing it. As a result, the possibility of the wrong job falling into the wrong hands is greatly reduced. Before President Grant became the Commander of the Army of the United States, he used to work as a tanner. Later on he became a renowned general and the president of this country. President Garfield was an ordinary schoolteacher previously. President Lincoln was a farmer's son, and he did every possible kind of work, from the lowly job of a woodcutter to the most exalted job of president of the country. Here every Tom, Dick, and Harry does not try to become a teacher, a clerk, a lawyer, or a government functionary. In our own country, the moment the sons of tradesmen such as goldsmiths, carpenters, and blacksmiths, as well as the sons of Brahmans, learn to read and write a bit, they start to demand a white-collar job and to think of such work as making pots and pans, sewing shoes, shaping wood, and so on, as belonging to inferior people. It is altogether the opposite here. Men and women who have graduated from the best schools here with advanced degrees do not hold back from doing whatever work they find to do. Here a person's industry and hard labor are respected; merely having a white-collar job (i.e., the kind marked by such cringing, dog-like servility[13] in our own country) is not respected. The respect that someone here who sweeps the streets or cleans the sewage drains has, not even the degree-holding bigwigs in our land — be they Raosahibs, Raobahadurs, Rajasahibs, Nawabsahibs, or whatever else — can have. Even in England, an ordinary merchant or laborer is shown great disrespect; I have even heard that the king or the queen would not meet such a person. And as for Hindusthan, there too the merchant and trading communities *(jātī)* are considered inferior. Why would

13. Trans.: *Śvavṛttī:* "Way or manner of a dog. 2 fig. Cringing and fawning" (Molesworth). — *KG*

any country retain its glory where this kind of disrespect is shown to industry and to those through whom the nation's wealth and advancement come?

Although day by day more and more industrious people are living in towns that have a lot of machinery and factories, that doesn't mean that everyone is coming to live in one particular place and just adding to the crowd there. If they do not make a success of themselves in one place, the roads are open to them to go to hundreds of other places. This country is vast, and it has innumerable industries too. In this great spreading land there is still plenty of space for settlement. So there is nothing to hinder a person from going somewhere new and settling down. For all these reasons, a person has no need to stay in one place here and add to the impoverishment of a city or die of starvation. Any person who possesses the strength to do some kind of work or other will not starve wherever he might go in the United States. If lazy people, those who disdain to work or who think too highly of themselves and say that they will work only if they get a certain kind of job, otherwise not at all, start to die of starvation, no one feels pity for them.

The growing populations, the growing cost of property, and the growing number of houses, stores, and factories in those cities that are important in terms of their burgeoning employment and commerce are all cause for astonishment. I will give here one or two examples of the growth of these cities. Among the fifty cities that were best known in 1880 for commerce and other significant factors like that, fifteen did not even exist in 1830. Open tracts of land might have been surveyed for the purpose of building these cities, but this land had not been leveled or had anything else done to it. Now these same towns have become so prosperous that even the smallest of them has a population of not less than forty thousand. The city of Chicago, which now has a population of over 700,000 people, was still awaiting its birth in the womb of the future in 1833. Thought was being given, however, to building a city there, and by 1834 there was quite a sizable settlement. They say now that the amount of money you would have needed during that year to buy the amount of land on which the entire city of Chicago is constructed today would be the same as the amount you would need to buy a mere six feet of frontage on one of its big streets today. The cost of land has gone up that much. This is all nothing less than the power of a growing population and of flourishing business. You can deduce to some extent the abounding prosperity of business in that city from the following figures. The trade in three commodities is very large in the city of Chicago: one is lumber, the second is food grains, and the third is animals. Four billion board feet of lumber,

900,000,000 board feet of finished boards and planks, 1,600,000,000 maunds[14] of food grains, 5,000,000 hogs, 2,000,000 head of cattle, and 1,000,000 sheep are sold there every year. In addition to this, the iron and steel mills there are by no means any less profitable and important. In Chicago, along with a town within thirty miles of it, there are three or four mills that manufacture steel rails for the railways, where 500,000 tons of rails are manufactured each year. That represents enough rails to ring our entire earth with one set of railway tracks.

The city of San Francisco is second only to Chicago in the remarkable way it grew. In 1844 there were only fifty people settled at the place where today the city of San Francisco is situated. Now there is a population of 250,000 there. In 1847 it cost only a hundred dollars to buy a piece of land there big enough to build a huge mansion. To buy the same amount of land now you would need twelve or fifteen thousand dollars. Goods worth $100,000,000, i.e., 300,000,000 rupees, are traded there nowadays. Across the Hudson River from New York City, there is a city by the name of Jersey City. The population of this city, which was 3,070 in 1840, now has grown to 120,722. The case is the same with Brooklyn, a city on the other side of New York City, which like Jersey City is called a suburb of New York City. The population of this city, which was 12,000 in 1830, reached 566,000 in 1880. There is a city by the name of Cleveland in the state of Ohio whose population, which was not more than 1,000 in 1830, reached 160,000 in 1880. The city by the name of Milwaukee in the state of Wisconsin, which consisted of two shanties in 1834, became a small village in 1835 and by 1880 had become a city with a population of 125,000. In 1840 the present state of Minnesota was nothing but uninhabited forest. In 1848 a total of 3,000 people were living in this entire state. Now there are 1,000,000 to 1,200,000 people settled there. The growth of the two cities of St. Paul and Minneapolis in this state is truly amazing. In 1880, St. Paul had approximately 41,000 people living in it, and 47,000 people were living in Minneapolis. By 1885 the population of St. Paul had grown to more than 111,000, and the population of Minneapolis had grown to more than 130,000. Every year 5,250,000 barrels of fine wheat flour are exported for sale all across the globe from Minneapolis. They say that the value of the commodities produced in Minneapolis in one year is more than

14. Trans.: A maund is now an obsolete unit of weight "used in India, Turkey, Iran, etc., varying from less than 20 to somewhat more than 160 pounds avoirdupois" *(Webster's New Universal Unabridged Dictionary)*. From a passing reference in Chapter 6, we can calculate that in Ramabai's usage of the term there are twenty-eight maunds to a ton and therefore slightly more than seventy-one pounds to a maund. 1.6 billion maunds represents about fifty-seven million tons. — *PCE*

180,000,000 rupees.[15] In 1884 246,985 railway wagons filled with goods came to Minneapolis, and even more than that number were sent out from the city. Business has flourished in exactly the same way in the city of St. Paul. And the story is no different in other cities that have been established in very recent times, such as Duluth, Indianapolis, Kansas City, Allegheny City, and so on. Go wherever you will in the United States, and you will see that even though cities like these came into existence and grew up like so many mirages,[16] almost as if overnight, they do not vanish when day returns but remain solidly in place — and are continuing to grow day by day.

All of this rapid growth that is taking place is the fruit of the industry of the people here. They don't have the leisure to dawdle and to take their own good time to do their work as the people in our country do. They know the value of time extremely well. In our country the shopkeepers sit in their shops leaning against bolsters and sell their merchandise in the most leisurely way. When a customer enters a shop, it takes the merchant a quarter of an hour just to adjust his scales. Then, ever so slowly — with the look on his face of a philosopher absorbed in mysterious thoughts, who when roused abruptly out of his trance looks around him with utter indifference toward material things — he gives the customer his merchandise. Even more time is lost then in haggling over the price. If the people of the United States had had this custom of wasting time and spending it leaning against a bolster, who knows if any trace would have been left of this nation by now?

One more thing that is worth bearing in mind is that these people do not sit around looking to the government to do each and every thing for them. Although the government of this country is appointed by the people and must, within the limits of the law, do whatever the people tell it to do, nobody is the least bit interested usually in going begging to the government for public services. Even if there are new factories to open, roads to construct, railway lines to lay, canals to dig, ships to build, or just some little shop to put up, these people come together, the many as one, and do the work.

In this country every variety of work has its own union.[17] Every possi-

15. Trans.: The currency exchange rate at that time, as we have seen earlier, was about three rupees to one dollar. So 180,000,000 rupees represented about $60,000,000. — *PCE*

16. Trans.: *Gandharvanagara:* "A city of the *gandharva* ["celestial choristers"], a celestial city affirmed to appear and disappear suddenly or in unexpected situations. . . . Fata Morgana" (Molesworth). — *PCE*

17. Trans.: *Maṇḍaḷi,* the all-purpose word Ramabai uses here, has been used in earlier chapters to render "association" (e.g., American Woman Suffrage Association), "guild" (e.g., Working Women's Guild), and even "union" (e.g., WCTU). In the present context "union" — as in "trade union" or "craft union" — seems the most appropriate sense. — *PCE*

ble kind of union exists: a union for tailors, for shoemakers, for cotton carders, for potters, for glass makers, and unions for makers of pens, needles, pins, thread, and so on and so forth. In my opinion "association in trade"[18] — which exists in our own land now only in name within the codes and compendia of law[19] created by Manu and others, and the very name of which has been all but forgotten by almost everyone — has reached a state of development and perfection in this country such as it probably has nowhere else. There is no work too big or too small that does not have some sort of union. And just as there are unions for every kind of work, there are also associations,[20] many of which are very large, of those people who are engaged in particular kinds of businesses. There are thousands of these associations: for example, of farmers, of cloth merchants, of traders in common commodities, of shoe manufacturers, of ready-made clothes merchants, of flour merchants, of fish and vegetable sellers, of liquor merchants, of dealers in cattle, horses, sheep, or hogs, of porters, of blacksmiths, of carpenters, of masons, of stonecutters, of tailors, of goldsmiths, and so on — and it must be borne in mind that "tailor," "goldsmith," and so on are not hereditary castes *(jātī)* here but merely names they assume in keeping with their occupations. The people in these associations lend a hand to other fraternal members; give each other the benefit of one another's experience; discuss among themselves subjects of importance to them, such as what can be done to make what they do first-rate, appealing, and profitable, what can be done to avoid falling victim to foreign interests, and so on; and then they adopt and follow a course of action that is decided upon by majority vote. This makes them very strong. Whether a team of two or an association with hundreds of thousands of members, these people know how to conduct their work properly and without a hitch and without either confusion or bickering. Almost all the services such as the telegraph, trains, ships, and mail have been created by independent, publicly instituted associations,[21] which have been granted the proper permits of au-

18. *Saṃbhūya samutthāna* is how they say in Sanskrit "many individuals coming together to do business and other practical affairs." — *PRS*

Trans.: *Saṃbhūya samutthānaṃ:* "engaging in business after joining partnership, association in trade" (Sir Monier Monier-Williams, *A Sanskrit-English Dictionary* [Oxford: Oxford University Press, 1982 (1899)]). — *PCE*

19. Trans.: *Smṛti:* "the body of law as delivered originally by *Manu* and other legislators . . . also any book, canon, or portion of this body or code" (Molesworth). — *PCE*

20. Trans.: *Maṇḍalyā* (sing. *maṇḍalī*) is the same word Ramabai uses previously for "union," but here the context suggests "trade association." — *PCE*

21. Trans.: Here once again Ramabai uses the word *maṇḍalyā* (sing. *maṇḍalī*), although the sense, it would seem in this context, might better be rendered "corporation." — *PCE*

thorization by the government. These associations are the fruit of the people's self-reliance, and through them the people are constantly receiving new lessons in self-discipline. Love of industry, unified efforts, self-reliance, and self-discipline — these four things are like the Philosopher's Stone. Whatever the nation in whose people they can be found, any object they touch is turned into gold. Indeed their touch is so extraordinary, strong, and effective that nothing they touch leaves their hands without turning into gold!

The railways and the waterways in this country — which through the tireless industry of these people have nowadays become as easy and comfortable to travel on as a king's highway — are proving to be invaluable to commerce. It is not easy even to imagine how far they extend. This large country *(mahādeśa)* is more than twice as big as our own Hindusthan — about two and half times larger. The 1880 Census informs us that the total area of this country then was 3,547,390 square miles. The way the country is naturally shaped is not the least of the numerous factors that unite this nation. Except for the state[22] of Alaska, the remaining 2,970,000 square miles of the country are one undivided whole. The four boundaries of this undivided part of the country are British America or Canada to the north, the Atlantic Ocean to the east, the Bay of Mexico and the independent state of Mexico to the south, and the Pacific Ocean to the west. There are large mountains both in the east and in the west, and the middle region is mostly plains. From the mountains on both sides and from the elevated regions to the north, numerous rivers flow down toward the middle of the country and for the most part flow into the Bay of Mexico in the south. Because almost all the rivers flow through the middle region, there is an abundant supply everywhere of freshwater for the arable land, and it is very fertile. These rivers are, moreover, the royal highways of commerce. They provide a tremendous service to internal commerce (i.e., trade within the country). The rivers here are also very long. The longest river in this country (when the Missouri and the Mississippi are combined) is the Mississippi. It is 4,500 miles long, and its bed is on the average 3,000 feet wide. Large steamboats sail up it about 3,900 miles. They say that the combined length of the waterways along it that can be used by boats (including all its tributaries and branches) is 35,000 miles. The meaning of the word Mississippi (in the language of our red brothers and sisters in North America) is "Father of Waters." When you see the vast expanse of this great river, you cannot help but feel that its name is altogether apt. According to the American

22. Trans.: *Saṃasthāna*, the word Ramabai mistakenly uses here, she has consistently used previously in the sense of "state." Her word for "territory" (which Alaska was at that time) has consistently been *upasaṃsthāna*. — *PCE*

writer Carnegie, "If all the rivers of Europe, excluding the Volga, were joined together, their size and the quantity of their water would be no more than that of the combined Missouri-Mississippi." This great river is three times bigger than the Ganga River in our own country. The combined length of the rivers that flow to the east of the Rocky Mountains is more than 40,000 miles and the land along their banks is twice that, i.e., 80,000 miles. And that is not even to mention the great rivers, such as the Columbia, Sacramento, San Joaquin, etc., that flow to the west of the Rocky Mountains for thousands of miles on their way to the ocean. By 1880, moreover, in order to increase the possibilities for commerce by connecting rivers together, 4,500 miles of canals had been dug in the United States, at a cost of $795,000,000. Seaports that are considered to be large and important, at such places as Philadelphia, Baltimore, New Orleans, and Portland, are located on the banks of rivers a good distance from the sea. Thousands of steamships come and go from them throughout the year. Huge docks have been built at these locations, and they are enormously important commercial centers.

If the rivers of this country are huge, so also are its lakes.[23] It would not be wrong to say that each one of America's Great Lakes (Superior, Huron, Michigan, Erie, and Ontario) is a freshwater sea. An enormous amount of trade is conducted on these lakes by means of numerous steamships and hundreds of smaller boats. The big cities that are located on the shores of these lakes, such as Duluth, Toledo, Buffalo, and Chicago, are successfully competing with enormous seaports such as New York, Boston, and New Orleans. Steamships are an invention of the American people; and the entire world is profiting from them. The first steamship that crossed the Atlantic Ocean and with the help of steam bound the people of the new and the old continents together sailed from America. Although this country's trade with other coun-

23. The length and area of the principal large lakes of the United States:

Lake Cayuga	38 miles long	104 square miles
Lake George	36 miles long	110 square miles
Salt Lake	75 miles long	240 square miles
Lake Ontario	190 miles long	6,300 square miles
Lake Erie	240 miles long	9,600 square miles
Lake Huron	250 miles long	21,000 square miles
Lake Michigan	340 miles long	22,000 square miles
Lake Superior	360 miles long	32,000 square miles

Apart from these, there are numerous lakes that are in the range of sixteen or seventeen miles in length or that are less than ten miles in length. With the exception of Salt Lake, all the rest are freshwater lakes, and it is said that one third of the freshwater in the entire world is contained in these lakes. — *PRS*

tries carried on by means of these steamships is not very large (because England has claimed control of almost all of it), the trade that goes on within the country itself is quite amazing. I have been informed by very knowledgeable people that trade worth 2,400,000,000 rupees is carried on each year on the Ohio River alone by means of steamships and smaller boats.

The endless railway tracks in this country are one more important instrument of commerce. Until 1850 the railway tracks and the trains here were very bad, and passengers suffered a great deal of inconvenience from them. Nowadays the inconvenience, the obstacles, the delays at the railway stations, and the dilatoriness of the trains themselves have all disappeared. In 1830 all of twenty-three miles of railway track had been laid in this country. In 1887 — i.e., within fifty-five years of railways beginning to be created in this country — 142,735 miles of railway track have been laid all across the country, and trains are running on them. Within the ten years from 1873 to 1883, 54,280 miles of these railway tracks were laid. The length of the railways in the whole of Europe put together is not as great as the length of the railways in the United States.[24] Excluding the United States, 150,012 miles of track had been laid in all parts of the world by 1887. If you were to look at this in terms of how rapidly railway tracks are being laid in the United States, it would certainly appear that within another ten or twelve years more railway tracks will exist in this country than in all the rest of the world. (In 1880, in the whole of Hindusthan, 273 miles of railway track had been completed; while the very next year 11,500 miles of track were laid in this country! It is very easy to see from this how far Hindusthan is lagging behind the United States!)

These waterways and railways are like the blood vessels in the nation's body. Through them the lifeblood of this nation's commerce flows unceasingly. It would be quite impossible to estimate the enormously important contribution these two instruments of trade make to the nation's commerce. The goods carried every year by boats and steamships on the largest lakes amount to 25,500,000 tons, i.e., 714,000,000 maunds;[25] the goods carried on boats and steamers on the nation's rivers amount to 34,000,000 tons, i.e., 952,000,000 maunds; and the goods transported overland within the country and everywhere else amount to 291,000,000 tons, i.e., 8,148,000,000 maunds! This enormous volume of trade that is being carried on within the United

24. I have learned from a reliable source that in 1880 the length of the railway tracks in the whole of Europe was 114,260 miles. So this establishes the fact that the length of the railway tracks in the United States is 28,475 miles longer than the length of the tracks in the entire continent of Europe. — *PRS*

25. Trans.: Ramabai continues to use a ratio of twenty-eight maunds to one ton here and throughout the remainder of the chapter. — *PCE*

States itself by means of its waterways and railways is six times greater than the trade Great Britain carries on with all foreign nations! And foreigners have no share in it at all.

There is one more astonishing thing in the United States that is a major contributor to this trade within the country and to the nation's prosperity; and if you ask what that might be, it is the telegraph service here — and one of its subsections, the telephone. An amazing web of 760,000 miles of telegraph wires is spread all across this country! Like the nervous system of the human body, it functions in the role of the nervous system of this country, and it is an extremely effective and important organ of the nation. Ever since Benjamin Franklin conducted his study of lightning, the people of this country have proceeded to use electricity to do innumerable things. Through the telegraph electricity does the work of their courier; through the telephone it does the work of personal envoy; it runs trains, lights lamps, runs machines, cures diseases, and even does gilding and plating! There must be very few things that it does not do. A telegraph machine is installed in every major store, warehouse, bank, and government office, as well as in major public venues. By this means — and of late nobody is needed actually to attend the machine — news sent from anywhere in the world is immediately printed! Hundreds of kinds of useful news — where the weather is changing, what the price of grain, cloth, metals, or coin is in various places, and so on — can be easily accessed by means of the telegraph and the telephone.

One more factor in making the trade within the country flourish is that, no matter where goods are sent within this vast country, no excise tax is levied on them. Goods can be shipped very cheaply by train and boat; and because there is none of the trouble of opening them up for inspection nor the expense of paying an excise levy in each and every place through which they pass, they can be delivered conveniently and at a reasonable cost — and even the seller makes a goodly profit. Goods entering the nation from foreign countries are taxed very heavily. Many people in this country say that if these tariffs on imported goods were abolished, trade would be greatly encouraged. As long as manufacturing[26] had not reached its present superior state in this country and as long as the industries and businesses here had not flourished, it was very beneficial to have tariffs on imported goods, the reason being that with their tariffs foreign goods would sell at higher prices; and the goods from their own country being thereby cheaper, most of the people would buy them. Now that

26. Trans.: *Śilpakalā:* although the word is nowadays used to mean "sculpture," Ramabai consistently uses it (as previously in Chapter 6) in the sense of "manual/mechanical arts," i.e., "manufacturing." — *PCE*

trade and business and manufacturing are thriving in the United States, there is not much reason to levy tariffs on imported goods. Nevertheless, almost everybody here is opposed to abolishing these tariffs. Whether it be trade or anything else, these people take the greatest of care not to fall under the influence of foreign countries and not to become the chattel of anyone. If particular goods are plentifully produced within the country and exported for trade to foreign countries, nobody hesitates to buy goods of that same kind *(jāta)* that are imported from other countries. The exchange of such commodities results not in loss; on the contrary, it produces profits. But if the trade in or use of some commodity has not yet flourished, these people do not allow the industries or businesses of their own country to be harmed by letting more than a modicum of that commodity be imported from foreign lands. Those people in our own land who keep looking expectantly to England[27] for each and every commodity, who cheerfully drink whatever mere handfuls of water England proffers them, and who harm their own country's industry and commerce by using English goods might do well to bear this matter in mind. The words as spoken by an American were, "Drinking tea imported from England and wearing clothes brought from there are harming my country's industries and businesses. So I refuse to drink that tea or wear English clothes, and I shall wear nothing but whatever rough homespun is available to me here." And his deeds were as good as his words! That is why this country is so affluent today. And what is it that we have done? We gave away our gold and got cheap English-made pots and pans of zinc; we closed down our looms and began to wear cheap English-made clothes; like the Indian people of North America we were bedazzled by the beauty of colorful sparkling glass beads, and in exchange for glass beads and glass bottles filled with liquor, we sold our jewel-bright land to a foreign people. And now we sit crying out for help because our lives are being wasted away by that liquor, and the now-broken glass is piercing our feet and wounding them grievously. That is why our country is in such a sorry state! From this it is only too clear that the United States and Hindusthan stand at polar opposites from each other.

Thus far I have given a cursory overview of those factors that have fostered trade and business in this country. Now we shall return to the intended topic of this chapter. The trade and business of this country can be classified in three general divisions: agriculture, manufacturing,[28] and mining.

27. Trans.: The word Ramabai uses for the first time here is *vilāyata*, an Arabic loan, meaning literally, "foreign country," but by the popular usage of that time meaning "England" specifically. — *KG*

28. Trans.: *Śilpakāma* is Ramabai's term here: literally, the work *(kāma)* of "[a] manual or mechanical art" (Molesworth). — *PCE*

Agriculture

This is the chief occupation of the people of the United States. As all other things, agriculture is also carried out in a scientific manner in this country, and it is continuing to advance day by day. The reason for this is that the farmers of this country are not enemies of literacy *(aksarasatru);* indeed, most of them can read and write. They read pamphlets, books, and so on about agriculture, and they put into use scientific processes and chemical applications that promote its advancement. The motto *e pluribus unum,* i.e., "many come together as one," is of use in agriculture just as in other things. There is an organization in this country called the National Grange, i.e., the "National Agriculturists' Committee."[29] We can learn what the fundamental principles are of those ethics upon the firm foundation of which this national agriculturalists' organization has been built from this organization's pledge, which is as follows: "In all the principal things, consensus; in all additional and common things, freedom of thought; and in all things, friendship.[30] We shall make a matter of the greatest concern whatever leads to the advancement of our occupation and of the fellow members of our occupation, and we shall work toward an equal division of labor among us and for just rewards for all, each according to his labor." It wouldn't be far wrong to say that this organization has branches in every town in this nation. Within the organization itself men and women are regarded as equals, and, at least in relation to the organization, women are given all the same rights that men have. The gentleman who is writing the history of this organization says, "The place where your wife or your sister can go is a place where impurity and immorality will not enter." It is for this reason that the National Grange has included respectable women as its members. Farmers who live in villages and on their own farms do not have available to them for entertainment *(tamāsha)*[31] the dramas, the vaudeville shows, the concerts, the best lectures, or the various other means of intellectual stimulation that people do in the cities. From sun-

29. Trans.: The National Grange of the Patrons of Husbandry, a fraternal society established in 1867 to advance the social, economic, and political interests of farmers, was at the forefront of postbellum agrarian protest in the United States. By 1874 more than 20,000 local granges existed. — *PCE*

30. Trans.: The original phrasing of the motto in the 1874 *Declaration of Purposes of the National Grange* is "In essentials, unity; in non-essentials, liberty; in all things, charity" (www.geocities.com/cannongrange/declaration_purposes.html). What follows this in the quotation in Ramabai's text is a rather drastic summing up of the *Purposes.* — *PCE*

31. Trans.: *Tamāśā:* "A diverting exhibition; a show, play, farce, mock-fight" (Molesworth). In Maharashtra the *tamāsā* is an extremely popular form of folk theater. — *KG*

rise to sunset their entire time is spent doing farm work. It is most desirable that they should have entertainment — but also that they should have the means of intellectual stimulation. The National Grange is constantly working toward this end. In keeping with the rules of this organization, lectures on a wide range of topics by public speakers of renown and learning are arranged several times a year. Provisions are made through the local granges for men and women who wish to do so to study a variety of subjects during their free time. As a result of their knowledge, both obtained through reading the agricultural information published by the Department of Agriculture of the United States and other books and born out of their own experience, as well as the many-faceted knowledge and benefits of unity available to them through the National Grange as mentioned above, the farmers of this country are day by day continuing to grow more industrious, advanced, happy, and wealthy.

Ever since this nation became independent, its citizens and its rulers have paid the greatest attention to the advancement of agriculture. Even though George Washington, the first president of this nation, was an extremely busy man, he insisted on supervising the Department of Agriculture himself. The most notable of men, who were the thinkers and political leaders of their day, such as Jefferson, Webster, Adams, and Clay, were themselves farmers. When people see such fine examples, it is only natural that they should think of farming as a respectable occupation and should feel enthusiastic about taking it up, and that farmers, as a consequence, should be universally respected. One fourth of the total wealth of the United States is invested in agriculture, and one fourth of what the country produces comes from agriculture.

Whether it be farmers or whether it be anyone else, it is not the practice here for the son to do exactly what his father did. That the countless men born into a certain family-line should, in keeping with some traditional prescription such as "Going by the same traditional path as one's ancestors,"[32] continue to do things exactly as their thousandth ancestor had done — the way he wielded his ax, the way he dug a water channel or a ditch, the way he set his plow in the ground, or the way he wove together a honeycomb or straw and made a bird's nest or constructed an anthill — is all quite impossible for the people here. Their ingenuity and scientific knowledge have been put to use in every matter of practical business. They use machines here even for farming. A steam-driven machine run by a couple of men that plows and

32. Trans.: *Yenāsyapitaro yātā/yena yātāḥ pitāmahāḥ* (*Manusmṛti* 4.178). Grateful acknowledgments to Gudrun Buhnemann and K. S. Arjunwadkar. — *PCE*

plants large fields can do the work of hundreds of people. On almost all farms, large or small, a machine run by one person that harvests and bundles the crops does the work of fifty or sixty people. There are hundreds of these kinds of machines being used for agricultural work, the very names of which nobody in our country would know or, by merely reading their descriptions in books, would understand what they are used for or how. The value of all the improved plows and machines that farmers in this country were using in 1880 was as much as $450,000,000, i.e., 1,350,000,000 rupees. There is not an overabundance of men to work the vast stretches of arable land in the United States, so farmers have no choice but to use machines. This very necessity has encouraged the inventiveness of the American people, and thousands of machines are being created by them. The people who are engaged in agriculture just as in other occupations are using the newly created machines with great enthusiasm.

We learn from the census of 1880 that the arable land in the United States (excluding the land in the large territory called Alaska) is 1,500,000 square miles. (The total area of our own Hindusthan is 1,383,500 square miles; so we must draw the conclusion that the arable land in the United States is larger in area than our entire country.) All the land in this country is new: before the English and other Europeans settled here no one had ever brought this land under cultivation. In all directions there were long-established forests and grasslands. From what information modern people have of the history of this country, we gather that from the beginning of creation until the Europeans settled here this land had never seen a plow. So it scarcely needs to be said that it is an extremely laborious and difficult job to clear land that has grown hard and compacted from forests growing on it from time immemorial, to plow it, and bring it under cultivation. But blessed is the industry and the energy of the people here! Up to the present time they have brought a minimum of 297,000 square miles of land under cultivation! At the beginning of this century, approximately 65,000 square miles of land in the United States had been brought under cultivation. During the following sixty years another 150,000 square miles of land were plowed and made productive. From 1860 to 1880, 82,000 square miles of land were brought under cultivation! I have mentioned earlier in the book that there are not very many large landholders (*jamīnadāra* or zamindars) with tenant farmers. The people living in the southern states had very large landholdings on which African slaves used to do the work. Now these black people have been emancipated, and almost all of them have continued to live where they were before. They rent small pieces of land from the large landowners and farm them. It is possible that when they have developed the means to buy farms, they will pay the owner the price of the land they have been renting and buy it for themselves. The laws concerning the purchase and sale of land are very simple in this country. Out in the western states many people own very large farms. But it does appear to be the wish of many people here that there should not be a system of large landholders supported by a class of tenant farmers in this country. Nowadays most of the farmers work small farms that they themselves have bought and own. Out of a total of about 4,000,000 farms in the United States, approximately three-quarters belong to independent owners; and it is their owners themselves who work them. Out of 4,005,907 farms here, 322,350 are tenant farms; 699,244 farms are owned by partnerships; and 2,984,306 farms belong to independent owners. The average farm is 134 acres. But there are at least 30,000 farms that are larger than 1,000 acres. Arable land is also very cheap to get here. Nowadays in some states an acre of land costs an average of 60 rupees. The cost of land in many of the northern states near the Atlantic Ocean ranges from 22 to 102 rupees an acre. As the population and the number of settlers continue to grow day by day, land is becoming more and more expensive. The cost of land more than doubled from 1850 to 1880.

Almost all of the land that is under cultivation and that is worth bringing under cultivation is flat, so machines are a great help in farming it. There is an abundant supply of water everywhere. Farmers are not lazy when it comes to putting in hard labor and using machines in their work. They strive in every possible way to make this fertile land even more productive. Owing to all these favorable factors, the agricultural wealth of the United States is even now very great, and it will continue to grow ever more abundantly. In 1880 approximately 2,700,000,000 maunds of food grains were produced on 118,000,000 acres of land, i.e., an average of twenty-three maunds thirty-six *seras* per acre.[33] Included among them were 1,750,000,000 maunds of maize, 460,000,000 maunds of wheat, and 407,000,000 maunds of oats, and the rest was other food grains. Maize, cotton, and wheat are the major crops of this country. Animals such as hogs, cattle, and horses are mostly given maize as feed, and hogs don't eat anything but maize. People also consume a good bit of maize. In 1880 the more than 30,000,000 rupees' worth of maize that was left over after filling the entire country's needs was exported to other countries. Up until 1860 the people of this country needed to import wheat from abroad. Now one fourth of the wheat produced in the entire world is produced in this country. In 1860 there were 173,000,000 maunds of wheat produced in this

33. Trans.: Ramabai makes a small computational error here. The actual amount comes to 22.88 maunds per acre. A *śera* is an obsolete measure amounting to somewhat less than two pounds. — *PCE*

country; in 1870 there were 287,000,000 maunds; in 1880, 459,000,000 maunds; and in 1884, 500,000,000 maunds! From this you can get some idea of how rapidly the production of crops such as wheat is continuing to grow here. Twenty-seven years ago the people of this country had to import wheat from abroad. But in 1880 the 590,000,000 rupees' worth of wheat left over after providing for all the people of this country was exported to other countries.

The people of this country started cultivating cotton in 1776. At first there was some doubt about whether it would be possible to produce cotton here and make a profit from it. But once they did decide to cultivate cotton, they did not do so in any half-hearted way. Very soon after this country became independent a man by the name of Eli Whitney created a machine to separate the cotton fiber from the cottonseed, and from that time the cultivation of cotton began to flourish. To allow this newly produced crop to be used within the country as a product within the domestic market, heavy tariffs were levied on cloth imported from abroad; so of course the number of domestic looms greatly increased, and cloth made from domestic thread began to be produced everywhere. Before 1830 almost all the cotton produced here was being consumed right here. But that year approximately 90,000,000 rupees' worth of cotton was exported abroad. In 1880 5,757,397 bales of cotton were produced in this country, out of which 660,000,000 rupees' worth was exported. Two-thirds of this cotton was sold in England. The cloth that England produces and sells in our country at a cheap rate is mostly made of American cotton. The thread made from this cotton is very thin and fine.

There is a grain called rye out of which they make bread. It, too, is produced here very plentifully. In 1880 20,000,000 maunds of this grain were produced. Forty-four million maunds of barley were also produced, as well as 407,000,000 maunds of a food grain called oats. The production of potatoes was 203,000,000 maunds. Both in the east and on the expansive plains in the west a great deal of excellent grass is produced. In 1880 1,008,000,000 maunds of grass were sold at market. Tobacco is also cultivated here a great deal. There are 638,000 acres of land sown in this calamitous crop, so there is a great deal of tobacco produced here. Half of it is sold in this country and half is exported. There is an abundance of many kinds of fruit everywhere in this country. In 1880 fruit worth more than 60,000,000 rupees was produced here. That year the total value of the crops produced in this country was more than 9,060,000,000 rupees. And in 1884, as I have learned from a reliable source, the value of the crops produced was 8,164,500,000 rupees.

I already mentioned earlier that animals such as hogs, cattle, and chickens are looked upon as vegetables here and are "cultivated" just as any other kind of crop. In 1880 there were 56,750,000 hogs and 46,000,000 head of cattle, of which 18,000,000 were milch cows. (The cows here are not like the cows in our land that yield a quarter *sera* or half *sera* of milk. They get plenty to eat, and constant efforts are being made in scientific ways to assure that they grow properly and that their condition and their health are the best. These cows truly are *ghaṭodhnī*,[34] i.e., their udders have the capacity of large water jars.) There were as many as 45,000,000 sheep and 12,000,000 horses in this country in 1880. By now their number must have increased a great deal. And there certainly is a use for all these animals in this country. The meat of these animals is supplied to the 55,000,000 meat-loving people here, and there is plenty left for export as well. Over the last few years they have started drying the meat of hogs and other animals to be exported for sale in foreign countries. The value of the meat of hogs, cattle, and sheep that is exported each year is more than 352,500,000 rupees. In 1880 3,000,000 maunds of wool were produced in this country. From the annual report of an organization called the Butter, Cheese,[35] and Eggs Association (the name is certainly a bit strange but there is no remedy for that!), we learn that the annual production of dairy products such as butter and cheese in the United States is more than 300,000,000 rupees. In 1880 the income of farmers in the United States (the profit left them after subtracting expenses) was more than 1,650,000,000 rupees. Everything belonging to the great is great!

Manufacturing

Before 1776 the thirteen English colonies in North America found themselves subjugated in every possible way. Because they were subject to the sovereign rule of the British government, strict laws were implemented in these thirteen colonies that would profit England and the people who lived there. At the time these states were about to become independent, George III was the king of England, and his rule became altogether intolerable to these people. Tariffs were levied on everything that was imported to and exported from the United States. They did not have the freedom to carry on trade independently with foreign countries and were restricted to trade done solely at English prices and with English merchants. It was the expressed opinion of a great number of English people that the Americans should mine iron and other metals for

34. Trans.: *Ghaṭodhnī:* "(a cow) having a full udder, Ragh. ii, 49" (Monier-Williams, *A Sanskrit-English Dictionary*). — *PCE*

35. Trans.: For want of an exact equivalent, Ramabai uses here the word *khavā:* "Milk conglobated by boiling" (Molesworth). *Khavā* is used in numerous Indian confections. — *PCE*

shipment to England, that they should not themselves use these metals to manufacture anything, that, indeed, the colonists here should not have even the right to have so much as a nail for shoeing horses produced in this country. Whatever products were made here and sent to England carried an onerous burden of tariffs. Tariffs on imports, tariffs on exports, taxes on the sale and on the purchase of goods, taxes every time they turned around — these people were ready to breathe their last from paying taxes. These people were tied hand and foot with this and numerous other rules like it that manifested their subjugation. There was nothing to encourage their trades and businesses. Their backs and heads were bowed under the burden of their taxes.

In the end, as a consequence of the Stamp Act and the tax on tea, their desire for independence grew strong, and they threw the yoke of England from off their necks and broke the fetters of English laws that had bound their hands and feet. In 1783 the War of Independence ended, peace was established in the nation, and soon the national government began to function smoothly. Laws encouraging the nation's trade were enacted one after another. And from that time forth their prosperity began. Commerce suffered a serious setback on the continent of Europe between 1790 and 1820 because of the numerous wars that took place there, but this only served to encourage commerce in the United States. From that time up until 1860 there was no obstacle to the trades and businesses here. But then the next five years brought all the desolation of war to this country, and commerce suffered enormous losses. Thereafter, from 1866 up to the present day, not only have the trades and businesses here advanced unhindered and made up for all their losses, but this nation has become even wealthier than England, which styles itself as the wealthiest country on the face of the earth. From the time of the earliest settlements here, the American people applied themselves to the advancement of manufacturing — and to such a degree that within a very few years of the establishment of the colonies the English grew alarmed and felt themselves obliged to enact strict laws to prevent the emergence of manufacturing here altogether. And so even as late as 1830 manufacturing had not flourished here that much. Up to that time the nation was entirely focused on establishing the peace and building a solid foundation for manufacturing and other trades and businesses. Nowadays anyone who hasn't personally seen what an advanced state manufacturing has reached in this country isn't likely even to begin to grasp it.

Manufacturing is growing more advanced every single day. Some years ago England was supreme in all the world in manufacturing. Nowadays the United States has taken over its supremacy in this field. Owing to the fact that machines have now begun to be used to do every kind of work, every industry is assuming quite monstrous proportions. The largest business of all is the milling of flour by means of machines. There are twenty-four thousand flour-milling machines in this country, which produce 5,000,000 pukka[36] maunds of flour every day. In 1880 the capital investment in this business was 532,200,000 rupees; and the value of the flour that was produced that year was 1,500,000,000 rupees. This quantity of flour is more than enough to supply the needs not only of the American people but of the people living on the entire continent of Europe. The flour produced by the American people is being marketed in large quantities in Europe, Japan, China, Hindusthan, and other countries.

The business of slaughtering animals is second in size only to the milling of flour. Machines are used on a large scale in this business as well. The animal to be slaughtered is brought to the near end of the machine, and within the space of one minute its throat is cut, its hide, intestines, and so on are removed, it is stuffed with flavorful and preservative substances,[37] packed, and made ready. Within five minutes it falls into the hands of the man standing at the other end of the machine. This very large slaughterhouse I have been describing is in the city of Chicago. There are many slaughterhouses just like it in other places as well. In Chicago in 1880 5,250,000 hogs and 2,500,000 head of cattle were slaughtered, their carcasses stuffed with preservative substances, processed, and sent out to be sold. The capital investment in this business is approximately 150,000,000 rupees, and the annual wages of the people employed in this work is more than 31,500,000 rupees. In one year 1,700,000 head of cattle, 2,200,000 sheep, and 16,000,000 hogs were slaughtered, stuffed with preservative substances, packed, and sent to markets all over the world as food for people.

The capacity of the United States is second only to England in the production of iron and steel products. One fifth of the iron products and one fourth of the steel products needed everywhere in the world are produced in the United States. In 1883 the value of the iron and steel products produced in the United States was 1,200,000,000 rupees. From the never-ceasing speed of wind with which this business is advancing and growing it would appear that by 1890 more iron and steel products will be produced in the United States than in England. In 1870 1,020,000 pukka maunds of steel products were manufactured here. And fifteen years later, i.e., in 1885, 38,458,364 pukka

36. Trans.: *Pakkā:* "Pukka" is the familiar Anglo-Indian rendering of this all-purpose adjective meaning, among other things, "of full weight." It is not clear here how or if a pukka maund differs from a simple maund. — *PCE*

37. Trans.: *Masālā,* literally, "drugs, medicines, spices" (Molesworth), is the very common word Ramabai uses here without elaboration. — *PCE*

maunds of steel products were manufactured! There are numerous iron mines in the United States; and given the extraordinary industry of these people, the metal from these mines will not be left to stay where it is but will be put to human use and will increase the wealth of this country. There are also large factories for manufacturing products and machines made out of such metals as copper, brass, and bronze. A great deal of capital has been invested in them, and in 1881 the value of the products manufactured in them was more than 642,000,000 rupees.

Cutting lumber and selling it for such uses as building houses is another very large business. I do not know whether this business exists in any other country or not, but I venture to guess that no other country has as many forestlands as the United States — or if they do, that the people in other countries have not ventured into the lumber business the same way. In 1880 forty thousand people were making a living in this business. The capital investment in it was about 600,000,000 rupees, and the value of the processed lumber was 699,806,187 rupees. There are very large forests in the states of Michigan, Wisconsin, Minnesota, Oregon, and northern California, and in the territory by the name of Washington Territory. There are areas of the country, indeed, where nothing can be produced but trees. In all these forestlands industrious people are felling enormous amounts of timber and becoming wealthy selling it within their own country as well as in other countries. Durable, beautiful, and valuable wood of many different species *(jātī)*, such as oak, cherry, maple, mahogany, and walnut, is produced on a large scale; it is felled, processed, and sent to Europe. In the golden land of the United States, four hundred different kinds of useful wood are produced!

Next in importance and size to this is the business of cotton. In 1880 the capital investment in this business was 624,000,000 rupees, and the value of the cotton products produced within the country was 382,000,000 rupees. The massive quantities of cotton grown in this country are sold in England and in other countries, so not that much cloth is produced here. But even so, more than enough cloth is produced to supply the needs of the people of this country. Next in importance to this is the wool business, the capital investment in which is 465,000,000 rupees, and I surmise that the value of the woolen products produced in this country must be about the same. More than eighty-six thousand people are making a living in this business. The value of domestic products woven from mixed wool, cotton, and other materials in 1880 was 198,750,000 rupees. In that same year the capital investment in the silk business was 57,000,000 rupees, and the value of domestically produced silk cloth was more than 55,500,000 rupees. The value of woolen or silk products or products such as socks and gloves woven out of wool, silk, or cotton that were produced that same year was as much as 186,000,000 rupees. It has not yet been even twenty-five years since these people began to manufacture carpets, but in this short period of time this business has truly flourished. The value of carpets manufactured in this country in 1880 was 65,250,000 rupees.

The shoe-making business is also very important. Just as other businesses, it has advanced enormously through mechanization. Fifty years ago a shoemaker in this country, in the same way as a cobbler in our own country, had to put a lot of labor and time into making shoes. In those days a shoemaker felt a great sense of accomplishment when he made one pair of shoes a day. Nowadays with the help of machines one man can make three hundred pairs of shoes a day! In 1880 there were three thousand large shoe factories in this country, and about 9,200,000 people were working in them.[38]

Just a few years ago all the watches that the people of the United States needed came from Europe. Nowadays so many watches are manufactured in the United States that they not only fill the needs of everyone here but are also sold in great numbers in most of the countries of Europe and in Hindusthan. Just like all the other industries here, the factories that make watches are very large, and they have reached a highly advanced state. Around 1850 when four or five watches a day were being produced in the best watch-making factories in this country, this was thought to be a lot. Nowadays in these kinds of factories twelve to thirteen hundred watches are produced every day. There are four or five large factories that produce this number of watches in a day, and there is never so much as a pause in their production. From just one factory six thousand watches are sent every month just to the city of London. In a few years all the people in the world will be the proud owners of these cheap, beautiful, and convenient watches. And in exactly the same way the sewing machines made by the American people will come into general use everywhere. In 1880 sewing machines worth 35,589,564 rupees were manufactured. Metal engraving — such as is used in making silver caskets and gold jewelry — is also of the finest quality here. And the artisans of the United States are very skilled in carving and engraving wood. There are hundreds of additional occupations besides. It would be quite impossible to give an adequate description of them all in this small essay. It is difficult to get a true sense of just how rapidly manufacturing has advanced and continues to advance. In 1850 the value of the products created through manufacturing was 6,180,000,000

38. Trans.: This number clearly seems to be mistaken as it would have represented almost one fifth of the population of the United States at that time. No doubt "ninety-two thousand" is meant. — *PCE*

rupees. In 1880 products worth 16,680,000,000 rupees were manufactured in this country. That same year the value of the products manufactured in England was 12,155,000,000 rupees, which goes to demonstrate that the value of the products manufactured in the United States is 4,525,000,000 rupees greater than in England.

Mines

The United States has not become the golden land it is solely by virtue of its visible surface fertility, either. In the same way that Mother Nature *(Srstidevi)* has made this independent nation visibly prosperous on its exterior surface with every comfort and convenience, she has placed under the ground, within the countless cellars of this nation's mines, imperishable treasures of gemstones and precious metals. Sitting in these countless vast cellars, Mother Nature is performing alchemy for the American people and turning the very earth into gold. Beneath the green pastures, beneath the delightful, fertile, verdant fields of grain, beneath the forests bedecked with lofty trees, beneath the comfortable, prosperous, populated towns, and beneath the plains that look so desolate and barren on the surface — all of them existing within the four boundaries, east, west, north, and south, of this nation — Mother Nature has stored in the earth's deep cellars numerous treasures such as limitless gold, silver, lead, copper, mercury, nickel, salt, coal, crude oil, natural gas, the best kinds of stone, sulfur, and more besides, all for the fortunate people of the United States. Just as when a suckling calf from time to time butts its head against its mother's udder she responds by releasing more milk, so also when the American people do nothing more than scratch the back of their motherland a bit she immediately shows her delight by taking countless metals and gemstones from out of her infinite horde and giving them to her children. Thanks to their industry and to their inquisitiveness these American people have been so blessed with good fortune that the very earth turns to gold in their hands.

Coal is the principal mineral resource of this country. They say that the total area of all the coalfields in the world is 400,000 square miles. Twelve thousand square miles of these are in the United Kingdom of Great Britain. I understand from a reliable source that the total area of the coalfields in the United States is 300,000 square miles! It is hard even to imagine that three-fourths of the coalfields in the entire world are in the United States. But it is true. It would not be wrong to say that the abundance of coal is in very large measure responsible for the extraordinary prosperity of every kind of business and industry in this country. Although this country has three-fourths of the coalfields in the world, they do not as yet mine as much coal as is mined in England. One reason for this is that it hasn't been that many years since they began to mine coal; and the other reason is that other precious mineral resources, such as gold, silver, copper, iron, petroleum, and so on, are found in vast quantities, and in the hurry and excitement of extracting them, nobody has felt that much of a necessity for coal. Even so, 2,446,800,000 pukka maunds of coal were mined last year.

They say that there is a total of 289,940 maunds of gold in the entire world. More than half of it has come from the continent of America. Since 1880, gold worth 93,775,000 rupees has been produced by the United States every year — which is one third of the gold produced in the entire world. Just as in every other industry, gold mining is also advancing with the greatest speed. Between 1851 and 1860 the average value of gold mined every year was 15,000,000 rupees. Nowadays gold worth 92,500,000 rupees is produced over the course of a year. The same story holds true for silver. Every year silver worth 138,750,000 rupees is produced here. They say that more than half the copper in the entire world is produced in the two countries of Chile and the United States. In 1880 756,000 maunds of copper were produced in this country; and only four years later more than twice that quantity had begun to be produced every year. In 1884 1,779,540 maunds of copper were produced! There are also numerous lead mines in this country. Around 1830 the mines were producing on average 225,000 maunds of lead a year. Nowadays, at the very minimum, 3,920,000 maunds of lead are mined over the course of a year. Before 1870 very little zinc was being produced from the mines in this country. Nowadays more than 1,275,000 maunds of zinc[39] are produced here over the course of a year.

Crude oil or petroleum is produced here in the greatest abundance. Some years ago plants were set up here to produce oil from coal, but then people realized that there were springs of crude oil at numerous places in the state of Pennsylvania from which the oil was flowing away with the river water; so they proceeded to dig large wells everywhere and to extract oil from them. Now petroleum from the United States is exported all around the world. When they were digging deep wells for crude oil, they also discovered a flammable mineral effluvium called "gas," which is abundant in this country. In some towns in the state of Pennsylvania, steam-driven machines in all the factories, the mills, and so on are run by means of this flammable gas.

39. Trans.: Whether as a misprint or through oversight, the word in the text here is *śiseṃ* (lead), but the context clearly shows that Ramabai means *jasta* (zinc). — *PCE*

Whether it be cooking, heating houses during winter, or lighting lamps, everything is done with gas. Another important use for gas is in chemical applications, and even glass, iron, and steel are refined using it. They say that just one well from among the hundreds of gas wells near the city of Pittsburgh produces 30,000,000 cubic feet of gas every day!

The moment gold was discovered in 1849 in the state of California people from the eastern states began to rush to the Pacific coast. Ever since then every Tom, Dick, and Harry has been going west to mine. In the uninhabited forested regions of Colorado, Nevada, California, etc., large towns sprang up overnight like so many mirages. Where once there was nothing but wilderness, towns began to appear; and on the vast plains where nothing but grass once grew, rich fields of grain began to appear. When these people find out about the discovery of some mining site or about some useful product that is to be had or can be produced somewhere, it's as if they become possessed. Then off they all run and, pushing their way past mountainous obstacles, accomplish their desires. If I were to sit here describing the industry and commerce of these people in detail, I would have to write several large volumes. But here are the details of this country's net annual produce from its industries and businesses (after deducting costs):

Produce from agriculture: 1,650,000,000 rupees
Produce from mining: 168,750,000 rupees
Produce from manufacturing: 61,500,000 rupees
Produce from fisheries: 21,750,000 rupees
Produce from lumber: 21,150,000 rupees
Produce from other products: 21,750,000 rupees

Thus the annual net produce of all industries and businesses is 1,944,900,000 rupees.

The British nation is famous for being the richest nation in the world. It is an old nation with a long history. Up to the present day, through its industries and businesses and other sources, it has accumulated in its treasury 130,800,000,000 rupees in wealth. The democratic nation of the United States is about 125 years old. In such a short period of time, by means only of its surpassing industry, it has accumulated in its treasury 146,850,000,000 rupees in wealth! Almost nobody would believe that the United States is wealthier even than England, but that is the truth.

The people who came to settle in this country were not rich to begin with; and those who are still coming to settle here also are not rich. But once they got here these industrious people, through the businesses and trades they engaged in, acquired all this wealth. Now the offspring of these wealthy people will be born rich. Many people here have begun to fear already that, just as those who are born rich in our country have acquired fame through their wild profligacy, as in the maxim, "By breaking pots or rending clothes or by riding a donkey, by this or by some other means,"[40] those who are born rich here will also make an evil name for themselves, bring down ruin on their homes and property, and utterly destitute themselves. Yet there doesn't seem to be any compelling reason here to fear that this country will reach such a sorry state as our own country has at the hands of such shining family exemplars (of nothing but familial disasters) as these. The United States as a country is like a beehive where only the honeybees that work will remain alive. There is no place for lazy male drones.[41] The industrious honeybees allow the sluggards to live only as long as they serve their purpose. But the moment their purpose is served, the workers sting these burdensome gluttons and kill them. Those people who originally were poor and who have made themselves wealthy today by virtue of their industry and education know the reason for their prosperity perfectly well. They do not shelter sluggards and idlers. And they do not waste their hard-earned money on such things as arranging weddings for pigeons or cats, base diversions and pleasures, hosting feasts for the sahibs, putting on fireworks displays, and watching plays, tamashas, and nautch girls. They make only the very best use of their money. There are plenty of wealthy people here who have so much money they could buy out not only all the richest moneybags[42] in the history of our own land but even entire kingdoms. As befits their wealth, they establish numerous first-rate institutions dedicated to the progress and the educational advancement of future generations. Wealthy men by the names of Trevor and Corcoran each gave 300,000 rupees to establish schools. Wilston, Walker, Hitchcock, and Winkley each donated 500,000 rupees; Colgate and Crozier each donated 800,000 rupees; Ciney and Busse each donated 1,000,000 rupees; Stone do-

40. Trans.: *Ghataṃ bhitvā paṭaṃ chitvā, kṛtvā rāsabharodanaṃ/yena kena prakāreṇa* [*prasiddhāḥ puruṣo bhavet*]. This is a commonly anthologized epigram of uncertain authorship. See Kashinath Pandurang Parab, ed., *Subhāṣita-Ratna-Bhāṇḍāgāra,* seventh ed., rev. Wasudev Laxman Pansikar (Mumbai: Panduranga Jawaji, 1935), section 3, verse 50. Grateful acknowledgements to Gudrun Buhnemann. — *KG* and *PCE*

41. Trans.: *Bhojanabhāū:* "a lazy or careless person who takes no share in the trouble of providing for the household, but who is always ready at mealtime; an eating brother . . ." (Molesworth). — *PCE*

42. Trans.: *Naūkoṭī Nārāyaṇa:* "(*Nava* Nine, *koṭī* Ten million, *Nārāyaṇa* Lord.) A term for one exceedingly rich; a *Croesus, Plutus, millionaire*" (Molesworth). — *KG*

nated 1,200,000 rupees; Phoenix donated 4,000,000 rupees; Vanderbilt and Vassar each donated 2,000,000 rupees; Clark donated 2,500,000 rupees; a gentleman by the name of Greene 3,000,000 rupees; a gentleman named Ritch donated 4,000,000 rupees; Parker donated 7,000,000 rupees; and Steven Gerard and Johns Hopkins each donated 10,000,000 rupees to establish schools. Leyland Stanford, the president of the Southern Pacific Railway and a senator from the state of California in the Senate of the United States, spent 90,000,000 rupees to establish a university in memory of his only son who had died. The great generosity of these extremely wealthy people is being put to use in the supremely praiseworthy cause of the advancement of education. As long as the wealthy people of this country spend their money this wisely and as long as education retains its ascendance here and people are inclined to use the knowledge they learn in school for practical purposes, there is no need for this country to have any fear of people like the headless wonders[43] who are born to wealth in our own land.

43. Trans.: *Śiraḥśūnya ketugrahasama:* literally, "like the headless ninth planet." The reference is to the story of the demon Rahu: "A *daitya* with the tail of a dragon whose head was severed from his body by Vishnu. The head and tail, retaining their separate existence, were transferred to the planetary heavens, and became, the first, the eighth planet, the second (or *ketu*) the ninth. To them are ascribed the eclipses of the sun and moon" (Molesworth). — *PCE*

Glossary

Abja: A thousand million, i.e., a billion.

Bāī: A Marathi term of respect for women generally, it is added as a suffix to either their given names or their surnames.

Brahmacārī: "A Brahman from his investiture with the sacrificial thread [at age 8] until marriage; during which period he is enjoined to observe the strictest chastity" (Molesworth).

Crore (Marathi *croḍa* or *koṭī*): Ten million.

Darśana: "Sight or seeing: also looking. 2 A dream or vision. . . . 4 Visiting any idol or sacred shrine" (Molesworth).

Deśabandhū: A fellow citizen, compatriot.

Gāṇapatya: A devotee of Ganapati or Ganesh.

Habaśī: Literally, Abyssinian; but used by Ramabai in the sense of African.

Jagadguru: A title conferred on the Shankaracharya, the chief proponent of the Advaita Vedanta philosophy, which means "teacher of the world."

Jahāgiradāra: The owner of lands or revenue that are assigned to him by the government or by a king.

Jaminadāra: A hereditary village officer with large landholdings.

Jāta (plural *jātī*): "Kind, sort, species, class, tribe. . . . 3 The well known *caste* of the Hindus" (Molesworth).

Kaikāḍī (fem. *Kaikāḍīṇa*): A wandering tribe of basket makers and stonecutters from eastern Maharashtra, who were formerly included among the "criminal tribes."

Lakh (Marathi *lākha* or *lakṣa*): One hundred thousand.

Lakṣmī: "The wife of Vishnu and the goddess of wealth, prosperity, splendor, elegance, etc." (Molesworth).

Mahāra: A formerly untouchable caste in Maharashtra. The Mahars were employed as village watchmen, gate-keepers, messengers, guides, and porters; they also performed the most degrading tasks in the community, e.g., disposing of the carcasses of dead animals.

Mahāravāḍā: The section of a village where the Mahars resided — always on the outskirts of the village.

Mahātma: "Magnanimous, nobleminded, large-hearted, generous, bold" (Molesworth).

Mantra: "An incantation or a mystical verse; a charm or spell. 2 A formula sacred to a deity" (Molesworth).

Manu: "The great legislator and saint, the son of Brahma or a personification of Brahma himself. . . . in every *kalpa* or interval from creation to creation there are fourteen successive *Manu*, presiding over the universe for the period of a *manvantara* respectively" (Molesworth).

Maund (Marathi *Maṇa*): An obsolete unit of weight. We can calculate that in Ramabai's usage of the term there are twenty-eight maunds to a ton and therefore slightly more than seventy-one pounds to a maund.

Pañcāyata: "An assembly of arbitrators (usually five)" (Molesworth). In present-day India it is the form of local self-government at the village level.

Pātāḷa: "Hell; the regions under the earth, the abode of the *nāga* or serpents" (Molesworth).

Purāṇa: "A . . . sacred and poetical text. There are eighteen. They comprise the whole body of Hindu theology. Each should treat of five topics especially: the creation, the destruction and the renovation of worlds, the genealogy of gods and heroes, the reigns of the Manus, and the transactions of their descendants" (Molesworth). Also, mythical legends.

Rānaṭī: "Wild, growing spontaneously. 2 Boorish, rustic" (Molesworth). "Uncultivated," in both an agricultural and a cultural sense, is the prevailing connotation of the word. "Savage," "uncivilized," or "barbarous" is the sense at which Ramabai is aiming.

Rao (Marathi *rāva*): "A title of honor, it is affixed to the names of persons eminent as soldiers, clerks, etc. . . . Applied also to the master of a house or establishment or to other respectable person" (Molesworth).

Raosahib (Marathi *rāvasāheba*): A title of honor reserved for a gentleman.

Sahib (Marathi *sāheba*): "A lord or master. 2 A gentleman. Esp. understood as an English or a European gentleman" (Molesworth).

Sarasvatī: "The wife of Brahma, the goddess of speech and eloquence, the patroness of music and arts and the inventress of the Sanskrit language and the Devanagari script. . . . 6 A term for an eloquent, or inventive, or excelling woman" (Molesworth).

Saubhāgyavatī (Abbr. *Sau.*): "A woman possessing *saubhāgya* or the excellence and blessedness consisting in the possession of a husband; a married and unwidowed woman" (Molesworth).

Śera: An obsolete measure of weight which varied greatly from place to place. From references elsewhere in the text we can calculate that Ramabai's *śera* was slightly less than two pounds.

Srīmadbhāgavata: The *Bhāgavata Purāṇa,* one of the eighteen canonical *Purāṇas*.

Tamahsa: "A diverting exhibition; a show, play, farce, mock-fight, etc." (Molesworth); a major form of folk theater in Maharashtra.

Yama: "The deity that judges the dead and sends them, according to their deeds, to Swarg or Narak, Elysium or Tartarus. . . . Hence applied to a fierce, savage, pitiless man" (Molesworth).

Sabhya: "Polite, well-bred, fit for good company" (Molesworth). Ramabai uses the word as the opposite of *ranati* ("uncivilized").

Smṛti: "Law, — the body of law as delivered originally by *Manu* and other legislators to their respective pupils . . . also any book, canon, or portion of this body or code" (Molesworth).

Svarājya: Self-rule.

Vidyā: "Knowledge, learning, science, esp. sacred" (Molesworth). "Education" in Ramabai's frequent usage of the term.

Vilāyata: "A foreign country, but understood esp. of England or Europe" (Molesworth).

Selected References

A. Ramabai's Own Words and Works

Bombay. Government of Bombay. Report of the Bombay Provincial Committee, with Minutes of Evidence Taken before the Committee, and Memorials Addressed to the Education Commission (Bombay: 1884), in 2 vols. (Appendix to the Report of the Education Commission appointed by Resolution of the Government of India, dated February 3, 1882.)

India. Government of India (Printed) Records. *Deposition before the Indian Education Commission* (Sir William W. Hunter Commission), given at Poona, on September 5, 1882, by Pandita Ramabai. (Originally in Marathi, immediately translated and put on sale: cf. Rachel L. Bodley's introduction to *The High-Caste Hindu Woman* [Philadelphia: Press of the J. B. Rogers Printing Co., 1887], pp. xiii-xiv.)

Ramabai Sarasvati, Pandita. *High-Caste Hindu Widows. Address by the Pundita Ramabai. . . .* Boston: Rand Avery, c. 1887.

———. *The High-Caste Hindu Woman.* Philadelphia: J. B. Rodgers Printing Co., 1887, with an introduction by Rachel L. Bodley. A new edition was published in 1901 by Fleming H. Revell, with an introduction by Judith W. Andrews (Chairman of the Board, American Ramabai Association).

———. *The Letters and Correspondence of Pandita Ramabai.* Compiled by Sister Geraldine; edited, with an introduction, by A. B. Shah. Bombay: Maharashtra State Board for Literature and Culture, 1977.

———. *Pandita Ramabai.* Madras: Published for the Christian Institute for the

Study of Religion and Society, Bangalore, 1979. Introduced by Shamsundar Manohar Adhav. No. 13 in the Confessing the Faith in India series.
———. *Pandita Ramabai Through Her Own Words: Selected Works.* Compiled and edited, with translations, by Meera Kosambi. New Delhi: Oxford University Press, 2000.
———. *Pandita Ramabai: The Widows' Friend.* Second ed. Melbourne: George Robertson and Co., 1903. (This is the Australian edition of *The High-Caste Hindu Woman,* with a sequel by her daughter, Manoramabai.)
———. "Sanskrit Ode to the Congress of Berlin, 1881." Translated by Monier Williams. London: Royal Asiatic Society of Great Britain and Ireland, 1882.
———. *Stree Dharma-Neeti.* Translated into English by Meera Kosambi in *Pandita Ramabai's Feminist and Christian Conversions: Focus on Stree-Dharma-Neeti.* Bombay: Research Centre for Women's Studies, S.N.D.T. Women's University, 1995. The original Marathi version of *Stree Dharma-Neeti* ("Morals for Women" or "Rules for Women") was published in Pune in 1882.
———. *Strīdharmanīti.* Ahmedabad: Union Press, 1895.
———. *A Testimony of Our Inexhaustible Treasure.* Kedgaon: Mukti Mission, 1907 (11th ed. 1992).
———. *United Stateschi Lakasthiti ani Pravas-Vritta* ("Conditions of Life in the United States and Travels There"). Bombay: Nirnaya Sagar Press, 1889.

B. Works about Ramabai

Appasami, Elisabeth Sornam. *Pandita Rāmābāyi Jīvika Caritra.* Translated from Marathi by F. L. Marler. Madras: Christian Literature Society for India, 1948.
———. *Pantitai Rāmāpāyi Sarasvati.* Sixth ed. Madras, 1969.
Athyal, Sakhi M. *Indian Women in Mission.* Madhupur, Bihar: Mission Educational Books, 1995. Mission Educational Books series, no. 7.
Butler, Clementina. *Pandita Ramabai Sarasvati: A Pioneer in the Movement for the Education of the Child-Widow of India.* New York: Fleming H. Revell, c. 1922.
Chakravarti, Uma. *Rewriting History: The Life and Times of Pandita Ramabai.* New Delhi: Kali for Women in association with the Book Review Literary Trust, 1998.
Clarke, Amy Key. *A History of the Cheltenham Ladies' College, 1853-1953.* London: Faber and Faber, 1953.

Dall, Caroline Wells Healey. *The life of Dr. Anandabai Joshee, a Kinswoman of the Pundita Ramabai.* Boston: Roberts Brothers, 1888.

Dongre, Rajas Krishnarao, and Josephine Patterson. *Pandita Ramabai: A Life of Faith and Prayer.* Madras: Christian Literature Society, 1963. Includes texts of Pandita Ramabai's *A Testimony* (pp. 47-86) and Sornamma Appasamy's "A Memoir" (pp. 87-100).

Dyer, Helen S. *Pandita Ramabai: Her Vision, Her Mission, and Triumph of Faith.* London: Pickering and Inglis, [1923].

———. *Pandita Ramabai: The Story of Her Life.* London: Morgan and Scott, 1913 (new edition).

Fuller, Jenny (Mrs. Marcus B.). *The Wrongs of Indian Womanhood.* New York: Revell, 1900. With an introduction by Ramabai.

Gardner, C. E. *Life of Father Goreh.* London: Longmans, Green, and Co., 1900.

Karve, D. D., trans. *The New Brahmans: Five Maharashtrian Families.* Selected and translated with the editorial assistance of Ellen E. McDonald. Berkeley: University of California Press, 1963. Includes I. D. K. Karve, "Social Reformer" (pp. 11-16), D. K. Karve, "My Life Story" (pp. 17-57), and Anandibai Karve, "Autobiography" (pp. 58-79).

Kosambi, Meera. *Pandita Ramabai's Feminist and Christian Conversions: Focus on Stree Dharma-Neeti.* Bombay: Research Centre for Women's Studies, S.N.D.T. Women's University, 1995. Chapter 2, pp. 53-109, contains the full text of Pandita Ramabai's *Stree Dharma-Neeti* translated into English.

Macnicol, Nicol. *Pandita Ramabai.* Calcutta: Association Press, 1926. From the Builders of Modern India Series.

———. *Pandita Ramabai: A Builder of Modern India.* New Delhi: Good Books, 1996. With a new introduction, "What Liberates a Woman?" by Vishal Mangalwadi.

McGee, Gary B. "'Latter Rain' Falling in the East: Early-Twentieth-Century Pentecostalism in India and the Debate over Speaking in Tongues." *Church History* 68, no. 3 (September 1999): 648-65.

Müller, Friedrich Max. *Auld Lang Syne, Second Series: My Indian Friends.* New York: C. Scribner's Sons, 1899.

———. *The Life and Letters of the Right Honourable Friedrich Max Müller.* Vol. 2. New York: Longmans, Green and Co., 1902.

———. *My Autobiography.* London: Longmans, Green and Company, 1902.

Nazareth, Malcolm J. "Reverend Narayan Vaman Tilak: An Interreligious Exploration." Ph.D. diss., Temple University, 1998.

Raikes, Elizabeth. *Dorothea Beale of Cheltenham.* London: A. Constable, 1908.

Ranade, Ramabai. *Himself: The Autobiography of a Hindu Lady.* New York: Longmans, Green and Co., 1938. Translated and adapted by Katherine

Van Akin Gates from a book written in the Marathi language by Mrs. Ramabai Ranade.

———. *Ranade: His Wife's Reminiscences.* Delhi: Publications Division, Ministry of Information and Broadcasting, Government of India, 1963. Translated by Kusumavati Deshpande from Ramabai Ranade's Marathi original, *Amchya Ayushatil Kahi Ashavai* (Pune: Dnyanaprakash Press, 1910).

Sengupta, Padmini. *Pandita Ramabai Saraswati: Her Life and Work.* Bombay: Asia Publishing House, 1970.

Sharpe, Eric J. "Ramabai Dongre Medhavi (Pandita Ramabai Sarasvati) (1858-1922)." In *Biographical Dictionary of Christian Missions,* ed. Gerald H. Anderson, p. 557. New York: Macmillan Reference, 1998.

Viswanathan, Gauri. "Silencing Heresy." Chapter 4 (pp. 118-52) in *Outside the Fold: Conversion, Modernity, and Belief.* Princeton: Princeton University Press, 1998.